Language and the Declining World in Chaucer, Dante, and Jean de Meun

Medieval commentaries on the origin and history of language used biblical history, from Creation to the Tower of Babel, as their starting-point, and described the progressive impairment of an originally perfect language. Biblical and classical sources raised questions for both medieval poets and commentators about the nature of language, its participation in the Fall, and its possible redemption. John M. Fyler focuses on how three major poets – Chaucer, Dante, and Jean de Meun – participated in these debates about language. He offers new analyses of how the history of language is described and debated in the *Divine Comedy*, the *Canterbury Tales* and the *Roman de la Rose*. While Dante follows the Augustinian idea of the fall and subsequent redemption of language, Jean de Meun and Chaucer are skeptical about the possibilities for linguistic redemption and resign themselves, at least half-comically, to the linguistic implications of the Fall and the declining world.

JOHN M. FYLER is Professor of English at Tufts University, Massachusetts.

CAMBRIDGE STUDIES IN MEDIEVAL LITERATURE

General editor
Alastair Minnis, *Ohio State University*

Editorial board
Zygmunt G. Barański, *University of Cambridge*
Christopher C. Baswell, *University of California, Los Angeles*
John Burrow, *University of Bristol*
Mary Carruthers, *New York University*
Rita Copeland, *University of Pennsylvania*
Simon Gaunt, *King's College, London*
Steven Kruger, *City University of New York*
Nigel Palmer, *University of Oxford*
Winthrop Wetherbee, *Cornell University*
Jocelyn Wogan-Browne, *Fordham University*

This series of critical books seeks to cover the whole area of literature written in the major medieval languages – the main European vernaculars, and medieval Latin and Greek – during the period c. 1100–1500. Its chief aim is to publish and stimulate fresh scholarship and criticism on medieval literature, special emphasis being placed on understanding major works of poetry, prose, and drama in relation to the contemporary culture and learning which fostered them.

Recent titles in the series
Ananya Jahanara Kabir and Deanne Williams, eds *Postcolonial Approaches to the European Middle Ages: Translating Cultures*
Mark Miller *Philosophical Chaucer: Love, Sex, and Agency in the Canterbury Tales*
Simon Gilson *Dante and Renaissance Florence*
Ralph Hanna, *London Literature, 1300–1380*
Maura Nolan, *John Lydgate and the Making of Public Culture*
Nicolette Zeeman *Piers Plowman and the Medieval Discourse of Desire*
Robert J. Meyer-Lee *Poets and Power from Chaucer to Wyatt*
Isabel Davis *Writing Masculinity in the Later Middle Ages*
John M. Fyler *Language and the Declining World in Chaucer, Dante, and Jean de Meun*

A complete list of titles in the series can be found at the end of the volume.

Language and the Declining World in Chaucer, Dante, and Jean de Meun

John M. Fyler

CAMBRIDGE
UNIVERSITY PRESS

CAMBRIDGE UNIVERSITY PRESS
Cambridge, New York, Melbourne, Madrid, Cape Town, Singapore, São Paulo

Cambridge University Press
The Edinburgh Building, Cambridge CB2 8RU, UK

Published in the United States of America by Cambridge University Press, New York

www.cambridge.org
Information on this title: www.cambridge.org/9780521872157

First published 2007

Printed in the United Kingdom at the University Press, Cambridge

A catalogue record for this publication is available from the British Library

Library of Congress Cataloguing in Publication data
Fyler, John M.
Language and the declining world in Chaucer, Dante, and Jean de Meun / John M. Fyler.
p.   cm. – (Cambridge studies in medieval literature)
Includes bibliographical references and index.
ISBN 13: 978-0-521-87215-7 (hardback)
ISBN 10: 0-521-87215-4 (hardback)
1. Bible. O. T. Genesis I – Criticism, interpretation, etc.   2. Language and languages – History – To
1800   3. Chaucer, Geoffrey, d. 1400.   4. Dante Alighieri, 1265–1321.   5. Jean, de Meun, d. 1305?
I. Title.   II. Series.
BS1235.52.F95   2007
809.1′934–dc22   2007002298

ISBN 978-0-521-87215-7 hardback

For Julia, Amanda, and Lucy

Contents

Acknowledgments

This book has been long in the making, and I am certain that I have inadvertently forgotten some debts that belong here: may their absence be attributed "to the defaute of myn unkonnynge and nat to my wyl." The John Simon Guggenheim Memorial Foundation awarded me a fellowship at the beginning of this project; resident fellowships at the Camargo Foundation and Clare Hall, University of Cambridge helped me bring it to an end. I am also grateful to the Faculty Research Awards Committee at Tufts University for assistance at various points along the way. I owe more than I can say to my teachers, official and unofficial. Charles Muscatine, my dissertation director, whose powerful book on the French tradition inspired me as an undergraduate and graduate student, set me thinking anew with his later work on the French fabliaux. Sir Richard Southern, in his 1968 Berkeley seminar on the twelfth century, introduced me to medieval intellectual history, and offered an inspiring but daunting example of brilliance as a teacher and lecturer. He helped make it possible for me to spend a year in Oxford, where Malcolm Parkes generously allowed me to audit his extraordinary courses in palaeography. I first read Chaucer in Talbot Donaldson's edition, and discovered years after the fact that he was the anonymous reader for my first published article on Chaucer; this was fitting, because he was always the audience I had in mind when writing, and like others, I have discovered uncomfortably often that something I had thought of as my own idea was in fact sketched out by one of his subordinate clauses. I owe a great deal to a number of fellow medievalists and friends: Elizabeth Archibald, C. David Benson, Larry Benson, Kenneth Bleeth, Rick Bogel, Clinton Bond and Shirin Davami, Susan Crane, Marilynn Desmond, Kevin Dunn, Robert Edwards, Janet

Acknowledgments

Gezari, Warren Ginsberg, Robert Hanning, Marshall Leicester, Donald Maddox and Sara Sturm-Maddox, Jim Maddox, Charles Moseley, Lee Patterson, Sue Penney, James Simpson, and Susan and Oscar Wood. I am grateful for my students, at Tufts and at the Bread Loaf School of English. At the Cambridge University Press, I owe much to Alastair Minnis and Linda Bree for their encouragement, and to the anonymous readers for their careful attention. I have revised some earlier publications, and thank *Mediaevalia*, Sewanee Mediaeval Studies, and Medieval Institute Publications for permitting me to reuse this material. I have depended on the great libraries with the resources necessary for my work, especially the Cambridge University Library and the British Library. Above all, I am grateful to the dedicatees for their encouragement and forbearance: to Julia for a long-continuing conversation and timely editorial advice; to Amanda and Lucy whose development into speech and then eloquence coincided with this years-long investigative descent into babble.

Abbreviations

AHDLMA	*Archives d'Histoire Doctrinale et Littéraire du Moyen Âge*
CCCM	*Corpus Christianorum, Continuatio Mediaeualis*
CCSL	*Corpus Christianorum, Series Latina*
CFMA	*Classiques Français du Moyen Âge*
ChRev	*Chaucer Review*
CNRS	Centre National de la Recherche Scientifique
CSEL	*Corpus Scriptorum Ecclesiasticorum Latinorum*
DS	*Dante Studies*
DVE	Dante Alighieri, *De Vulgari Eloquentia*
EETS	The Early English Text Society
JMRS	*Journal of Medieval and Renaissance Studies*
LCL	Loeb Classical Library
M&H	*Mediaevalia et Humanistica*
MLQ	*Modern Language Quarterly*
MLR	*Modern Language Review*
MS	*Mediaeval Studies*
PG	*Patrologia Cursus Completus: Series Graeca.* Ed. J.-P. Migne. Paris, 1857–66
PL	*Patrologia Cursus Completus: Series Latina.* Ed. J.-P. Migne. Paris, 1841–64
PMLA	*Publications of the Modern Language Association of America*
PQ	*Philological Quarterly*
RA	*Recherches Augustiniennes*
RS	Rolls Series (*Rerum Britannicarum Medii Aevi Scriptores*)
RTAM	*Recherches de Théologie Ancienne et Médiévale*

List of abbreviations

SAC	*Studies in the Age of Chaucer*
SATF	Société des Anciens Textes Français
SD	*Studi Danteschi*
SP	*Studies in Philology*
ST	Thomas Aquinas, *Summa Theologiae*
UTQ	*University of Toronto Quarterly*
YFS	*Yale French Studies*

I

The Biblical history of language

Ferdinand de Saussure and the structuralists, by making language the paradigm for large areas of inquiry, almost inevitably provoked a new interest in an age-old question: how, when, and where did language originate? This question elicited responses throughout the Middle Ages and Renaissance – indeed, to the end of the eighteenth century, as the famous discussions by Rousseau and Herder attest. From the late seventeenth century on, however, the responses became increasingly speculative, largely because Genesis lost its status as the infallibly authoritative account of early human history.[1] No longer restricted by a unitary Biblical truth, linguistic speculations could increase and multiply, mixing the plausible with the implausible. To defend against the deluge, the inaugural bylaws of the Société de linguistique de Paris (1865) stipulated that no papers of any sort concerning the origin of language would be accepted. Now that the question has regained some of its former popularity, we may sympathize with the Society's position.[2]

Yet resuscitating this question has brought some earlier views into sharp focus and given them new interest. When we consider patristic and medieval comments on the origin of language, two things are immediately apparent. First, discussion focuses inevitably on the opening eleven chapters of Genesis, from the Creation to the Tower of Babel; second, Augustine's extensive comments on language dominate and provide the framework for later commentary. In Neil Forsyth's synopsis, Augustine's "system of symbolic interpretation" comes of age in *De Doctrina Christiana*, where he describes the effects on language of the Fall. "Adam and Eve found that now they could communicate only by the clumsy method of language and gesture. A dislocation of consciousness produced the distance between the inquiring intellect and the object of its search. The word of God was veiled, in order to exercise the seeker. This veil, the language of sign and symbol, was both the distance of the mind from God and the avenue by which the philosophic searcher might reach him."[3]

The veil of language, according to context and the temperament of its beholder, may be understood as permeable or impermeable, translucent or opaque. All three of the later medieval poets with whom this book is concerned – Jean de Meun, Dante, and Chaucer – make use of, and significantly add to, the commentarial and Augustinian traditions. They differ, however, in their particular responses to these traditions. Dante is the most thoroughgoing Augustinian of the three; but Augustine and the tradition of Biblical commentary also had a profound effect on the way Jean de Meun and Chaucer thought about language, as both the tool and the resistant material of their craft.

These three poets are also of course indebted to the classical tradition, which intersects at many points with the Judaeo-Christian. Almost everything I have written on Chaucer explicitly or implicitly has concerned the myth of the Golden Age and declining world; once again, as I have come to realize, I am returning to that myth, though this time through the lens of its Biblical analogue in the opening chapters of Genesis. The authoritative summary of this material, in all of its wide-ranging manifestations, has now appeared in James Dean's *The World Grown Old in Later Medieval Literature*[4]; his thorough look at the larger picture allows me to focus more narrowly on its linguistic details, in four chapters that are meant to be cumulative but can also stand alone. This first chapter summarizes the patristic, rabbinical, and medieval Christian commentaries on language at the beginning of the world, in the first eleven chapters of Genesis; I also look at what these commentaries say about Pentecost and the promised renewal of language by the Word as the world nears its end. Chapter 2 analyzes Jean de Meun's discussion of language in the *Roman de la Rose*, framed as it is by Genesis and the Ovidian myth of the Golden Age. Chapter 3 outlines Dante's Augustinian review of linguistic history in *De Vulgari Eloquentia* and the *Commedia*. It then looks at the *House of Fame*, in which Chaucer upends Dante's confident poetry of the redemptive Word; instead, like Jean de Meun, he resigns himself with skepticism and comedy to the ambiguities of fallen language. Chapter 4 describes the movement from the *Second Nun's Tale* to the *Canon's Yeoman's Tale*, as Chaucer's final, bleak reprise of how language and meaning disseminate themselves in the fallen world, a world in which the word can no longer be cousin to the deed.

Virtually all medieval accounts of language begin with the authorized account: the story in Genesis of its origin and rapid participation in the Fall. The Genesis narrative offers three historical foci for linguistic commentary, one before and two after the loss of Eden; they provide useful points of reference for categorizing the habitual concerns of medieval linguistic thought. The first is the origin of language – Adam's naming of the birds and animals in Paradise (Gen. 2.20); this episode raises broader issues of signification in general, and of the differences between man's language and God's. Next, showing the effects of the Fall, are the sins of Cain, the first murderer and city-builder, and of his descendants, especially Lamech the inventor of bigamy and his children, to whom we owe the arts of civilization (Gen. 4.19–24). The scholia on their words and deeds are akin to pagan remarks on the loss of the Golden Age, and take up such issues as the abuse of language for sophistry or even outright lying. The third and most notorious linguistic event is the building of the Tower of Babel and the consequent confusion of tongues (Gen. 11.1–9), in which the dismaying linguistic results of original sin, already evident in Cain's descendants, become hardened further into the division that will last until Judgment Day. Only then will the restored unity promised by Pentecost, the antitype of Babel, be achieved at last.

There are actually four languages, hierarchically arranged, at the beginning of Genesis. The first is God's, since the Biblical account of language begins even before the beginning of time, with John's elaboration on the first two words of Genesis, "In principio erat Verbum, / Et Verbum erat apud Deum, / Et Deus erat Verbum" (John 1.1) [In the beginning was the Word, and the Word was with God, and the Word was God],[5] and with God's speech before the creation of humankind, his "Let there be light" and assigning of names to Day, Night, Heaven, Earth, and Seas. The second language is Adam's, when he gives names to the birds and animals, and the third the speech he hands on to his descendants after the Fall. The fourth and most depraved comprises our diverse tongues after Babel. We reascend only with difficulty even to Adam's fallen speech; his Edenic language, let alone God's true Word, is entirely or almost entirely inaccessible.

I take some risks in outlining this hierarchy with such clarity. It accurately describes Milton's portrayal of linguistic history in *Paradise Lost*, but may partially misrepresent the patristic and medieval commentaries on Genesis – and for that matter, Genesis itself – since they do not differentiate between these successive states of language in a unanimous or wholly consistent fashion. If, for example, Hebrew was in fact Adam's language, as almost all the commentators agree, then the Hebrew names for the birds and animals must be their true names, perfectly matching signifier and signified, and logic would suggest that we might recover a linguistic Eden, if not Eden itself, simply by taking a crash course in the true tongue. This is certainly not, however, what Clement V had in mind in 1311 when he asked that Hebrew be taught at every university, even though John Wyclif does argue that traces of Adam's power – the power to evoke obedience from the creatures he named – do survive in the language of magic and incantation: "I believe Hebrew sounds [*voces*] to have greater efficacy than manifold others."[6] Dante is more akin to Milton when he changes his mind between *De Vulgari Eloquentia* and *Paradiso* 26: in the earlier work Hebrew is Adam's language; in the latter, Adam speaks a language that alters radically after the Fall. By contrast, many medieval commentators take no account of linguistic change and decline when they discuss the gap between the Logos and human words: their sight is firmly set on the gulf between the divine and the human, not on calibrating relatively minor variations in the extent of that gulf. Genesis does, however, offer a number of cues for linguistic speculation, and the commentaries give us licence to use its text as the springboard for antiquarian theorizing. Milton is, after all, the heir of this commentarial tradition, which was in full force throughout the seventeenth century[7]; and Milton's medieval predecessors are often surprisingly modern in their linguistic concerns.

To be sure, any attempt to describe the origin of language faces a notable conceptual problem, akin to the definitions of God according to what He is not, or the difficulties Dante and Paul lament in describing Heaven: since their instruments of discourse are themselves affected by the Fall, fallible human beings cannot easily contemplate, and certainly cannot easily describe, what the unfallen language must have been. Our efforts to do so, tinged by retrospective longing as they are, must participate in the quest that Derrida has so attentively undermined: the quest for a primal unity of sign and thing, an immanence in spoken language that writing keeps pallidly at a distance, and that our speech itself keeps deferring continually beyond our grasp. Earlier exegetes would agree with Derrida when he says that "The sign is always a sign of the Fall. Absence always relates to distancing from God."[8] According to Thierry of Chartres, God can only be spoken of metaphorically [*translatiue*].[9] And the first language in Genesis, God's, is of course not really a language, for the speech of Creation is not really speech in any human sense of the term. With his characteristic brilliance and thoroughness, reflecting the central position of the divine *Verbum* in his theology, Augustine asks a series of questions in *De Genesi ad Litteram* about God's "Fiat lux":

> And how did God say, *Let there be light*? Was this in time or in the eternity of His Word? If this was spoken in time, it was certainly subject to change. How then could we conceive of God saying it except by means of a creature? For He Himself is unchangeable . . .
>
> And was there the material sound of a voice when God said, *Let there be light*, as there was when He said, *Thou art my beloved Son*? . . . And, if so, what was the language of this voice when God said, *Let there be light*? There did not yet exist the variety of tongues, which arose later when the tower was built after the flood. What then was the one and only language by which God said, *Let there be light*? Who was intended to hear and understand it, and to whom was it directed? But perhaps this is an absurdly material way of thinking and speculating on the matter.
>
> What then shall we say? Is it the intellectual idea signified by the sound of the voice, in the words, *Let there be light*, that is meant here by the voice of God, rather than the material sound? And does this belong to the Divine Word . . .?[10]

Yes is the answer, of course. And for Augustine this eternal language, in which to utter is the same as to act,[11] establishes the origin and goal of all human discourse. The eternity and unity of the Word, set against the transience and partiality of human speech, become a characterizing preoccupation of Augustine's writings. This preoccupation appears, for example, in his comments on knowing things "in the Word of God," as angels do, instead of knowing "the same thing in itself,"[12] and his remark in the *Confessions*: "we returned to the sound of our own tongue, in which a word has both beginning and ending. For what is like to your Word, Our Lord, who abides in Himself forever, yet grows not old and makes all things new!"[13] It is central to his disquisition, in Book Fifteen of *De Trinitate*, on the relation of the Incarnate Word to human speech: the inner word, the word of the human heart, and not the outer, audible or legible one, is the true similitude [*similitudo*] of the divine Word. This inner word has powers that no human language has ("this is the word that belongs to no language, that is to none of what are called the languages of the nations, of which ours is Latin"), and we may apprehend it "not only before it is spoken aloud but even before the images of its sounds are turned over in thought . . . For when we utter something true, that is when we utter what we know, a word is necessarily born from the knowledge which we hold in the memory, a word which is absolutely the same kind of thing as the knowledge it is born from."[14] Yet this likeness in a word – "that word of man, the word of a rational animal, the word of the image of God which is not born of God but made by God" – conceals "a great unlikeness [*dissimilitudo*] to God and the Word of God"; and even after the Last Judgment, when we shall be in the company of God again and have the powers of angels, likeness will be far from identity.[15]

God obviously makes allowance for our limited powers when He uses any human language, even a perfect one[16]; according to a commentary incorrectly attributed to Thomas Aquinas, "God truly speaks to us in human fashion just as a lisping [*balbutiens*] mother condescends to her son."[17] Such divine condescension was once, if only for a brief time, hardly necessary, as Augustine argues in his fascinating reading of Genesis 2.5, "for the Lord God had not rained upon the earth." Now, Augustine says, God does rain upon the earth, "that is, he makes souls grow green again by his word; but he waters them from the clouds, that is, from the Scriptures of the Prophets and Apostles. They are, moreover, rightly called clouds, because those words which resound and pass through the beaten air, with the darkness of allegories also added as if they were covered in some manner by a mist, become like clouds." But before the Fall, God made the "plant of the field" and "herb of the ground," that is to say, the human soul, green by watering it "by an inner spring, speaking in its intellect, so that it might receive words not from the outside, as if they were rain from the clouds spoken of above; but instead be filled from its own spring, that is from the truth flowing from its own innermost depths."[18]

In the world we inhabit, however, the Fall and Redemption of humankind have extensive linguistic repercussions, in the gap signalled by wordplays on the Word such as Aquinas' hymn "Pange Lingua"[19] and Dante's announced intention to talk about human language "inspired by the Word that comes from above."[20] When Augustine sets forth his scheme of providential history, he elaborates on his predecessors, who had argued that while Eve "conceived the word of the serpent," Mary willingly accepted God's Word: "For unto Eve, as yet a virgin, had crept the devil's word, the framer of death. Equally, unto a virgin was introduced God's word, the builder of life."[21] Marcia Colish has outlined in detail the Augustinian paradigm of history, in which human language falls farther and farther from its divine exemplar, until Christ the Incarnate Word, the second Adam born of the second Eve, graces us with the possibility of redeemed speech.[22] For Augustine the Fall is centrally defined by its linguistic aspect, the lapse into dissimilitude. God says, as he creates man: "Faciamus hominem ad imaginem et similitudinem nostram" (Gen. 1.26) [Let us make man to our image and likeness][23]; but in Augustine's memorable phrase, we now live in the fallen world far from God "in regione dissimilitudinis" [in a region of unlikeness].[24]

Similitude and image, *similitudo* and *imago*, are crucial words in the Genesis text, and they link the origin of language with the Creation. Although Calvin argues that the two terms have identical meanings since "the Hebrues commonly use to repeate one thinge with diverse wordes,"[25] almost all patristic and medieval commentaries argue for a hierarchical distinction between them. But the Greek and Latin traditions offer contradictory accounts of that hierarchy. With the notable exception of Gregory of Nyssa, who uses the terms interchangeably, "similarity, even more than the image, is the dominant relation which links man to God in all Greek patristic thought."[26] In the Latin tradition, by contrast, "image" is superior to "similitude." Augustine thus comments on Genesis 1.26 in *De diuersis quaestionibus* 51, and he also remarks in *quaestio* 74 on the differences between *imago, aequalitas*, and *similitudo*.[27] Aquinas argues "that the idea of image involves likeness, and that 'image' adds something to 'likeness,' namely the idea of being a sort of print taken from another"; *similitudo* is "preliminary" to image, "covering a wider class of things," whereas *imago* involves "the properties of intelligent nature [*naturae intellectualis*]."[28]

Even at the moment of Creation, the shift from unity to division, as from identity to image or similitude, has moral as well as ontological implications. Almost inevitably, and despite the need to emphasize the good of Creation, patristic exegesis reflects its Neoplatonic origins by marking out analogous hierarchies of original unity and subsequent loss. Divine language vs. human and thing vs. word are the linguistic correlatives of the human being Adam as both "imago et similitudo" of God, vs. woman created as the *imago* of man, but in some versions merely the *similitudo* of God.[29] The divide between One and Many of course exists even before the divide between divine and human. Jerome in fact argues that the omission of "And God saw that it was good" on the second day of Creation, the summation that appears on each of the other days, is intended to show us that "a double number is not good, because it divides from union, and prefigures the marriage contract"[30]; and Bede associates this second day with the second age of the world, and with the division of tongues at the Tower of Babel.[31] Guibert of Nogent only mildly embellishes the traditional reading when he relates "In the beginning God created heaven and earth" to the division within human beings between spirit (heaven) and flesh (earth); for Philo Judaeus had, long before, given a more literal gendered marking to this division: "The first man originally existed in a state of unity or oneness, and so long as he remained in this state, he was like both the world and God in his singleness . . . But this original state of oneness or singleness was interrupted by the appearance of woman."[32]

Although Philo differs in emphasis from the Christian patristic writers, they are all responding to the inconsistent Creation narratives of the Jahwist and Priestly scribes, which underlie the connection between the creation of woman and the invention of language. The Jahwist account, the earlier of the two by perhaps four centuries,[33] describes the creation of Eve and her naming in the context of Adam's naming the animals and birds (Gen. 2.18–24): in part because of this context, the Jahwist writer implies that Eve is subordinate to Adam, and sufficiently differentiated from him that he can assign her a name.[34] The Priestly account, on the other hand, which comes first in the Genesis text, appears to suggest, or can at least be taken to suggest, that male and female, both subsumed under the term *adam* or *homo*, are coeval and implicitly equal: "Et creavit Deus hominem ad imaginem suam: ad imaginem Dei creavit illum, masculum et feminam creavit eos" (Gen. 1.27) [And God created man to his own image; in the image of God he created him. Male and female he created them]. Elizabeth Cady Stanton's barbed comment is on the mark: "The first account dignifies woman as an important factor in the creation, equal in power and glory with man. The second makes her a mere afterthought. The world in good running order without her. The only reason for her advent being the solitude of man."[35]

Of course, for patristic and medieval commentators the two Creation narratives are a single one, the work of Moses; and what we now see as discrepancies between them are to be understood as merely apparent discrepancies, variants within a single unified account that require interpretative reconciliation. Even recently, Pope John Paul II's 1988 apostolic letter *Mulieris Dignitatem* argues that there is no "essential contradiction between the two texts."[36] Once one rejects the notion that Genesis 1.27 describes a single androgynous human being,[37] the usual exegetical maneuver to make these two texts congruent is to distinguish, as Augustine does, between the seminal creation (*informatio*), the "seminal reasons" [*rationes seminales*], of the human being (*ha'adam* or *homo*), and the formation in time (*conformatio*) of the two sexes (*vir* and *femina*).[38] Andrew of St. Victor argues that the plural "them" [*eos*] in Genesis 1.27 shows that the original human was not an androgyne, but that, although the woman was not yet divided from the man, she was "substantially pre-begotten" [*materialiter praeseminata*], her bodily creation proleptically referred to in this text that shifts so abruptly from "him" to the "male and female" of "them."[39] Significantly, Jesus echoes this verse in his argument against divorce: "Have ye not read that he who made man from the beginning made them male and female?" (Matt. 19.4).[40] This Genesis verse also becomes a crucial authority for the equality of all human souls, as in Peter Lombard's heavily Augustinian commentary on 1 Corinthians: the image of God is not in the body, but in the "rational mind, where there can be knowledge of God, and where there is no sex, . . . because in either sex the image of God is fulfilled, from which image woman [*femina*] is not disjoined, just as she is not excluded from the grace of the renewal and the reformation of the image of God."[41] Thus Jean de Meun's Genius and the narrator of Chaucer's *Troilus* (5.1835–40) explicitly state that women and men both are made in the image of God.[42]

Even so, this verse becomes entangled in opposing currents of Biblical exegesis, notably in the twelfth and thirteenth centuries, as Philippe Buc has shown.[43] On the one hand, and certainly the majority view, given extra weight by the widespread influence of Isidore and the *Glossa Ordinaria*, female is subordinate to male in Paradise as well as after the fall, though this subordination to a genial prelacy differs entirely from the violence of post-lapsarian servitude, epitomized according to Peter Comestor by the wounds of defloration.[44] But such a reading of Genesis 1.26–28 is countered in the course of the thirteenth century by Dominicans such as Hugh of St. Cher and Nicholas de Gorran, who argue that there was no prelacy in Paradise[45]: dominion over the fishes of the sea does not extend to *prelatio* over other human beings. And already in the twelfth century Andrew of St. Victor and others posit an original equality between male and female,[46] in line with the ameliorating commonplace – in Hugh of St. Victor, Abelard, Peter Lombard, and the *Bible Française*, and repeated in the *Parson's Tale* – that Eve is, significantly, created from Adam's side, not his head or his foot.[47]

Even with such divergent interpretations, the harmonizing impulse in Biblical commentary accords with the text it comments on; for the Genesis narrative insists on similitude, likeness bridging a gap of difference, in God's creation of man.[48] The question of similitude in turn dominates the account of man's relationship to the rest of creation, because the search for a mate for Adam "like unto himself" [*simile sibi*][49] provokes Adam's first use of language:

> And the Lord God said: It is not good for man to be alone[50]; let us make him a help like unto himself. And the Lord God having formed out of the ground all the beasts of the earth, and all the fowls of the air, brought them to Adam to see what he would call them: for

whatsoever Adam called [*vocavit*] any living creature the same is its name [*ipsum est nomen eius*]. And Adam called all the beasts by their names, and all the fowls of the air, and all the cattle of the field: but for Adam there was not found a helper like himself. (Gen. 2.18–20)

Modern critics have remarked on the "extraordinary naiveté" of this passage, which implies that "the whole animal creation is the result of an unsuccessful experiment to find a mate" for Adam.[51] But for earlier commentators, Adam realizes here his superiority to the other creatures[52] or becomes aware, when he sees that they are all sexually differentiated and paired, of his own solitariness.[53] As the *Legenda Aurea* puts it, man was "not perfect till the woman was made"; and Aquinas notes: "Now just as variety in the grading of things contributes to the perfection of the universe, so variety of sex [*diversitas sexus*] makes for the perfection of human nature."[54] In this context of Adam's search for his similitude, his naming the birds and animals involves a complicated interplay between his intuitive understanding of their natures and his rational awareness that they are different from him, and not possible mates "like unto himself." For since his name for an animal was, as Rashi says, "to be its name forever," his understanding of their natures is almost beyond intellection, a perfect matching of name and thing[55]; yet the act of naming itself requires the articulation of difference, since to name something is to recognize its otherness. Augustine's comment on Genesis 1.4–5 contrasts "the clattering and diversity of tongues" with the "pure understanding" of God: just as God divided light from darkness and "called the light Day, and the darkness Night," so He "thus divided and arranged all things so that they might both be discerned and receive their names."[56]

Abelard wrestles ingeniously with these problems of naming and language in his *Expositio in Hexaemeron*. Was the command against eating the forbidden fruit audible and comprehensible to Adam, since he is said to have invented language only later, at the naming of the animals? Abelard decides that probably, as often happens in the Bible, strict chronological order does not apply to the various instances of language use in Paradise. Indeed, if Adam and Eve did not spend enough time there to develop an entire language, which would have taken several years, the scene of naming the animals anticipates what largely happened later, outside Paradise, just as Genesis 1.27 anticipates the actual creation of Eve in Genesis 2. And since Eve too is first named *adam* – "He created them male and female; and blessed them; and called their name Adam, in the day when they were created" (Gen. 5.2) – she too may have had authority to name the animals.[57] In any case, both Adam and Eve, as "rational animals," have powers that no mere animal has. Alcuin, following Augustine, notes that "the serpent spoke words which he did not understand." And Honorius Augustodunensis compares the devil's speech through the serpent to the similarly uncomprehending Balaam's ass or modern-day madman.[58]

The Hebrew text of Genesis vividly marks the origins of differentiation and division by its pseudo-etymologies, which are often repeated in later commentaries. The first, God-given name for human beings connects us etymologically to the earth from which "adam" was made: as Jerome glosses, "Adam, man [*homo*] or earthen, or native, or red earth."[59] But the names Adam gives to his helpmate, one name before and one after the Fall, play on similitude and difference, registering a shift first from unity to multiplicity – mirroring God's own act of Creation – and then, dismayingly, from integral connection to alienation. Adam copies God's verbal economy and assertion of similitude when he names his mate *isha* (Gen. 2.23), for the name itself shows her near-identity with the man, *ish*, from whom she was made, "woman" from "man," "bone of my bones, and flesh of my flesh."[60] According to Rashi, this Adamic word-play on *ish/isha* in fact proves that the world was created in Hebrew.[61] If so, English might have a better claim than Greek or Latin to be a sacred language, because "man" and "woman" translate this wordplay so readily. Augustine notes that the term "mulier" in the Vetus Latina translation of Genesis loses the verbal effect that "virago" or "virgo" would preserve[62]; and Jerome's Vulgate in fact uses "virago" to copy the mirroring in the Hebrew text.[63] Eve may be so called, Peter Comestor says, because "virago" means "a viro acta" [brought forth from man]; and this etymology, which also appears in the standard medieval dictionaries, is widely disseminated.[64] Abelard comments: "*Virago, because from vir*, so that she might also be connected by name just as she is by nature, collecting her name, to wit, just as her substance from the man, so that from the very names themselves they might be admonished how much they ought to love those who are so connected to themselves."[65]

As the *OED* notes, "virago" in this sense appears in the Middle English *Cursor Mundi* and in the Wycliffite translations of Genesis: in one version, Genesis 2.23 reads "this schal be clepid virago, for she is takun of man"; the other expands on the received etymology: "this shal be clepid mannus dede, for she is takun of a man."[66] The first *OED* citation of the word in its now usual meaning is Chaucer's *Man of Law's Tale*: "Virago, thou Semyrame the secounde!" (359). Yet a pejorative sense previously occurs in Latin, as is evident in Isidore's use of the term to describe "corrupt women" [*corruptae mulieres*], and in Geoffrey le Baker's characterization of Queen Isabella, just before Edward II's murder, as a "ferrea virago," a "femina crudelis," because she will not respond to the king, a "new Orpheus," as he wanly sings for her return.[67] Nicholas of Lyra thus argues that *virago* incorrectly translates *isha*, "because *virago* does not signify a woman taken or derived from man, but more a woman acting manfully"[68]; *vira*, he says, would be a better choice, if Latin permitted it. The same suggestion was made earlier by Andrew of St. Victor[69]; Isidore had in fact argued that *vira*, following the pattern of *serva* and *famula*, was the ancient word for *femina*.[70]

Up to the point of the Fall, God's injunction "Increase and multiply" (Gen. 1.28) has a wholly benign effect, as in the doubling of *adam* into *vir* and *virago*; for the Creation, mirroring the original act of its Creator, divides and subdivides, but with the bond of virtuous similitude holding together its disparate, multiple parts. Aquinas, speculating on whether there would have been procreation in the state of innocence, answers the objection that "once the human race were multiplied by procreation, division of ownership would have had to follow":

> In this state when owners multiply there has to be a division of possessions, because possession in common is fraught with discord, as the Philosopher says. But in the state of innocence men's wills would have been so disposed that they would have used in common, without any danger of discord, and in the measure and manner that suited the situation of each, the things that came under their ownership [*dominio*]; even now, after all, this may be observed to be the case among many good men.[71]

As the Wakefield *Noah* play sums up God's benign Creation: "Adam and Eue, that woman, / To multiplie without discord, in Paradise put he thaym" (30–31).[72] Or so we must infer, following the commentators, since there is hardly time for this benign process to advance very far before the Fall turns its play of likeness and difference into a cancerous multiplication – first, to the two genealogies from Adam, of Seth and of Cain; then, to the division at Babel of the one true tongue into seventy-two.

Having a name is as distinctively human as the power of naming. In fact, according to Honorius Augustodunensis, the elevated status of the unfallen angels means that they have no need for names: the names Michael, Gabriel, and Raphael, like the name Satan, are properly speaking "second names," *agnomina*, given to them by human beings, and not their proper *nomina*.[73] In Milton, who insists on the distinctions between unfallen and fallen speech, and particularly unfallen and fallen names,[74] "Satan," meaning "Adversary," is emphatically a fallen name, Satan's true name having been expunged from the Book of Life; the *Monk's Tale* also makes this distinction: "O Lucifer, brightest of angels alle, / Now arthow Sathanas, that mayst nat twynne/ Out of miserie, in which that thou art falle" (2004–6).[75] Indeed, Milton marks the invention of Satan's fallen name by a remarkable visual, hence silent, display when it first proclaims itself in an acrostic, working its way "sidelong," athwart language, at exactly the moment when the Adversary is about to tempt Eve:

> Scipio the height of Rome. With tract oblique
> At first, as one who sought access, but feared
> To interrupt, sidelong he works his way.
> As when a ship by skilful steersman wrought
> Nigh river's mouth or foreland, where the wind
> Veers oft, as oft so steers, and shifts her sail.[76]

The effects of the Fall on human language are no less pronounced; they first manifest themselves in sexual division and divisiveness. Peter Comestor notes that "Adam" and "virago" or "isha" were proper names at first, but are now common nouns; an otherwise innocent change from singular to plural, needed to differentiate the first woman from her progeny, has a darker significance because woman's renaming occurs after the Fall, when Adam gives her the proper name Eve.[77] The similitudes of Paradise quickly become demonic: Satan disguises himself as a serpent with "a maiden's face, because like applauds like"[78]; and Chaucer's Merchant uses Genesis 2.18 – "Lat us now make an helpe unto this man/ Lyk to hymself" (*Merchant's Tale* 1328–29) – only sarcastically, because such paradisal likeness is now a chimera. What the Parson says about Ire applies more generally: it "wasteth and destroyeth the liknesse of God – that is to seyn, the vertu that is in mannes soule – / and put in hym the liknesse of the devel" (*Parson's Tale* 544–45). The name Eve implicitly plays on such dissimilitude within itself, in effect a kind of punning, which mirrors the dissimilitude the Fall brings to Adam and Eve separately, in their division from God, and together, in their division from each other.[79] Its positive meaning, "Living" or "Life," appears in the immediate explanation "because she was the mother of all the living" (Gen. 3.20)[80]; in fact, in the Vetus Latina translation that Augustine quotes, Adam simply gives his wife the name "Life," *Vita.*[81] But there are more sinister connotations within her name: Augustine discusses the paradoxes in Adam's renaming her, of the name "Life" being imposed at the moment when death entered the world, and Jerome glosses "Eua calamitas aut uae uel uita" [Eva, calamity, or woe, or life].[82] As the *Middle English Genesis* summarizes the change:

> Adam abraid, and sag ðat wif;
> Name he gaf hire ðat is ful rif:
> Issa was hire firste name,
> Ðor-of ðurte hire ðinken no same;
> Mayden, for sche was mad of man,
> Hire first name ðor bi-gan.
> Siðen ghe brocte us to woa,
> Adam gaf hire name eua.[83]
>
> (231–38)

According to Luther, Adam's renaming woman as Eve is part of her punishment, a further token that she must be subjected to the power of her husband; and this punishment survives in women's loss of their surnames when they marry.[84]

Jerome's gloss, with its alternative and contradictory possibilities, sets the stage for Isidore to expatiate on the doubleness within Eve's name and self:

Eva is interpreted as life or calamity or woe. Life, because she was the source of being born; calamity and woe, because by her transgression the condition of dying appeared. For she took the name "calamitas" because of her falling [*A cadendo enim nomen sumpsit calamitas*].[85] Some say, moreover: Eva is called life and calamity, because often woman is the cause of well-being for man, often the cause of calamity and death, which is woe.[86]

This simultaneous reading of Eve's name *in bono* and *in malo* is worthy of Chauntecleer, for whom the "sentence" of "Mulier est hominis confusio" is its contradiction (*Nun's Priest's Tale* 3163–66). Isidore's wordplay on *a cadendo*, on grammatical ending and another kind of Fall, is copied word-for-word by Rabanus Maurus, and leads to the kind of grammatical punning that Lehmann has described, in which "declining" takes on a double meaning as Adam and Eve become "oblique" nouns after their Fall or "declension."[87] The name "Eva" opens itself to various kinds of deconstruction: the most famous is the "Eva"/"Ave" reversal, in which the three letters of the angel Gabriel's first word to the Virgin, the linguistic prelude to the Redemption, signal a cosmic peripeteia.[88] But in the context of mere fallen language, there are more acerbic possibilities. Robert Holkot argues, when he discusses the mystical meaning of the letters in *AVE*, that "A is called the first letter by all nations, because according to Papias" it is the first sound babies make.[89] But Innocent III divides Eve's name into post-partum syllables of woe:

> We are all are born crying so that we might express the misery of nature. For the newly born male says "A," the female "E." "All are born of Eva saying 'E' or 'A'." What is "Eva" therefore? Either syllable is the interjection of one in pain, expressing the magnitude of the pain. Hence she deserved to be called *virago* before sin, "Eva" after sin, because of which she heard said to her: "In sorrow shalt thou bring forth children."[90]

In his versified Bible, the *Aurora*, Peter Riga sums up our fall and redemption in the letters of Eve's name:

> The woman was previously named *virago*; after the Fall she is called *Eva*, as if that sound gives birth to *woe* [*ue*]. Eva gave death to the world; this name reversed will become *ave*, through which deliverance shone in the world. For the "ave" of Gabriel dissolves the whole woe

[*ue*] of Eva, when the Holy Virgin conceives her own Father through her ear. Every male brings forth "a" when he is born, every female "e." Adam the father bestows "a," Eve the mother creates "e."[91]

Eva might in the end have more easily escaped this obsessive wordplay as the palindrome Eve, even though Adam's first bad pun after his Fall plays on her now monosyllabic name: "O Eve, in evil hour thou didst give ear/ To that false worm" (*Paradise Lost* 9.1067–68).

This line of thought, connecting "woman" and "woe," has its peculiarly English variant in the pseudo-etymology of "woman" as the "woe-man" who brought woe to man. But in Chaucer's poetry, which predates this misogynistic joke, "woe" is something that women typically suffer, not cause: Custance the "woful womman" of the *Man of Law's Tale* (522) or the women whose fate is "oure owen wo to drynke" (*Troilus* 2.784) rather than the Wife of Bath as the dispenser of "wo that is in mariage" (*Wife's Prologue* 3).[92] Either way, the common noun "woman" joins the proper name "Eve" in English as a linguistic signal of the Fall. In other languages, the name "Eva" alone gives enough room for moral comment. Dante is almost certainly thinking of the "Eva" supposedly in babies' cries when he discusses Adam's first sound, which must have been "El," the name of God: "for if, since the disaster that befell the human race, the speech of every one of us has begun with 'woe!' [*heu*], it is reasonable that he who existed before should have begun with a cry of joy."[93] The first *lapsus linguae*, in other words, is a result of Adam's fall, as "El" becomes "eu" and "virago" becomes "Eva."

PLATO, ARISTOTLE, AND AUGUSTINE

These obsessive speculations on the name and nature of Eve, as language slips after the Fall, crystallize larger linguistic issues. In philosophical terms, what slips is the way language signifies reality. Christian exegesis in effect rehearses the ancient debate on the origin and nature of language, and succeeds in taking both sides by aligning them diachronically. Plato had argued in the *Cratylus* that at least some words have direct links to the things they signify.[94] Other names – Aristotle in *On Interpretation* would say all names – are imposed *ad placitum*, that is, arbitrarily or by convention, and without any natural connection to things.[95] Aulus Gellius sums up the differences between the two views; but their

definitive statements for the Middle Ages are Boethius' two commentaries on *De Interpretatione*, which translate Aristotle's text and expand
on his ideas, and Isidore's *Etymologiae* 1.29.2, which argues that most
words have origins according to the nature of the things they signify,
but some according to convention [*Non autem omnia nomina a veteribus
secundum naturam inposita sunt, sed quaedam et secundum placitum*].[96]
In Abelard's variation on this debate, words imitate things, with the
crucial stipulation that language was instituted by human invention. In
certain cases, etymology shows connections between names that corre-
spond to connections between things; but if a name is given to a thing
because the thing has a certain quality, the name is not given in order
to manifest that quality expressly. A name – and here Abelard opposes
Isidore – gives only a very partial view of what a thing truly is: we cannot
turn knowledge of words directly into knowledge of things.[97]

Despite an unflagging medieval delight in delving for etymologies, the
Boethian position on the nature of signification is certainly the majority
view, and etymology can often appear not "as a tool of epistemological
inquiry," but "in an essentially rhetorical way, as a place of invention."[98]
Yet the ancient debate found a compromise in which current usage
can offer "the key to uncovering the archeological layers of derived
meaning, the history of each word, and etymologically arriving back
at its original, natural meaning."[99] Thus Augustine, who generally sees
language as conventional, can say: "The Stoics believed that these cases
where the impression made on the senses by the things is in harmony
with the impression made on the senses by the sounds are, as it were, the
cradle of words."[100] John of Salisbury suggests such a compromise in his
Metalogicon, in a chapter entitled "Although it is not natural, grammar
imitates nature":

> Since grammar is arbitrary and subject to man's discretion [*ad
> placitum*], it is evidently not a handiwork of nature. Although nat-
> ural things are everywhere the same, grammar varies from people to
> people. However, we have already seen that nature is the mother of
> the arts . . . The very application [*impositio*] of names, and the use
> of various expressions, although such depends on the will of man
> [*arbitrio humano*], is in a way subject to nature, which it probably
> imitates [at least] to some modest extent.[101]

It would seem then, as several scholars have argued, that Howard Bloch "posits too sharp a contrast" between later medieval nominalism and "an 'early medieval grammar' of 'proper' signification"[102]; but there are equal risks of oversimplification in the claim that "people of the Middle Ages were basically anti-cratylistic in their conception of verbal signs."[103] Medieval logicians and speculative grammarians certainly take an ahistorical view; and by any interpretation, exegetical or scientific, language after Babel must be conventional. But the Genesis text makes countering demands on exegetes contemplating its literal meaning. In fact, Cratylism and conventionalism coexist in medieval thought, if in somewhat different fields of discourse,[104] and Bloch accurately describes an "anguished ambiguity provoked by a deep split between what medieval writers *knew* about verbal signs and what they *desired* to believe about them – a split evident in the easy copresence of what seem like mutually exclusive explanations of linguistic origin (natural versus conventional) as well as in an even more pervasive dichotomy between semiological theory and practice."[105] Indeed, I will argue in Chapter 2 that even Jean de Meun, at first sight one of the most vehement arguers for conventional signification, shows himself in one crucial passage to be deeply indebted to the Cratylist tradition.

After all, Genesis offers a special case, since the perfection of Adam's language in Eden implies a primal connection of name and thing. As Aquinas says, "And names ought to fit the nature of the things named; so Adam understood the natures of all the animals."[106] Nicholas of Lyra likewise explains that Adam names the birds and animals "in accordance with their nature, from which it is revealed that he had knowledge of the natural properties of living things, because names if they are obliged to be well given are given according to the properties of things."[107] And Meister Eckhart, in his *Expositio* on Genesis, argues that "Adam gave names to individual things according to the properties of those things, in such a way that the names themselves made known the natures and natural properties of the things."[108]

This correspondence between word and thing cannot easily survive the Fall, if Eve's name itself cannot be univocal and signs have become equivocal: Augustine notes that the lion can signify either the devil or Christ.[109] The loss of Eden implies among all else a shift to naming *ad placitum.*[110] The first instance of the shift is innocent enough. If Adam named "all the beasts of the earth, and all the fowls of the air" in Eden, the commentators ask, when did the fish receive their names? Peter Comestor says that they are perhaps to be included among "the beasts of the earth"; but he also supplies the usual answer, that the fish were discovered and named only later, according to convention and the usages of various languages.[111] Indeed, Isidore suggests that this delay in naming explains the number of marine creatures that are, like the sea horse, named "from their likeness to land animals."[112] The naming of the fish, Augustine says, presaged what is now true of all names:

> If we examine the various languages of mankind, we see that these living beings are called by names men have given them in their ordinary speech. And this is true not only of creatures in the water and on the earth but also of the earth itself, the water, the sky, what appears in the sky, and what does not appear but is believed to be there; all are called by different names in the different languages of the world. We know, of course, that there was originally just one language before man in his pride built the tower after the flood and caused human society to be divided according to different languages. And whatever the original language was, what point is there in trying to discover it? It was certainly the language Adam spoke; and in that language, if it has survived to our time, there are those words that were uttered when the first man named the beasts and the birds.[113]

In such discussions as these, the effect on language of the Fall is of secondary interest, more or less ignored in a spirit of scientific inquiry. And in fact Adelard of Bath's account of the "maiden" Grammar and her civilizing work, "essentially a mythologised version of the early chapters of Boethius' commentaries on the *De Interpretatione*," cannot be reconciled with the Genesis account: "For this maiden, when mortals first wandered about here and there in the countryside like beasts, without mutual courtesy and with their reason silent, and no one could convey to his fellow what he understood either about himself or about the objects around him – this maiden, I say, by putting names to single objects (*res*), first blessed mortals with the distinction of mutual conversation."[114] But if one believes that naming was originally a perfect intuition of the thing named, naming *ad placitum* marks a sinister divorce of name from thing, mirroring the flux and instability of the fallen world. Dante explores this divorce, as his thoughts on language change and develop.[115] In *De Vulgari Eloquentia*, human instability explains the variability in human language:

> Since, therefore, all our language (except that created by God along with the first man) has been assembled, in haphazard fashion [*a nostro beneplacito*], in the aftermath of the great confusion that brought nothing else than oblivion to whatever language had existed before, and since human beings are highly unstable and variable animals, our language can be neither durable nor consistent with itself; but, like everything else that belongs to us (such as manners and customs), it must vary according to distances of space and time.[116]

Here Dante agrees with most of the Genesis commentators that Adam spoke Hebrew, and that Hebrew is the one language exempt from change. But in *Paradiso* 26, where Adam repeats almost exactly this lament on human instability (26.127–29 and 136–38),[117] the original language is noticeably different, extinct long before the Tower of Babel (26.124–26). In Dante's revised view the language God gave to Adam must suffer, with everything else, the results of Adam's Fall.

Paradiso 26 essentially pushes several widespread assumptions about primitive language to their logical conclusion, assigning the great dividing point in linguistic history to a time well before the confusion of tongues, and presumably before the Flood. Because of Augustine's authoritative commentaries, the abrupt and universal collapse of likeness into unlikeness had come to be the central defining quality of the Fall. In linguistic terms, dissimilitude manifests itself in three related ways that are familiar to us from any theoretical discussions of language, since all theories of signification, medieval or modern, are of necessity theories of signification in the fallen world. The first is the inherent disposition of signs to float freely, as it were, separated from thought as well as from the things they signify. Augustine speaks for fallen humanity when he laments: "I grieve over the inability which my tongue has betrayed in answering to my heart."[118] The second is the gap between writing, as a simulacrum of speech, and speech itself. The third (an extension of the first) is the divorce of fallen words from the Truth – the potential in language for misused rhetoric or sophistry, and worse, for outright lying.

Since words are signs, separate at once from thought and external reality, they point to another distinction between naming according to the nature of a thing and naming *ad placitum*. In effect the distinction is between a grammatical view of signification and a logical one, the latter being the more widely current in later medieval thought, notably among the speculative grammarians.[119] The grammarian Priscian, on the one hand, argues that language refers directly to reality, and Anselm's *Monologion* makes this argument by consciously echoing the Creation narrative: all words are the "similitudines et imagines" of the things they signify.[120] In contrast Aristotle argues, with Boethius following him, that written words are signs of spoken words, spoken words signs of "affections or impressions of the soul," and those "mental affections . . . the same for the whole of mankind, as are also the objects of which those affections are representations or likenesses, images, copies."[121] Aristotle thus succeeds in explaining an evident point of unity within differing languages: that different words refer to the same universal "mental affections."[122] Even more important, his categories of written words, spoken words, mental states, and external objects readily turn into a hierarchy of value: in many classical and medieval accounts, spoken words are superior to written, and things are superior to words of either sort.[123] Writing was instituted, Augustine says, for commendable reasons: because men "could not hear the words of those not present," "and to tie together the things that tend to drop out of memory by the bond of writing, so to speak, by which they can be retrieved."[124] But in the Aristotelian view, especially if it is added to a Platonic distrust of writing,[125] our words are thus at a double remove from reality – or a triple remove, if they are written words. As Augustine says, written words are merely the "signs of words," that is, "the signs, therefore, of signs."[126]

In an alternative model, offered by Vincent of Beauvais, words are intermediaries between thoughts and things: "Furthermore, significant speech [*significativus sermo*] has a double relation. One, namely, to the thing signified, which is outside the soul. The other in truth to that image which is in the intellect or imagination."[127] But this doubleness of reference has much the same effect as reference at two or three removes. In Dante's powerful statement, our place in the hierarchy of being between animal and angel is mirrored in our language, which is similarly set between mere sound and pure meaning.[128] The neither/nor condition of language – suspended between mind and thing as a signifier, and between mind and body by its very nature – suggests all too well its implication in human frailty.

The most notable mark of contingency in language, in Augustine's widely influential analysis, is its temporality. We are separated from ourselves, or from the Truth within ourselves, and this separation appears inevitably in our speech: as Augustine repeatedly stresses, the fact that human speech must occur in time makes it the very image of division and mortality, set against the unity and wholeness of the Word. In an especially forceful example, he shows the fragile transience of an hour and of even the briefest of syllables:

> Of this very hour which is now passing, what will you give me, to which you will venture to apply the word, *it is*? When you say the very word '*est*' (it is), it is but one syllable, but one single motion, and the syllable has but three letters; in the very sounding of the word, you do not arrive at the second letter of the word, unless the first is finished. The third letter will not sound, except when the second also shall have past. Of this single syllable what will you give me? And can you retain the days, who cannot retain a syllable?[129]

Language is centrally implicated in this analysis of what the meaning of *is* is, since language and time together characterize our fallen state. Augustine laments that "the intellectual apprehension diffuses itself through the mind with something like a rapid flash, whereas the utterance is slow, and occupies time, and is of a vastly different nature" [*illa autem locutio tarda et longa est, longeque dissimilis*].[130] Though he moved beyond his early belief (in *De Genesi contra Manichaeos* 2.5) that "the fall made necessary signs themselves, not just the diversity of signs," hence that "language itself is a consequence of the fall,"[131] he continued to maintain that language would have been unnecessary in Paradise, because human beings then had the power to know God inwardly and directly. Likewise, in the world to come as in Momus' glass, "The thoughts of our minds will lie open to mutual observation," and speech will once again be beside the point.[132]

In our world, the extension of speech in time and the multiplication of significant sound are equally symptomatic of our fallibility. For if the one syllable "est" has such reverberations, what may one say of the multitude of words? Hugh of St. Victor laments that "many are the words [*sermones*] of man, because the heart of man is not one."[133] In Augustine's powerful phrasing, we contemplate "the significations of words, and the voices subjected to the authority of your Book which fly like the fowls of the air under the firmament – interpreting, expounding, discussing, disputing, praising You and calling upon You, words coming from the mouth and sounding forth that the congregation may answer Amen. That all these words have to be corporeally uttered is by reason of the abyss of this world and the blindness of our flesh, whereby thoughts cannot be seen but need to be sounded in our ears."[134] The multiplicity of our words, extended in time and space, marks our division from ourselves, from each other, and from God; and it drowns in noise the divine silence, toward which the rhetoric of redemption tends. "For the law is read, because we have not as yet reached that Wisdom which filleth the hearts and minds of those who look upon it: and there will be no need for us to have any thing read to us when there. For in what is read to us, syllables sound and pass away: that light of Truth passeth not away, but remaining stedfast satisfieth the hearts of those who witness it . . . For reading is only necessary, as long as *we know in part, and prophesy in part* [1 Cor. 13.9.10]."[135] After the Last Judgment, Bernard of Clairvaux says: "we will not have to use words even to each other where we will all run together into one perfect man. Fittingly therefore tongues shall cease; nor shall a mediating interpreter be required, where that unique Mediator shall by charity have done away with absolutely every middle term, that we also may be made one in them who are truly and eternally one, God the Father and the Lord Jesus Christ Himself."[136]

Language, when it forgets the silence from which it derives its truth and toward which it tends, risks a too great attention to itself, and neglect of the reality that it merely signifies. Bonaventure warns: "The thing [*res*] is not subject to the word, but the word [*sermo*] to the thing."[137] From Augustine on, in fact, commentators stress the ontological and moral primacy of the thing over the word.[138] For Hugh of St. Victor, "the significance of things is far more excellent than that of words, because the latter was established by usage, but Nature dictated the former. The latter is the voice of men, the former the voice of God speaking to men."[139] Abelard argues that there is a fundamental disjunction between words and things: a word is a *vox significativa ad placitum*; language is conventional, not natural, and it reflects mental structures, not real ones.[140] And John of Salisbury thus comments on the declining world: "Our age has expired and is reduced almost to nothing; not knowing the degrees of honor, it puffs itself up with honors; it is charmed by the vanity of names, while despising the truth and fruitful consequence of realities [*uanitate nominum delectatur contempta rerum ueritate et fructu*]."[141]

Augustine argues that all learning is in effect a kind of remembering, since we must learn the meaning of words from the things they refer to, not from other words:

> The utmost value I can attribute to words is this. They bid us look for things, but they do not show them to us so that we may know them . . . From words we can learn only words. Indeed we can learn only their sound and noise. Even if words, in order to be words really, must also be signs, I do not know that any sound I may hear is a word until I know what it means. Knowledge of words is completed by knowledge of things, and by the hearing of words not even words are learned. We learn nothing new when we know the words already, and when we don't know them we cannot say we have learned anything unless we also learn their meaning. And their meaning we learn not from hearing their sound when they are uttered, but from getting to know the things they signify. It is sound reasoning and truly said that when words are spoken we either know or do not know what they mean. If we know, we do not learn, but are rather reminded of what we know. If we do not know, we are not even reminded, but are perhaps urged to inquire.[142]

But if this argument suggests the risks of a language detached from a solid mooring in reality, the infected will can make matters worse, by consciously distorting the relation between word and thing – that is to say, by lying. Thierry of Chartres warns: "He who says the truth says that which is in the thing. He who speaks falsehood, wanders outside the thing."[143] And Augustine underlines the moral implications of lying by stating that falsehood was impossible in Eden before the Fall,[144] whereas now, truth is unavailable to us except by divine grace: "For I do not think that I could utter truth save by your inspiration, seeing that You *are true, and every man a liar. And when he speaks a lie, he speaks of his own* [Rom. 3.4; John 8.44]."[145]

That such ideas on signification are widely current is apparent in this scattering of quotations; but they also receive an extended, coherent, powerful statement in Augustine's account of his early life. As he makes clear in the *Confessions*, each human being can exemplify the plight of us all. Augustine's rhetorical training, which provides him with his vocation until his conversion gives him his true calling, marks his special affinity with words, for good or for ill: "it was impressed upon me as right and proper in a boy to obey those who taught me, that I might get on in the world and excel in the handling of words [*excellerem linguosis artibus*] to gain honor among men and deceitful riches" (1.9; trans. p. 12). But the distasteful effects he chronicles in himself characterize every human being, because we are all handlers of words, and original sin appears in everyone's development from infancy to speech.[146] A child, Augustine remembers, learns to speak primarily in order to satisfy his infected will more successfully than cries and gestures will allow him to do (1.8). The rhetorician, in this context, simply carries the duplicitous potentialities of language to their implied ends. As a teacher of his students, Augustine says, "without guile I taught them guilefulness" [*eos sine dolo docebam dolos*]: "I honestly did my best for men who loved vanity and sought after lying: and in truth I was one with them" (4.2; trans. p. 62).

His account of his conversion is an account of fallen eloquence giving way to redeemed speech, of words ceding place to the Word. He is inspired by Victorinus' example, when Julian made it illegal for Christians to teach literature and rhetoric: "Victorinus had obeyed the law, preferring to give up his own school of words [*loquacem scholam*] rather than Your word, by which You make eloquent the tongues of babes" (8.5; trans. p. 164). And such innocent eloquence is at the heart of his own famous conversion, when he takes as a command the mysterious voice of an unseen child of indeterminate sex, saying the words *Tolle lege*: "I snatched it up, opened it and in silence read the passage [*arripui, aperui et legi in silentio capitulum*] upon which my eyes first fell" (8.12; trans. p. 179).[147] The aftereffects of this heart-directed reading are specifically verbal, as Augustine gives up fallen language for redeemed speech and the rhetoric of silence: now the reason can compare "these words sounding in time with Your eternal Word and its silence" [*haec uerba temporaliter sonantia cum aeterno in silentio uerbo tuo*] (11.6; trans. p. 265), and it does so in a beautiful rhapsody:

> If to any man the tumult of the flesh grew silent, silent the images of earth and sea and air: and if the heavens grew silent, and the very soul grew silent to herself and by not thinking of self mounted beyond self: if all dreams and imagined visions grew silent, and every tongue and every sign and whatsoever is transient – for indeed if any man could hear them, he should hear them saying with one voice: We did not make ourselves, but He made us who abides forever; but if, having uttered this and so set us to listening to Him who made them, they all grew silent, and in their silence He alone spoke to us, not by them but by Himself: so that we should hear His word, not by any tongue of flesh nor the voice of an angel nor the sound of thunder nor in the darkness of a parable, but that we should hear Himself whom in all these things we love, should hear Himself and not them . . . (9.10; trans. pp. 200–1)

Augustine gives up his professorship of Rhetoric, or as he puts it, quietly withdraws his "tongue's service from the speech market" (9.2; trans. pp. 183–84); and he tells the people of Milan to hire another "seller of words" [*venditorem verborum*] to teach their students (9.5).[148]

SIGNS OF DECAY: CIVILIZATION AND ITS DISCONTENTS

In *The Confessions* Augustine recounts his deeply personal experience of the ambiguities in civilized speech, with codified rhetoric and verbal eloquence set against the tongues of babes and the solecisms in Scripture, offensive to the classicist but inconsequential to the Christian.[149] At several points, here and in his other works, Augustine comments on the fallen language of the earthly city; and the habitual paradox in his thought, attacking classical rhetoric while being drawn to it and exploiting it masterfully, sets the pattern for later discussions. The familiar tension between classical culture and Christian belief manifests itself in a careful culling of pagan culture or in rejecting that culture altogether, as when Jerome warns Eustochium against the cultivated married women who love "adultery even of the tongue" [*adulterium etiam linguae*].[150] But this tension itself hearkens back to a venerable tradition in Genesis commentary. In this tradition the arts of discourse, with their potential for misuse, typify the moral ambiguities in civilization. Speech and naming, Cassirer notes, characteristically have a central place in myths of Creation, in the "emergence from the vague fullness of existence into

a world of clear, verbally determinable forms."[151] After the Fall, however, speech becomes capable of sophistry and lying, and names manifest
fallen duplicity. The divisions of the Creation from its Creator, and of
the human race into sexes, are innocent. But the two meanings of the
postlapsarian name "Eva," that is, "life" and "woe," present a referential
doubling that forecasts the fate of Eve's children. The genealogies of
Cain and Seth, which mark the beginning of Augustine's Two Cities,
are identical in several of their names (Genesis 4–5) but in nothing else;
Philo stresses the fact that "each of the names mentioned has a meaning
that can be taken in two ways" (2.351), given its two contrary posses-
sors. For later medieval readers, Peter of Poitiers makes the opposition
between the two genealogies vividly clear in his popular *Compendium
Historiae*, especially when as often happens they are illustrated in adjoin-
ing parallel columns.[152]

Etymology signals character. Philo argues that Cain means
"Possession, because he thinks he possesses all things," whereas Abel's
name means "one who refers (all things) to God."[153] According to a
Midrash in *Genesis Rabba*, "Cain and Abel divided the world, Cain taking the immovables and Abel the movables."[154] The implications of this
distinction between the settled and the nomadic are explored in a later
Biblical book, Hebrews 11, where Abel heads the list of Old Testament
figures who were holy wanderers, "pilgrims and strangers on the earth"
(11.13). "But now they desire a better, that is to say, a heavenly country.
Therefore God is not ashamed to be called their God: for he hath prepared for them a city" (11.16). Cain, on the other hand, is the founder
of the first earthly city (Genesis 4.17). Philo comments that this cannot
literally be true, but means "that Cain resolves to set up his own creed,
just as one might set up a city," and that "Cain's buildings are demon-
strative arguments." With these arguments Cain "repels the assaults of
his adversaries, by forging plausible inventions contrary to the truth."
The inhabitants of Cain's city are "men ignorant of real wisdom," whose
"sophistic devices" God will finally punish when he destroys the Tower
of Babel. "By a 'tower' is meant a discourse working up each (immoral)
doctrine which they introduce."[155]

When later commentators imagine Cain's city, they make explicit
Philo's implied distrust of urban civilization. Although in many early
modern writings the arts of civilization serve as reparation for the Fall,[156]

to medieval moralists with few exceptions (notably Adelard of Bath) they are also severely affected by that Fall. Hugh of St. Victor proclaims that the liberal arts intend "to restore within us the divine likeness, a likeness which to us is a form but to God is his nature"; Peter Lombard confirms that Christ, the New Adam, "by divine inspiration, . . . was master of all sciences and arts."[157] But Remigius of Auxerre argues that as fallen human beings we in effect "do nothing more than recall" the arts when we learn them; and later, the scholastic theory of knowledge represents "the task of learning as a laborious reconquest of that which the human mind had once held without effort."[158]

Wyclif says that none of us would have need of the liberal or mechanical arts were we still in the state of innocence.[159] Hugh of St. Victor, who distinguishes among "three works – the work of God, the work of nature, and the work of the artificer, who imitates nature," names Adam and Eve's "aprons" of fig leaves as the first examples of "The work of the artificer," which is "to put together things disjoined or to disjoin those put together, whence we read, 'They sewed themselves aprons.'"[160] If by implication the arts are meant to restore some of our primal powers, they are tainted by their origin in Cain's city, a first city that is in fact a second city, perversely differentiating itself from the city of God.

Cain's initial sin is that "he did not rightly divide" his harvest.[161] But Cain quickly becomes a master of division and deviser of categories, walling the city and dividing the land: in the English translation of Trivet's *Chronicles* "he was the furste that deuysed the londe and walled the Cytees and gadered to geder rychesse by streynght and be Rauyne."[162] Josephus, in a much-quoted passage, adds that he "also changed, by his invention of weights and measures, the simplicity with which men previously lived, their life innocent because of their ignorance of such things; and he turned magnanimity into cunning artifice and corruption."[163] The only remedy for the arts misused, at best a partial remedy, is in the paradox that Gower outlines, by which *divisio*, the rational articulation of scholastic discourse, can try to undo the effects of *divisio* in the fragmentation of speech and minds at the beginning of human history.[164]

The extreme result of this continuing process of division is of course the Tower of Babel, when the one true tongue becomes garbled and confused into seventy-two.[165] But division, obsessively multiplied, also defines the last of the Cainite line before the flood, Lamech, who shares the name of Noah's father[166]:

> ... and Mathusael begot Lamech. Who took two wives: the name of the one was Ada, and the name of the other Sella. And Ada brought forth Jabel: who was the father of such as dwell in tents, and of herdsmen. And his brother's name was Jubal; he was the father of them that play upon the harp and the organs. Sella also brought forth Tubalcain, who was a hammerer and artificer in every work of brass and iron. And the sister of Tubalcain was Noema. And Lamech said to his wives, Ada and Sella: Hear my voice, ye wives of Lamech, hearken to my speech: for I have slain a man to the wounding of myself, and a stripling to my own bruising. Sevenfold vengeance shall be taken for Cain: but for Lamech seventy times sevenfold.[167] (Gen. 4:18–24)

The usual medieval explanation of this song, to explain the pleonasm of murdered "man" and "stripling," comes from the Jewish apocrypha by way of Jerome.[168] In Calvin's unsympathetic summary: "The Jewes, according to their manner, have imagined a vaine fable: as, that Lamech was a hunter, and blinde, and for the same cause had a boy to guide his hande. Nowe Caine lurking in the wood, was slaine by him with an arrowe: because the boy deeming him to be a wilde beast, directed his hande to shoote at him. Wherefore he revenged him selfe on the ladde, who through his wante of discretion, was the cause of the murder."[169] (The boy, according to Rashi and other commentators, was Lamech's own son Tubalcain.) The story appears in many commentaries in the earlier Middle Ages,[170] and is even more widely diffused after its appearance in the *Historia Scholastica*.[171] It appears in a number of visual representations as well, among them a roof boss in Norwich Cathedral and the illuminations of the Holkham Bible Picture Book and B. L. MS Egerton 1894.[172] Lamech's crime fittingly ties him, as the last in Cain's line, with Cain himself – both killers, but Lamech doubly guilty of parricide and infanticide, and to be punished not seven, but seventy-seven fold.[173]

Lamech's other infamous act is another form of doubling – his sexual innovation, bigamy. Alcuin says that when Adam and Eve covered their nakedness with fig leaves, it was "because they lost the glory of simple chastity, they flew to the duplicitous itch of lust" [*duplicem libidinis pruriginem*].[174] This "duplicitous itch" pervades the fallen world; many commentators note that Lamech's daughter Noema is the last named before the Flood,[175] and the fact that she and Lamech's wives are all named, while there are no female names given among Seth's descendants, shows that Cain's line is the earthly city of carnal generation.[176] Bigamous Lamech, the last of the Cainite line, makes explicit the fall from unity, as he turns duplicity into doubleness. The *Middle English Genesis* sums him up as one cursed by "twin-wifing ant twin-manslagt" (485): the double murderer is also a double husband. His sexual doubling, much remarked upon by the commentators,[177] is the detail Chaucer mentions in his three references to Lamech. The Wife of Bath takes pains to differentiate herself from "shrewed Lameth and his bigamye" (*Wife of Bath's Prologue* 54).[178] The betrayed falcon in the *Squire's Tale* compares her false lover to Lamech, "that alderfirst bigan/ To loven two" (550–51). And in *Anelida and Arcite*, he sums up the amorous duplicity of men:

> But nevertheless, gret wonder was hit noon
> Thogh he were fals, for hit is kynde of man
> Sith Lamek was, that is so longe agoon,
> To ben in love as fals as evere he can;
> He was the firste fader that began
> To loven two, and was in bigamye,
> And he found tentes first, but yf men lye.
>
> (148–54)

In the final verse, Chaucer assigns to Lamech the work of his son Jabel. The confusion is understandable because Lamech offers a malign paternal model for the accomplishments of his children, who carry further the Cainite division and subdivision, parodies of the innocent divisions in the Creation narrative.[179] One of the illustrations in Egerton 1894 represents the scene vividly: Lamech has two wives, Oda [Ada] and Sella; each of the two wives has two children; and the four children are the inventors of the arts, which themselves all enact articulation and division.[180]

Jabel the first shepherd, according to Peter Comestor, "discovered the portable tents of shepherds for changing pasture, set the flocks in order, and divided them by their branding marks, and separated according to their kinds the flocks of sheep from the flocks of goats, and also according to their nature he distinguished them," dividing them by color and by age. He is the master of "sundring and samening," according to the *Middle English Genesis*; and his name, Jerome says, means "separating" or "sending in different directions" [*dimittens*], "or changed, or it will pass away."[181] His brother Jubal, who is often called Tubal, is Ada's other son, "the father of them that play upon the harp and the organs" (Gen. 4.21). He is described as the inventor not of instruments but of music, "that is, of harmonies"; and his name means "brought down, or separating."[182] In many accounts, including the *Historia Scholastica* and Higden's *Polychronicon*, Jubal discovered music by listening to Tubalcain banging metals at his forge, thus inventing the art that the Greeks attribute "fabulously" [*fabulose*] to Pythagoras.[183] Chaucer himself, citing Peter Riga, refers to this story when the Man in Black names Tubal as the discoverer of "the art of songe":

> For as hys brothres hamers ronge
> Upon hys anvelt up and doun,
> Therof he took the firste soun –
> But Grekes seyn Pictagoras,
> That he the firste fynder was
> Of the art (Aurora telleth so);
> But therof no fors of hem two.[184]
> (*Duchess* 1160–70)

Jubal's other famous accomplishment, much commented on, alters a detail in Josephus. According to the *Jewish Antiquities*, the descendants of Seth were expert in astronomy and, fearing Adam's prophetic vision of the world's end, wrote down the rules of the arts on two columns, one to survive flood, the other fire. In Higden's *Polychronicon* the last in Seth's line, Enoch, is paired with Lamech – each the seventh in descent from Adam, one the best, the other the worst. In this account the Sethites invented the arts of learning – particularly Enoch, the "fyndere of lettres" who "wroot som bookes."[185] But many medieval commentaries, often citing Josephus as their source, assign this work to Jubal, Cain's descendant, giving it a more sinister significance.[186] John Cassian's version of the story explains how evil arts could survive the Flood: Ham "knew he could not bring a book on these subjects into the ark," so "he carved these evil arts and profane writings on various metals and hard stones which could not be worn away by the water. When the deluge was finished he searched them out with the same curiosity with which he had hid them and transmitted to posterity the seeds of sacrilege and profanity."[187]

The first of Sella's children, Tubalcain, is often linked with Jubal, and sometimes confused with him as the inventor of music.[188] In the Middle English metrical version of Methodius' *Revelations*, Jubal and Tubal are "þe fyrste men of all/ þat euer fonde crafte ჳonge or olde"[189]; and they are harshly treated in the early apocryphal literature.[190] Tubalcain himself – in the standard account by Josephus, which was widely disseminated by the *Glossa Ordinaria*, Peter Comestor, and Peter Riga – discovered ironworking, skillfully practiced and taught the arts of war, and made sculptures in metal for the delight of the eyes (by discovering the art of casting).[191] According to Jerome, the name Tubal means "drawn to lamentation"; and Rashi argues that Tubalcain is so named because "He seasoned and improved the work of Cain in making implements of war for murderers."[192] In the *Middle English Genesis*, "Of irin, of golde, siluer, and bras/ To sundren and mengen wis he was" (467–68); like his half-brothers, who divide flocks and harmonies, Tubalcain is a master of differentiation. So is his sister Noema, the last of Lamech's children: she discovered "the art of particolored weaving" [*artem variae texturae*], or as Caxton translates the phrase, "the craft of diverse texture."[193] Her name itself sums up the sexual license before the Flood.[194]

Each of the arts thus manifests division and subdivision, marking a universal lapse from innocent unreflecting identity to duplicity and alienation, and mirroring the separation of word from thing in the fallen world. Tubalcain's art, given the commentators' emphasis on its bellicose effects, is the most conspicuously tainted; but his link with Jubal soils the art of music by association, and the art of singing itself may suggest the fallen state of language.[195] Jabel's art would seem innocent enough, but the *Glossa Ordinaria* talks of the "instability" symbolized by the shepherd's nomadic life, and Bede says that Jabel's name appropriately means "mutatus" because in the Flood Cain's progeny was "changed in punishment."[196] Noema's discovery is not simply of weaving, since Eve the weaver predates her, but of weaving as a decorative art. According to the Knight of the Tower, Noah's Flood "was bycause of the pryde and desguysynge of men and specially of wymmen/ that counterfeted them self of newe and dishonest rayments," led by Satan in "their grete pryde and their desguysynge/ . . . to falle in the fylthe of the stynkyng synne of lecherye."[197] Noema is often specifically identified as one of "the daughters of men" from Cain's line who seduced "the sons of God" from Seth's (Genesis 6.1–2).[198]

In this Genesis narrative, as it is elaborated upon by the commentators, the arts are morally ambiguous in themselves and because of their origins. Hugh of St. Victor suggests with particular forcefulness the implications of this universal division: "Thus, once it had begun to lose its integrity through its earthly desires, the human heart, which had hitherto kept its stability in cleaving to divine love and remained one in the love of the One, was as it were divided into as many channels as there were objects that it craved, once it had begun to flow in different directions through earthly longings. And that is how it happens that the soul, not knowing how to love its true good, is never able to maintain its stability."[199] Vincent of Beauvais warns us to "spoil the Egyptians" by using the fruits of the arts without falling prey to their evils.[200] Bede's discussion, expanding on Augustine, is especially eloquent on the way we may do so. The moral taint of the civilizing arts, he says, comes from their worldly focus, because they all "pertain to the refinement or ornament or allurements of this life." Abel and the descendants of Seth, by contrast, lived "a simple life," as if they were "pilgrims on the earth." For although Abel was a shepherd, he did not wish to "give himself up to this duty" to the extent of inventing shepherds' tents, as Jabel later did. In the fallen world the arts are needed: metalworking would not have been invented had "humankind observed natural law properly." Yet even if the arts are innately culpable, they may nonetheless be put to good use by the holy. For example, "the patriarchs lived in tents, but as if they were pilgrims in the world, in contrast to those who were accustomed to live in cities and houses as if they were citizens of the earth. The psalmists used the cither and organ, but in order to praise the Lord."[201] Even so, we must remember that the arts were first misused just before the cleansing Flood; and Bede says that on the Day of Judgment we will need to account for the ways in which we have used them.

NIMROD THE IDOLATOR AND THE TOWER OF BABEL

When Chaucer's lyric "The Former Age" mentions Nimrod and "Jupiter the likerous" (56) in the same breath, it insists on a parallel between classical mythology and the Genesis narrative of early human history.[202] In doing so, Chaucer follows a long-standing tradition: the ninth-century *Ecloga Theoduli* corrects Pseustis' fable of the giants' rebellion against Jove with Alithia's true account of the Tower of Babel, a kindred rebellion by Nimrod the giant.[203] Dante follows this tradition in *Inferno* 31, where Nimrod appears with the giants Ephialtes and Antaeus. It also colors his account of the gigantic Old Man of Crete, who sums up the decaying world by his physical recapitulation of the four ages of gold, silver, brass, and iron, and by his embodiment of the shift from unity to division: "Every part except the gold is cleft by a fissure that drips with tears" (*Inferno* 14.112–13). These insertions of classical myth enrich the context of the Babel story: if language fell with Adam, if it implicitly participates in further corruption with Lamech and his children, the decisive event for language in later history, in effect a second Fall, is the building of the Tower of Babel. Before, "the earth was of one tongue, and of the same speech" [*Erat . . . terra labii unius, et sermonum eorumdem*] (Gen. 11.9); afterwards, God punishes proud men by deciding: "let us . . . there confound their tongue, that they may not understand one another's speech" [*confundamus ibi linguam eorum, ut non audiat unusquisque vocem proximi sui*] (11.7). "And therefore the name thereof was called Babel, because there the language [*labium*] of the whole earth was confounded" (11.9).[204]

Augustine describes God's wrath as the result of a mad human pride: "This pride is signified by the famous tower raised towards heaven at the time when wicked men justly received incompatible languages [*voces dissonas*] to match their incompatible minds."[205] Nimrod particularly embodies this pride; for although Genesis offers no suggestion that he is the builder of the tower, other than that Babylon is named as "the beginning of his kingdom" (Gen. 10.10), he is universally so identified in the commentaries.[206] He brings with him the unsavory associations of his being "mighty on the earth" and "a stout hunter before the Lord" [*robustus venator coram Domino*] (Gen. 10.8–9),[207] two characterizations that serve to link him with his sinful predecessors. Cain, as

Isidore notes, was the first city-builder before, Nimrod the first after the Flood.[208] The association is made even stronger because Ham, the name of Nimrod's grandfather, is often confused in its medieval spelling Cham with Cain.[209] Nimrod also, as at least one commentary notes, follows Lamech's example by being a hunter[210]; and Bonaventure links them together as Antichrists.[211] The association of Nimrod with Cain and Lamech is predictable, because he begins anew the corrupting processes of civilization. His name itself, Jerome says, means "tyrant, or fugitive, or transgressor,"[212] his hunting and tyranny being related sides of his character: Nimrod is called a "mighty hunter" because he "laid hold of an unaccustomed tyranny as if by hunting."[213] Although the beginnings of warfare are usually attributed to his descendant Ninus,[214] the two of them are sometimes confused, and Philippe de Mézières describes Nimrod's "jardin horrible et perilleux," in which there is no "justice, amour, regle ne policie," whose inhabitants are heretics, magicians, and astrologers, and which figures forth "all the instances of the shedding of human blood since the beginning of the world."[215] *Paradise Lost* describes Nimrod's dominion as a perversion of the Golden Age:

> . . . till one shall rise
> Of proud ambitious heart, who not content
> With fair equality, fraternal state,
> Will arrogate dominion undeserved
> Over his brethren, and quite dispossess
> Concord and law of nature from the earth,
> Hunting (and men not beasts shall be his game)
> With war and hostile snare such as refuse
> Subjection to his empire tyrannous.[216]
>
> (12.24–32)

Nimrod, in a tradition deriving from the apocryphal literature, is also associated with astronomy and arcane knowledge. According to the *Revelations* of Pseudo-Methodius, translated into Latin in the eighth century, Noah had a fourth son named Ionitus, who was expert in astronomy and became Nimrod's teacher.[217] Peter Comestor copies this story, and his account is widely diffused in the later Middle Ages: it appears in the text that accompanies the illustrations of Egerton 1894,[218] and in Holkot's commentary on the Book of Wisdom.[219] Hugh of St. Victor identifies "Nemroth the Giant" as "the greatest astrologer," and

Gower describes him as one of the first writers about astronomy.[220] His building of the Tower of Babel, in part to further his expertise in star-lore, characterizes his presumptuous quest of forbidden knowledge.[221] His most extreme punishment, in *Inferno* 31, is utter solipsism: he blows his horn, speaks a completely unintelligible language, and cannot understand anyone else's speech. In several medieval accounts, his linguistic punishment is much less severe: he must give up Hebrew and spend the rest of his life speaking Chaldaean.[222]

Nimrod's final exploit, which is – I will argue – of particular relevance to the *Canon's Yeoman's Tale*, is as the first worshipper of idols, specifically the tyrant who compelled the Chaldaeans to worship fire.[223] This story originates in the pseudo-Clementine *Recognitions*, and from there receives a wide dissemination in the Middle Ages, especially through the medium of such works as Isidore's *Chronica*.[224] As Hugh of St. Victor sums up Nimrod's achievements: "he began to exercise power [*dominium*] over others through violence, and led them into idolatry, so that they might worship fire as God, because he saw the very great uses by the benefit of the sun, which is fiery, affecting the earth. Which error the Chaldaeans followed afterwards."[225] In many accounts idolatry begins two generations later, with Nimrod's grandson Ninus, who makes idols in honor of his dead father Belus.[226] But because the *Recognitions* confuses Nimrod and Ninus – "Nimrod, . . . whom the Greeks also called Ninus, and from whose name the city of Nineveh took its name"[227] – Nimrod himself is the more strongly associated with idolatry, as in *Mandeville's Travels*: "Nembroth . . . was the firste kyng of the world. And he leet make an ymage in the lykness of his fader & constreyned all his subgettes for to worschipe it. And anon begonnen othere lordes to do the same. And so begonnen the ydoles & the symulacres first."[228]

The confusion here of idolatrous fire-worship with Ninus' solider images probably contributes to the more general condemnations of Nimrod's work. In several accounts, Nimrod orders Abraham to be thrown into the fire because he refuses to worship it as the Chaldaeans do[229]; and he is also associated with the beginnings of pyromancy.[230] Higden says: "De ortu idolatriae omnia pene figmenta manarunt," a statement that is rendered differently in the two translations of his work: "Of þe bryngynge forþ of mawmetrie com wel nyh al þe feyninge of poetrie"; and "Alle figmentes toke begynnenge allemoste of ydolatry."[231] The context makes apparent that Higden is referring especially to the poets' portrayals of the gods; and a similar concern lies behind an opinion, reported by Boccaccio, "that poetry was far older than Moses, having had its origin about the time of Nembroth," the founder of idolatry. "For when he saw that fire was useful to men, and that he could, to some extent, foretell the future from its various motions and sounds, he averred that it was a god; wherefore he not only worshipped it instead of God, and persuaded the Chaldeans to do likewise, but built temples to it, ordained priests, and even composed prayers," in which he used "formal, polished discourse." Yet even if the Assyrians did invent "religious worship, the study of philosophy, and the glory of arms," Boccaccio adds, "I cannot easily believe, without more trustworthy evidence, that an art so sublime as that of poetry arose first among peoples so barbarous and wild."[232] Deschamps too associates Nimrod with the arts: his quick synopsis of human history, as "Memoire" remembers it, sums up the division of the world among the three sons of Noah, the confusion of tongues, Nimrod's tyranny, the beginning of war, and the articulation of the seven liberal arts, "each in its practice."[233] Such an account comes predisposed to find in Genesis history the myth of the Golden Age.

Nimrod's most famous reputed accomplishment, and the one at the center of his other sinister deeds, is his building of the Tower of Babel. In turn, the linguistic effects of Babel take on even more sinister coloring from Nimrod's tyranny, fire-worship, and idolatry.[234] The story has a central place in the Western imagination,[235] owing in part, no doubt, to its potential for visual representation: like the Ark and Abraham's sacrifice of Isaac, it lends itself to striking visual images such as Brueghel's painting or the illumination in Egerton 1894. Its prominence is also in part due to the identification of Babel with Babylon in Biblical geography. The symmetrical design of the famous mappamundi in Hereford Cathedral makes Eden, Babylon, Jerusalem, Rome, and Gibraltar equidistant from each other, as points marking the major events in the history of humankind.[236] More important still is typological symmetry, for Babel is the symbolic type of Pentecost (Acts 2.1–12); and in the *Speculum Humanae Salvationis*, the two scenes are represented side by side.[237] As the *Glossa Ordinaria* explains, "That confusion is contrasted with the confusion of tongues, from which the name Babel was obtained. Thus the humility of the Apostles answers to human pride"; "The dispersion of tongues was done in the tower, but what pride scattered, humility gathers together again: in pride the dispersion comes to be, in humility concord."[238] In this typological view, the hellish extremes of linguistic division are countered by heavenly possibilities: the confusion of tongues, like Adam's Fall, has its ordained place in the history of redemption. Babel thus has symbolic meaning as "pride of the world, or the doctrines of heretics," which will give way at last to "unity of confession and faith."[239]

In later and earlier – that is to say, early modern and early apocryphal – speculations on linguistic matters, various languages lay claim to being the first one of all. In the apocryphal *Book of the Cave of Treasures*, for example, Syriac takes the place of Hebrew as the first language, in part because of the symbolic implications of the way it is written: "In the writing of the Syrians the left hand stretcheth out to the right hand, and all the children of the left hand (*i.e.* the heathen) draw nigh to the right hand of God."[240] Richard Verstegan reports arguments that Teutonic was the first language, as "proved" by the Germanic meanings of "Adam," "Eve," and other names in Genesis.[241] Herodotus' story of Psammetichus, King of Egypt, recounts a notorious linguistic experiment with infants; in its medieval analogue, Frederick II "wanted to find out what kind of speech and what manner of speech children would have when they grew up, if they spoke to no one beforehand. So he bade foster mothers and nurses to suckle the children, to bathe and wash them, but in no way to prattle to them or to speak to them, for he wanted to learn whether they would speak the Hebrew language, which was the oldest, or Greek, or Latin, or Arabic, or perhaps the language of their parents, of whom they had been born. But he laboured in vain, because the children all died. For they could not live without the petting and the joyful faces and loving words of their foster mothers."[242]

The less experimentally inclined patristic and medieval commentators are nearly unanimous in their view that Hebrew was the language that Adam spoke, and the sole language prior to Babel: indeed Vincent of Beauvais, copying Augustine, argues that "before the division of tongues it was not called 'Hebrew,' but 'human' [*humana*] simply, seeing that all men used it in common."[243] Isidore, like many others, says that Hebrew was the only language before Babel, and that Adam named the birds and animals in Hebrew.[244] According to several medieval narratives, Hebrew survived the confusion of tongues because Shem, or his descendants Heber and Peleg, did not participate in the building of the Tower.[245] There are other, more thoroughgoing explanations: God's plan for the redemption of human beings explains why Hebrew survived. According to Haimo of Auxerre, "it was fitting that, in the language in which Adam had heard the persuasive eloquence of the Devil [*diaboli suasionem*], in that same language he should receive the preaching of the Savior"[246]; and Dante echoes this line of argument in *De Vulgari Eloquentia*.[247]

In medieval accounts, Latin and Greek join Hebrew to make up the three sacred languages, the ones that appear on the Cross (John 19.20) and in which Holy Scripture is recorded and authoritatively translated. Augustine explains why these three should be the ones represented on the Cross, and "dominate there above the others: Hebrew, because of the Jews glorying in the law of God; Greek, because of the pagan sages [*gentium sapientes*]; Latin, because of the Romans ruling over many or nearly all peoples until then." Brunetto Latini remarks that after the confusion of tongues, the three sacred languages sum up linguistic and national divisions in the world, with those who live in the East speaking from the throat as the Hebrews do, those in the middle of the earth speaking from the palate like the Greeks, and those in the West following the Italians by speaking through their teeth.[248] Knowledge of all three – "eminent to the highest degree in the whole world," according to Hugh of St. Victor – is invaluable to the Biblical exegete, since comparing their renderings of Scripture can illuminate its obscurities.[249] Hugh sidesteps a question that Jerome had raised: whether a translation of the Bible – into Latin, let alone a vernacular language – can claim the divine inspiration of its original. But the view of Gregory the Great, who argues for inspired translation (hence for the authority of the Vulgate), is the usual one until the Reformation.[250] Indeed, the work of the Septuagint translators is seen from early on as a reparation for Babel – their number, seventy-two, and the days they take to accomplish their task, also seventy-two, equalling the number of languages into which the first language disintegrates.[251] And in one eccentric commentary, Latin differs significantly from the vernacular languages and succeeds in escaping the corruption of Babel. Henri de Crissey argues that the meanings of vernacular words are imposed *ad placitum*, while Latin, deriving from Greek, which in turn derives from Hebrew, goes back to the words given by God.[252] The standard view, however, is that while Latin is more stable because more fixed in form – Dante describes Latin as "grammatica," more perfect than the vernacular (*DVE* 1.1.2–3) – it too suffers the effects of all languages after Babel.

The immediate effects of Babel were of course confusion and division. In a pungent comment on language after Babel, Augustine remarks that

> if two men meet, and are forced by some compelling reason not to pass on but to stay in company, then if neither knows the other's language, it is easier for dumb animals, even of different kinds, to associate together than these men, although both are human beings. For when men cannot communicate their thoughts to each other, simply because of difference of language, all the similarity of their common human nature is of no avail to unite them in fellowship. So true is this that a man would be more cheerful with his dog for company than with a foreigner [*linguarum diuersitas hominem alienat ab homine . . . ita ut libentius homo sit cum cane suo quam cum homine alieno*].[253]

When Holkot comments in passing on Babel, arguing that "any men whatever, if they have to cohabit, require an idiom for communicating together their thoughts in diverse matters," he cites the *Nicomachean Ethics* (8.12): "all friendship consists in communication" [*omnis amicitia consistit in communicatione*][254]; and the loss of such friendship and human association becomes vividly apparent in the commentaries on Genesis 11, often with humorous effect. Verstegan imagines the scene of one language suddenly becoming seventy-two: people race around "lyke mad men, euery one labouring (in that great & confused multitude) to seek out such as himself could vnderstand," until all the members of the various language communities assemble, ready to disperse into the wider world.[255] Verstegan has his medieval antecedents: the thirteenth-century *Histoire Universelle* describes the workmen at Babel suddenly unable to communicate, with one asking for fire or water, only to be given earth or a stone; and this story is repeated in several of the early commentaries on Dante.[256] The *Mistére du Viel Testament* shows us this scene as it unfolds: the workmen abruptly begin to speak nonsensical languages, incomprehensible to each other; even worse, according to apocryphal account, "If a mason told a hod-carrier 'Give me mortar!', the carrier would hand him a brick instead, with which the mason would angrily kill the hod-carrier. Many were the murders done in the Tower; and on the ground also, because of this confusion; until at last work slowed to a standstill."[257] In *De Vulgari Eloquentia*, the confusion of tongues is a confusion of professional jargons:

> Only among those who were engaged in a particular activity did their language [*loquela*] remain unchanged; so, for instance, there was one for all the architects, one for all the carriers of stones, one for all the stone-breakers, and so on for all the different operations. As many as were the types of work involved in the enterprise, so many were the languages by which the human race was fragmented [*tot tot ydiomatibus tunc genus humanum disiungitur*]; and the more skill required for the work, the more rudimentary and barbaric the language they now spoke [*tanto rudius nunc barbariusque locuntur*].[258]

Nimrod's presumption above all is punished by incomprehension, in Augustine's version of *contrapasso*: "Since a ruler's power of domination is wielded by his tongue, it was in that organ that his pride was condemned to punishment. And the consequence was that he who refused to understand God's bidding so as to obey it, was himself not understood when he gave orders to men."[259] The loss of friendly communication and unanimity of voice has more universal, distressing consequences, in the strange tongues [*diverse lingue*] that Dante hears at the entrance to Hell (*Inferno* 3.25). And in the Prologue to the *Confessio Amantis*, Gower presents the confusion of tongues as the supreme example of division, the "moder of confusioun,"[260] epitomizing the discord in the kingdoms of the declining world and within the human body. Division is indeed at the heart of fallen man's mortality, since "his complexioun/ Is mad upon divisioun" of the elements and humours; this is a war that "ferst began in Paradis" with the Fall, and will not finally end until the Day of Judgment.[261]

Inevitably, the very nature of naming has changed with the division of languages: "Adam imposed names on all things in Hebrew. But after the division of tongues was accomplished, separate peoples were accustomed to name all things according to their properties, and their own pleasure."[262] In an especially influential reading, Alcuin argues that there was no new creation involved; as the *Glossa Ordinaria* paraphrases his argument: "In this division of tongues God made nothing new, but divided the modes of speaking and forms of language among different peoples. Whence we find the same syllables and letters of the same meaning joined in different ways in different tongues, and often the same nouns or verbs other in significance."[263] Language has decomposed as part of a general decay, its original unity disintegrating into fungible particles: indeed, our speech differs from God's precisely because human language continues to change. Chaucer's phrasing in the proem to Book Two of *Troilus and Criseyde* is very close to *De Vulgari Eloquentia* 1.9.6 and *Paradiso* 26.127–32; Constance in the *Man of Law's Tale* speaks "a maner Latyn corrupt" (519), late Latin or even Italian[264]; and the courtly compliment to Queen Anne, that our first letter is now an *A* (*Troilus* 1.171), may imply that in other languages and at other times, this was not the case. Dante's interest in these matters is in many respects precocious, tied as it is to his desire to rehabilitate the "illustrious" vernacular; but it has some parallels in Ranulf Higden's famous lament concerning the decline of English from its original purity because the English, unlike the Scots and Welsh, have adulterated their language: "as a result of mixture, first with the Danes and then Normans, by a corruption of their language in many respects, they now incorporate strange bleatings and babblings."[265]

Higden laments a decay largely beyond remedy: in the fallen world after Babel, grammar serves as a palliative, staving off further decline[266] because to some extent it can ground discourse: as Anne Middleton argues, "Grammar reflects the structure of mind, but, more important, the relation of concepts in the human mind corresponds to relationships of real entities in the universe, to what eternally is."[267] The effort to restore language to its original purity and simplicity is typically a seventeenth-century enterprise, as in the Royal Society's search for a scientific prose style. To counter the "extravagance" of prolixity, Sprat says, the Society's members will try "to return back to the primitive purity, and shortness, when men deliver'd so many *things*, almost in an equal number of *words*," striving for "a close, naked, natural way of speaking."[268] For medieval commentators, the restoration of such linguistic purity, though forecast by Pentecost, must await the Last Day: in one extreme version, "Hebrew was the mother of tongues and would be the current speech in heaven, even though the blessed would be able to speak all languages."[269] More commonly, Hebrew is awarded a privileged position among the languages on earth. For Jerome, "The beginning of speech and of public communication and all that we speak is the Hebrew tongue, in which the Old Testament was written"; and John of Salisbury praises Hebrew as a language "more natural than the others, having been, so to speak, taught by nature herself."[270]

At scattered points in the long expanse of time between Babel and Pentecost, issues of language come to the fore in the Bible – as exceptions to the rule of obscure prophecy and double meaning, as manifestations of God's power, and as forceful reminders of a largely vanished clarity. The Lord descends in a pillar of cloud and reproaches Aaron and Miriam for speaking against Moses: "Hear my words: If there be among you a prophet of the Lord, I will appear to him in a vision, or I will speak to him in a dream [*in visione apparebo ei, vel per somnium loquar ad illum*]. But it is not so with my servant Moses who is most faithful in all my house. For I speak to him mouth to mouth, and plainly: and not by riddles and figures [*non per aenigmata et figuras*] doth he see the Lord" (Numbers 12.6–8; cf. Deuteronomy 34.10).[271] Bruno de Segni, alluding to Jesus' explanation of why he speaks in parables (Matt. 13.9–14), identifies Moses allegorically with Christ, but Miriam and Aaron with the Jewish people and priests who do not understand the riddles and figures that they hear.[272] Partly to keep itself unsullied by the uncomprehending, truth generally appears to the prophet in vision or dream, or in the *aenigmata Prophetarum* and "the words of the wise, and their mysterious sayings" [*verba sapientium et aenigmata eorum*] (Proverbs 1.6).[273] Ambrose explains this obscurity in his comment on Psalm 61.12 (AV 62.11), "God hath spoken once. These two things have I heard" [*Semel locutus est Deus, duo haec audivi*]:

> God has spoken once, and many things were heard, because he has not spoken through letters and syllables. He has spoken through mysterious sayings, he has spoken through visions, he has spoken through the distribution of charisms, he has spoken of single things through the Spirit. We, however, say many things and scarcely are

heard. Once he has spoken in the Law, and likewise a second time he has spoken in the Gospel. Or perhaps, as I think, because he has spoken in many places in the prophets, he has spoken lastly in his Son . . . To us, therefore, that is, to the Church, he has spoken once, and two things were heard, because we have both heard and understood those things that they had not understood who read them: they did not hear, who heard them. For Christ alone opened the human ear for understanding mysteries; he alone undid the seal of the book, and unravelled the mysterious sayings of the prophets.[274]

Augustine likewise justifies the multiplicity of meaning in the Bible, where "problems and ambiguities of many kinds" create problems for "casual readers": "In some passages they find no meaning at all that they can grasp at, even falsely, so thick is the fog created by some obscure phrases. I have no doubt that this is all divinely predetermined, so that pride may be subdued by hard work and intellects which tend to despise things that are easily discovered may be rescued from boredom and reinvigorated."[275] Language is to be the means for clarifying obscurities within language.

If the Incarnation resolves the Prophets' riddles, Pentecost offers a paradigmatic image for that resolution.[276] The Holkham Bible Picture Book, like the Wakefield *Second Shepherds' Play* and the *N-Town Play*, uses speaking in tongues to depict the access of new light in the world. In the top panel of folio 13, the angel appears to the shepherds, singing "Gloria in excelsis." One of the shepherds says in reply: "Glum glo ceo ne est rien. Allums la, nous la sauerums been"; his cousins in the *N-Town Play* garble Latin into "Gle, glo, glory," and "Gle, glo, glas, glum."[277] But when the Holkham shepherds approach the Virgin and Child, in the bottom panel, they suddenly have the gift of tongues. "E le chant qe le angel out chaunte. En le honour de la natiuite. Songen alle wid one steuene. Also þe angel song þat cam fro heuene." Miraculously, the shepherds proceed to sing "Gloria in excelsis deo et in terra" and "Te Deum laudamus." What begins as a joke about a rustic's illiteracy turns, after the startling introduction of English into this Anglo-Norman text, into the benign confluence of languages and a miraculous linguistic comprehension in the presence of the divine.[278]

Such language barriers appear in a number of texts, pointedly framed by the glossolalia of Pentecost. In one of three twelfth-century saints'

lives in which an English speaker is given the miraculous gift of understanding and speaking French or Latin, Godric "could only suppose
that, as it happened to be Pentecost, the gift had come to him from
the Holy Spirit."[279] The *Summoner's Tale* parodies Pentecost when a
rustic punctures the intellectual and social pretensions of friars by com-
monsensically solving a philosophical conundrum: how to divide a fart
equally.[280] Two lines in particular – "The rumblynge of a fart, and every
soun, / Nis but of eir reverberacioun" (2233–34) – could almost be from
the *House of Fame*, where the Eagle's reductive lecture turns significant
speech into mere *flatus vocis*.[281] In the Summoner's hands, rhetorical
pretense is reduced to impotent silence, and plain speech elevated to
eloquence.

Yet the use of French, English, and Latin to allude to Pentecost –
registering as they do the various levels of social class and discourse –
shows that the promise of the Incarnation, and of Pentecost, must remain
a promise until the Day of Judgment: until then, in Augustine's phrasing,
Babel continues to coexist with Jerusalem, *Confusio* with *visio pacis*, Cain
with Abel. The two cities "are mingled [*permixtae sunt*], and from the
very beginning of mankind mingled they run on unto the end of the
world."[282] For that reason, he argues, the Church speaks in all languages,
"and in whatsoever it speaketh not, it will speak. For the Church shall
increase till it filleth every tongue . . . I dare to say to thee, I speak in the
tongues of all men: I am in the Body of Christ, in the Church of Christ:
if the Body of Christ now speaketh in the tongues of all men, I also am in
all tongues: mine is the Greek, mine the Syrian, mine the Hebrew, mine
the tongues of all nations, because I am in the unity of all nations."[283]
But God divided human languages at Babel, sparing human beings by
preventing a "destructive unity" [*perniciosam unitatem*], as Augustine
says in his comment on Psalm 54.10 (AV 55.10) ("Cast down, O Lord,
and divide their tongues: for I have seen iniquity and contradiction in
the city"):

> Through proud men, divided were the tongues; through humble
> Apostles, united were the tongues. Spirit of pride dispersed tongues,
> Spirit Holy united tongues. For when the Holy Spirit came upon the
> disciples, with the tongues of all men they spake, by all men they
> were understood: tongues dispersed, into one were united. Therefore

if still they rage and are Gentiles, it is expedient for them divided to have their tongues. They would have one tongue; let them come to the Church; because even among the diversity of tongues of flesh, one is the tongue in faith of heart.[284]

When Paul talks about the charismata, among which are the *genera linguarum* (kinds of tongues) and the *interpretatio sermonum* (interpretation of speeches) (1 Cor. 12.10 and 12.28), he does so in the context of "diversities of graces, but the same Spirit" (12.4). The display of language, even "If I speak with the tongues of men, and of angels" (13.1–2), means nothing without charity; prophecy by itself also means nothing, because "We know in part; and we prophesy in part" (13.9) but charity endures. Even so, in a world of language barriers and human division, prophecy is preferable to speaking in tongues: "So likewise you, except you utter by the tongue plain speech [*manifestum sermonem*], how shall it be known what is said? For you shall be speaking into the air. There are, for example, so many kinds of tongues [*genera linguarum*] in this world; and none is without voice. If, then, I know not the power of the voice, I shall be to him, to whom I speak, a barbarian: and he that speaketh, a barbarian to me" (14.9–11). In these exhortations Paul sets forth a complex interplay between unity and diversity, and between communication and incomprehension. Paradoxically, "tongues are for a sign, not to believers, but to unbelievers: but prophecies, not to unbelievers but to believers" (14.22).[285]

Aquinas considers the question of whether Christ himself possessed the various charisms, specifically the gift of tongues. Scripture is silent, he argues, because whereas the Apostles "were being sent out to teach all the nations," Christ "wished to preach personally to one nation only, to the Jews." "And so he did not have to speak several languages. And yet he knew all languages. For not even the innermost thoughts of men were hidden from him . . . ; and spoken words are simply signs of these thoughts."[286] Aquinas certainly has in mind and is elaborating on the prophecy of Ezekiel 3.4–7, which Paul also echoes: "Son of man, go to the house of Israel, and thou shalt speak my words to them. For thou art not sent to a people of a profound speech and of an unknown tongue [*ad populum profundi sermonis et ignotae linguae*], but to the house of Israel: Nor to many nations of a strange speech [*populos multos profundi sermonis*] and of an unknown tongue, whose words [*sermones*] thou canst not understand." The prophet, ironically, would be more effective with the "many nations of a strange speech": "if thou wert sent to them, they would hearken to thee. But the house of Israel will not hearken to thee, because they will not hearken to me: for all the house of Israel are of a hard forehead and an obstinate heart."

As the Incarnate Word, Christ redeems language and redefines its significance and purpose, above all in the sacraments, since each sacrament is like redeemed language in being, as Hugh of St. Victor notes, "a sign of a sacred reality"; "What on the outside is visible and material, is a sacrament; what on the inside is invisible and spiritual, is the reality or power of a sacrament."[287] Christ's power over language is exempt from normal human constraints. But the charism of speaking in tongues, as it is displayed by the Apostles, also and even more explicitly counters the effects of Babel.[288] Pentecost is forecast, according to the commentators, by Psalm 18 (19): "The heavens shew forth the glory of God: and the firmament declareth the work of his hands. Day to day uttereth speech [*eructat verbum*]: and night to night sheweth knowledge. There are no speeches nor languages [*Non sunt loquelae, neque sermones*], where their voices are not heard. Their sound hath gone forth into all the earth: and their words unto the ends of the world" (2–5). In Augustine's reading, "the heavens" are the Evangelists and the Psalm describes Pentecost, "seeing that the Gospel was preached in every tongue [*omnibus linguis*]"[289]; and his reading becomes conventional after its wide dissemination by the *Glossa Ordinaria* (*PL* 114:789). Dispersion is to be countered by dispersion, the confusion of tongues by the wide transmission of the Gospel.[290]

The commentaries on Acts 2.1–4 also wrestle with the paradox that unity and multiplicity are connected underneath their apparent opposition. The outward remnants of Babel can mask an inward unity, a single language of the human heart as it reaches toward the divine, when worship of God replaces idolatry and, Aquinas says, "the gift of tongues was the remedy to be applied to the diversity of tongues." Yet even in the display of this gift, a vestigial taint of Babel remains. Aquinas notes that we should not be surprised at the special powers of native fluency, when he begins his comment on Paul's Epistle to the Hebrews by quoting the

Glossa Ordinaria: "It is not surprising that this Epistle is more eloquent than others: it is indeed natural for one to speak better in his own tongue than in a foreign tongue. Now the other Epistles were composed by the Apostle in a foreign tongue, i.e. in Greek, but this one he wrote in Hebrew." Hence, Aquinas argues: "So Paul and other Apostles were instructed by God in the tongues of all peoples as much as was needful for the teaching of the faith. But as regards certain embellishments of human art and eloquence in speech the Apostles were instructed in their own language, not in another."[291]

Nonetheless, when Augustine glosses Acts 2.1–4, Pentecost prefigures all the future languages of the universal Church: "That wind cleansed hearts of their carnal chaff; that fire consumed the hay of ancient concupiscence; those tongues by which the ones filled by the Holy Spirit spoke, marked beforehand the Church to be with the tongues of all the nations. What discord had scattered, charity could collect, and the scattered members of the human race, as of a single body, could be brought back, joined together with one head, Christ, and forged by the fire of love into the unity of a holy body."[292] For Bede, "spiritually the variety of tongues signifies the gifts of various charisms [*varietas linguarum dona variarum significat gratiarum*]. Not unfittingly indeed is the Holy Spirit understood to have given the gift of tongues on that account to men in whom human wisdom is publicly both learned and taught, so that it might show how easily it can make men wise through the wisdom of God that is within them."[293] In the N-Town Pentecost play, accordingly, the Apostles parcel out their speech among themselves, one word or phrase for each Apostle in succession, the words taken together making up a unified meaning; and in the Chester play, the Credo is recited bit by bit, in Latin, with an English paraphrase, the dispersed coming together to make a unified whole.

As the Last Judgment approaches, when the author of the Bible's final book prophesies "a great multitude, which no man could number, of all nations and tribes and peoples and tongues [*omnibus gentibus, et tribubus, et populis, et linguis*]" (Apoc. 7.9), the reunification of language is of central importance. The prophecy of Sophonias (Zephaniah) had promised such an outcome: "Because then I will restore to the people a chosen lip [*labium electum* – translated as 'pure language' in the Authorized Version], that all may call upon the name of the Lord and may serve him with one shoulder" (Soph. 3.9).[294] Hence Augustine describes two opposing songs, of this world and of Jerusalem:

> *Let my tongue cleave to my jaws, if I remember not thee.* That is, let me be dumb, he saith, if I remember not thee. For what word, what sound doth he utter, who uttereth not songs of Sion? That is our tongue, the song of Jerusalem. The song of the love of this world is a strange tongue, a barbarous tongue [*lingua aliena, lingua barbara*], which we have learnt in our captivity. Dumb then will he be to God, who forgetteth Jerusalem.[295]

But paradoxically, language becomes one again at the very point when the book of Nature and the Book itself are closed. "I am Alpha and Omega, the first and the last, the beginning and the end" (Apoc. 22.13); the closing of the Book, framed by the Alpha of Creation and the Omega of Judgment, signals the end of human language. Honorius Augustodunensis expands on Jesus's description of the Last Judgment (Matthew 25.34–46), wondering whether the Judgment will "be said with the sounds of words."[296] As Augustine elaborates on the difference between angels and human beings, he envisages the end of time when we too will be face to face with God, no longer dependent on Scripture, a "firmament" now stretched out "as a skin" over us,[297] but to be rolled up with the book of the heavens at the Last Judgment (Apoc. 6.14):

> There are, as I believe, other waters above this firmament [of Scripture], waters immortal and kept clear of earthly corruption. Let the super-celestial hosts of Your angels praise Your name, let them praise You for they have no need to look upon this firmament nor to read it in order to know Your word. For they ever see Your face, and in Your face they read without syllables spoken in time what is willed by Your eternal will. They read it and they choose it and they love it; they read it without ceasing, and what they read never passes away. For by choice and love they read the very immutability of Your counsels. Their scroll is not closed, their book is not folded together, for their book is Yourself and You eternally are . . . The clouds pass, but heaven remains. The preachers of Your word pass from this life to the next, but Your Scripture is stretched over the peoples until the end of time. *Heaven and earth shall pass, but Thy words shall not pass*; the scroll shall be folded, and the grass over which it was spread shall pass

with its glory, *but thy Word endures forever*; now we see in the darkness of clouds and in the mirror of heaven, and not *as it is*; because though we are now beloved by Your Son, *it has not yet appeared what we shall be.* He has seen us through the lattice of flesh and has caressed us and inflamed us, and *we run after the odor of his ointments.* But *when He shall appear, we shall be like to Him, because we shall see Him as He is.* It will be ours, O Lord, to see Him as He is: but it is not for us yet.[298]

FALLEN LANGUAGE

Describing Biblical history as the history of language presents a powerful paradigm of a fallen world characterized by loss, disquiet, and hopeful expectation. In his book on romance, "the secular scripture," Northrop Frye memorably describes the central romance focus on identity as having "some connection to a state of existence in which there is nothing to write about. It is existence before 'once upon a time' and subsequent to 'and they lived happily ever after'": the intervening space is the romance world, of alienation, disguise, anxious questing, and desire.[299] Frye's account equally fits the linguistic contours of the unsecular Scripture, framed by an eternal God before language – or before, at least, the necessity of language – and an eternity after the Last Judgment, when language will again be unnecessary, when there will be nothing to write about and no need to speak. A recent summation of the Bible nearly duplicates Frye's phrasing, however unwittingly: "the whole of history, from creation to apocalypse, can be viewed as a passage from one moment of full presence to another, an epoch of signs and interpretation."[300] The intervening time is in effect the time of wandering, error, and trial, as Milton powerfully and pointedly shows – though to be sure, the romance paradigm especially fits Milton's very unmedieval emphasis on the moral necessity of the active life.[301]

The Augustinian account of these linguistic contours is an extraordinarily compelling one, building on and deepening the meanings of the Biblical text itself; and the rest of this book will be largely concerned with how three major later medieval poets come to terms with that text and that account. In each, the Genesis text, given its authoritative status as the word of God, works against the grain of a more secular grammatical analysis of linguistic history, and gives that analysis added complexity. Dante is the one of the three who most exactly reproduces the logocentrism at the heart of the Augustinian view, stated succinctly by Bonaventure as the historical variation on three versions of the Word, *increatum*, *inspiratum*, and *incarnatum*: "Just as mankind came into being through the uncreated Word and fell into sin by abandoning the inspired Word, so it should rise from sin through the incarnate Word."[302] In the *Commedia* the journey to redemption pulls language along in its wake; Jean de Meun and Chaucer share a more tentative response, which constitutes what Hanning in another context has called a "lapsarian poetic." Let me conclude this first chapter by exploring briefly what such a phrase might mean.

In part, it responds to a quality that most readers have sensed in the *Roman de la Rose* and the *Canterbury Tales*, the poetic delight, even revelling, in the centrifugal forces of multiplicity, and the difficulty of reining that multiplicity in, of reducing it to a single, unifying message – in effect, of condensing the profusion of words to a single Word. There is no doubt a confluence of forces at work here. The later medieval version of multiplicity is often and aptly characterized as Gothic; Larry Benson, for example, notes "the late Gothic ability to maintain contradicting attitudes and to derive aesthetic pleasure from the tension of unresolved conflicts."[303] Jean de Meun and Chaucer are especially attracted to the inconclusive and the dialogic,[304] in part probably reflecting "a new pluralism" in philosophical thought,[305] in part manifesting their inherent skepticism about confidently dogmatic conclusions.[306] For his part, in his response to Dante, Chaucer enacts some impulses already evident in Boccaccio and Petrarch, the poet of the *rime sparse*.[307] In Chaucer this is a quality that I characterized in *Chaucer and Ovid* as quintessentially Ovidian, of *impetus* (energy) perpetually undoing – or at least complicating – *ratio* (order or system); and Jean de Meun is equally indebted to Ovid's ironic perspective. But this Ovidian paradigm is also colored by the Biblical context, which both Chaucer and Jean de Meun have in mind as they conflate classical and Christian versions of the Fall.

When the two poets resist or undermine the dominant Augustinian paradigm of language, they may seem surprisingly or even implausibly modern; and indeed I will note in Chapter 4, as others have noted, that the *Canon's Yeoman's Tale* has some striking affinities with Samuel Beckett.[308] One would expect, however, and there are in fact powerful differences within these affinities. John Freccero outlines the Augustinian view, which reins in the "unlimited semiosis" described by Saussure and Peirce:

> Anterior to the written text is the spoken text, anterior to that is the acoustic image, in turn dependent upon a concept which is itself linguistically structured. Our attempt to make the leap from words to things seems doomed to a continual feedback that looks like infinite regression . . . For Augustine, the central metaphor of Christianity provided the grounding for this infinite regression. Reality itself is linguistically structured . . . The metaphor of God's Book halts the infinite series by ordering all signs to itself.[309]

In Jean de Meun and Chaucer, as in Dante, this grounding exercises a powerful pull. But if they share the common medieval nostalgia for a primeval state of innocence, which we are unable and perhaps should not wish to recover,[310] they also seem more content than Dante is with the post-lapsarian constraints on language and vision; they are at least more resigned to writing and thinking within those constraints.

Traugott Lawler argues that "the complementary relationship in the *Canterbury Tales* between unity and diversity, oneness and multiplicity – between the one and the many . . . is the most pervasive issue in the poem, and its major unifying force."[311] And Robert Myles so describes the opening of the *General Prologue*: "Chaucer's words imply a classic dialectic: there is an initial unity, a subsequent motion away from unity, and a return to unity – from stasis to motion to stasis."[312] While I whole-heartedly agree that the relationships between unity and multiplicity are pervasive, I am more doubtful about the implications of Lawler's phrase "unifying force,"[313] because positing such a force may so comfortably lead to a reductively Augustinian reading.[314] A number of critics have found a Biblical paradigm, moving from Genesis to Apocalypse, in the structure of the *Canterbury Tales*.[315] But the work in fact ends, not in the New Jerusalem, but on the road to a Canterbury that has taken on the shadowy outlines of the heavenly city, not all that far away but definitely not yet immanent. If we cannot go home again, we also cannot get to or see clearly where we are going from here, not even at this final moment in Chaucer's poetry where mortality is most pressing and there is nothing left to say.

Dante's response to Babel, his remedy for the dispersal of the one true language into seventy-two, is the "illustrious vernacular," the effort to shape human poetry to the purposes of the divine, and to restore to language some of its original power. Tellingly, Chaucer and Jean de Meun are by contrast poets of the inconclusive *débat*, poets of the earthbound and partial (sometimes devastatingly ironic) vision – and in Chaucer's case, of the unfinished poem. They are, self-consciously and by others' account, translators, for whom translation implies, as it does more generally, a variety of linguistic issues.[316] To the extent that Latin is the language of authority, of fixed "grammar," its rendering into the vernacular echoes, at least by analogy, the mediation performed by Christ as the Incarnate Word.[317] Derek Pearsall has aptly described Chaucer's practice, specifically in his prose translations, "of absorbing major works of the European intellectual tradition into his imaginative repertoire" by translating them; and of course, Chaucer follows Jean de Meun's lead when he translates Boethius.[318] For Chaucer, such a translation can serve as an *aide-mémoire* and as a crib, as well as the means to disseminate an authoritative work to a larger audience. But he also uses translation as the occasion for creative augmentation, in which word-for-word copying gives way to verbal generation. Sometimes he "has in effect created his source" by amalgamating several sources into one.[319] Elsewhere, the dreamer in the *House of Fame* dreams Dido's lament – "Non other auctour alegge I" (*HF* 314); and the narrator of *Troilus* can give, not simply the gist of Troilus' first love song, all that Lollius provides, but word for word, "save oure tonges difference," all "that Troilus/ Seyde in his song" (*Troilus* 1.395–97), at a point when he is actually translating and adapting one of Petrarch's sonnets.

Latin can also be merely a foreign language – to be translated laterally instead of on a vertical axis. In the preface to the *Astrolabe*, translation works both ways: from learned Latin to "full light reules and naked wordes in Englissh" (26–27) for the benefit of his young son; but also, in phrasing closely akin to the preface to the Wycliffite Bible, from Latin as in effect simply one more vernacular, itself the product of translation (*Astrolabe*, 28–40). For Chaucer, Latin may simply provide, as French and Italian do, a source for adapted or directly translated poetry. His translations of the *Romaunt of the Rose* and, in bits and pieces, of Dante, Boccaccio, Petrarch, and Froissart, are not in most respects qualitatively different from his use of Ovid and Vergil. Vergil can be at once an authoritative source on the Trojan War and its aftermath – in *Troilus and Criseyde* Chaucer pretends that Vergil, Ovid, and Statius are history books, available to a Trojan reading, and listening, public[320] – and a questionable authority on the crucial matter of Dido.[321] Chaucer's translations muddy the conventional associations of Latin with authority and of prose with factuality[322] – most conspicuously, perhaps, in the peregrination of the Griselda story from Italian to Latin to French to English, from prose to verse, and back and forth between domestic and spiritual (and perhaps political) contexts. But this dislodging of Latin also occurs in the Wife of Bath's unmooring of Jerome from his position of supposedly disinterested, impersonal authority,[323] or in the double use of a single passage on wives' good counsel from Albertanus of Brescia's Latin text, once straight (in the *Tale of Melibee*), and once with deadly irony (in the *Merchant's Tale*).

The proliferation of the one into the many, the collapse of authority into contingency – these are evident even in the material presence of the text. Richard de Bury voices the complaint of books against the fallen world:

> Alas! how ye commit us to treacherous copyists [*falsis scriptoribus*] to be written, how corruptly ye read us and kill us by medication, while ye supposed ye were correcting us with pious zeal. Oftentimes we have to endure barbarous interpreters [*interpretes barbaros*], and those who are ignorant of foreign idioms [*qui linguarum idiomata nesciunt*] presume to translate us from one language into another; and thus all propriety of speech is lost and our sense is shamefully mutilated contrary to the meaning of the author! Truly noble would have been the condition of books, if it had not been for the presumption of the tower of Babel, if but one kind of speech had been transmitted by the whole human race.[324]

Chaucer of course makes precisely this lament in his lyric "Adam Scriveyn," addressed to the scribal descendant of the first Adam,[325] whose errors the poet must constantly "renewe"; these are errors in two "translations," one true ("Boece"), the other pretended, since "Troylus" is supposedly taken from a Latin source Lollius, whose own authority becomes more undermined the farther the poem progresses. Errors of transcription compound the uncertainties of translation and of language change[326]; if mistakes are more easily fixed than uncertainties, an irremediable contingency remains at the heart of earthly discourse.

Appropriately, a defining symptom of language in the fallen world is equivocation, the fact that a word is capable of having multiple meanings.[327] This possibility is not simply taken into account by Biblical exegesis, but is indeed at the heart of its enterprise, because it entails the different levels of meaning within a single word.[328] In the Bible, however, equivocations are fruitful, not malign; they require resolution by interpretation. The Prologue to the Wycliffite Bible talks of the need for accuracy in translating "wordis equivok, that is that hath manie significacions vndur oo letter," but as G. R. Evans argues, "Wyclif draws the moral Peter the Chanter had drawn in the late twelfth century: *in sensibus equivocis non est contradictio*. There can be no contradiction between statements where the same term is used in different senses." She cites Bonaventure's comment: "As Augustine says, equivocation does not create contradiction; rather it differentiates for the sake of agreement (*non facit contraria sed pro congruitate facit diversa*)."[329] Since the Bible is by its very nature an authoritative utterance, the word of God filtered through human voices, its interpreter can be certain that a single meaning underlies the variousness of its utterances; equivocation is merely seeming equivocation.

Even so, as Rita Copeland points out, "rhetorical language, the inherent nature of which is indirection and ambiguity," creates problems for exegetical programs, whether of Wyclif or Aquinas, because "At its root, rhetoric and its tropological dimension is about the impossibility of there being a manifest, plain truth."[330] Nonetheless rhetoric too, despite its recalcitrance, can be subdued to divine purposes. Augustine thanks God for teaching him

> that a thing was not bound to be true because uttered eloquently, nor false because the utterance of the lips is ill-arranged [*quia incomposite sonant signa labiorum*]; but that on the other hand a thing is not necessarily true because badly uttered, nor false because spoken magnificently. For it is with wisdom and folly as with wholesome and unwholesome food: just as either kind of food can be served equally well in rich dishes or simple, so plain or beautiful language [*verbis autem ornatis et inornatis*] may clothe either wisdom or folly indifferently.[331]

For Augustine, Christian uses of rhetoric are a central instance of "spoiling the Egyptians," of using the arts of the pagan classical world for Christian purposes.[332]

In merely human uses of language, on the other hand, equivocation may imply contradiction, may create ambiguity, may in fact become antiphrasis, which Isidore defines as "an expression [*sermo*] to be understood by its contrary."[333] It may become sophistry and even prevarication. Equivocation may become, or verge on, all the sins of the tongue.[334] Even in a more innocent guise, it creates by its very nature the "binarism" that, Patterson argues, constitutes the "basic narrative structure" of the *Canterbury Tales*.[335] It lies at the heart of medieval dream theory and dream visions, Jean de Meun's *Roman* as much as Chaucer's early poems, in which dreams sum up the uncertain relation between authority and experience, and the proliferation of dream categories matches the uncertainties of dream interpretation. And equivocation is centrally important in the doubles and twinning at the heart of *Troilus and Criseyde*, a poem of "amphibologies" (4.1406) and "ambages" (5.897) – two terms that Chaucer introduces into English.

Equivocation is in fact the crucial issue at stake in rhetoric as an art; and the question of rhetoric's grounding in truth becomes a crucial one. Alain of Lille accuses Venus of moral and grammatical turpitude, because "she kept turning her art into a figure and the figure into a defect" [*suam artem in figuram, figuram in uicium transferebat*].[336] Even at its best, however, the rhetorical figure is a solecism: as William of Conches paraphrases Isidore's definition, "The figure is a fault with a reason" [*Figura est vicium cum ratione*], and the same definition appears in John of Salisbury's *Metalogicon* 1.18.[337] John of Salisbury indeed tries to reclaim figurative language:

> This reciprocity between things and words, and words and things, whereby they mutually communicate their qualities, as by an exchange of gifts, is more commonly accomplished by words used in a metaphorical sense [*translatiuis sermonibus*] than by those of secondary origin [*institutio secondaria*] . . . This force of transferred meaning [*translationis*], whereby properties of things are ascribed to words, and vice versa, gives birth to a certain tolerance, which permits the use of words in varying senses [*quandam loquendi parit indifferentiam*]. The latter license serves the learned as a shortcut; yet it confounds and

virtually slays the unlearned, preventing them from comprehending the truth. For one who wants to know the truth must weigh, with a judicious mind, even what those who speak in an obscure and faulty way [*qui balbutit*] are trying to say as the latter very often speak the truth.[338]

Cicero had argued long before that "The words we employ then are either the proper and definite [*propria et certa*] designations of things, which were almost born at the same time as the things themselves; or terms used metaphorically and placed in a connexion not really belonging to them [*aut eis quae transferuntur et quasi alieno in loco collocantur*]; or new coinages invented by ourselves."[339] If this definition leaves some space for proper designation, it consigns much language use to the metaphorical and inherently problematic.

The problem is compounded by the fictional, which a moral response, medieval or modern, is inclined to discount as a lie, "a turning away of language from its extralinguistic reference" as Peter Haidu describes it: "Fiction is man's disruption of language from its divinely ordained intentionality . . . By withdrawal of its referential function, language becomes self-referential, and obtains its *littérarité*, not as an additional aesthetic complexity, but by the withdrawal of another function, the subtraction of divine purpose."[340] Chaucer's apparent answer to this charge is his twice-repeated quotation of Romans 15:4: "For Seint Paul seith that al that writen is, / To oure doctrine it is ywrite, ywis" (*Nun's Priest's Tale* 3441–42); "For oure book seith, 'Al that is writen is writen for oure doctrine,' and that is myn entente" (*Retraction* 1083). But this reading of Paul is only partially accurate, since the writing to which Paul refers is evidently the Old Testament: "that by pacience and comfort of scripturis we han hope."[341] Chaucer's interpretation, a common one in the fourteenth century, conspicuously extends Paul's meaning, and the meaning of "scripturis," to include secular literature as well.[342]

In the *Nun's Priest's Tale*, this apologia is immediately followed by the injunction: "Taketh the fruyt, and lat the chaf be stille" (3443); but the tale has served up a dizzying multiplicity of perspectives, which seem to suggest that fruit and chaff are nearly inseparable. If the tale, according to its narrator, must not be disparaged as simply a "folye, / As of a fox, or of a cok and hen," it also cannot easily be reduced to a simple, univocal "moralite" (3438–40). Rhetorical playfulness is indeed its dominant feature, tailor-made for Richard Lanham's differentiation of *homo rhetoricus* from *homo seriosus*, and his argument that "Rhetoric is always ritualizing, stylizing purpose in order to enjoy it more."[343] The tale also illustrates the way in which "the schools give a license to poets" – in Nicolette Zeeman's argument that "classical and medieval theories of figuration" are "constantly generative of language and its provisional claims to meaning."[344] The play space of the *Nun's Priest's Tale* suggests a larger Chaucerian ambivalence between the lure of the univocal and the exuberance of the multiple. The lure of the unequivocal is most powerfully evident at the end of the *Canterbury Tales*; but before I reach that ending, more provisional than comfortingly unifying, the next two chapters will look at the multivocal sources for Chaucer's ideas.

2

Love and language in Jean de Meun

Love and language are both contaminated by the Fall from Paradise or from the Golden Age: commentators and poets who are preoccupied with love almost necessarily become preoccupied with language as well. Both originate in Paradise as defining human faculties; both now exhibit a gap between will and performance, and between the natural and the artificial. In Paradise, according to Honorius Augustodunensis' *Elucidarium*, an infant would have been able to walk and to speak *absolute* [clearly] from birth[1]; and in the Golden Age love was natural and innocent. Now we must learn to walk and learn to use language; and for the medieval poets schooled by Ovid, the language we use is not only analogous to but directly implicated in the domain of sexual difference and heterosexual desire. As Bloch argues, language – that is, language in the fallen world – engenders narrative, desire, and especially narratives of desire.[2] And Augustine says that the "word uttered inside ourselves," as it manifests itself in spoken words and deeds, is a word of love:

> This word is conceived in love of either the creature or the creator, that is of changeable nature or unchangeable truth; which means either in covetousness [*cupiditas*] or in charity [*caritas*] . . . Now this word is born when on thinking over it we like it either for sinning or for doing good. So love, like something in the middle, joins together our word and the mind it is begotten from, and binds itself in with them as a third element in a non-bodily embrace, without any confusion.[3]

This chapter will focus on Jean de Meun's complex and intriguing account of language in relation to love; like Chaucer, he develops that account from the Augustinian tradition, but even more powerfully from Ovid's insights on love in the fallen world.

LOVE AND THE DECLINING WORLD: OVID,
GENESIS, AND CHAUCER

Whatever ambivalence Augustine and the other Latin Fathers feel about classical rhetoric and classical literature, their impulse to "spoil the Egyptians," to appropriate pagan material for Christian purposes, becomes fully evident when early Christian poets use the story of the Golden Age to expand on the Genesis narrative. Their purposes in doing so are primarily stylistic, adapting poetic descriptions of Arcadian simplicity to adorn their own accounts of Paradise.[4] Later medieval poets, however, use classical myth more to enhance meaning than to ornament poetic form, as they portray the decline from natural simplicity to civilized decadence, both sexual and rhetorical.

In "The Former Age," Chaucer conflates the two venerable accounts of early human history. When he describes the world declining from its Golden Age of virtuous simplicity to the corrupt present, a time of "covetyse,/ Doublenesse, and tresoun, and envye,/ Poyson, manslawhtre, and mordre in sondry wyse" (61–63), he assigns blame for this decline in equal measure to "Jupiter the likerous,/ That first was fader of delicacye" (56–57) and to "Nembrot, desirous/ To regne" (58–59), who built the Tower of Babel. Deschamps makes a similar conflation in one of his *balades*, which dates the end of the First Age to the time after Noah's Flood and the division of tongues at Babel: appropriating familiar tropes from the classical myth for his version of Genesis history, he describes a fall into carnivorousness, weapons, vineyards, harvesting wheat, avarice, the building of castles, "seignourie et possession."[5] Certainly neither Chaucer nor Deschamps, when they fuse the narrative in Genesis with the one in Ovid's *Metamorphoses* (and with its copy in Boethius), means to suggest that these are equally authoritative as historical accounts of the First Age. But this fusion does show very clearly that the two poets – like Dante in *Purgatorio* 28 – find the pagan mythological narrative to be a helpful elaboration of Genesis, consonant with its moral purpose and its historical truth.[6]

More pointedly, Chaucer combines mythical and Biblical history when he thinks about the sexual dimensions of the decline from natural simplicity to civilized decadence; so does Jean de Meun when he retells the myth of Saturn's castration. Ovid, Chaucer's favorite classical

source, has a great deal to say on this subject; and Chaucer uses Ovid's
ideas to bolster his own thinking not only about the Golden Age, but
about the early chapters of Genesis. Any reader of Ovid must be struck
by the parallels between the Genesis account and the version of Creation
and the Flood in Book One of the *Metamorphoses*. *Metamorphoses* and
Genesis also seem to manifest parallel attitudes toward the invention of
the civilizing arts: the loss of the Golden Age inaugurates bodily excess
and amorous duplicity as much as it does the arts of metalworking, agriculture, and navigation. The vineyards of Deschamps' declining world
find their Biblical correlative in Noah's drunkenness; similarly, the early
chapters of Genesis provide more than one analogue for "Jupiter the
likerous."

In Book Two of the *Ars Amatoria*, Ovid advocates sexual intercourse
as a way to mollify an angry mistress, and to introduce this bit of
advice he summarizes – in a startling digression from up-to-date Roman
modernity – the early history of the world and of human sexuality:

> First there was a confused mass of things without order, and stars and
> earth and sea had only one shape; presently the sky was set over the
> earth, the land was encompassed by the sea, and empty chaos retired
> to its own place; the forest received wild beasts, the air birds to keep;
> you lurked, fishes, in the liquid waters. Then humankind wandered
> in the lonely fields; brute strength was theirs and forms uncouth;
> woodland was their home, their food grass, their bedding leaves; and
> for long none knew his fellow. Beguiling pleasure is said to have
> softened those fierce spirits: a man and a woman had tarried together
> in one spot; what they were to do, they learned themselves with no
> teacher: without art Venus accomplished the sweet act.[7] (2.467–80)

This passage echoes Lucretius' remarks on the same subject,[8] but it also
evidently alludes to and parodies Cicero's account of eloquence as the
beginning of civilization:

> At this juncture a man – great and wise I am sure – became aware of
> the power latent in man and the wide field offered by his mind for
> great achievements if one could develop this power and improve it
> by instruction. Men were scattered in the fields and hidden in sylvan
> retreats when he assembled and gathered them in accordance with a
> plan; he introduced them to every useful and honourable occupation,

though they cried out against it at first because of its novelty, and then when through reason and eloquence they had listened with greater attention, he transformed them from wild savages into a kind and gentle folk.[9]

For the *magister amoris* the first teacher of human beings is sexual desire, not the "great and wise" man who substitutes the power of rhetoric for brute force.

The comically improbable analogy between the origin of the world and the sexual pacification of an enraged mistress gives Ovid the pretext for his digression on early history. It comes just after his description of the lovers' détente in "the treaty of a love embrace" [*concubitus foedera*]: "Concord dwells there, when weapons have been put down; there, believe me, was Reconciliation [*Gratia*] born" (*Ars* 2.463–64). Just as the primal chaos gives way to order, with each species at home in its proper element, so in turn does the brutal life of primitive humanity give in to the softening influence of love. From the standpoint of this "hard" primitivism, history is progressive and civilizing; indeed, Ovid says, the sexual act serves even now to assuage the atavistic *furor* of a jealous woman. There is a characteristic Ovidian joke here: such *furor* obviously survives very near the civilized surface. As if to show precisely that, Ovid immediately proceeds with a catalogue of beasts in heat – "the hound is joined in clinging lechery to the bitch; . . . the snub-nosed goat supports her unclean lord; mares are excited to frenzy, and through regions far removed follow the stallions, though streams divide them" (2.484–88). This list makes it all too apparent that the placatory effects of coitus in human beings and in animals are uncomfortably akin. The artlessness with which Venus first accomplished "the sweet act" is close to blind instinct. In this respect Augustine is a thoroughgoing Roman when he thinks of sexuality as a marker of the Fall: a deeply disruptive force, "a profoundly undomesticated, unmodifiable drive."[10]

Though Ovid often argues that the move from the confusion of chaos to order is civilizing, he simultaneously implies that it constitutes an alienating series of distinctions and separations: the isolation of birds, beasts, and fish within their separate and unbridgeable realms, and of primitive human beings in their lonely fields, isolated one from another. That is to say, the dire effects attributed to civilization by "soft" primitivism actually begin earlier, and Chaos becomes the true Arcadian freedom, supplanted by alienating categories – above all, by the division of animals into two sexes, which try by instinctive force to reunite.[11] Ovid's account may well remind us of the four-legged hermaphrodite that Aristophanes posits in the *Symposium*, but he pushes the primal unity back before the beginning of history, even as he implies Aristophanes' conclusion: "Love is always trying to redintegrate our former nature, to make two into one, and to bridge the gulf between one human being and another."[12] Even more strikingly, Ovid calls to mind the idea associated with Empedocles (and alluded to in canto 12 of the *Inferno*),[13] that without the resistance of Hate, which separates and orders the elements, Love would return them to their primal, chaotic lack of differentiation.[14]

Thus, according to Ovid, the sexual act at once moves us away from Chaos and returns us to it. The paradox implied here is, in broad terms, at the heart of Ovid's poetry: order and energy, reason and passion, stasis and flux are continually at odds, and the forces of energy and flux summed up by the libido refuse to acquiesce placidly in their own suppression. This paradox appears most strikingly in Ovid's characteristically double-edged comparison of early times with the present. Ovid displays a self-conscious, half-comic ambivalence about yearning for the Golden Age, summed up in the conflicting suppositions of "hard" and "soft" primitivism. On the one hand, he portrays the Golden Age as a time when the libido could vent itself uninhibitedly; the civilized present, by contrast, is an age of repressed sexuality, artificially dampened and artificially stimulated both. The fame and widespread literary influence of the love-doctor's advice for the lovelorn, "otia si tollas, periere Cupidinis arcus" (*Remedia Amoris* 139) [Take away leisure, and Cupid's bow is broken], may partially obscure its joke: the work of Roman civilization – law, war, agriculture – serves to divert the mind from indolence, but the indolence of a fallen world was in fact, back in the Golden Age, the *otium* of innocent leisure.

Yet Ovid also exults that modern artfulness may remedy such repression as much as cause it. His delight in modernity follows inevitably as a side-effect of his delight in poetry, since the verbal arts go hand in hand with civilized, sophisticated game-playing and deception. He tells unhappy lovers to stop reading love poetry: "eloquar inuitus: teneros ne tange poetas;/ summoueo dotes ipsius ipse meas" (*Remedia* 757–58) [Unwillingly I speak: touch not the poets of love; with my own hand I take my own gifts from you]. In his notorious lament:

> non ego diuitibus uenio praeceptor amandi;
>   nil opus est illi, qui dabit, arte mea.
> secum habet ingenium qui, cum libet, 'accipe' dicit;
>   cedimus, inuentis plus placet ille meis.
> pauperibus uates ego sum, quia pauper amaui;
>   cum dare non possem munera, uerba dabam.
>
>   (*Ars* 2.161–66)

> [I do not come as the preceptor in love for the rich: he who will give has no need of my art; he has enough wit about him who when he pleases says "Take." I yield; he will please more than my devices. I am the poet for the poor, because I was poor when I loved; since I could not give gifts, I gave words.]

The poet gives the words of his poems, but his art is implicitly one of trickery: the joke here depends on *uerba dare* being an idiom meaning "to deceive."[15] In the world Ovid describes, simplicity survives – except in naturally beautiful women – only in debased forms. The drunkard, in whom wine creates the openness of mindless abandon – "tunc aperit mentes aeuo rarissima nostro/ simplicitas, artes excutiente deo" (*Ars* 1.241–42) [Then simplicity, most rare in our age, lays bare the mind, when the god dispels all craftiness] – displays one kind of modern directness. The only other is that of the rich man, whose presents exceed the poet's best efforts because, he says, "aurea sunt uere nunc saecula: plurimus auro/ uenit honos, auro conciliatur amor" (*Ars* 2.277–78) [Now truly is the age of gold: with gold comes many an honor, with gold is love procured].

If Ovid claims to celebrate sophisticated modernity, medieval literary works usually argue that the world has declined – that is to say, that the "soft" version of primitivism is truer than the "hard." There are, to be sure, some very interesting exceptions to this rule. In the *De Mulieribus Claris*, Boccaccio has it both ways, as he expresses an ambivalent view. Ceres is extolled as the founder of agriculture and a civilizing force: "Who will condemn the fact that wild, wandering men were led out of the woods and into cities? Who will condemn the fact that men who were living like beasts were led to a better life? . . . The fact that barbarous times were changed into a civilized age? The fact that man's mind was aroused from idleness to thought?" On the other hand, "who will praise the fact that" primitive vegetarians, "having no worries, satisfied by the laws of nature, sober, modest and without deceit, enemies only of beasts and birds, were attracted to delicate and unknown foods?" With civilization come vices, Boccaccio laments, boundaries to the fields that had previously "been common to all," "the words 'mine' and 'yours,' which are certainly inimical to public and private peace. From this came poverty and slavery, as well as quarreling, hatred, bloody wars, and burning envy which flies about everywhere." In the end, Boccaccio decides in favor of "those golden centuries, although primitive and uncivilized."[16] But for Christine de Pizan in her rewriting of Boccaccio, women are heavily involved in the civilizing process, with "originary powers . . . in every area of life," and she sees that process as an unalloyed good.[17]

Yet there is a surprising analogue to Ovid's particular version of soft primitivism – the idea of progressive alienation and subdivision into categories – in the opening chapters of Genesis: the division of *homo sapiens* into two sexes, the genealogies of Cain and Seth after the Fall, and most particularly, the account of Lamech the first bigamist and his children, the inventors of the arts, all of them marked by division and categorization. Sexual duplicity and the arts of civilization are, for the Genesis commentators, closely linked; and when Chaucer refers to Lamech, he too uses bigamy and amorous deceit as a way of summing up moral decline, and identifying duplicity with division. What Chaucer adds to this Biblical view of early history is a specifically Ovidian awareness of the way in which language and poetry are implicated in decline, especially as they serve as vehicles for expressing love. Of the four instances in Chaucer's poetry in which the word "double" means "duplicitous" instead of "twofold," two refer to sexual deceit (*Anelida and Arcite* 87, *House of Fame* 285), and two describe verbal equivocation: "the synne of double tonge" (*Parson's Tale* 644), and the "ambages" of Calchas, "That is to seyn, . . . double wordes slye,/ Swiche as men clepen a word with two visages" (*Troilus* 5.898–99). Love and poetry both signify the fallen state of the world – love in its post-Edenic doubleness, but also its earthly manifestation as unsatisfiable desire; poetry because, as the *House of Fame* most clearly shows, language is always at a remove from the reality it uncertainly attempts to reveal. In both love and language, the effects of simple consciousness, and even more of self-consciousness, compound the division: to be aware of alienation adds to the pain of experiencing it.

Chaucer also adopts Ovid's inference that sophistry and deception are an inherent part of love poetry; and in many of his gestures toward the Golden Age he evinces a distrust of rhetorical ornament as a sign of the fallen world. In the *Book of the Duchess*, the Man in Black's first, poetically naive lyric reveals an innocent simplicity that befits his role as an ideal lover (1171–82). Troilus struggles with the *ars dictaminis* and the affected-modesty trope when he writes to Criseyde for the first time (2.1077, 1083). When he is about to speak with her at long last, he carefully plans his tactics – "Thus wol I pleyne unto my lady dere;/ That word is good, and this shal be my cheere" (3.53–54) – but becomes flustered and forgets his "lessoun" (3.83) as soon as she appears. (She, for her part, responds wholeheartedly to his innocence: she "loved hym nevere the lasse,/ Al nere he malapert, or made it tough,/ Or was to bold, to synge a fool a masse" [3.86–88].) Even the artful Diomede backhandedly makes this point: he takes pains to mimic the halting cadences of the innocent (5.925–31) and the rhetorical naiveté that Troilus unselfconsciously reveals.

In this context, the Man in Black's preface to his recital of his first song is particularly interesting, as he describes his lack of musical and poetic skill:

> But for to kepe me fro ydelnesse,
> Trewly I dide my besynesse
> To make songes, as I best koude,
> And ofte tyme I song hem loude;
> And made songes thus a gret del,
> Althogh I koude not make so wel
> Songes, ne knewe the art al,
> As koude Lamekes sone Tubal,
> That found out first the art of songe.
> (*Book of the Duchess* 1155–63)

Though the *Book of the Duchess* is full of apparently irrelevant expositions, the mention of Lamech here does firmly place "the art of songe" in the fallen world – even if as a stay against idleness, "the ministre and the norice unto vices" (*Second Nun's Prologue* 1), and suggests metaphorically that the Man in Black belongs to an earlier, more golden world, before civilized deceit and sexual duplicity. As the *Squire's Tale* says, "Lameth" was the first bigamist (550–51), and his name is bracketed in that tale by the falcon's complaints of sexual betrayal and "doublenesse" (543, 556). Even more emphatically, in *Anelida and Arcite* the false lover accuses his lady of "doublenesse" (159), in order to hide his own copying of Lamech's example (148–54).

Like Ovid, then, Chaucer implies some connections between love poetry and the deceptive purposes speech can serve in the declining world. The Man in Black and Blanche inhabit a world of plain speech, in which courtship does not require the tricks of verbal artifice. Likewise, the innocent Dorigen, in a tale full of reminiscences of the golden past, who "nevere erst hadde herde speke of apparence" (*Franklin's Tale* 1602), is confronted with the courtly seducer Aurelius; and this would-be lover is an expert in singing and the composition of love poems (944–52). The Franklin's effort to present a marriage of equals, in effect a reversion to the first age before sexual hierarchies, is matched by his distrust of rhetorical ornament and its magical abilities for sophistry and deception. Duplicity, in this view, is best countered by striving for a simple mode of expression that is appropriate to a Golden Age unanimity of spirit; but in both poems such expression is hedged in by the inadequacy of words in the face of mortality and by the threats posed by illusion, including verbal illusion.

Chaucer also follows Ovid, however, in suggesting that the present is not simply a corruption of past simplicity; our motives in believing so are often suspect. Several examples come to mind: the hypocritical piety of pilgrims like the Man of Law and the Physician, as they affect a plainness of style to match their ancient stories and invented purity of pious motive; the complicated interplay between instinct and consciousness in the *Parliament of Fowls*; and the equally complex relation between primal simplicity and human complication at the beginning of the *General Prologue*. Above all Lamech's doubleness, when he appears in Chaucer's poetry, has a double effect. The Wife of Bath distinguishes her serial multiplicity of marriage from Lamech's cursed "bigamy"; but the ease with which she demolishes this straw man in argument sophistically evades the more substantial case against her sexual excess. In the *Squire's Tale* and *Anelida and Arcite*, Lamech is cited as part of an exaggerated female polemic against the duplicity of all men (he is, in this respect, the opposite number to Proserpina and May, in whom the Merchant finds the source for the duplicity in all women). Doubly the sign of our alienation and fall, Lamech also becomes a rhetorical trope in the unending battle between the sexes. He provides at once an exuberant token of the delights of rhetoric and sophistry, and an ancient marker of our unlikely efforts to escape the divisions in our discourse and experience.

SATURN AND THE DISSEMINATION OF LANGUAGE

As I will show in detail in Chapter 3, Dante in the *Commedia* powerfully recapitulates an Augustinian linguistic paradigm. As he moves from the dark wood of the world to Hell and on to Paradise, he echoes the Biblical movement from Paradise, the Fall, and the Tower of Babel to the Last Judgment, from the one true language divided from itself in a "land of unlikeness" and then dispersed into seventy-two, to the redemption of the Word and the salvific promise of alienation giving way to unity. Despite Chaucer's constant attention to the *Commedia* in the *House of Fame*, the great differences between the two works suggest that he is not altogether comfortable with the Augustinian view of language that Dante so powerfully puts into action. Understandably, the towering examples of Augustine and Dante have cast their shadow over much late medieval poetry; and many critics have found the redemptive Word to be at the heart of Chaucer's meaning as well – whether with complacent approbation or dismay. I think instead that Chaucer continually shows himself to be more skeptical, as his poetry not only exposes a fallen world of multivocality and dissemination but rests in them as all that we have available to us. To be sure Chaucer, because he is a medieval Christian poet, contemplates the hope of ultimate redemption, of the promise set forth by Pentecost that all languages will become a single Word at the end of time. But entirely in keeping with his usual ironic pose, he refuses to adopt a perspective of superlunar certainty, and the promise of redemption has little or nothing to do with the actualities of his poetic practice. To put the *Canterbury Tales* or the *House of Fame* side by side with the *Commedia* is to feel the difference immediately. Instead of Dante's certainty of moral and eschatological judgment, we find unresolved – and unresolvable – debates, and the ironic perspective, ultimately traceable to Ovid, that refuses to rest in certainty. In the *House of Fame*, Chaucer's fullest exploration of poetics, the fragmentation of the Word is much in evidence in the competing versions of Dido's story, and in the unsolved, and unsolvable disputes about truth and meaning in Part Three.

One could say some of the same things about the Boccaccio of the *Decameron*, and it may well be – as Holly Wallace Boucher has argued – that the skepticism of both writers reflects the influence of fourteenth-century nominalism.[18] But Chaucer's great medieval source for his ironic view of language is Jean de Meun; and indeed, in an authoritative essay on the passage I am concerned with here, David Hult has called Jean's writing "a poetics of dismemberment."[19] Jean also has been lined up on the Augustinian/Dantean side of things, most forcefully and eloquently in the books of John Fleming[20]; and of course, whether or not Dante actually authored the *Fiore*, he was himself a reader of the *Roman de la Rose*.[21] Like the *Canterbury Tales*, the *Roman* is a work with many competing voices; and its central conundrum is whether any of these voices is authoritative. Alan Gunn argued that Nature, with her Chartrian case for procreation, is the compelling figure.[22] For Fleming, Reason's voice should drown out all the others, though it does not, in this fallen world, manage to do so: "Reason alone of all the Lover's teachers in the *Roman de la Rose* commands the authority to be trusted"; "hers is the one voice within the poem to which we can confidently listen for the moral adjudication of the poem's amatory doctrine"; she is "associated in the poem with the *Sapientia Dei Patris* or Christ."[23] In this adulation of Reason Fleming follows the precedent of Pierre Col[24] and echoes D. W. Robertson: "Raison speaks with the voice of Patristic authority, Boethius, and Cicero. She is, as it were, Lady Philosophy, who is described by Guillaume as the Image of God. He who seeks Jean de Meun's opinions will find them here, not in the discourses of the other characters who, with Ciceronian decorum, speak as their natures demand."[25] Joan Ferrante makes much the same argument – "Reson is rejected by the lover in no uncertain terms, but she is the only character in the poem who is not undercut by the author" – as does Per Nykrog, who says that Reason is "a being who is close to God, in prelapsarian innocence."[26]

I agree instead with those who argue that Reason herself is subjected to irony,[27] and that, as happens so often in Chaucer, the great debate in Jean's *Roman* is purposely inconclusive.[28] Because so much rests on our interpretation of Reason's role, this controversy needs to be rehearsed briefly. One might begin with Aquinas' comment on the nature of dreaming in the Garden of Eden: "What happens in sleep is not imputed to a man, because he has not got the use of reason [*usum rationis*] then, and that is the proper act of man."[29] If this is true even in Paradise, how much more is it true of the fallen world, in which reason survives as the image of God in man, but in which our knowledge is hampered by all the symptoms of our corruption: "But a full and lucid consideration of God's intelligible effects is made practically impossible for man in his present state by the sensible ones which distract and engross his attention."[30] In particular, "the use of reason [*usus rationis*] depends in some way on the use of the powers of sense; so when the senses are locked and the inner sense capacities are blocked, a man does not have the untrammelled use of reason, as you can see with sleepers and maniacs [*homo perfectum usuum rationis non habet, ut patet in dormientibus et phreneticis*]."[31] Hult notes, appositely, that "a passing comment by Reason" in the *Roman* "suggests that the very appeal to reason in such debates [on the meaning of dreams] is quite possibly an indispensable illusion of the interpreter's own folly"; Reason argues: "but the fool sees nothing in his folly but sense and reason combined [*fors que sen et reson ensemble*]: this is how his foolish heart perceives it" (6564–66).[32] Is a dreamed Reason identical with Reason herself? This supposedly prophetic dream is after all a dream of desire and desire's fulfillment, in a medium that demands interpretation.[33] Its dream-character Nature expresses skepticism about the nature of dreams, including the kind in which a lover "feels his sweetheart in his arms although she is not there" (18357–58). Can a Reason dreamed of in a state that by definition lacks reason be Reason in actuality? Can a dreamed Reason be entirely disentangled from the carnal appetites that subvert it in the fallen world – appetites that are fully in play within the dream and constitute its origin?

For in us the sensual urge [*appetitus sensualis*], where the feelings are located, is not completely subordinated to the reason, with the result that feelings in us sometimes jump in ahead of rational judgment [*judicium rationis*] and hamper it; though sometimes too they follow upon the rational judgment, in so far as the sensual urge to some extent obeys the reason. But in the state of innocence the lower appetite was completely subordinate to the reason, so that there were no feelings of soul in that state except such as followed upon rational judgment.[34]

These questions might seem to be merely pirouettes above a *mise-en-abyme* of modern invention, except that Jean de Meun himself has Nature speculate on frenzies and the uncertain nature of dreams within the very dream we are supposed to accept as truly prophetic; and her speculation inevitably undermines the truth value of the dream in which she and Reason appear. But the conflicting definitions of Reason herself also undercut her authority. First, Reason is among other things the *ratio* or system of the *Ars Amatoria*, by which the Ovidian *magister amoris* claims to have harnessed if not defeated *impetus*, chaotic emotion[35]; and she shows her Ovidian aspect in the *Roman*, to Christine de Pizan's dismay, by repeating the teacher's injunction that "it is better to deceive than to be deceived"[36]: "There are those," Reason says, who "pretend to be true lovers [*fins amanz*] while disdaining to love *par amour*, and they make fools of ladies, promising them their bodies and souls and swearing false and deceitful oaths [*mençonges et fables*] to those whom they are able to deceive, until they have had their pleasure" (4359–67).

> Mes cil sunt li mains deceü,
> car adés vient il mieuz, beau mestre,
> decevoir que deceüz estre,
> meesmemant en ceste guerre,
> quant le maien n'i sevent querre.
> (4368–72)

[But these are the least deceived, for it is always better, fair master, to deceive than to be deceived, especially in this war in which they cannot seek a compromise.]

Yet as in Ovid, the cynicism of this consummately "rational" advice undercuts itself; as I argued some years ago,[37] Ovid shows that the complete triumph of *ratio* in amatory matters is both impossible and, finally, not something to be wished. To the extent that Jean's Reason partakes of the Ovidian *ratio*, she reveals the same difficulty, even inhumanity, in pure rationality, however much we know that the Lover's willing irrationality is comic or morally reprehensible. Her case for deception is, indeed, immediately repeated by Friend, that stand-in for the Ovidian *magister*:

> si sachiez que cil font bone euvre
> qui les deceveors deçoivent;
> sachiez qu'ainsinc fere le doivent
> tretuit amant, au mains li sage.
>
> (7312–15)

[you may be sure that those who deceive the deceivers do well, and that all lovers, at least the wise ones, should do so.]

Even within the context of Christian discourse, however, Reason needs to be defined with more nuance than simply as "the image of God" or "*Sapientia Dei Patris*." To be sure, Guillaume de Lorris says that Reason was created by God "a sa semblance et a s'image" (2975) [in his own likeness and image] in Paradise (2970–74). But although Reason may be the same faculty after the Fall as before,[38] her efficacy is impaired, as is everything else; and as Hult says, "Reason's own position is seriously compromised" because she cannot "comprehend man's condition after the Fall, including its direct linguistic result, the appearance of obscenity."[39] *Honte*, Shame, is after all her daughter (2821–28, 3012). Gillian Rudd's book on *Piers Plowman*, examining other later medieval texts, offers some useful pointers for our thinking about Reason in Jean de Meun. She quotes the *Cloud of Unknowing* to support her point that "Reason's function is thus one of discrimination only":

> Reson is a myȝt þorou þe whiche we departe þe iuel fro þe good, þe iuel fro þe worse, þe good fro þe betir, þe worse fro þe worste, þe betir fro þe best. Before er man synned, myȝt reson haue done al þis by kynde. Bot now it is so blendid wiþ þe original synne þat it may not kon worche þis werk bot ȝif it be illuminid by grace.[40]

She points out that Boethius distinguishes between divine intelligence and human reason (*Boece* 5.pr.5.35–36): just as imagination and wit are subordinate to reason, so "mannys resoun oughte to summytten itself and to ben bynethe the devyne thought" (5.pr.5.93–95). Similarly, as Sarah Kay notes, Alain de Lille's *Summa Quoniam Homines* "distinguishes *ratio* ('reasoning power which is exercised upon human and earthly things. Natural science or *naturalis philosophia* is its field') from *intellectus* (understanding of spiritual beings, angels and souls) and *intelligentia* (by which man can have some comprehension of the Trinity)."[41] Reason can at best suggest "the preferred course of action in view of the prevailing conditions"[42] – exactly what Jean's Reason does when she argues that it is better to deceive than be deceived. Rudd also points to John of Trevisa's distinction between intellect and reason, in *De proprietatibus rerum*, by which the natural intuition of the good in Paradise has declined into "a fallen or temporal virtue at best"; hence, "reason must be superseded if wisdom as *sapientia* is to be achieved."[43]

Reason inhabits Nature, as Jean de Meun learned in part from Alain de Lille. The two female authority figures are in many respects allied and offer congruent advice, though as Chaucer implies in the *Parliament of Fowls*, they do not always necessarily agree on matters of love and marriage (632). In *De Planctu Naturae* Nature defines her differences from Theology by their differing relationships to Reason: "I establish the truths of faith by reason, she establishes reason by the truths of faith. I know in order to believe, she believes in order to know."[44] Nature's relation to the supernatural is equivalent to Reason's relation to the super-rational, that is, to human Reason before the Fall. Because of the limits on Reason's scope, her discourse cannot stand as the normative authority in the *Roman*.[45]

Her colloquy with the Lover about language and signification offers the best opportunity for considering her claims. Reason, from the Lover's viewpoint, is an altogether too aggressive female voice. She offers herself to be his *amie* (5771), without any of the coyness that the decorum of *fine amour* demands. And he finds her diction to be objectionably frank, when she introduces the myth of the declining world:

> Joutice, qui jadis regnot,
> au tens que Saturnus regne ot,
> cui Jupiter coupa les coilles,
> ses filz, con se fussent andoilles,
> (mout ot ci dur filz et amer)
> puis les gita dedanz la mer,

dont Venus la deesse issi,
car li livres le dit issi.

(5505–12)

[Justice reigned formerly, in the days when Saturn held sway, Saturn,
whose son Jupiter cut off his balls as though they were sausages (a
harsh and bitter son indeed) and flung them into the sea, whence
sprang the goddess Venus, as the book says.]

If Reason had to name them, the Lover says, she should at least have
spoken of them with "some courteous word, as a virtuous woman would
when speaking of them" ("par quelque cortaise parole,/ si con preude
fame en parole" [6905–6]). (The *Ovide Moralisé* and Gower would perhaps win the Lover's approval: in Gower's version, Jupiter "kutte of with
his oghne hond/ Hise genitals"; in the moralized Ovid's, "Les genitaires
li trencha,/ Et dedens la mer les lança" [cut off his genitals, and threw
them into the sea].⁴⁶) And in the famous debate on the *Roman*, both
Jean Gerson and Pierre Col refer to Cicero's *De Officiis*, which discusses
decorum [propriety] in this context: "and in the case of those parts of
the body which only serve Nature's needs, neither the parts nor the
functions are called by their real names [*suis nominibus*]. To perform
these functions – if only it be done in private – is nothing immoral; but
to speak of them is obscene."⁴⁷

Reason responds that she can "openly" call by its "proper" name
[*apertement par propre non*] anything that is good, and that she has the
power of naming, sinlessly, "in plain and unglossed language" [*par plein
texte sanz metre gloses*] the "noble things," the *coillons* and *viz* that God
made with his own hands in Paradise, and to which He gave the power
of generation (6915–40).⁴⁸ "Now that is worse than before," the Lover
replies, "for I now see clearly by your bawdy talk [*parleüre baude*] that
you are a foolish and loose woman" (6949–52):

car, tout ait Dex les choses fetes
que ci devant m'avez retretes,
les moz au mains ne fist il mie,
qu'il sunt tuit plein de vilenie.

(6953–56)

[even though God may have made the things you have just told me
about, at least he did not make the words, which are altogether vile.]

75

(He is, of course, following Amor's earlier command in Guillaume de Lorris' part of the poem: "be sure never to use rude words [*orz moz*] or coarse expressions [*ribaudies*]: your mouth should never be opened to pronounce the name of anything base [*vilainne chose*]. I do not consider a man to be courteous if he names filthy, ugly things" [2097–102].[49]) Reason counters that God taught her the habit of plain speech (7048–50). As for the Lover's claim that God made the things but not the words, she argues that her power to name when she pleases extends to giving names as she pleases, that is to say, *ad placitum* (7056–66). Hence the Lover misunderstands what God has given to Reason as the inventor of names:

> Et quant tu d'autre part obices
> que lez et vilain sunt li mot,
> je te di devant Dieu qui m'ot,
> se je, quant mis les nons aus choses
> que si reprendre et blasmer oses,
> coilles reliques apelasse
> et reliques coilles clamasse,
> tu, qui si m'en morz et depiques,
> me redeïsses de reliques
> que ce fust lez moz et vilains.
> Coilles est biaus nons et si l'ains,
> si sunt par foi coillon et vit,
> onc nus plus biaus guieres ne vit.
> Je fis les moz, et sui certaine
> qu'onques ne fis chose vilaine.
> (7076–90)

[And if you object on the other hand that the words are ugly and base, I tell you before God who hears me that if, when I gave things the names that you dare find fault with and condemn, I had called "balls" "relics" and "relics" "balls," then you who thus attack and reproach me would tell me instead that relics was an ugly, base word. *Coilles* is a good name and I like it and so, in faith, are *coillon* and *vit*; none more beautiful have ever been seen. I made the words and I am certain that I never made anything base.][50]

Why should we not, she asks, call such things by their proper names? "They had to have names, or men would not have been able to name them, and therefore we gave them names, so that they might be called by those very names. If women do not name them in France, it is only because they are not accustomed to do so" (7097–102):

> car li propres nons leur pleüst,
> qui acoutumé leur eüst;
> et se proprement les nomassent,
> ja certes de riens n'i pechassent.
> (7103–06)

> [for they would have liked the proper name had it been made familiar to them, and in giving them their proper name they would certainly have committed no sin.]

Women are welcome, Reason says, to use all the names they employ – "purses, harness, things, torches, pricks" (7113) – and not to "name properly" [*proprement nomer*], so long as she herself is not constrained by their prudish reliance on euphemism, "quant riens veill dire apertement,/ tant conme a parler proprement" (7121–22) [when I want to say something openly and call things by their proper names]. Anyway, Reason concludes, she did not mean *coilles* to be understood literally:

> Certainly in our schools many things are said in figurative expressions [*paraboles*] which are very fair to hear, and not everything one hears should be taken literally [*a la letre*]. My words, at least when I spoke of "balls," which I wished to mention briefly, had a different meaning from the one you want to give them, and anyone who understood the literal meaning well would find a meaning in the text that would clarify the obscure discourse [*fable occure*]. The truth concealed within would be clear if it were explained; you will certainly understand it if you recall to mind the integuments on the poets. (7123–38)

There are some justifications, certainly, for taking Reason's speech at face value. Her position in favor of plain speech, the "rational" position, echoes such fabliaux as "The Damsel Who Couldn't Stand to Hear the Word 'Foutre,'" which expose the hypocrisy of courtly euphemism and the taboo against vulgar speech.[51] Certainly the end of the *Roman*, with its elaborately allegorical description of sexual intercourse, shows that periphrasis may in fact be at least as obscene, and much more pornographic, than plain speech. As Christine de Pizan comments: Jean names the sexual organs "by poetic but nonetheless explicit words [*mos poetiques entendables*] which are a hundred times more enticing and more alluring and more sensual [*delicteus*] to those who are inclined in that way, than if he had named them by their proper names."[52] Instead of turning a statue into a woman, as Pygmalion did in what Rosemond Tuve calls "a brilliant satire on the basic pretenses of 'courtly' love," the Lover succeeds in turning a woman into a statue and a building, the Castle that he storms and penetrates.[53] As in the *Franklin's Tale*, plain speech offers a clear-sighted alternative to such euphemistic delusion.

Euphemism has a paradoxical effect, however; as Simon Gaunt notes of the fabliau, the damsel's "reaction is to the word *foutre*, not to the act ... What the damsel appears to be seeking is either a means of having sex without talking about it explicitly, or training a lover to talk in a way which she finds arousing."[54] The linguistic joke here is analogous to Ovid's comment on makeup: that it uses art to make the unpalatable palatable, to deceive and self-deceive both. In this respect, it also echoes the Chartrian view of Venus, who embodies the sentimental notions of love and romance we require to do Nature's work of procreation. In the *Roman* Reason agrees with Nature that the only legitimate purpose for sexual activity is procreation; but her plain-speech movement has certain problems because euphemism serves eros as much as it serves prudery. After all, in Swift's "Strephon and Chloe" the hovering Cupids of a papier-mâché pastoral fly away forever when the newly wedded couple learn to "call a Spade, a Spade."[55]

The problems in the "plain speech" argument become evident when we bring to bear two sources for Jean's thinking: first, the Augustinian tradition of commentary on Genesis, specifically on language and sexuality before and after the Fall; second, Ovid's account of love before and after the mythical equivalent of the Fall, the end of the Golden Age. For Jean as for Chaucer, the Golden Age serves as a poetic integument for the Biblical narrative. Jean's meaning in particular requires our understanding of this myth, to which he repeatedly recurs over the course of the *Roman* as the key to his central concerns.

Jupiter's castration of Saturn marks the end of the Golden Age, and Reason's summary of the myth provokes the debate on words and things.[56] It is the first of three shocking instances of castration, the others being Origen and Abelard, though the only one with mythic, extra-literal significance; in those two other narratives, the offending word "balls" has a merely literal meaning (8766 and 17022).[57] Reason uses Saturn's castration to support her argument that Love, at least the proper kind of Love, is more essential than Justice (5526–33). Her use of the myth risks creating confusion, since Venus, born from Saturn's spilled seed, is evidently not the kind of love Reason is praising; and the justice of positive law in the fallen world is not identical with the justice defined by the goddess Astraea.[58] Natural Justice and natural Love – accompanied by communal property and communal affection – characterize the Age of Saturn: Friend's description seems more or less straightforward, even within his partial and often suspect discourse. But Justice and Love both change after Jupiter castrates his father. Venus, in the fallen world, stands not for an idealized Love but for a more narrowly circumscribed desire, in the *Roman* specifically feminine desire[59]; and her son Amor, who is the code-carrying god of masculine desire, reminds us of her limits by recalling his remarkable genealogy: "But I swear by holy Venus, my mother, and by her old father, Saturn, who begat her when she was already a young girl, though not on his espoused wife" (10797–800). Reason then tells the story of another violent cutting off, which answers the disappearance of Justice with a fearsome version of Love: Virginius' concern for his daughter's honor makes him decapitate her rather than hand her over to the corrupt judge Appius (5559ff.).[60] Significantly, Reason's argument from this exemplum that Love is more necessary than Justice is specifically an argument about the fallen world; the tension between the two is impossible in the Golden Age.

Her use of an integument to convey her meaning follows a long tradition of covering mysterious meanings by a fiction. Macrobius justifies such use of fable: philosophers "know that Nature loathes an open, naked exposition of herself: just as she has withheld herself from the contemplation of crude men by covering herself in motley array, so too she has wanted prudent men to discuss her secrets only by way of fabled narratives."[61] But Macrobius also says that not all fabled narratives are appropriate for this use, and names Saturn's castration of Caelus as a preeminent example of what is not permissible.[62] Since, as Peter Dronke explains, a "fable both preserves the secret meaning intact and leaves it inaccessible to those intellectually ill-equipped to comprehend," Jean de Meun's Lover seems to be one of this ignorant company.[63] But Reason does not bother to explain to him that this integument of Saturn's castration and the birth of Venus actually concerns the Fall, or indeed, that integument and polite diction are. made necessary by the fallen world. In the garden of Eden, Nature did not need to be hidden, and obscenity was impossible. But when Reason uses an integument that contains an obscenity, she concocts a volatile mixture of the figurative and the literal, as well as of the fictive and the historical. She does not reduce its volatility when she says that she was speaking figuratively when she mentioned "balls," but then insists that the Lover understand the offending word literally:

> Mes puis t'ai tex. II. moz renduz,
> et tu les as bien entenduz,
> qui pris doivent estre a la letre,
> tout proprement, sanz glose metre.
> (7151–54)

[But afterwards I gave you two words which you well understood and which must be taken literally and exactly, without any gloss.][64]

Reason's discussion of the Golden Age is the first of four extended treatments of the myth in Jean's *Roman*, and it needs to be read in the context of the other three. For Friend, who gives an Ovidian description of the first age – characterized by vegetarianism, sobriety, and simplicity – this was a time in which "love was loyal and true [*fines*], free from covetousness and rapine, and the world was a very simple place" [*mout precieus*] (8329–31). "At that time the earth was not ploughed" (8351),[65] a description that becomes decidedly comic later, when Genius vehemently exhorts all males to plough arduously for the perpetuation of the species. In this age of an "eternal springtime" (8376), on their simple couches of leaves or moss or grass, "those who enjoyed the games of love embraced and kissed each other, free from greed and rapaciousness" (8402–4). This is an age in which:

> these simple, secure folk would have their dances, games, and gentle amusements, free from every care except to enjoy their loyal and

loving pleasures. No king or prince had as yet committed the crime of robbing or stealing from others. All were accustomed to be equal and did not want to have anything of their own [*ne riens propre avoir ne voloient*]. They well knew the saying, which is neither false nor foolish, that love and lordship never bore each other company nor dwelt together: the one who dominates always separates them.[66] (8411–24)

In the modern world, by contrast, "true love [*bone amour*] cannot last" (8433), and marriage leads to misery, with the jealous husband who "wants to be master of his wife's body and possessions" (8435–36). Language and what it signifies also suffer an estrangement in this declining world: Jean has superimposed the history of language, as outlined in the Genesis commentaries, on the classical myth. Indeed, as Brownlee and Huot argue, "the dissociation of words and things opens up new possibilities for linguistic figuration. In a very real way, the birth of erotic desire and of figurative discourse is what makes poetry possible."[67]

For Fleming, however, this account of the Golden Age is utterly ironic, a wish-fulfillment vision from a self-deluding, fallen perspective of an entirely imaginary original free love.[68] But elements of this idea are, I believe, certainly taken seriously in Deschamps' ballade CX, "La loy souvent contraire à la nature,"[69] and in the *Franklin's Tale*, and they are at the heart of the *Book of the Duchess*: in all of these works love in the Golden Age is described as occurring between equals, before the hierarchies and political corruption consequent on the Fall.[70] Within the *Roman* itself such nostalgia is certainly without irony in the account of *amicitia*, which Cicero praises as the highest form of human love. The Lover disputes Reason's injunction that he should spurn Amor "por ne soi quele amor sauvage" (5347) [for some primitive love], and claims that this kind of love disappeared when the giants put the gods to flight, and when Right, Chastity, and Faith left the earth: "That love was so dismayed that it also fled and was lost, while Justice, weightier than the rest, was the last to flee" (5363–66); "Fraud [*Baraz*], who has inherited the earth through his strength and excesses, drove them all away" (5372–74). Friendship, traditionally male, and heterosexual love are here blurred together – both of them losing their ideal forms after the Golden Age. Indeed, Aelred of Rievaulx in *De amicitia spirituali*, which revives and Christianizes the Ciceronian ideal, explicitly makes the connection[71]:

> And when God created mankind afterward, in order to commend more highly the good conferred by human society he said, "It is not good for a man to be alone; let us make for him a helper fit for him." Certainly divine virtue did not simply form this helper from similar or even from the same material, but woman was created expressly as an incentive for happiness and friendship [*sed ad expressius charitatis et amicitiae incentivum*], from the very substance of the man himself. And so it is beautiful that the second created being was taken from the side of the first, so that nature might teach that all are equals, as it were "collateral." In human affairs there is to be neither superior nor inferior; this is the appropriate mark of friendship. [*Pulchre autem de latere primi hominis secundus assumitur, ut natura doceret omnes aequales, quasi collaterales, nec esset in rebus humanis superior vel inferior, quod est amicitiae proprium.*]
>
> So from the very beginning nature impressed upon human minds the emotional desire for friendship and affection [*amicitiae et charitatis*], a desire which mankind's inner sense of love increased with a certain taste of sweetness. But after the fall of the first humans, when affection grew cold and greed had crept in [*cum refrigescente charitate cupiditas subintrasset*] and made mankind prefer private property to the common good, avarice and envy corrupted the splendor of friendship and affection, and brought disputes, rivalries, hatred, and suspicion to our corrupted human nature. Then those who were good began to distinguish between affection and friendship [*charitatem et amicitiam*], noticing that affection ought to be given even to those who are enemies and perverse, although among the good and the bad there can be no fellowship [*communio*] of wills or counsel. And so friendship, which like affection was first preserved among all and by all, remained among a few good people according to natural law. [*Amicitia itaque, quae sicut charitas inter omnes primum et ab omnibus servabatur, inter paucos bonos naturali lege resedit.*][72]

Aelred provides the outline here for the later medieval ideal in which a happy marriage can exemplify *amicitia*.[73] But Jean adopts something even more interesting from *De amicitia spirituali*: just as Aelred conflates the Biblical account of the Fall with the myth of the Golden Age, so likewise does Jean's phrase *amor sauvage*, which evokes Ovid's *rusticitas*, the primitive virtues of ancient Rome that the *magister amoris* dismisses as uncouth simplicity.[74]

The third version of the Golden Age comes from the Vieille, the old woman who gives Ovidian advice to Fair Welcome; she wants Fair Welcome "to call me his lover without loving me *par amour*" ("quant vost que fusse amis clamez/ sanz estre par amors amez") (12961–62). She talks about Jupiter as a notorious liar in love, who laughs at lovers' perjuries (13095–104). She points to all the women deserted by men in the fallen world because they were mistakenly loyal to one man – among them Dido, Phyllis, Oenone, and Medea. Golden Age equality is implicit in her argument that women were "born free" (13845): "loi les a condicionnees,/ qui les oste de leur franchises/ ou Nature les avoit mises" (13846–48) [the law has bound them by taking away from them the freedoms Nature had given them]. In the state of nature, by contrast, she finds the free love that Friend has previously described:

> ains nous a fez, biau filz, n'en doutes,
> toutes por touz et touz por toutes,
> chascune por chascun conmune
> et chascun conmun a chascune.
> (13855–58)

[on the contrary, fair son, you may be sure that she has made all women for all men and all men for all women, every woman common to every man and every man to every woman.]

Marriage and law were instituted to "prevent dissolute conduct, quarreling, and killing, and to facilitate the rearing of children" (13861–63); Helen of Troy was neither the first nor the last woman for whose sake war and killing have occurred (13893–905).[75] She uses the analogies of the caged bird that escapes, and of a cat chasing a rat it has never seen, to explain the natural desire for freedom in married women who have love affairs: "for it is Nature, drawing them towards their freedom [*franchise*], who makes them do this. Nature is very strong, stronger even than nurture [*nourreture*]" (14005–8). All men and women desire each other, she says, as she returns to her advice on love in the fallen world, which comes directly from the *Ars Amatoria*.[76]

Genius, who presents the final exposition of the Golden Age, begins his sermon with the sexual metaphors of hammers and anvils, "and sharp-pointed ploughshares fit for her ploughs, and fallow fields, not stony ones but fertile and grassy, which need tilling and digging if they are to be enjoyed" (19517–22). This is a fallen world of plowing and agriculture, but with fertile and grassy fields, a world in which without such plowing Death will overtake all life. Hence Genius makes his enthusiastic injunction – "Plough barons, plough for God's sake, and restore your lineage" (19671–72) – which ushers in a series of outrageous double entendres, elaborating on the Ovidian joke that love and agriculture are parallel pursuits. Genius suggests in fact that they are identical pursuits, both summed up in the postlapsarian figure of Cadmus (19706–22). Winthrop Wetherbee argues that Saturn's castration marks "the severing of human life from its paradisal origins . . . , an act which brought into the world death and the obligation of labor, including the labor of procreation. As Jean makes plain it also meant the divorce of natural man from rationality, and perhaps from aspiration toward anything beyond sexual fulfillment."[77] Jean returns to this defining historical moment when he describes the park of the Good Shepherd, released from the vicissitudes of time: "For the blazing sun which always shines there fixes the day at a single point, such that no one ever saw so fair nor so pure an eternal springtime, not even in the reign of Saturn, who ruled over the age of gold and on whom his son Jupiter inflicted such injury and torment as to cut off his balls" (19997–20006).[78] But this glimpse of the ideal is immediately occluded, because Genius limits the myth's significance to the effects, physical and psychological, of castrating a "worthy man" [*prodome*] (20008): "car escoillié, certain an somes,/ sunt couart, pervers et chenins,/ por ce qu'il ont meurs femenins" (20028–30) [for we can be sure that castrated men are cruel, perverted cowards, because they have feminine characteristics]. "And although the one who castrates [*escoillierres*] is neither a murderer nor a thief and has committed no mortal sin, he has at least sinned in that he has greatly wronged Nature by stealing the means of procreation" (20039–44). Jupiter cares about none of this: he is only concerned with grabbing power; and his proclamation to the world "que chascuns pense d'estre aese" (20067) [that everyone put his mind to achieving happiness] is in fact a prescription for selfish self-indulgence, for which Jupiter the mock-Epicurean sets the pattern himself:

> car deliz, si conme il disoit,
> c'est la meilleur chose qui soit
> et li souverains biens en vie
> don chascuns doit avoir anvie.
>   (20075–78)

> [for delight, as he said, is the best thing in the world and the chief good in life, and everyone should desire it.]

Fleming notes the oddity here, that Genius "strangely characterizes the *end* of the Golden Age as the beginning of the reign of pleasure."[79] The characterization seems less odd when we consider Genius' speech in its Ovidian context. In Genius' account, Jupiter the enforcer is responsible for the loss of the golden world; and significantly, "avant que Jupiter venist,/ n'iert nus qui charrue tenist" (20089–90) [no one ever ploughed until Jupiter came]. This might seem, comically, to suggest that sexual intercourse first occurred in the Silver Age (true enough, according to the Biblical commentaries on Paradise), but it certainly implies that here is the beginning of fallen sexuality, with its fraudulence, Ovidian deception, and need to counter the forces that spill life (Jupiter himself notably, but more urgently, Death and decay in Jupiter's new world). Jean repeats a number of commonplaces from Biblical tradition conflated with classical myth; Jupiter began the division of land by boundaries and he gave snakes venom: "He created various new arts; he named and numbered the stars; he caused traps and nets and limes to be set to catch wild beasts, and cried the first dogs after them, something no one had done before" [*don nus n'iert avant coustumiers*] (20109–14). He invented the arts of falconry and of culinary complexity: "This was the beginning of the arts, for everything can be conquered by work and by grinding poverty, which is why the people are worn with care" (20145–48). He also shortened the springtime and divided the year into seasons:

> summer, spring, autumn, and winter, those are the four different seasons that used to be part of a constant spring. Jupiter wanted no more of that, and when he came to the throne, he destroyed the age

of gold and created the ages of silver and later of bronze, for men were so eager to do wrong that they went into a permanent decline. Now the condition of the age is so altered that it has changed from bronze to iron, a cause of great rejoicing to the gods in their halls of everlasting grime and gloom, who are jealous of mankind as long as they see them alive. (20163–78)

The pagan pantheon have become the demonic keepers of human black sheep, who need the redemption promised by the Shepherd of the heavenly park – set in contrast, at the end of Genius' sermon, to the garden of false felicity and transience at the beginning of Guillaume's *Roman*.

These four expositions of the Golden Age – by Reason, Friend, the Vieille, and Genius – have slightly different emphases, but together they make manifest Jean's central reliance on Ovid and Augustine for his meaning. At the beginning of the *Remedia Amoris*, Ovid claims to have reduced the blind emotion of love to a rational science: "what is now *ratio* was *impetus* before" (10); and in his tongue-in-cheek scheme, reason or system lines up with sophistication, *cultus*, art, poetry, and deception against primitive emotion, rusticity, and the lost simplicity of the Golden Age. Amor, winged and willful, must be restrained and educated by the *magister amoris*. Guillaume de Lorris picks up the story after Amor's education is complete. The god of love has become the *ratio*, the system, gendered masculine, on the side of the male lover. As in the *Ars Amatoria*, *ratio* competes with authentic emotion, above all because of its predisposition to objectify and implicitly dehumanize the beloved, the *quod* (*Ars* 1.35) or the *materia* (*Amores* 1.3.19) on which the art of love can try to work its will. Jean adds the definition of Venus as *impetus* to the mix, specifically as feminine sexuality.[80] Venus in the Golden Age could accomplish the "sweet work" of love "without art" (*Ars* 2.480); in Jean's fallen world, "art," Amor's system, is required, but Venus has to be called in to finish the job. Jean wittily sets female desire against an Ovidian male *ratio*, itself rendered irrational by the conduct of the Lover; both female *impetus* and male *ratio* are products and symptoms of the fallen world. In this Ovidian ambience, Reason is inevitably contaminated by the art of love's *ratio*, with its element of scheming and emotionally detached seduction; and this is so even if she attacks the system's preferences for courtly euphemism, with its potential for deception and self-deception.[81]

If for Ovid, *impetus* has now supposedly become *ratio*, for Augustine the opposite holds true. What was once *ratio* is now *impetus*: the Edenic subordination of the sexual organs to the rational will has lapsed into an involuntary, violent rebellion of body against soul. In Paradise, *impetus* and *ratio* are indivisible; in the fallen world, they perpetually find themselves at odds, and love has turned into the oxymorons and warring contraries that Reason decries in a long catalogue. Jupiter's castration of Saturn has brought into being a world of alienation, hierarchy, and division – the world of the seasons, the arts, and land divided into ploughed parcels. The birth of Venus makes this the world of desire, a world in which the act of love has itself become labor, and the Herculean ploughman-Lover breaks into a sweat.[82]

Inevitably, the fallen world infects our terms of discourse; and here the Genesis commentaries are especially pertinent to Jean's argument. For Jean effects another conflation of classical and Christian when he implicitly attaches the Biblical history of language to the myth of the declining world.[83] Jean shows his debt to the "grammatical Platonism" of the twelfth century,[84] the idea "that names are not arbitrary, that there is a primordial, divinely ordained harmony between names and things," and "that the relationships expressed in grammar mirror those that subsist in truth, that the reciprocities in language depend upon, and are valid because of, their counterparts in reality."[85] Aquinas tries to reconcile a grammatical Platonism with naming *ad placitum* in his commentary on Aristotle's *Peri hermeneias*:

> Some, however, have said that although nouns do not signify naturally in so far as their signification is not from nature, as Aristotle says here, still they do signify naturally in so far as their signification accords with the natures of the things, as Plato said. Nor is it any impediment that one thing is signified by many names, for there can be many copies [*similitudines*] of one thing, and similarly many diverse names can be imposed on one thing in accordance with diverse properties.[86]

Thierry of Chartres attempts an analogous reconciliation when he speculates on a crucial question: Who was the one who imposed names on things? He notes that Biblical commentators "assert that Adam gave names to things by means of the Holy Spirit. For he could not otherwise have discerned the primeval union of names and forms. In like manner

Cicero in the *Tusculan Disputations* calls him most happy and blessed who first imposed names on things. Victorinus confirms this, saying that *names make things real [nomina essentiant res]*."[87] And he also notes that "Form and name accompany each other. For there cannot be a form without a name . . . Indeed, *nomina essentiant res*":

> For names were united in the divine mind from eternity before the 'imposition' made by men. Afterwards man imposed them on things to which they were united in the divine mind. He imposed them, as it seems to us, at the instigation of the Holy Spirit. Whence it is said that *he was most wise who imposed names on things*. Moreover, Moses the most expert of philosophers notes this union in Genesis, where he says: *And he called the light Day and the darkness Night and the gathering together of the waters Seas*. All this was done in the divine mind. Through which it is denoted that words were united to things in the divine mind. Whence the divine wisdom is called the Word . . .[88]

Thierry speaks in particular about Adam here, as the human imposer of names, though he appears to imply a more universal connection of name and thing, unaffected by temporal change or the Fall. But for most commentators, and I think for Jean, temporal change and the Fall are crucially important. Adam's Reason had the power of naming before the Fall; and Reason still has the power of naming in the fallen world. But the names Reason assigns are no longer the true names of things, even if any name she chooses is a correct or proper name, arbitrary but assigned by convention. The issue is vividly highlighted by the relationship between language and sexuality. In a correspondence that Jean de Meun translated into French, and hence knew exceptionally well, Abelard rejoices to Heloise that "divine grace cleansed rather than deprived me of those vile members which from their practice of utmost indecency are called 'the parts of shame' [*pudenda*] and have no proper name of their own."[89] In this view of fallen language he agrees with Andrew of St. Victor, who thus explicates Genesis 2.25: "*and were not ashamed [Et non erubescant]*. Those parts of the body that we now call 'pudenda' because of their illicit and bestial movement descending from sin, are rightly called by such a name, because in truth both their movement and the act are filled with diffidence and shame."[90]

Jean may well have had in mind both Abelard's text and its ultimate source, *De Civitate Dei* 14.15–28, in which Augustine discusses the Fall and human sexuality.[91] In Augustine's view, it was "after the sin that this lust arose"[92]; there would have been sexual relations between an unfallen Adam and Eve, but without shame. The fallen state also affects our ability to talk about sexual matters, even when we imagine them before the Fall.

> Then the instrument created for the task would have sown the seed on 'the field of generation' as the hand now sows seed on the earth, and there would be no cause for modesty to object when I wish to discuss this subject in detail, no reason for decency to insist on my asking pardon, with an apology to pure ears. Discussion could then have free scope, without any fear of obscenity, to treat of any idea that might come to mind when thinking about bodily organs of this kind. Nor would there be any reason for calling the actual words obscene; in fact whatever was said on this subject could be as respectable as any talk about other parts of the body.[93]

Augustine defers to Paul as he embarks on his account of prelapsarian sexuality: "What I am saying will not shock the reader who is not horrified at the Apostle's attack on the horrible vices of the women who 'instead of natural practices have changed to practices contrary to nature' [Rom. 1:26), especially as, unlike the Apostle, I am not now mentioning and condemning abominable obscenities. Nevertheless, in explaining, to the best of my powers, the processes of human generation, I must endeavour, like him, to avoid obscene words."[94] Even so, "The activities I am discussing are bound to induce a feeling of shame, under present conditions. And although I am doing my best to imagine the state of affairs before these activities were shameful, nevertheless, in present circumstances, my discussion must be held in check by the restraining appeal of modesty instead of being furthered by such little eloquence as I command . . . This is the reason why a sense of shame inhibits my speech, though reason supplies abundant material for thought."[95]

Alain de Lille's Nature expresses a similar concern with obscenity and decorum, when she responds to the dreamer's request that she explain "what unreasonable reason, what indiscreet discretion, what indirect direction forced man's little spark of reason to become so inactive that, intoxicated by a deadly draught of sensuality," he rebelled against Nature's laws, both of sexuality and of language. She refuses "to explain my theme on the plain of plain words or to vulgarise the vulgar with vulgar neologisms," to make the word cousin to the deed, but chooses rather

> to gild things immodest with the golden trappings of modest words [*pudenda aureis pudicorum verborum phaleris inaurare*] and to clothe them with the varied colours of graceful diction. The result will be that the dross of the above-mentioned vices will be beautified with golden phrases and the stench of vice will be balsam-scented with the perfume of honey-sweet words, lest the great dunghill stench should spread too far on the breezes that carry it and should induce in many a vomiting from sickening indigestion. Nevertheless, as we experienced above, since the language of our discourse should show a kinship with the matters about which we speak, there should be at times an uncouthness [*deformitas*] of style to conform to the ugliness of the subject-matter. In the following disquisition, however, it is my intention to contribute a mantle of fair-sounding words to the above-mentioned monsters of vice to prevent a poor quality of diction from offending the ears of readers or anything foul finding a place on a maiden's lips.[96]

Hence her euphemisms of hammers and anvils, pens and pages, when she advocates heterosexual reproduction, asking Venus her deputy to "not allow the hammers to stray away from their anvils in any form of deviation," or the "pen to wander in the smallest degree from the path of proper delineation into the byways of pseudography."[97] Hence, too, her description of homosexual acts as grammatical solecisms – as Maureen Quilligan wittily puts it, men behaving "unspeakably"[98] – carrying on the elaborate play of, for example, Matthew of Vendome's description of the male genitalia as a dactylic foot (/uu).[99]

Jean de Meun's Lover appears at first sight to be a literal reader of Alain's Nature, echoing her concern for decorum and the avoidance of obscenity, because he rather prissily accuses Reason exactly in Nature's terms:

> Si ne vos tiegn pas a cortaise
> quant ci m'avez coilles nomees,
> qui ne sunt pas bien renomees
> en bouche a cortaise pucele.

Vos, qui tant estes sage et bele,
ne sai con nomer les osastes,
au mains quant le mot ne glosastes
par quelque cortaise parole,
si con preude fame en parole.

(6898–906)

[Also, I do not think it was courteous of you to pronounce the word
"balls": no well-bred girl should call them by their name. I do not
know how you dared name them, you who are so wise and fair, without
at least glossing the word with some courteous utterance, as a virtuous
woman would when speaking of them.]

Since the opening lines in this passage might be translated, more pro-
vocatively, as "you have just used the word 'balls,' which are not of good
repute in the mouth of a courtly maid," or "they are not well thought
of in the mouth of a courteous girl," the Lover may be referring here, as
Carolyn Dinshaw says, "to dirty sex as well as to dirty language," even
if he seems oblivious to this obscene double entendre lurking within his
insistence on decorous language.[100]

The point of Jean de Meun's irony here is not simply to advocate free
and unadorned speech,[101] though Jean repeatedly alludes to the concerns
expressed by Alain de Lille's Nature.[102] On this issue I think Quilligan,
in her very interesting essay on "Words and Sex," goes slightly wrong in
her account of Jean's meaning. She argues that Reason's disagreement
with Nature, though comic, has a serious point – that "Direct language
is necessary for allegory":

To speak in euphemisms about sexuality, Jean shows, is to limit the
non-literal meaning of language to the carnal, the merely erotic . . . In
the polite diction of the religion of love, the "allegorical" level of
meaning attached to any metaphor is merely physical. One calls a
testicle a "relic" and asks the reader by innuendo to translate the term
"relic" into the physical object which has no natural association with
the term itself. The "reasonable" use of language, however, which calls
the naturally numinous objects by their traditional names, permits an
allegorical meaning which is truly spiritual. If one calls a testicle a
testicle one has the opportunity to show what spiritual purpose these
physical objects in themselves may indeed "witness". . . Euphemism
subverts the allegorical use of metaphor.[103]

This argument does accurately characterize the effect of euphemism at the end of the poem; and Reason's discourse, as Fleming has most forcefully argued, shows the ironic effects of the polite euphemism that the god of Love enjoins on the Lover. "Courteous" utterance, as the elaborately periphrastic description of sexual intercourse reveals, can be far more obscene than the direct, "unglossed" language that Reason employs. And in a characteristic Ovidian maneuver, Jean shows that such language has the effect of disguise, of hiding a lover's motives from himself as well as from the woman he is attempting to seduce.

Yet Quilligan's argument assumes that "coilles," a French word, is the proper because traditional French name for testicle (this is itself an arguable point) even though the Latin etymology or pseudo-etymology of "testes" as "witness" suggests that the Latin name may be a *more* proper name than the French: John of Trevisa defines "þe ballockes þat hatte *testiculi* in latyn, dyminutif of *tistibus* 'witnesses'."[104] Jean's joke in fact depends on the fact that if Saturn's "coilles" are "testes," they are in fact also "relics," both in literal physical terms (this is the basis of the Host's sally at the end of the *Pardoner's Tale*)[105] and metaphorically, as the vestiges of the simple, just, equitable, and innocently amorous Golden Age, disseminated into the iron world as multiplicity (Ocean), deceit, and Venus Anadyomene. Calling them "relics" might encourage an idolatry of the physical – certainly in evidence at the end of the poem when the Lover worships his lady's genitals as "relics" (21214, 21555, 21570) – but the word *reliques* does suggest the integumental meaning of Saturn's castration quite effectively, if less shockingly than the emphatically physical *coilles*.

Jean's presentation of the myth brilliantly sums up the issues involved. The impact of the word "coilles" is heightened by its couplet rhyme "andoilles," which forces upon our imagination the hard, literal factuality at the surface of the myth, and recapitulates the brutal matter-of-factness of Jupiter's act. Once cut off, however, Saturn's balls are diffused and disseminated in the ocean foam that produces Venus at the birth of the fallen world. The Lover is shocked by "coilles"; we may be shocked as much by "andoilles," itself a word with bawdy overtones.[106] At the end of her argument, Reason says that we should not understand "coilles" (and for that matter, "andoilles") literally in any case, since she means us to read the myth as an *integument*. But this proviso cannot completely undo the shock of the literal, even though in its movement from literal to metaphorical it echoes tonally the shift from Saturn's sausage-hard testicles to the sea foam of Venus' generation.

Since integument, translation, and the metaphorical are themselves linguistic symptoms of the fallen world, Reason's discourse contains within it the signs of its own failings. Reason pointedly says that God gave her the power to name things *ad placitum*:

> Par son gré sui je coutumiere
> de parler proprement des choses,
> *quant il me plest*, sanz metre gloses.
>   Et quant me reveuz opposer
> tu, qui me requierz de gloser –
> veuz opposer? ainceis m'opposes
> que, tout ait Dex fetes les choses,
> au meins ne fist il pas le non,
> ci te respoing: espoir que non,
> au meins celui qu'eles ont ores
> (si les pot il bien nomer lores
> quant il prumierement cria
> tout le monde et quan qu'il i a),
> mes il vost que nons leur trovasse
> *a mon plesir* et les nomasse
> proprement et conmunement
> por craistre nostre entendement;
> et la parole me dona,
> ou mout tres precieus don a.
>   (7048–66; emphasis added)

[It is by his will that I am accustomed to call things by their names when I want to, without glossing them. And when in your turn you wish to raise an objection and require me to supply a gloss – raise an objection do I say? – rather you do in fact object that although God made things, at least he did not make their names – this is my reply: perhaps he did not, or at least not the names they now have (although he could certainly name them when he first created the world and everything in it), but he wanted me to find proper and common names for them as it pleased me, in order to increase our understanding, and he gave me speech, a most precious gift].[107]

In the context of the Genesis commentaries, this passage suggests that Reason herself is limited by the constraints of the fallen world, since her names differ from the original ones. Within these constraints, her argument is perfectly rational (as one would expect!), but nonetheless the names she invents are of necessity arbitrary and interchangeable, divorced from the integral relation of word and thing in the Adamic language. She can speak of things by their "proper names," (7103) or "speak properly [*proprement*] of things," without gloss (7049–50), or name genitals as she does all other things "properly" (7063, 7105, 7118, 7122), but truly proper names no longer exist, and her invented words are by their very nature a gloss.[108]

In Douglas Kelly's account of the *Roman*, "human language has become so corrupt in usage since the Golden Age ended with Saturn's castration that the proper noun for testicles has become improper"[109]; in this view words have apparently remained the same, but they now have the taint of obscenity. But Jean implies instead, I think, that the original, Adamic "proper" noun no longer exists. Christine de Pizan's reply to Pierre Col is precisely on the mark here:

> Then you go on to say that if the thing, therefore, makes the name dishonorable, what name can one give to the thing which would not be dishonorable? Without more ado, I will answer this bluntly, for I am no logician. To be honest, there is no need for such rationalizations [*persuacions*]. Indeed, I do admit to you that, because of corrupted will, I could in no way speak of a dishonorable thing, whether the secret members or some other ignoble matter, whatever name I should give them, without the name becoming dishonorable. Nevertheless, if in the case of sickness or some other need, it were necessary to refer specifically to the secret members or whatever else, and if, in such a situation, I were able to make myself clearly understood by using some other name [*j'en parloie en maniere que on m'entendist et non nommer par propre non*], then I would not at all be speaking dishonorably. The reason is that the purpose for which I spoke in such a case would not be dishonorable. Yet, even in such a case, if I were to name them by their proper names [*leur propre non*], I would indeed be speaking dishonorably, for the primary associations of the thing have already made the name dishonorable.[110]

If Jean's Reason is correct, she goes on to say, "I ask you sincerely, you who are his very especial disciple as you say, why you do not name them openly [*plainnement*] in your own writing without beating around the bush [*sans aler entour le pot*]?"[111]

Embedded in this discourse is a wordplay on "propre" as meaning "decent" and "decorous" as well as grammatically "proper," the distinction that in a somewhat less highly charged context appears in the *Manciple's Tale*.[112] In the *Roman*, Fleming argues, "Reason defends both thing and word – the thing because it was made by God in paradise, the word because it is the 'proper name' of a thing. In the case of *coilles*, incidentally, this latter claim would seem to be fully justified in the light of the etymological history of Latin *culleus* in the Romance languages."[113] Whether "etymological history" alone matters may itself be problematic.[114] Even more important, this argument misses the point and the joke of the debate, which depends on the fact that naming *ad placitum* is a defining characteristic of the fallen world, after the Adamic language has disappeared and after the diffusion of languages at the Tower of Babel. Reason admits that the names God gave to things may not be the names they now have (7056–60), their current "proper names" being the ones she has imposed *ad placitum*; and in the fallen world she is right to argue that one name is as good as any other, at least as far as signifying power is concerned. But the fallacy in her argument is that naming "proprement" is at once rationally possible and, from an Adamic perspective, impossible.[115] The proper names of things are lost, or if they survive, they survive only in Hebrew. "Coilles" is no more the proper name for what it refers to than "reliques" would be – nor is it less proper; the differences between them are differences of decorum, of the "proper," the human registers of delicacy that are themselves corrupted and fallen.

As I will argue at the end of Chapter 4, the meaning of "words being cousin to deeds" mimics this linguistic change from the true propriety of the Adamic name to a suspect but necessary social decorum. In a fallen world, all names are allegorical: that is to say, they refer to things by *alieniloquium*, since the primal connection between sign and thing could not survive the Fall. Since this is the case, Reason's argument, however rational, constitutes another version of deluded nostalgia for the Golden Age: to use unclothed words is no more likely for us than to go around unclothed – whatever euphemism and clothing may say about our spiritual state.[116] Friend's lament for a lost Golden Age of free love is suspect because of his fallen perspective.[117] But Reason, though she may be rational, is herself guilty of an analogous partiality when

95

she argues that there are, in a sense, no such things as *pudenda*, and no shameful words. Instead, Adam and Eve's covering of "leurs secrés membres" [their secret parts], as Christine de Pizan terms them in the *Mutacion de Fortune*,[118] foreshadows the use of euphemism to name them. Just as the shame and sinful desire of the fallen world require that the things be covered – and as Augustine says, require that the sexual act be committed in private – so must the names be covered by euphemism. These are the bodily parts, Statius says, "whereof to be silent is more seemly [*più bello*] than to speak," even as he, Virgil, and Dante approach the earthly paradise at the top of the purgatorial mountain (*Purgatorio* 25.43–44).

Christine de Pizan, in the *Débat* on the *Roman*, complains of Jean de Meun's "personnage que il claime Raison, laquelle nomme les secréz membres plainement par nom" [the character he calls Reason, who names the secret members plainly by name].[119] To the response that God made these things, hence they and their names must be good, "je dy et confesse que voirement crea Dieu toutes choses pures et nectes venans de soy, n'adonc en l'estat d'innocence ne eust esté laidure les nommer; mais par la pollucion de pechié devint homme inmonde" [I say and confess that truly God created all things pure and clean coming from himself and that in the State of Innocence it would not have been wrong to name them, but by the pollution of sin man became impure].[120] She discusses Lucifer's name as a point of comparison: "God made Lucifer beautiful above all the angels and gave him a very solemn and beautiful name, but then Lucifer was reduced by his sin to horrible ugliness; whereupon, the name, albeit very beautiful in itself, now, because of the impression of the person, creates horror in those who hear it."[121] As for the "relics" argument that Reason makes: "je vous confesse que le nom ne fait la deshonnesteté de la chose, mais la chose fait le nom deshonneste" [I suggest to you that the name does not make the thing dishonorable, but the thing, the name].[122]

In a sense, Christine is playing off Boethius' argument in the *Consolation of Philosophy* 3, pr. 12, that the word must be cousin to the deed. In Jean de Meun's translation, "Comme tu aies apris par la sentence de Platon qu'il couvient que les paroles soient cousinez aus chosez dont il parlent"[123]; in Chaucer's: "sith thow hast lernyd by the sentence of Plato that nedes the wordis moot be cosynes to the thinges of whiche thei speken" (*Boece*, p. 439). Indeed Jean's narrator himself, like Chaucer after him, paraphrases this argument as an excuse for any lapse of decorum that he may have commmitted:

> se mi dit sunt de tel maniere
> qu'il soit droiz que pardon an quiere,
> pri vos que le me pardoignez,
> et de par moi leur respoignez
> que ce requeroit la matire
> qui ver tex paroles me tire
> par les proprietés de sai;
> et por ce tex paroles ai.
>
> (15139–46)

[if my words are such that I should ask pardon for them, I beg you to pardon me and to reply on my behalf that they were called for by my subject, whose intrinsic properties drew me to such language; that is why I use these words.]

For, as he goes on to say, citing Sallust as his authority:

> "car quiconques la chose escrit,
> se du voir ne nous velt ambler,
> li diz doit le fet resambler;
> car les voiz aus choses voisines
> doivent estre a leur fez cousines."
> Si me convient ainsint paler,
> se par le droit m'an vuell aler.
>
> (15158–64)

["Whoever does the writing, if he is not to deprive us of the truth, his words must echo the deed, for when words rub shoulders with things, they should be cousins of the deeds." And so I must speak in this way if I want to proceed correctly.][124]

The trouble with this argument is that it cuts both ways. If one agrees that certain body parts are, in the fallen world, *pudenda*, then Christine is quite right in arguing that the words that are cousin to them are also inevitably contaminated. In this respect Alastair Minnis is just slightly misleading in his witty imagining:

If Raison is right, then presumably one is free to imagine Adam going around the garden of Eden cheerfully using the primordial equivalents of terms like "shit" and "fuck" (if I may work further Jean's vein of humour). Doubtless someone may retort that such terms would have been innocent in Paradise – which rather misses the point that, particularly when imagined in such a context, they are a source of amusement to Adam's not-so-innocent descendants.[125]

For Jean is not, I think, constructing a bawdy version of Milton's brilliant effort in *Paradise Lost* to imagine the unfallen meanings that reside, if only etymologically, within fallen words such as "mazy," "wanton," and "errant." In the Augustinian view there are no primordial equivalents to our four-letter words, because word and thing in Paradise are both unimaginably, or nearly unimaginably, different from their fallen descendants; indeed, even our digestive systems and their residue were, as Wyclif points out, themselves unimaginably different, having in Paradise "neither offense to God nor nuisance [*nocumentum*] to man."[126]

In a fallen world in which names are assigned *ad placitum*, then, language is purely conventional; and convention has to do with decorum, standards of civility or gentility, precisely with a social agreement on meaning. In this respect allegory is created by, but also sums up the dilemma of language and signification in the fallen world. Like parable and indeed all figurative language, it serves to denature the otherwise dangerous assumptions of literality: it forces us to think about meanings that we might too easily think we understand in the "literal." But it suggests too that even the literal is in fact a version of *alieniloquium*, since literal meaning has lost its substantial pre-fallen connection with the thing it signifies. As Augustine insists in his tracing of every human's passing from infancy (the infant as *infans*, "not speaking") to speech, all of our speech is tainted by our infected will.

In this context Reason is evidently being somewhat disingenuous. If God did not name the pudenda, "or at least not the names they now have," then the names Reason has imposed on them are not their true names; and as Augustine makes clear, the fallen state ensures that the human mind will contaminate any names assigned to them just as it does the things. That is to say, Christine de Pizan and Gerson are right on target when they accuse the *Roman* of obscenity; they simply miss Jean's irony at Reason's expense. For what Reason's discourse reveals, in part despite herself, is how radically language has changed. In Paradise, when Adam gave the animals and birds their true names, there was a single name for each thing; proper and common nouns were identical. In the fallen world, language participates in the universal lapse into multiplicity and division: a single name can signify several things; yet several names can signify a single thing. And as Jean wittily spells out this paradox, he once again elaborates on both Augustine and Ovid, on both Biblical commentary and pagan myth.

Single names can signify several things in at least three respects:

1) As I noted in Chapter 1, ambiguity in a proper name begins with the name "Eve," or so Jerome argues. Jean de Meun in fact calls into question our ready assumption that any names can be proper names, by fiddling around with the meaning of "Rose" and the identity of the Dreamer/Lover who pursues that rose. At the beginning of Guillaume de Lorris' part of the *Roman*, the woman with whom the Lover falls in love is so rose-like "qu'el doit estre Rose clamee" (44) [that she ought to be called Rose]; similarly, in the fourteenth-century marguerite poems of Machaut and others, the marguerite/daisy of the poem is also, presumably, a woman named Marguerite. But who or what is it that ought to be called "Rose"? As Kay asks, "Is it a lady? her love? her virginity?" By the end of the poem the name for this "mysterious and eroticised object"[127] has been reduced to signify her genitalia – as if the poem, which has anatomized her into her various qualities, personified as (usually male) characters, has emptied her of her psychologically complex identity, and allowed her reduction to a sexual body part.

2) Augustine had noted in *De Doctrina Christiana* 2.24 that the same sound may have different meanings in different languages (Greek *beta* is a letter, Latin *beta* a vegetable). Accordingly, we are told in a medieval French joke that the dirtiest word in the Latin Psalter is *conculcavit* [he has trampled under foot], because it contains three obscene monosyllables – in French.[128] Within French itself, one of the fabliaux on verbal taboo hinges on the fact that *vit* has a number of innocuous meanings along with its "obscene" one.[129] And Hult has wittily shown how sound patterns of obscenity, "based upon a type of verbal contagion," are similarly at work in the *Roman*, when *coilles*, once named, reappears many times in the rest of the poem, as a complete word and

as an obtrusive fragment buried within other words such as "cueillir," "Bel Acueil," "escoillier," and "escollier."[130]

3) Most of all in the *Roman*, "a single name for several things" sums up the confusion or blurring of literal and figurative language (a predictable confusion in a *somnium*, which is by definition an enigmatic dream open to various interpretations). Reason understands the literal *coilles* of Saturn figuratively, or integumentally; the Lover understands the word literally, and takes offense; Origen takes the injunction to be a "eunuch for the Kingdom of Heaven's sake" literally, and cuts off his own *coilles*.[131]

As for several names signifying a single thing: this is, after all, a poem with two titles, the *Romanz de la Rose* (37) and the *Miroër aus Amoreus* (10621), and also two names for the *je* who has dreamed this dream and is narrating this poem: Guillaume de Lorris has metamorphosed into Jean Chopinel.[132] Guillaume, as written by Jean de Meun, is also supplanted by him; and Jean, among other things, seems to be making Ovid's joke about the danger of letting one's friend act on one's behalf, even in a dream.[133] Jean shows us the consequences of naming *ad placitum*: if language is conventional, then all names are allegorical, a version of *alieniloquium*. Meaning requires agreement, custom, the *acoustumance* that makes the women of France call male genitalia "purses, harness, things, torches, pricks," instead of what Reason says are their "proper" names. But in the fallen world, this is the agreement of human beings who are divided against themselves and each other, between and within languages. This is precisely the place where Jupiter's hierarchies of alienation intervene with categories that did not exist in Eden or the golden world: the distinctions of social class and decorum, or of euphemism vs. obscenity. These are categories we are unable to escape; and if calling "balls" "relics" does risk an idolatry of the physical, for Saturn's "coilles" at least, "relics" may in fact be the better name.[134] For these are indeed vestiges left behind from the former world and disseminated into the sea, and *testes* or witnesses to lost plenitude,[135] the lost plenitude of a universal language and an innocent world before the Fall, and before the invention of fallen desire.

3

Dante and Chaucer's Dante

ADAM'S LANGUAGE AND OURS

Of the writers to whom Chaucer is indebted, Dante is the most inter-
ested in the history and theory of language, and the most inclined to
examine such matters fully. At the beginning of the *Convivio* and in his
treatise on eloquence in the vernacular, Dante explains his theories of
language at some length; ideas about the history and signifying power of
speech even more notably pervade the *Commedia*. Whether Chaucer's
debt is to Dante's prose exposition of his ideas, or more probably to his
poetic treatment of them, that debt is apparent in the *House of Fame*,
which attends carefully to Dante's views primarily to subvert them. The
House of Fame constitutes Chaucer's first and most exhaustive thinking
through of Dante's work, as he skeptically examines and makes use of
the *Commedia*. The ideas that he adapts and reacts to in this early poem
continue to appear in his later poetry, in more distilled and abstract
forms. As befits their prominence in his thought and poetic practice,
Dante's ideas on language have been examined by many critics, but they
have a particular resonance in a Chaucerian context, as well as in the
context of medieval Genesis commentaries; and they provide a useful
reference point for discussing all of Chaucer's major poems from the
House of Fame on.

Dante's thinking on language begins from a powerful commonplace,
which he no doubt took from Aquinas and which also appears in Augustine and Cicero: that speech is the distinguishing trait of human beings,
the attribute that manifests our reason and our isolation from the other
forms of life on earth,[1] and from the angels as well. In Dante's words,
that distinguishing attribute appears "in those operations that are proper

to the rational soul, into which the divine light radiates most freely: that is, in speech [*nel parlare*] and in those gestures which are customarily called bearing and conduct. Here we should know that among the animals man alone speaks and has conduct and gestures which are called rational, because he alone has reason within himself" (*Convivio* 3.7.8–9; p. 107).² The primacy of speech explains one of the names for a human being, *fante* – etymologically, "one who speaks"³; this name is particularly appropriate because speech was the first gift of God to Adam, after the breath of life itself (*DVE* 1.5), and Adam's fitting response was to say God's name as his first word, "in the form either of a question or of an answer" (*DVE* 1.4.4). The gift of speech is one that each of us owes, secondarily, to our parents; and a major component of Dante's patriotic attachment to the vernacular is in fact simple familial gratitude, in thanks for his own begetting: "This vernacular of mine was what brought my parents together, for they conversed in it, just as it is the fire that prepares the iron for the smith who makes the knife; and so it is evident that it has contributed to my generation, and so was one cause of my being" (*Convivio* 1.13.4; p. 31).

Given the centrality of this idea in Dante's thought, one is hardly surprised at the extent to which language in the *Commedia* itself serves as a sign of sin or redemption. As the souls in Hell make a willed descent to the bestial, their language – the most distinctive mark of their humanity – becomes increasingly debased. The distinctively human may in fact disappear altogether into wailings and sighs, and the other inarticulate "natural" signs that we share with the animals.⁴ Many of the damned souls are specifically marked by "sins of the tongue," the varieties of which are extensively treated in medieval penitential literature;⁵ indeed, Giuliana Carugati argues, Dante signals his own implication in this sin, the one "by which man, endlessly repeating the enterprise of Babel, erects monuments of words, in perpetual defiance, and deferral, of God's silence."⁶ In either case, inarticulate sound or perverted language, for these inhabitants of Hell "speech has lost the power to communicate in a normal way . . . Either they make sounds without meaning or their words convey a meaning they did not intend."⁷

The hellish inversions of language are memorable: they are, indeed, among the most vivid details of the *Inferno*. Pier delle Vigne, the thorn tree from whose broken limb "parole e sangue" [words and blood] (13.44) escape together, stands out among those to whom speech is now difficult. When a brief silence makes his wound fill with blood, Pier must puff hard to clear the way for his voice (13.91–92); and his verbal difficulty is part of his punishment as a suicide, denied normal self-expression as well as an embodied self. The suicides, who willfully separated soul from body, will forever be denied reunion with their flesh: after the Last Judgment, the corpse of each will hang on the tree that entombs its soul (107–8). Their eerie wailing (22) can voice itself in words only when their branches are brutally broken off by others: by Dante's breaking a twig; by the Harpies' foul feeding on their leaves, which gives "dolore, e al dolor fenestra" [pain and to the pain an outlet] (102); or by the demonic chase, which drives the squanderers of possessions to crash headlong into these squanderers of self (109–21).

The punishment by *contrapasso* is still more vehement elsewhere. The would-be prophets who presumed to speak of the future are now silent (20.8), compelled to look behind them because their necks are twisted as by a palsy (16): Dante's word for "palsy," "parlasia," is "an odd word for paralysis," Joan Ferrante notes, "probably to incorporate the pun on speech."[8] A voice Dante hears, "a parole formar disconvenevole" [ill-suited for forming words] (24.66), leads him to the circle of the thieves, specifically to Vanni Fucci, whose curse at God is cut off by the snake coiled around his neck, "come dicesse 'Non vo' che più diche'" [as if it said, "You shall say no more"](25.6). His companions among the thieves are punished by continual metamorphoses, which steal from them their human form and their human capacity for speech, in a phantasmagoric exchange between human shade and reptile:

> e la lingua, ch'avëa unita e presta
>   prima a parlar, si fende, e la forcuta
>   ne l'altro si richiude; e 'l fummo resta.
> L'anima ch'era fiera divenuta,
>   suffolando si fugge per la valle,
>   e l'altro dietro a lui parlando sputa.
>   (25.133–38)

[and the tongue, which before was whole and fit for speech, divides, and in the other the forked tongue joins up; and the smoke stops. The soul that was become a brute flees hissing along the valley; and the other, speaking, spits after it.]

The most extensively portrayed deformation takes up the next two
cantos, where the fraudulent counsellors appear wrapped in flames.
Dante ties these cantos to the preceding one by patterns of verbal reminiscence. The thieves of canto 25, who are robbed of their capacity for
speech, suggest the phrasing Dante uses to describe the flames in cantos
26 and 27, each of which "steals away" (*invola*, 26.42) a sinner, and also
the terms by which Minos judges Guido da Montefeltro: "Questi è d'i
rei del foco furo" [This is a sinner for the thievish fire] (27.127). In turn,
Ulysses as "Lo maggior corno de la fiamma antica" [The greater horn of
the ancient flame] (26.85), along with the "corno aguto" [pointed horn]
(27.132) of Guido's speaking flame,[9] presage the horn of Nimrod, its
inarticulate blast (31.12, 31.71) providing his only means of expression,
"quand' ira o altra passïon ti tocca!" [when rage or other passion takes
you] (31.72).[10] Although Ulysses' preeminence in fraudulent counsel
may explain the relative ease with which he gives voice to his sonorous
rhetoric – and Dante is certainly aware that he himself is at risk because
of rhetoric's dangers[11] – Guido's expressive plight would seem to be
the more typical in this circle: first a "confuso suon" [confused sound]
(27.6) like that of the Phalarian bull; then the fire's effort to change the
attempted words into its own "linguaggio" (14), the language of moving
flame; then at last the escape of Guido's words from the vibrating tips
of the flame that engulfs him (17–18). Bad counsel is punished by the
denial of easy access to any words at all.

Those who are free to speak in lower Hell tend to do so in coarse and
debased terms; and Dante's own speech becomes, as Singleton points
out, "deliberately nasty, violent, derisive, and taunting."[12] The damned
souls mechanically copy the devils' vulgarity (21.100–2), and they soon
enough descend below any speech at all. Vanni Fucci is reduced to
making the fig at God with both hands (25.1–2), much as the patrol of
devils exchange signs with their leader:

> Per l'argine sinistro volta dienno;
> > ma prima avea ciascun la lingua stretta
> > coi denti, verso lor duca, per cenno;
> > ed elli avea del cul fatto trombetta.
> > > (21.136–39)

[They wheeled round by the bank on the left, but first each pressed his tongue between his teeth at their leader for a signal, and he had made a trumpet of his arse.]

If Dante has never yet heard "sì diversa cennamella" [so strange a pipe] (22.10) or seen such a "segno" (12), there are stranger signs yet to come. Nimrod's horn blasts away in canto 31; in the lowest pit of hell the sounds are of chattering teeth (32.36) and savage barking (32.106–8); instead of speech, Ugolino's gnawing on his persecutor's skull serves as the "bestial segno" [bestial sign] (32.133) of his hatred.[13]

When Virgil and Dante find all the bridges broken at the sixth bolgia, after the devil Malacoda has lied to them in canto 21, the ruin is in a sense of language itself, as truthful communication, as a binder of human beings, and as the means we have of making our thoughts known to one another. Dante says in *De Vulgari Eloquentia*:

> Since, therefore, human beings are moved not by their natural instinct, but by reason, and since that reason takes diverse forms in individuals, according to their capacity for discrimination, judgement, or choice – to the point where it appears that almost everyone enjoys the existence of a unique species – I hold that we can never understand the actions or feelings of others by reference to our own, as the baser animals can. Nor is it given to us to enter into each other's minds by means of spiritual reflection, as the angels can do, because the human spirit is so weighed down by the heaviness and density of the human body.
>
> So it was necessary that the human race, in order for its members to communicate their conceptions among themselves, should have some signal based on reason and perception [*rationale signum et sensuale*]. Since this signal needed to receive its content from reason and convey it back there, it had to be rational; but, since nothing can be conveyed from one reasoning mind to another except by means perceptible to the senses, it had also to be based on perception. For, if it were purely rational, it could not make its journey; if purely perceptible, it could neither derive anything from reason nor deliver anything to it.
>
> This signal, then, is the noble foundation [*ipsum subiectum nobile*] that I am discussing; for it is perceptible, in that it is a sound, and yet also rational, in that this sound, according to convention, is taken to mean something [*rationale vero in quantum aliquid significare videtur ad placitum*].[14]

The broken bridges are, not surprisingly, at the circle of the hypocrites, whose meaning was once as painted as they themselves now are (23.58). Hypocrisy and lying – notably the startling fraud of Gianni Schicchi's pretending to make a dead man speak (30.42–45) – frustrate the purpose of language as an intermediary between people, a medium of exchange repeatedly associated in the poem with coinage.[15]

Francesca's famous line, "Galeotto fu 'l libro e chi lo scrisse" [A Gallehault was the book and he who wrote it] (5.137) shows that words may also act as another kind of go-between, like the "galeoto" Phlegyas (8.17), the "boatman" who transports the damned to the infernal city of Dis. When Boccaccio twice offers "Prencipe Galeotto" as an alternative title for the *Decameron*, in the opening epigraph and at the end of the Epilogue defending his tales and the sexual euphemisms within them, he is perhaps implying backhandedly that Francesca, like his own audience of women, should take more responsibility for her readerly actions. For his part, Dante repeatedly makes problematic the relation of poetry and truth: as Singleton's famous dictum goes, "The fiction of the *Divine Comedy* is that it is not fiction."[16] Virgil at one point accuses Dante of not having given enough credence to the *Aeneid*: he would not have broken off a twig from Pier delle Vigne "S'elli avesse potuto creder prima . . . ciò c'ha veduto pur con la mia rima" [If he . . . had been able to believe before . . . what he had never seen save in my verses] (13.46–48), that is to say, Polydorus' eerie metamorphosis. But Virgil also, explaining the origin of Mantua, enjoins Dante not to believe another account: "la verità nulla menzogna frodi" [let no falsehood defraud the truth] (*Inf.* 20.99) – the other account being what he himself had said about Manto and Mantua in the *Aeneid*. Dante tells Lucan and Ovid to be silent, because the metamorphoses they describe, *poetando* [poetizing], cannot match the double metamorphosis he witnessed (*Inf.* 25.94–102). In all of these instances the poetic and implicitly fictive bump up against Dante's autopsy – what he claims to have seen and heard himself.

When lying or hypocrisy defeats the communicative function of language, the effect is perniciously apparent: Malacoda's lie differs absolutely from the "vere parole" [true words] (2.135) of Beatrice and Virgil's "parlare onesto" [noble speech] (2.113), as directions to set Dante on the true path. Yet as Malacoda's example also shows, lying in the *Inferno* is not effective, or becomes unwitting self-exposure. Vanni Fucci does not, and cannot dissemble: he must answer what Dante asks (24.136). The dissemblers on earth must tell the truth in the afterlife, or at least reveal their true states with transparent self-deceptions.[17] In this respect they copy the first liar, Cain, who was no more successful in his effort to deceive God (Genesis 4.9–10).

If Malacoda's lying may echo the impotence of Cain's, Dante also reminds us at several points in the *Inferno* of the most notorious instance of linguistic pride and impotence in the Old Testament.[18] The first such allusion to Babel and its aftermath is matter-of-fact: Dante remarks how many "diverse lingue" [strange tongues] (3.25) there are among the wailing dead. The second allusion is somewhat more pointed, if only because the queen it celebrates is so closely tied to sin and to Babylon: Semiramis

> fu imperadrice di molte favelle.
> A vizio di lussuria fu sì rotta,
>   che libito fé licito in sua legge,
>   per tòrre il biasmo in che era condotta.
>
> (5.54–57)

[was empress of many tongues. She was so given to lechery that she made lust licit in her law, to take away the blame she had incurred.]

For as Ferrante notes, Semiramis thus "changes one letter and makes lust legal in her law."[19] But the most striking reminiscences of Babel are, of course, the representations of strange tongues: Plutus' "Pape Satàn, pape Satàn aleppe!", said "con la voce chioccia" [with a clucking voice] (7.1–2)[20]; and Nimrod's "Raphèl maì amècche zabì almi," cried out by "la fiera bocca, / cui non si convenia più dolci salmi" [the fierce mouth, to which sweeter psalms were not fitting] (31.67–69).[21] Nimrod's outburst, as Virgil explains, is in a language with only one speaker:

> questi è Nembrotto per lo cui mal coto
> pur un linguaggio nel mondo non s'usa.
> Lasciànlo stare e non parliamo a vòto;
>   ché così è a lui ciascun linguaggio
>   come 'l suo ad altrui, ch'a nullo è noto.
>
> (31.77–81)

[this is Nimrod, through whose ill thought one language only is not used in the world. Let us leave him alone and not speak in vain, for every language is to him as his is to others, which is known to none.][22]

Nimrod's five words are, Hollander argues, "a reproduction of what 'fallen Hebrew' sounded like," but if so, a Hebrew that has relinquished its communicative function altogether.[23] This reduction of language to solipsism, wonderfully imaged in the stupefied giant whose pride destroyed our primeval linguistic unity, carries the decay of language as far as it can go. The only possible further descent is to the silence and cold of innermost Hell, with Satan's flapping wings, his biting and clawing of Judas, Brutus, and Cassius (34.49–60), and Virgil's explanation, by a parody of *Vexilla regis*, of this horrible sight that Dante, first among living men, sees.[24]

In this respect as in others, Dante recapitulates Scriptural history: the vivid concreteness of his journey depends on this figural quality in his allegory. The *Commedia* makes evident what Genesis proclaimed: the implication of language in the world of sin and death brought about by the Fall.[25] Unsurprisingly, language takes part in the more general rehabilitation in the *Purgatorio*; and the comparison with the debased speech in Hell is at times an explicit one, in the subversion and redemption of "hymn" and "psalm." Nimrod's "psalms" [*salmi*] (31.69) are preceded by the hymns of the sluggish and sullen, which fit their nature: "Quest'inno si gorgoglian ne la strozza, / ché dir nol posson con parola integra" [This hymn they gurgle in their throats, for they cannot speak it in full words] (*Inf.* 7.125–26).[26] In Purgatory, by contrast, the more souls rise above the constraints of earth and the flesh, the more their speech becomes noticeably choral: the hymn is the quintessentially purgatorial form of discourse. This is a world filled with "group movement" and "choral speech,"[27] where hymnal poems mark the transition points from one stage of penitence to the next:

> Ahi quanto son diverse quelle foci
> da l'infernali! ché quivi per canti
> s'entra, e là giù per lamenti feroci.
> (*Purg.* 12.112–14)

[Ah, how different these passages from those of Hell, for here the entrance is with songs, and down there with fierce laments.]

The change in tone is emphatic; appropriately, the word *canto*, both as a song and as a self-referential pointing at Dante's poem itself, appears many more times in the last two-thirds of the work.[28] Divine poetry marks the shift to human salvation.

Human poetry does too, if in a more tentative fashion. Purgatory is full of poets: Sordello, Statius, Bonagiunta, Guido Guinizelli, and Arnaut Daniel – all of them for Dante poets of a single Romance tongue, which Purgatory serves to re-unify.[29] Indeed, the only conspicuous examples of poets elsewhere – except of course for the ancients in Limbo – are Bertran de Born (*Inferno* 28) and the love-poet turned Cistercian, Folco, in *Paradiso* 9.[30] If speech, degraded in hell, is to be redeemed and purified in the other world, the poet's language must participate in that redemption: "Ma qui la morta poesì resurga" [But here let dead poetry rise again] (*Purg.* 1.7). The poets, especially the poets of love, are especially suited to this second *cantica*: even disregarding the purgatorial state of their souls, the nature of their vocation makes their presence here appropriate. For poetry, in Dante's view, evidently sums up the ambiguities of human speech, and its capacity to be used for either good or evil purposes. On the one hand, we have the example of Paolo and Francesca, led on by the pandering book;[31] and for that matter, of Dante himself, who explores the risks of poetic pride, the dangers of reading and writing when he implicitly compares himself to Ulysses, and supplies his false counterpart with such seductive rhetoric.[32] On the other hand, Dante shows us that the poet can rise to the demands of "'l poema sacro/ al quale ha posto mano e cielo e terra, / sì che m'ha fatto per molti anni macro" [the sacred poem to which heaven and earth have so set hand that it has made me lean for many years] (*Par.* 25.1–3). In Purgatory, the mediating function of poetry fits the mediating world of the purgatorial mountain. When Statius blesses Dante for his "tanto labore" [great labor] (*Purg.* 21.112), his words seem to refer as much to the sacred poem as to the soul's progress, even though this is a world – as Cato's rebuke reminds Casella (*Purg.* 2.120–23) – in which listening to beautiful poetry, even to Love's discourse, "Amor che ne la mente mi ragiona" [Love that discourses in my mind] (2.112), is no substitute for diligent attention to the cleansing ascent.

Although the poets in Purgatory are saved and the ones in Limbo are not, the lessons of the great pagan poets – which Statius sums up in his fervently acknowledged debt to Virgil – stand in opposition to the horrors of Hell and transcend them. Just as the natural reason of the virtuous pagans lights up their eternal abode, and distinguishes it from the surrounding darkness, so their measured rationality, gentility, and decorous calm stand against the torments soon to follow; Virgil, as Dante's guide, constantly reminds us of those virtues and keeps them to the foreground. The inhabitants of Limbo lament only with "sospiri/ che l'aura etterna facevan tremare" [sighs, which caused the eternal air to tremble]; and they are sighs of "duol sanza martìri" [sadness, without torments] (*Inf.* 4.26–28). In contrast, when Virgil and Dante leave Limbo, "fuor de la queta, ne l'aura che trema" [out of the quiet, into the trembling air] (4.150), they come to a place where

> . . . molto pianto mi percuote.
> Io venni in loco d'ogne luce muto,
> che mugghia come fa mar per tempesta,
> se da contrari venti è combattuto.
> (5.27–30)[33]

[much wailing smites me. I came into a place mute of all light, which bellows like the sea in tempest when it is assailed by warring winds.]

The catachresis of "d'ogne luce muto" defines what has just vanished, the luminous quiet sounds of Limbo, its measured speech:

> giugnemmo in prato di fresca verdura.
> Genti v'eran con occhi tardi e gravi,
> di grande autorità ne' lor sembianti:
> parlavan rado, con voci soavi.
> (4.111–14)

[We came to a meadow of fresh verdure, where there were people with grave and slow-moving eyes and looks of great authority; they spoke seldom and with gentle voices.]

Behind this scene lie the traditional moral injunctions on the virtues of silence, and dangers in talking too much.[34] Dante has learned and continues to learn this lesson, as the example of the virtuous pagans continues to influence his moral behavior. In Limbo itself, he refuses to tell us what he and the other poets discussed:

Così andammo infino a la lumera,
   parlando cose che 'l tacere è bello,
   sì com' era 'l parlar colà dov' era.
                                    (4.103–5)

[Thus we went onward to the light, talking of things it is well to pass
in silence, even as it was well to speak of them there.]

In the deeper parts of Hell, we see Dante and Virgil moving "Taciti, soli,
sanza compagnia" [Silent, alone, without escort] (23.1), having escaped
from the squabbling demons. Virgil once again repeats the moral lesson:

"Altra risposta," disse, "non ti rendo
   se non lo far; ché la dimanda onesta
   si de' seguir con l'opera tacendo."
                                    (24.76–78)[35]

["Other reply," he said, "I do not give you than the doing, for a fit
request should be followed by the deed in silence."]

In violent contrast to the silence and gentle voices of Limbo, Master
Adam and Sinon carry on their punch-up (*Inferno* 30), fittingly in the
canto just before Nimrod appears; and Virgil rebukes Dante for pausing
to listen to their flyting, "ché voler ciò udire è bassa voglia" [for the wish
to hear that is a base wish] (30.148).

   The joke here is, of course, that Dante recounts for us at some length
a dispute that Virgil attacks him for listening to – as if his base wish to
eavesdrop needs to be acted out before it can be expunged. This pro-
cedure after all lies at the center of what Dante's journey means as an
itinerarium mentis: the path of purgation must lead through his witness-
ing of the infernal torments. It also explains how Dante places himself in
the poetic tradition, as he internalizes the example of the poets in Limbo
and the continuing advice of their exemplary representative Virgil. For
if the poets are among those who "parlavan rado, con voci soavi," they
are also of necessity breakers of silence, who are implicated – as Dante
is in canto 30 – in the baseness or virtue of what they recount. Moreover, though, as Statius says, the poet's fame lasts the longest of all (*Purg.*
21.85), it still needs revivification: a living poet must restore to dead poets
their voices by his acts of indebtedness and imitation. As Singleton and
others have noted, Dante marks his debts by specific acts of imitation:

he copies the style of other poets, for example Guido Guinizelli, when he introduces them in the poem.[36] (The extreme of this practice, of course, is later in the same canto 26 of the *Purgatorio*, when Arnaut Daniel speaks in Provençal.)[37] This need for revivification partly explains why Virgil is, at his first appearance, described as "chi per lungo silenzio parea fioco" [one who seemed faint through long silence] (*Inferno* 1.63), and one of the most powerful meanings of his return to speech as Dante's guide[38]; the *Aeneid* will resonate again in its rewritten and revivified form.

For the *Commedia* imitates the *Aeneid* both in obvious ways – the topography of the underworld, the resemblance of Pier delle Vigne to Polydorus – and more subtly as well. Dante laments, "Io non Enëa, io non Paulo sono" [I am not Aeneas, I am not Paul] (*Inf.* 2.32), but he in fact becomes another Aeneas in his visit to the realm of the dead, and as a future exile.[39] Most touchingly, he recapitulates Aeneas' experience in *Paradiso* 15–17, when his ancestor Cacciaguida is described as another Anchises (15.25), with the proviso "se fede merta nostra maggior musa" [if our greatest Muse merits belief] (15.26) about the truth of *Aeneid* 6; like Anchises, he greets his progeny with a somber vision of the future. When Virgil takes his leave of Dante in the Earthly Paradise, "Tratto t'ho qui con ingegno e con arte" [I have brought you here with understanding and with art] (*Purg.* 27.130), his leave-taking includes a specifically linguistic, that is to say poet's lament: "Non aspettar mio dir più né mio cenno" [No longer expect word or sign from me] (139); and the final line of the canto, "per ch'io te sovra te corono e mitrio" [wherefore I crown and miter you over yourself] (142) implies Dante's newfound ability to stand alone as poet as well as redeemed soul. Both are indeed summed up in Beatrice's saying his name (*Purg.* 30.55), the only time that it appears in the poem.[40] But even this apparent point of transcendence is premature, since she is rebuking Dante for weeping at Virgil's departure; and the canto has fully shown how complex such a departure must be. Dante quotes in Latin from the Song of Songs (30.11); inserts a Latin phrase of his own, "*ad vocem tanti senis*," into his Italian verse (17); seems to defy Biblical source and grammatical gender by the address of Beatrice as "*Benedictus qui venis!*" (19); and caps these Latin insertions with "*Manibus*, oh, *date lilia plenis!*" (21) – the "oh" adapting Vergil's Latin to his own metrical needs, and with this quotation from

Anchises' lament for Marcellus (*Aeneid* 6.883) now turned into joyful anticipation of Beatrice's arrival.[41] When, at his first sight of Beatrice, Dante turns like a frightened child to his mother, and finds that Virgil has disappeared, the words he says to Virgil as he turns, "conosco i segni de l'antica fiamma" [I know the tokens of the ancient flame] (30.48), are of course taken from Dido's speech to her sister (*Aeneid* 4.23). And his anguish at Virgil's disappearance, which repeats the name "Virgilio" three times in as many lines (49–51), almost certainly echoes the fourth *Georgic* (525–27), which names Eurydice three times in as many lines as she returns to the underworld.[42] Virgil's influence endures beyond his actual presence, though this influence is one that Dante must at times correct and in the end leave behind.

Virgil's impact on Dante is urgent as well as profound: in Ulrich Leo's attractive hypothesis, Dante's rereading of the *Aeneid* in a time of personal crisis provoked his writing of the *Commedia*.[43] Much the same thing happened twelve centuries earlier, when as *poeta* – an epithet often used for Virgil in the *Purgatorio*[44] – he led Statius to poetry and then to the Christian faith: "Per te poeta fui, per te cristiano" [Through you I was a poet, through you a Christian] (22.73). Dante's allusion to Dido in *Purgatorio* 30 imitates Virgil while it implicitly makes distinctions – between true and false love, and true and false gods. Statius too reminds us that Virgil accomplished more than he knew, especially when he wrote the *Fourth Eclogue*:

> Facesti come quei che va di notte,
>   che porta il lume dietro e sé non giova,
>   ma dopo sé fa le persone dotte.
>   (22.67–69)[45]

[You were like one who goes by night and carries the light behind him and profits not himself, but makes those wise who follow him.]

Virgil's reward for serving as a beacon is, appropriately, visionary and poetic, though temporary and beyond his full comprehension: he is granted the sight of the true Earthly Paradise – of which the ancient poets perhaps dreamed when they sang of the Golden Age (28.139–41) – and can look on with Statius at the vision staged for Dante's benefit in canto 28.

As others have pointed out, this sequence of cantos paradoxically pays homage to Virgil in the process of one-upping him; Statius in fact owes his salvation to a misreading of a line from the *Aeneid* (3.57), when he takes *sacra* to mean "holy" instead of "accursed" (*Purg.* 22.40–41). In these cantos of the *Purgatorio* the lines of poetic descent and arguments about method establish the ground for Dante's transcendence of his tradition, and of human poetry itself, in the *Paradiso*. There is, first, a tension between the moral equality of souls – Statius calls Virgil and Dante "frati miei" [my brothers] (*Purgatorio* 21.13), Guido Guinizzelli calls Dante "frate" (26.115) – and a carefully calibrated scale of poetic value. Statius defers to Virgil; so does Dante, though he must also move beyond him. Dante learns poetic lessons from the talk of Virgil and Statius (22.128–29). Bonagiunta defers to Dante, admitting that his own verse failed to break the knot – "il nodo" (24.55) – of artificiality and win through to the beauties of the "dolce stil novo" [sweet new style] (24.57), the style that Dante attributes to direct inspiration, and will allow him in the *Commedia* to rise beyond the earthbound:

> E io a lui: "I' mi son un che, quando
> Amor mi spira, noto, e a quel modo
> ch'e' ditta dentro vo significando."
> (24.52–54)

> [And I to him, "I am one who, when Love inspires me, takes note, and goes setting it forth after the fashion which he dictates within me."]

Dante defers to Guido Guinizzelli, and to his own unnamed "betters" (26.98) who, along with him, copied Guido's style – standing in the relation to Guido that Statius does to Virgil. Guido himself defers to Arnaut Daniel as the "miglior fabbro del parlar materno" [better craftsman of the mother tongue] (26.117). Though Dante will prove that there is no singing-school for the would-be rhapsodist of Heaven, the poet must nonetheless train himself in monuments of the soul's magnificence, to put himself on the path to transcendence.

This tension between the poetic and the noetic is one that Dante resorts to repeatedly in the *Paradiso*, as he phrases the *topos* of inexpressibility in a variety of ways.[46] Dante has led us further and further beyond the limits of human speech: notably, in the *visibile parlare* of *Purgatorio* 10, in which the truth of God's poetry is set against the limits of its human imitators[47]; in the need to ask for the Muses' divine assistance (*Purg.* 29.37–42); and in the hymn that he hears but does not understand in the Earthly Paradise (32.61): "Io non lo 'ntesi, né qui non si canta" [I did not understand the hymn, and it is not sung here]. Dante does not understand it, one assumes, because it is sung in the primal language, in which signifier and signified are directly connected, beyond our powers to comprehend. At the beginning of *Paradiso* 7, two of the three sacred languages, Latin and Hebrew, fuse together in Justinian's celebratory hymn:

> "*Osanna, sanctus Deus sabaòth,*
> *superillustrans claritate tua*
> *felices ignes horum malacòth!*"
>   (7.1–3)[48]

Seven cantos later, light and sound form a more transcendent fusion:

> E come giga e arpa, in tempra tesa
>   di molte corde, fa dolce tintinno
>   a tal da cui la nota non è intesa,
> così da' lumi che lì m'apparinno
>   s'accogliea per la croce una melode
>   che mi rapiva, sanza intender l'inno.
> Ben m'accors' io ch'elli era d'alte lode,
>   però ch'a me venìa "Resurgi" e "Vinci"
>   come a colui che non intende e ode.
>   (*Par.* 14.118–26)

[And as viol and harp, strung with many cords in harmony, chime sweetly for one who does not catch the tune, so from the lights that appeared to me there a melody gathered through the cross which held me rapt, though I followed not the hymn. Well I discerned it to be of lofty praise, for there came to me: "Rise" and "Conquer," as to one who understands not, but hears.]

In the move toward the inexpressible, however, Dante also reminds us that the poet's skills, however imperfectly expressive, are the only ones available – and the skills are those of the vernacular poet, since as Ferrante notes, "Many of the plays with meaning and sound that are so essential to the success of the *Paradiso* are not possible in Latin."[49] Yet his vision of transcendence is emphatically in the past or future, his present state one of exile and hopeful expectation for the "triumph of caesar or of poet" (*Par.* 1.29). If his "poema sacro" can win his return to Florence, he will, "con altra voce omai, con altro vello/ ritornerò poeta" [with changed voice now and with changed fleece a poet will I return] (*Par.* 25.7–8). Within the *Paradiso* the point of demarcation between poetry and the super-poetic is precise. The heaven of Venus, the last one touched by the shadow of the earth, is the one inhabited by Folco, the last poet named in the *Commedia* (*Par.* 9); here too is the last of the several references to Dante's earlier poetry (8.36–37).[50] Afterwards, the songs are heavenly and beyond the powers of human verse:

> canto che tanto vince nostre muse,
>   nostre serene in quelle dolci tube,
>   quanto primo splendor quel ch'e' refuse.
>
> (12.7–9)

> [song which, in those sweet pipes, as much surpasses our Muses, our Sirens, as a first splendor that which it throws back.]

Part of the project of the *De Vulgari Eloquentia* had been to make certain that the illustrious vernacular might, like grammatically fixed Latin, serve as a counter to the Fall.[51] Yet even a language purified by the purgatorial ascent is evidently inadequate to the description of Heaven. Dante, like Paul in 1 Corinthians, makes apparent the insufficiency of our human powers to describe the eternal; and when he prepares a holocaust to God "Con tutto 'l core e con quella favella/ ch'è una in tutti" (*Par.* 14.88–89) [with all my heart, and with that speech which is one in all men], the universal speech he uses is clearly the silent communication of Augustine's "inner word." Sense perception is necessarily prior to understanding (*Par.* 4.41–42), and sense perception is precisely what fails. At one point, Dante cannot hear "la dolce sinfonia di paradiso" [the sweet symphony of Paradise] (21.59) because, as Peter Damian explains to him, "Tu hai l'udir mortal sì come il viso" [You have the hearing as the sight of mortals] (21.61). Like Paul, Dante hears *arcana verba* that cannot be repeated:

> Ne la corte del cielo, ond' io rivegno,
>   si trovan molte gioie care e belle
>   tanto che non si posson trar del regno;

> e 'l canto di quei lumi era di quelle;
>> chi non s'impenna sì che là sù voli,
>> dal muto aspetti quindi le novelle.
>>> (*Par.* 10.70–75)

[In the court of Heaven, whence I have returned, are many gems so precious and beautiful that they may not be taken out of the kingdom, and of these was the song of those lights. Let him who does not wing himself so that he may fly up thither await tidings thence from the dumb.]

Indeed, they cannot be understood by a mortal, even one who has been granted a heavenly journey.

After such comments, the meeting with Cacciaguida is the more striking because once Dante's ancestor descends to the level of human language, he does so in an emphatically homely way, by speaking in the old Florentine dialect.[52] The emphasis on the *segno d'i mortal* suggests a concern with signification as much as with boundaries:

> Indi, a udire e a veder giocondo,
>> giunse lo spirto al suo principio cose,
>> ch'io non lo 'ntesi, sì parlò profondo;
> né per elezïon mi si nascose,
>> ma per necessità, ché 'l suo concetto
>> al segno d'i mortal si soprapuose.
> E quando l'arco de l'ardente affetto
>> fu sì sfogato, che 'l parlar discese
>> inver' lo segno del nostro intelletto,
> la prima cosa che per me s'intese,
>> "Benedetto sia tu," fu, "trino e uno,
>> che nel mio seme se' tanto cortese!"
>>> (15.37–48)

[Then, a joy to hearing and to sight, the spirit added to his first words things I did not comprehend, so deep was his speech; nor did he conceal himself from me by choice, but of necessity, for his conception was set above the mark of mortals. And when the bow of his ardent affection was so relaxed that his speech descended toward the mark of our intellect, the first thing I understood was, "Blessed be Thou, Three and one, who show such favor to my seed."]

Though Dante's mind will finally break through its mortal barriers of
sense like lightning (23.40–45), what he sees and hears is beyond the
power of memory to repeat (23.45, 20.11–12), in part because of the
self-consuming effects of heavenly fulfillment:

> Nel ciel che più de la sua luce prende
>   fu' io, e vidi cose che ridire
>   né sa né può chi di là sù discende;
> perché appressando sé al suo disire,
>   nostro intelletto si profonda tanto,
>   che dietro la memoria non può ire.
>   (*Par.* 1.4–9)

> [I have been in the heaven that most receives of His light, and have
> seen things which whoso descends from up there has neither the
> knowledge nor the power to relate, because, as it draws near to its
> desire, our intellect enters so deep that memory cannot go back upon
> the track.]

The letter to Cangrande explicates this passage in terms that explicitly
set the inner word in contrast with its spoken simulacrum:

> And so the author saw, as he says, something he on returning "neither
> knows how nor is able to relate." Now it should be carefully noted
> that he says that he "neither knows how nor is able"; he does not
> know how because it was forgotten, he is unable because even if he
> had remembered and could retain the content [of his vision], the
> words would be lacking. For we see many things with the intellect for
> which there are no verbal signs. This fact Plato makes plain enough by
> the use he makes of metaphors in his books: for he saw many things
> by the light of the intellect which he was unable to express in the
> appropriate words.[53]

Poetry and perhaps speech itself depend by their very nature on separation, incompletion, and loss.[54] If Dante becomes metamorphosed
after the manner of Glaucus (*Paradiso* 1.68) (cf. the *trasmutato* at 22.10),
the metamorphosis is one that words cannot trace:

> Trasumanar significar *per verba*
>   non si poria; però l'essemplo basti
>   a cui esperïenza grazia serba.
>   (1.70–72)

[The passing beyond humanity may not be set forth in words: therefore let the example suffice any for whom grace reserves that experience.]

Dante is forced to push language beyond its limits: the word *trasumanar* is itself a coinage, and neologism becomes one way of trying to describe the indescribable.[55] In a realm where *del suo verbo* refers to the unspoken thoughts of Cacciaguida and his descendant (*Par.* 18.1),[56] language works in odd ways, such as the Latin angelic skywriting in heaven (18.91 and 93). But whatever the poet's ingenuity, however much he calls on "lo 'ngegno e l'arte e l'uso" [genius, art, and practice] (10.43), he finally yields to inexpressibility. This yielding is phrased most memorably in the final canto of the poem, in the final failure of the "alta fantasia" [lofty phantasy] (142), but also earlier on, in an image of great power and ingenuity, as the souls in formation as wheeling spheres dance and sing before Beatrice:

> Di quella ch'io notai di più carezza
>   vid' ïo uscire un foco sì felice,
>   che nullo vi lasciò di più chiarezza;
> e tre fiate intorno di Beatrice
>   si volse con un canto tanto divo,
>   che la mia fantasia nol mi ridice.
>   (*Par.* 24.19–24)

[From the one I noted as the richest I saw issue a fire so joyful that it left there none of greater brightness; and it revolved three times round Beatrice with a song so divine that my phantasy does not repeat it to me; wherefore my pen leaps and I do not write it, for our imagination, not to say our speech, is of too vivid color for such folds.]

Thus, the general outlines of Dante's linguistic theory are evident. His ideas, first worked out theoretically in *De Vulgari Eloquentia* and then revised, are central to the structure and meaning of the *Commedia*. Speech takes part in the degradation of the Fall, and the eternal reprobation of the damned in Hell. It even more centrally defines the particular levels of Purgatory, by its ambiguities and mediating nature. And though it cannot wholly achieve the necessary transcendence to describe Paradise, Dante invests it and poetry with the nobility of an effort pushed to the limits of human powers[57]:

> e così, figurando il paradiso,
>   convien saltar lo sacrato poema,
>   come chi trova suo cammin riciso.
> Ma chi pensasse il ponderoso tema
>   e l'omero mortal che se ne carca,
>   nol biasmerebbe se sott' esso trema:
> non è pareggio da picciola barca
>   quel che fendendo va l'ardita prora,
>   né da nocchier ch'a sé medesmo parca.
>   (*Par.* 23.61–69)

[and so, depicting Paradise, the sacred poem must needs make a leap, even as one who finds his way cut off. But whoso thinks of the ponderous theme and of the mortal shoulder which is laden therewith, will not blame it if it tremble beneath the load. It is no voyage for a little bark, this which my daring prow cleaves as it goes, nor for a pilot who would spare himself.]

Ferrante shows how the poem moves "from the staccato cacophony of Hell towards the fluid harmony of heaven," given the "tendency towards fewer speakers but longer speeches in Paradise than in Hell." In sum, "we have the failure of language as a mode of communication in Hell, the unification of language in Purgatory, and the creation of language in Paradise."[58]

ADAM'S LANGUAGE IN *PARADISO* 26

In *De Vulgari Eloquentia* Dante had followed the traditional belief that Adam spoke Hebrew, which allowed a neat typological symmetry. Just as, according to legend, the Cross was made of wood from the Edenic Tree, so there was an opportune identity of Adam's speech and Christ's. For Dante, the original purity of Hebrew survived the confusion of tongues so that Christ, who was born from the Hebrews "(in so far as He was human) should not speak the language of confusion, but that of grace" (*DVE* 1.6.6). But in *Paradiso* 26, Dante's thinking is noticeably different. Adam says:

> La lingua ch'io parlai fu tutta spenta
>   innanzi che a l'ovra inconsummabile
>   fosse la gente di Nembròt attenta:

ché nullo effetto mai razïonabile,
  per lo piacere uman che rinovella
  seguèndo il cielo, sempre fu durabile.
Opera naturale è ch'uom favella;
  ma così o così, natura lascia
  poi fare a voi secondo che v'abbella.
Pria ch'i' scendessi a l'infernale ambascia,
  I s'appellava in terra il sommo bene
  onde vien la letizia che mi fascia;
e *El* si chiamò poi: e ciò convene,
  ché l'uso d'i mortali è come fronda
  in ramo, che sen va e altra vene.
                    (*Par.* 26.124–38)

[The tongue which I spoke was all extinct before the people of Nimrod attempted their unaccomplishable work; for never was any product of reason durable forever, because of human liking, which alters, following the heavens. That man should speak is nature's doing, but whether thus or thus, nature then leaves you to follow your own pleasure. Before I descended to the anguish of Hell the Supreme Good from whom comes the joy that swathes me was named *I* on earth; and later He was called *El*: and that must needs be, for the usage of mortals is as a leaf on a branch, which goes away and another comes.][59]

Many others have noted the closeness of Dante's phrasing here to Aquinas' on the conventional nature of language: "significare conceptus suos est homini naturale, sed determinatio signorum est ad placitum humanum" [Man naturally expresses his ideas by signs, but how these are determined depends upon human agreement].[60] Yet elsewhere in the *Summa* Aquinas also describes an Adamic language that is in essence Cratylistic: "In the state of innocence men would not have needed animals to supply their bodily wants . . . But what they needed them for was to acquire an experiential knowledge of their natures. This is suggested by God leading the animals to Adam for him to give them their names, which designate their natures [*ut eis nomina imponeret, quae eorum naturas designant*]."[61] In *Paradiso* 26, Adam's language is presumably a primordial version of Hebrew, but a Hebrew that itself has since undergone devastating alteration.[62] In a narrow but decisive adjustment of his earlier view, Dante says that Adam's first word, which in *De Vulgari Eloquentia* was "the name of God, or *El*, in the form either of a question or of an answer" (1.4.4), was in fact an earlier version of God's name, the iconic sign of Oneness "I," the name that survived until Adam's death, sometime after which it became "El." Dante's reasons for inventing this name are readily apparent, since it has an innate correspondence with the God it signifies, as an iconic representation of His singularity and unity.[63] It marks a primal transparency in words that has since been lost in Hebrew, never to be found in any other language.

This is a moment of crucial importance for my argument, and a moment in the *Commedia* that has, I think, been widely misunderstood to mean that "mutability was a feature of language from the very beginning" and that "language was changing from the time of creation," given that "Adam does not seem to differentiate between his pre- and post-lapsarian linguistic activity."[64] In this view, Adam's language even in Paradise is a language subject to change, a language of "ultimately arbitrary original signs,"[65] a language subject to all the variation that Horace poignantly describes in the *Ars Poetica*, in a passage that Dante adapts with his image of language as falling leaves: "As forests change their leaves with each year's decline, and the earliest drop off: so with words, the old race dies, and like the young of human kind, the new-born bloom and thrive. We are doomed to death – we and all things ours . . . All mortal things shall perish, much less shall the glory and glamour of speech endure and live [*mortalia facta peribunt, / nedum sermonum stet honos et gratia vivax*]."[66] Accordingly, Colish argues: "Dante removes the claim that any language might be able to make to superiority over the vernacular, which he can now treat as the equal of the Hebrew of Eden as well as the Latin of the classical authors."[67] But there is in fact no "Hebrew of Eden"; what we might call instead the "proto-Hebrew of Eden" was the perfect, Adamic language, a language that as Dante makes evident is lost and irrecoverable. In the fallen world, the world of mortals, there is not any longer a perfect language; but there was one, for a very brief moment, in the Garden of Eden.[68]

The briefness of that moment comes as a surprise to the modern reader. For by Adam's own account, in the lines that immediately follow his discussion of language, he spent no more than a few hours in Paradise:

Nel monte che si leva più da l'onda,
    fu' io, con vita pura e disonesta,
    da la prim' ora a quella che seconda,
    come 'l sol muta quadra, l'ora sesta.
               (*Par.* 26.139–42)

[On the mountain which rises highest from the sea I lived pure, then guilty, from the first hour to that which follows, when the sun changes quadrant, next upon the sixth.]

The brevity of this stay – insisted on by such works as Peter Comestor's *Historia Scholastica* and the *Elucidarium* of Honorius Augustodu-nensis[69] – allows Dante to imagine a perfect Adamic language that falls along with its inventor. The effect is to reduce Hebrew, before and after Babel, to a vernacular like any other, and to modify Dante's earlier views on *grammatica* in *De Vulgari Eloquentia*.[70] Because Adam's language is now irrecoverable (and was not in fact Hebrew), any vernacular, like eloquence itself, has the power to be used for good or for ill.[71] Thus in *Paradiso* 27, the *Gloria Patri* can with no violation of heavenly decorum be sung in Italian; even more conspicuously, when Dante quotes Psalm 9.11 in *Paradiso* 25, as Brownlee points out, "it is as if the Latin were (paradoxically) presented as a 'translation' of the Italian," because the Italian rendering of the complete verse comes before its fragmentary citation in Latin.[72]

Dante thus implies in *Paradiso* 26 that *I* is the true name of God, given by Adam with an intuitive understanding such as he manifests in naming the animals; and if this true name survives the Fall, it does not survive Adam himself. Dante's invention is in accord with and almost certainly expands on some earlier Biblical commentaries, and for that matter, the Genesis text itself, since *I* as Adam's first word becomes the inaugural instance of image and similitude in the human world, prior to the bodily creation of Eve as Adam's similitude, and its visual demonic variant, the serpent with the maiden's face. Guerri noted nearly a century ago that *I* is the first letter of the name Iehovah and also denotes unity, and he cites apposite texts from John of Garland and Ubertino da Casale.[73] Damon understands *I* to be "an attempt at a non-vocalic transliteration of the tetragrammaton," and hence to stand for God's "incomprehensibility and ineffability."[74] Mazzocco uses *Convivio* 4.6.3–4, which says that the vowel "i" characteristically evolves into "e," to argue that Dante reinforces the mystical implications of the name with philology: "Since it is in the nature of *I* to evolve into *E*, Dante must have concluded, by engaging in a bit of what today we might characterize as historical phonology, that the linguistic base for *El* could not be anything else but *I*."[75]

Even in the names for God, then, the shift from Edenic Cratylism to a naming *ad placitum* manifests itself, in the changeability of language naming the One. Indeed, Dante's invented history of God's name gains added poignancy because he is evidently indebted to Isidore's *Etymologiae* 7.2–3, which talks about *El* as a name for God. Isidore begins his account of the ten names (including *Eloi*, *Sabaoth*, *Adonai*, and the Tetragrammaton) by which God is called among the Hebrews with: "Primum apud Hebraeos dei nomen El dicitur" [The first name of God among the Hebrews is called *El*]; and this is evidently the source of Dante's comment in *De Vulgari Eloquentia*.[76] But at a much later point in Isidore's encyclopedia, after he has outlined the geographical location of Persia, he notes: "The magic art first arose in Persia, to which Nimrod the giant went after the confusion of tongues, and there he taught the Persians to worship fire. For all in those parts worship the sun, which is called *El* in their language [*qui ipsorum lingua El dicitur*].[77] This is an astonishing moment, with implications for Dante that I think no one has noticed previously. If the Hebrew name for God has now also become the Persian name for the idolatrously worshipped Sun, in a context that specifically mentions Nimrod and his fire worship (which I will have more to say about in Chapter 4), the devastating change in the nature of language has become all too apparent. Dante himself invokes the Sun as "Elïòs" (*Par.* 14.96); and Huguccio of Pisa had remarked: "From *Ely*, that is God, the sun is called *elyos*, having been considered a god in former times."[78] In *Paradise Lost* as well, "Thou Sun" (8.273) are Adam's first words, and first act of naming. Virgil explains to Sordello the sin of omission by which "ho perduto/ a veder l'alto Sol che tu disiri/ e che fu tardi per me conosciuto" (*Purg.* 7.25–27) [I lost the sight of the high Sun that you desire and that was known by me too late]. Idolatrous sun-worship in effect takes literally the familiar symbol of Christ as the Sun. Even Virgil's prayer to the Sun (*Purgatorio* 13.16–21) seems to hover between pagan idolatry and Christian truth, between the letter and the spirit.[79]

Dante also signals the calamitous shift from *I* to *El* by the various transformations and debasements *I* itself has undergone in the fallen world. At its basest, in *Inferno* 24.100, *i* is merely a graphic sign that can be written very quickly[80]:

> Né o sì tosto mai né i si scrisse,
>   com' el s'accese e arse, e cener tutto
>   convenne che cascando divenisse.
>   (*Inf.* 24.100–02)[81]

> [and never was *o* or *i* written so fast as he took fire and burned, and must sink down all turned to ashes.]

In *Paradiso* itself, Dante leads up to Adam's speech with two variations on the letter *I*. In the sky-writing of *Paradiso* 18, which marks a "substitution of visual for auditive forms of language,"[82] the souls of the Just spell out in their flight the letters *D*, *I*, and *L*, and then proceed to spell out a complete word (*Par.* 18.78 and 91). Dante's emphasis on the stately progress of these letters – the spirits halt for a while in silence after each one (81) – raises the issue of how perception colors meaning, since at first sight the three letters – "nostra favella" [our speech] (*Par.* 18.72), our human language, which Singleton glosses as "letters of the alphabet" – could instead be Roman numerals. Only when the complete words "DILIGITE IUSTITIAM" begin to appear, when "figure" (86) become unambiguously "vocali e consonanti" (89) [vowels and consonants], is a possible misunderstanding or double meaning dispelled, though of course *I* serves as both vowel and consonant in these two words. We have in fact been prepared for such ambiguous word and number play by the "cinquecento diece e cinque" of *Purgatorio* 33.43, when the written number collapsed into numeral form, DXV, becomes an obscurely prophetic anagram for the DVX, the Leader who will slay the whore of Babylon. And indeed, in *Paradiso* 18 significations explode when the final *M* of the command, as if playing on the double signification of *M* as letter and number, becomes more than a thousand [*mille*] lights (103–4), forming first an eagle's head and neck and a lily, and then the entire eagle.

In the following canto, *Paradiso* 19, *I* itself appears as a numeral, phrased as a letter, along with *M*, set in opposition to it in the immediately following line:

> Vedrassi al Ciotto di Ierusalemme
>   segnata con un i la sua bontate,
>   quando 'l contrario segnerà un emme.
>   (19.127–29)

> [It will show the Cripple of Jerusalem, his goodness marked with an *I*, while an *M* will mark the opposite.]

The early commentators, notably Benvenuto da Imola, read *i* and *emme* as Roman numerals, though Francesco da Buti argues that the relative size of the two letters is the issue, *i* being the smallest letter in the alphabet, and *m* in effect *i* repeated three times.[83] Moreover, the Greek *iota* is a well-known symbol of the minimal, as in Matthew 5.18: "I say unto you, till heaven and earth pass, one jot or one tittle [*iota unum, aut unus apex*] shall not pass of the law, till all be fulfilled."[84] Dante's point is precisely that the true name of God in the Adamic language has, in the postlapsarian world, become merely a sign like any other, arbitrary and imposed *ad placitum*. Thus it no longer serves as God's sole name; its successors among the various names for God are themselves also open to double meaning or misuse, as in the Chaldaean *El*. One version of Cratylism that does survive in and mark the fallen world is the OMO (*Purgatorio* 23.32) imprinted on the face of sinful man. As Vincent argues, "The identification of word and thing can surely go no further than this when the thing is stamped and labelled with its word"[85]; but significantly, OMO is revealed by the process of purgation, as the glutton's face is stripped down to its hollowed essence.

Adam is, as a user of language, analogous to Cacciaguida, who speaks to his descendant, "non con questa moderna favella" [not in this our modern speech] (*Paradiso* 16.33), but in the old Florentine idiom. The two of them together exemplify Dante's continuing preoccupation with linguistic change, in the broad sweep of human history and more locally as well: according to *Convivio* 2.13.9, the moon is the sphere of grammar because, as Horace pointed out at the beginning of the *Ars Poetica*, words continually disappear and reappear in human history; there are indeed, Dante laments, changes even in the space of fifty years (*Conv.* 1.5.9).[86] Adam's instability, however, was the cause of all the rest. He is to blame not simply for the difference in dialect between Cacciaguida and Dante, but for the very fact that they do not speak the Edenic language. Famously, Adam's explanation of his Fall stresses this linguistic dimension:

> Or, figliuol mio, non il gustar del legno
> fu per sé la cagion di tanto essilio,
> ma solamente il trapassar del segno.
> (*Par.* 26. 115–17)

> [Now know, my son, that the tasting of the tree was not in itself the cause of so long an exile, but solely the overpassing of the bound.]

The overpassing of the *segno* is punished by the corruption of the sign, until the process of degradation reaches its close in Nimrod's horn blast or Ugolino's "bestial segno" (32.133), just before the silence in the bottom-most pit of Hell. By contrast, *Paradiso* 26 implies a linguistic reunification at the end of time, within the bounds of the one true language: as in the Biblical text of the Apocalypse (1.8, 21.6, 22.13), God is "Alfa e O" (*Paradiso* 26.17), in Mazzotta's phrasing "the boundaries of the letters of the alphabet which can be combined in and produce all possible words" within the Book of the Universe with whose rebinding the poem ends (*Paradiso* 33.85–87).[87]

What Dante does in the *Commedia*, then, is to take the ideas of language in Genesis and the New Testament – that is, the relation of speech to the fall and redemption of humankind – and give them concrete particularity. If, as Singleton and Freccero have argued, Exodus is the type of Dante's journey, language too follows this figural pattern of exile and return.[88] Dante also follows a Vergilian paradigm of exile: his leaving "proud" Florence is analogous to Aeneas' leaving "proud" Troy, even as his Comedy answers and rewrites Vergil's "high tragedy." In each instance, exile makes possible return, a fall makes possible a rise. For Dante the tower of Babel, the division of one language into many, is also a paradigm for the political collapse marked by the loss of a single ruler, into the factionalism and division of warring city-states and dialects in Italy.[89] As Corti says, the Tower of Babel marks "the disappearance from the face of the earth of a language that was simultaneously natural and universal. Henceforth languages could not be other than natural and non-universal, or universal and non-natural"[90]; and she also argues that Babel is a typological figure for the Florence of violently warring factions.[91] One solution to the linguistic problem (*De Vulgari Eloquentia* 1.9.11) is the construction of a *grammatica*, an artificial, unchanging, fixed language.[92] Another, which Dante embraces in different ways at different points in his life, is the rehabilitation of language within the vernacular itself,[93] which he implicitly connects with a political program to bring unity to Italy.

Speech, in its various debased and redeemed forms, is a defining feature of specific places along Dante's journey; and the unrolling of linguistic change in history finds its copy in Dante's progress through Hell, Purgatory, and Heaven. But the diachronic movement also hides a synchronic tension: the paradoxes in the poet's craft and in human speech itself – most apparent in the *Purgatorio* – are continuing ones. Just as the pure light of Paradise is the effect of an unearthly clarity – and Dante reminds us that he has returned to earth and exile, even as he tries to recapture that ethereal purity – so, for the poet and for the rest of us, the difficulties of language persist, whatever heights a momentary vision may have attained.

Chaucer never tries for such effects of transcendence, of language pushed to its upper limits of referentiality. But he evidently attended closely to Dante's progressive revelation of his linguistic ideas over the course of the *Commedia* – ideas on linguistic change, and also on related problems of speech, style, and meaning. Although he was almost certainly unacquainted with Dante's impassioned defense of the vernacular in *De Vulgari Eloquentia*, he had taken its lesson to heart before he ever read Dante. But when Dante notes in the *Convivio* that Latin is stable, while the vernacular changes even within the space of fifty years,[94] he sounds very much like the opening of Book Two of *Troilus and Criseyde*:

> Ye knowe ek that in forme of speche is chaunge
> Withinne a thousand yeer, and wordes tho
> That hadden pris, now wonder nyce and straunge

Us thinketh hem, and yet thei spake hem so,
And spedde as wel in love as men now do.
(2.22–26)

Another of Dante's preoccupations bears even more directly on Chaucer's interests: the variance among different vernaculars, the divisive legacy of Babel, which Chaucer at the end of *Troilus* phrases as a nervous awareness of human instability:

And for ther is so gret diversite
In Englissh and in writyng of oure tonge,
So prey I God that non myswrite the,
Ne the mysmetre for defaute of tonge;
And red wherso thow be, or elles songe,
That thow be understonde, God I biseche!
(5.1793–98)

In Dante the differences between vernaculars mark the assertion of political, moral, and poetic communities, but also the risk of mutual alienation. Dante's speech gives him away as a Tuscan, as Farinata says: "La tua loquela ti fa manifesto" (*Inferno* 10.25)[95]; the line has added pungency because it translates Matthew 26.73, when Peter is identified as one of Jesus' followers: "nam et loquela tua manifestum te facit" [for even thy speech doth discover thee]. Dante is recognized as Tuscan and Virgil as Lombard (*Inf.* 22.99); and this difference between them defines a curious and much debated passage in the *Inferno*. Dante wishes to hear Ulysses speak; Virgil assents eagerly to his request, but says "Lascia parlare a me" (*Inf.* 26.73) [leave speech to me], giving a cryptic reason: "ch'ei sarebbero schivi, / perch' e' fuor greci, forse del tuo detto" (74–75) [perhaps, since they were Greeks, they would be disdainful of your words]. Why should they be more favorably disposed to Virgil? His address to them suggests one reason, that they owe part of their fame to the commemorative powers of his poetry, and he addresses them in a decorously lofty style[96]:

s'io meritai di voi mentre ch'io vissi,
s'io meritai di voi assai o poco
quando nel mondo li alti versi scrissi,
non vi movete . . .
(26.80–83)

129

[if I deserved of you while I lived, if I deserved of you much or little when in the world I wrote the lofty lines, move not.]

But as Pagliaro and others have noted, there may be a linguistic issue as well: that Dante, as a Tuscan, is identified with the descendants of Troy, and is hence the enemy of the two Greeks, in a way that a Lombard is not.[97] The likelihood of some such explanation becomes greater given the evidence of canto 27. Guido da Montefeltro notes that Virgil spoke Lombard in dismissing the two Greeks (27.20–21); and Virgil tells Dante that he should now speak for a specifically linguistic reason: "Parla tu; questi è latino" (27.33) [You speak: he is Italian]. This verse, in pointed comparison to Virgil's comment in the previous canto, suggests that if Dante can speak Tuscan to an Italian, Virgil must be able to speak Lombard to Greeks, and they to understand him.[98] In any case, these cantos emphasize linguistic division as one expression of human bonds and human hostilities.

In the *Purgatorio* and the *Paradiso*, the unitive qualities of a vernacular are emphasized; these qualities are of course centrally important in *De Vulgari Eloquentia*. Sordello and Virgil embrace, with a greeting that has especially patriotic overtones, which Dante moralizes upon at some length (*Purgatorio* 6.74–84). Both are Mantuans, both are poets, both are in fact poets who chose to write not in the Lombard dialect but in another tongue, Sordello in Provençal and Virgil in Latin.[99] And Cacciaguida, as befits his discourse on the better, simpler past in Florence, speaks in the old Florentine dialect, marking the binding continuities of family and tradition that tie him to his descendant.

Chaucer's view of these issues has some interesting points of contrast, beginning with the question of Latin and the vernacular. As in Dante, the issue centers on whether Latin was ever itself a vernacular language. For us the answer is clear, but evidently for a number of medieval writers, Latin had always been what Dante calls "grammar," a learned language.[100] Indeed, Nicole Oresme is almost unique when he describes Latin as the "maternal tongue" of the Romans.[101] Latin has an even more elevated status, as one of the three languages written on the Cross (John 19.19–20), joining the other two in which the Bible was written. Since Jerome himself argued that "inspirational translation does not exist" (i.e., that God does not speak through the translator as he does through the original),[102] there is some irony in Jerome's translation of the Hebrew and Greek Bible into the Latin vernacular of his Italian audience. For soon enough, to a wider European audience, his translation itself becomes an inspired, holy text, in a learned and indeed sacred language.

If Latin is a sacred language, then by implication the Bible in Latin should not be tampered with by further translation into a vernacular. Not surprisingly, then, the preface to the fourteenth-century Wycliffite translation of the Bible into English insists on Latin's vernacular status:

> ʒit worldli clerkis axen gretli what spiryt makith idiotis hardi to translate now the bible into English, sithen the foure greet doctouris dursten neuere do this? This replicacioun is so lewid, that it nedith noon answer, not but stillnesse, eithir curteys scorn; for these greete doctouris weren noon English men, neither thei weren conuersaunt among English men, neithir in caas thei kouden the langage of English, but thei ceessiden neuere til thei hadden holi writ in here modir tunge, of here owne puple. For Jerom, that was a Latyn man of birthe, translatide the bible, . . . and Austyn, and manie mo Latyns expouniden the bible, for manie partis, in Latyn, to Latyn men, among whiche thei dwelliden, and Latyn was a comoun langage to here puple aboute Rome, and biʒondis, and no this half, as Englishe is comoun langage to our puple, and ʒit this day the comoun puple in Italie spekith Latyn corupt, as trewe men seyn, that han ben in Italie.[103]

And the first chapter of the Wycliffite "Tractatus de Regibus" opens: "Sythen witte stondis not in langage but in groundynge of treuthe, for þo same witte is in laten þat is in Grew or Ebrew, and trouthe schuld be openly knowen to alle maneres of folke, trowthe moveþ mony men to speke sentencis in yngelysche þat þai hav gedirid in latyne, and her fore bene men holden heretikis."[104]

Interestingly, Chaucer's preface to his *Treatise on the Astrolabe*, with a prayer to the King, "that is lord of this langage" (56–57) (implying an un-Italian unity of vernacular and realm), justifies translation into "naked wordes in Englissh" in much the same terms:

> But natheles suffise to the these trewe conclusions in Englissh as wel as sufficith to these noble clerkes Grekes these same conclusions in Grek; and to Arabiens in Arabik, and to Jewes in Ebrew, and to Latyn folk in Latyn; which Latyn folk had hem first out of othere dyverse

langages, and writen hem in her owne tunge, that is to seyn, in Latyn.
And God woot that in alle these langages and in many moo han
these conclusions ben suffisantly lerned and taught, and yit by diverse
reules; right as diverse pathes leden diverse folk the righte way to
Rome. (*Astrolabe* 28–40)

This preface clearly conceives of Latin as another vernacular, open to
translation, and reduced to one among many "pathes" to understanding;
likewise for love, we are told in *Troilus and Criseyde*, there is not just
one path to Rome, "Forthi men seyn, 'Eech contree hath his lawes'"
(2.36–37 and 42). Latin's status as a learned language pertains, then, not
to grammatical status but to difficulty of subject matter, the "subtile
conclusiouns" in Latin that Chaucer will try to reproduce with naked
English words, "in my lighte Englissh" for his son (51–53): "I n'am but a
lewd compilator of the labour of olde astrologiens, and have it translatid
in myn Englissh oonly for thy doctrine. And with this swerd shal I sleen
envie" (61–64). A mere compiler, with the blunted sword of a vernacular
language, can have no pretensions to magisterial authority.

The intersection of the vernacular and eloquence, which has rich
implications for Chaucer, is one of Dante's preeminent concerns. Dante
uses and redefines the three levels of style, the staple of classical rhetoric.
He works out in the *Commedia* a group of paradigms in series, with
analogous though not exactly corresponding terms; and, following the
precedent of the Church Fathers, he inverts our normal expectations
of the values that they should be assigned. This inversion of expected
values has implications for the history of human speech, both for every
individual and for the human race. One might expect the baby's prattle –
the *pappo* and *dindi* of *Purgatorio* 11.105 – to count for less than mature
speech, certainly in its ability to describe evil:

> ché non è impresa da pigliare a gabbo
> discriver fondo a tutto l'universo,
> né da lingua che chiami mamma o babbo.
> (*Inferno* 32.7–9)

[for to describe the bottom of the whole universe is not an enterprise
to be taken up in sport, nor for a tongue that cries mamma and daddy.]

But having such adult powers of description is in fact a token of severely corrupted innocence; and Dante describes the shocking effects of original sin on the speech of every human being:

> Fede e innocenza son reperte
>   solo ne' parvoletti; poi ciascuna
>   pria fugge che le guance sian coperte.
> Tale, balbuzïendo ancor, digiuna,
>   che poi divora, con la lingua sciolta,
>   qualunque cibo per qualunque luna;
> e tal, balbuzïendo, ama e ascolta
>   la madre sua, che, con loquela intera,
>   disïa poi di vederla sepolta.
>
> (*Paradiso* 27.127–35)

[Faith and innocence are found only in little children; then each flies away before the cheeks are covered. One, so long as he lisps, keeps the fasts, who afterward, when his tongue is free, devours any food through any month; and one, while he lisps, loves his mother and listens to her, who afterward, when his speech is full, longs to see her buried.]

Paradoxically, the poet must try to divest himself of the evil embedded in human language while he keeps its descriptive powers.[105] Dante uses precisely this image of infantile speech as an *aporia* for his account of the Beatific Vision:

> Omai sarà più corta mia favella,
>   pur a quel ch'io ricordo, che d'un fante
>   che bagni ancor la lingua a la mammella.
>
> (*Paradiso* 33.106–8)

[Now will my speech fall more short, even in respect to that which I remember, than that of an infant who still bathes his tongue at the breast.]

But his implication in sin enhances Dante's ability to describe what he sees in Hell, even without the reprobate assistance of "rime aspre e chiocce" (*Inf.* 32.1) [harsh and grating rhymes].[106] The poet must act out the linguistic effects of Adam's fall, even in his effort to repudiate it.

Just as Dante chooses the vernacular instead of Latin, so he chooses a version of Augustine's *sermo humilis* as the stylistic level for his poem, or more exactly, a style that embraces a variety of stylistic registers. (He may of course be indebted to a recent version of the *sermo humilis*: St. Francis' fusion of *sublimitas* and *humilitas*.)[107] The work is to be a *comedìa* (*Inf.* 16.128 and 21.2),[108] in contrast to Virgil's "alta ... tragedìa" (*Inf.* 20.113); and his style is directly opposed to that of Virgil's "alti versi" (*Inf.* 26.82) [lofty lines].[109] This opposition constitutes a change in Dante's conception of his poetic career, one that he acts out over the course of the poem; for when he thanks Virgil in the opening canto – "tu se' solo colui da cu' io tolsi/ lo bello stilo che m'ha fatto onore" (*Inf.* 1.86–87) [You alone are he from whom I took the fair style that has done me honor] – as the sole pattern for his previous work, he is echoing what he has previously said elsewhere. In *Convivio* 1.4.13 Dante argues that he needs to make his work seem less familiar to the Italians: "it is fitting that I should add, with a loftier style [*più alto stilo*], a little weight to the present work, so that it may seem to take on an air of greater authority"; and his purpose accords with what he says in 1.5.14, that "the vernacular follows custom [*uso*], while Latin follows art," that Latin, the language of art, is more beautiful than the vernacular, the language of common use.[110] His shift of thought between the *Convivio* and the *Commedia* appears in particular details as well: as Pagliaro notes, one of the words Dante condemns in *De Vulgari Eloquentia* as a parochial Florentine dialect form, *introcque* (1.13.2), is given an emphatic position in the *Commedia* as a rhyme word (*Inferno* 20.130).[111] Indeed, in *De Vulgari Eloquentia* 2.7, Dante rejects as childish and inappropriate for the illustrious vernacular several words that he then uses in the *Commedia*.[112]

Dante's redefinition of style sums up the other ways in which he must go beyond Virgil. As Hollander has persuasively argued, *Inferno* 2 – when Virgil and Dante have their opening, extended conversation – might properly be called "the canto of the word": *parola* appears five times in the canto, more than in any other in the *Commedia* (countering the five instances of *paura* in canto 1); and this canto also has the most spoken words of any.[113] The canto provides the setting for a Christian redefinition of what the greatest pagan poet had accomplished, just as Augustine's *sermo humilis* redefines classical rhetoric,[114] even as he tries to describe a properly Christian eloquence that may come in rich serving dishes as well as simple, beautiful language as well as plain (*Confessions* 5.6). Later on, Dante intimates the issues at stake when he sees Ulysses, and gives a Miltonic account of the spuriously heroic. Classical notions of epic heroism are shown to be insufficient, an almost bombastic counterpoint to a humbler, more passive Christian heroism. For Ulysses contrasts with Dante as a spiritual explorer; and his rhetorical skill, bound up with the "alti versi" that Virgil claims to have given him, explains his punishment as a fraudulent counsellor, and contrasts with the humbler style that Dante adopts.[115] Dante implicitly answers Ulysses elsewhere, showing that the *sermo humilis* is appropriate to a purgatorial mode of expression.[116] Benvenuto da Imola suggests the serious purposes in Dante's stylistic humility: "the divine style is sweet and plain [*suavis et planus*], not lofty and proud [*altus et superbus*] as that of Virgil and the poets."[117]

Dante tends in the *Commedia* to express a certain distrust of rhetorical ornament and stylistic pretension, to show up the eloquent for "their moral and intellectual failings."[118] If Brunetto Latini is famous, according to Villani, for being "the master who first taught refinement to the Florentines and the arts of speaking well and of guiding and ruling our republic according to the science of politics,"[119] we are also made aware of the easy slide into excess, in the elaborate rhetoric of Pier delle Vigne.[120] In addition to Ulysses' fraudulent rhetoric, we are shown the fraudulent hyperbole of flattery. Dante's straightforwardness compels a pander to explain his punishment, however unwillingly: "tua chiara favella, / che mi fa sovvenir del mondo antico" (*Inf.* 18.53–54) [your plain speech, which makes me remember the former world]. And like Chaucer's Parson, who castigates the "shiten shepherde" (*General Prologue* 504), Dante fittingly uses the excremental *merda* (18.116) to describe the flatterers' place of punishment: "Qua giù m'hanno sommerso le lusinghe/ ond' io non ebbi mai la lingua stucca" (18.125–26) [Down to this the flatteries wherewith my tongue was never cloyed have sunk me]. Plain speech is the way to address a pander, naked words the way to respond to the flatterer's verbal fraudulence. Even in the sunlight of *Purgatorio* 1, Cato marks the entry into a new realm by his level-headed, even cold response to Virgil's attempt to ingratiate himself: "Ma se donna del ciel ti move e regge, / come tu di', non c'è mestier lusinghe" (1.91–92) [But if a lady of Heaven moves and directs you, as you say, there is no need of flattery]. Beatrice in particular is a user of plain speech, from her first direct address to Dante (*Purgatorio* 30.55–57), and her speech is like a sword: "volgendo suo parlare a me per punta, / che pur per taglio m'era paruto acro" (31.2–3) [turning against me the point of her speech, which even with the edge had seemed sharp to me]. Like St. Cecilia in the *Second Nun's Tale*, whom I will discuss in Chapter 4, she needs no rhetorical ornament to prettify her true discourse. The increasing clarity of the higher realms makes possible a speech uninflected by vanity or deception.

This last association, of humility with a plain style, voices a long-standing prejudice, the usual expression of which is that ornament is inappropriate to theological discourse. According to Alain of Lille, for example, theological language should be "intellectu perceptibilis" [perceptible to the intellect], that is, it should not use "involucra verborum" [*involucra* of words].[121] Such attitudes survive in the Parson's refusal to recite a tale in verse: "I kan nat geeste 'rum, ram, ruf,' by lettre, / Ne, God woot, rym holde I but litel bettre" (*Parson's Prologue* 43–44); and the Parson no doubt reflects the climate of opinion that also produced Wycliffite attacks on rhetorical ornament, and the belief that prose is a more neutral idiom than verse for the conveying of ideas.[122] In a series of images that are of special interest for the *Canterbury Tales*, notably the *Clerk's Tale*, Dante talks about speech as clothing, jewelry, or decoration. In *Convivio* 1.10.12 he uses such an image to argue that the ornaments of poetry, "that is, rhyme and meter," distract our attention from the natural beauties of the vernacular: "just as the beauty of a woman cannot be perfectly expressed when the adornment of her preparation and apparel do more to make her admired than she does herself."[123] There is a certain irony involved in his stance: in the *Commedia*, as here, he usually criticizes rhetorical ornaments and clothing with precisely the images his early commentators use to praise him.[124] For example, the *Ottimo Commento* argues that one of Dante's intentions in the *Commedia* was "to demonstrate the ornate speech [*l'ornato parlare*] of rhetoric in verse"; and according to Guido da Pisa, first among Dante's purposes was "that men might learn to speak elegantly and in an orderly manner [*ordinate*]."[125] And Boccaccio's *Accessus* states that Dante's style, despite its being in the vernacular and hence inferior to Latin, "è nondimeno ornato e leggiadro e sublime" [is nonetheless ornate and graceful and sublime].[126] In the *Inferno*, ornateness can be either praised or scorned. Beatrice asks Virgil to guide and help Dante "con la tua parola ornata" (2.67) [with your fair speech]; but we learn that Jason seduced Hypsipyle "con segni e con parole ornate" (*Inf.* 18.91) [with tokens and with fair words].[127] The juxtaposition in usage implies the ambiguous purposes of rhetoric, but also – given Dante's own comments later – suggests that Virgil's "parola ornata" cannot be the final stylistic resting place for the Christian poet.

Dante makes this point even more emphatically by the kindred images of rhetorical "color,"[128] and the notion of words as clothed or naked. The hypocrites, whose punishment makes literal the image, are "una genta dipinta" (*Inf.* 23.58) [a painted people]. And by contrast, Cacciaguida speaks to Dante in a redeemed language, "nè per ambage" (*Par.* 17.31) [in no dark sayings], like the ones in which the pagans ensnared themselves, "ma per chiare parole e con preciso/ latin" (34–35) [but in clear words and with precise discourse].[129] Not surprisingly, the siren in Dante's dream is made fair by the poet's coloring gaze:

> Io la mirava; e come 'l sol conforta
> le fredde membra che la notte aggrava,
> così lo sguardo mio le facea scorta
> la lingua, e poscia tutta la drizzava
> in poco d'ora, e lo smarrito volto,
> com' amor vuol, così le colorava.
> (*Purg.* 19. 10–15)[130]

[I gazed upon her: and even as the sun revives cold limbs benumbed by night, so my look made ready her tongue, and then in but little time set her full straight, and colored her pallid face even as love requires.]

But even purified speech is by nature too vivid, with too much color [*troppo color vivo*], to describe Heaven (*Par.* 24.23–27). Likewise, Dante emphasizes the damned soul's nakedness when the pander's flatteries and fraudulent hyperbole are punished by *contrapasso*,[131] but Beatrice offers instead a verbal nakedness, in her promise of simplicity:

> Veramente oramai saranno nude
> le mie parole, quanto converrassi
> quelle scovrir a la tua vista rude.
> (*Purg.* 33.100–2)

[But henceforth my words shall be as simple as may be needful to make them plain to your rude sight.]

At first glance, Chaucer may seem to be replicating Dante's distinction between Virgil's high tragedy and his own humble *Commedia*, when at the end of *Troilus and Criseyde* he offers a valediction to his poem using the same terms:

> Go, litel bok, go, litel myn tragedye,
> Ther God thi makere yet, er that he dye,
> So sende myght to make in som comedye!
> But litel book, no makyng thow n'envie,
> But subgit be to alle poesye;
> And kis the steppes where as thow seest pace
> Virgile, Ovide, Omer, Lucan, and Stace.
>
> (5.1786–92)

But the phrase "litel tragedye," followed by the demand that this "litel book" pay obeisance to the great poems of classical antiquity, undercuts with a diminutive its implicit claim to high style. Chaucer's tragedy and comedy are both in the vernacular, and both enjoined to be humble, not as in Dante, divided between two levels of style and two different languages competing for authority.

There is, however, another possibility in this stanza, which moves Chaucer closer to Dante's high claims for the vernacular. The standard reading, as in the Riverside edition, understands "makyng" and "poesye" to be near-synonyms, and the verb "envie" to mean "contend with": in this reading, Chaucer is commanding his poem not to compete with, but to bow deferentially to all poetry, Latin or vernacular, ancient or modern. But "envie" can mean simply "envy," and in Chaucer's lexicon "making" and "enditing" describe modern poems in the vernacular, like the comedy Chaucer hopes to "make." Ancient poems, by contrast, are "poems," written by authors for whom he almost exclusively reserves the elevated and unenglished term for poetic makers, "poetes."[132] (This stanza is the only appearance of the word "poesye" in his work, though "poetrie" appears several times.)[133] If the lines are accordingly construed as "Do not envy [hence, do not feel inferior to] any modern vernacular poem, but be subject to all of the great ancient epics," Chaucer has complicated the claim in the *Astrolabe* that "with this swerd shal

I sleen envie" (preface, 64), his sword being the vernacular and his self-description as a compiler, not an author. Many readers have felt, even accepting the usual reading, that this stanza feels a bit disingenuous, that at the very least, Chaucer claims a place next to the classical poets, "subject to them, but in their company"[134] – that he is making a more modest reprise of Dante's poetic conversations in Limbo, where a nearly identical quintet of poets (with Horace taking the place of Statius) "mi fecer de la loro schiera, / sì ch'io fui sesto tra cotanto senno" [made me one of their company, so that I was sixth amid so much wisdom] (*Inferno* 4.101–2). But if Chaucer may be claiming, in a backhanded way, an elevated status for his humble poem, just as Dante does more overtly, he does so with a quite different overall effect. Chaucer never proclaims himself *poete*, as Dante does.[135] Although *Troilus and Criseyde* implies a lofty status for itself by its division into books and invocations to various Muses, it maintains a notable variety of style, high and less high, particularly because of Pandarus' down-to-earth loquaciousness.[136] And the *Canterbury Tales*, the promised comedy, though it does indeed offer a plentiful diversity of styles and voices, high style set against low and decorous against indecorous, does not – as I will argue in Chapter 4 – move to the Dantean transcendence of world and language at the end of *Paradiso* 33. The replication of terms conceals a world of difference: Chaucer's comedy, unlike Dante's *Commedia*, is earthbound.

NAME AND FAME

Ever since Lydgate, if in fact his phrase "Dante in Inglissh" means to describe the *House of Fame*, Chaucer's debt to Dante in this poem has been evident.[137] The nature of the debt has at times no doubt been misstated, in nineteenth and early twentieth-century efforts to make the *House of Fame* into a parody of the *Commedia*, or in B. G. Koonce's often illuminating though I think fundamentally mistaken description of Chaucer's poem as an English replica of Dante's.[138] Nonetheless, as I became increasingly aware when I edited the poem for the *Riverside Chaucer*, Chaucer "does sustain an ironic counterpart to Dante's poem" and reacts to the *Commedia* with his own versions of Dante's persistent interests.[139]

The specific indebtednesses have often been cited: the Invocations at the beginnings of Book Three (1091–109), from *Paradiso* 1.13–27, and of Book Two (520–26), from *Inferno* 2.7–9; Chaucer's Eagle, in the context of the several eagles in the *Commedia* (and also in *Epistola* 6)[140]; the adaptation in line 81, "And he that mover ys of al," of *Paradiso* 1.1 ("La gloria di colui che tutto move" [the glory of the All-Mover]).[141] Chaucer's expression of modesty, as someone unsuited to a celestial vision (588–92), imitates but contrasts strikingly with Dante's protest that he is not Aeneas, and not Paul (*Inf.* 2.32). Dante's claim to Brunetto Latini that he awaits the workings of Fortune with equanimity (*Inferno* 15.91–93) is closely akin to Chaucer's expressed indifference to the effects of Fortune's sister Fame (1873–82). And Chaucer's response to his celestial journey in Book Two – "For more clere entendement/ Nas me never yit ysent" (983–84) – is very close to Dante's, when he learns the earthly location of the Purgatorial mountain: "unquanco/ non vid' io chiaro sì com' io discerno" [never did I see so clearly as I now discern] (*Purg.* 4.76–77).

There are a number of other parallelisms, important because they show Chaucer's careful attention to Dante's text while he was engaged in composing his own. Chaucer owes a great deal to Dante's various explanations of "kyndly enclynyng."[142] The "Frend" who speaks to him (1871–72) seems to understand Chaucer to be an embodied sound – as we have been told are all the visitants to the House of Fame (1074–85): Chaucer is evidently thinking of the several instances when shades come to realize that Dante is a living human being.[143] Instead of Virgil, Chaucer gets the Eagle as a guide, though as Clemen notes, both guides are mind-readers.[144] And as I argued at greater length in *Chaucer and Ovid*, Chaucer makes us remember that the *Commedia* too is a book of Fame – Cacciaguida explicitly tells us so; and Dante's suffused emphasis on Fame is certainly among the sources, if not the only one, for Chaucer's exposition. Even Statius' account of his fame as a poet, "col nome che più dura e più onora" (*Purgatorio* 21.85) [with the name which lasts longest and honors most], has its equivalent in the relatively exalted position of the poets and historians in Fame's palace (*House of Fame* 1419–26).

In this Dantean poem, Chaucer notably copies Dante's interest in one of the most basic, even primitive functions of language: the names we are given by our parents and those that language offers us to describe the exterior world. Adam's naming of the animals in Genesis is his first task, and almost his first use of God's supreme gift of speech. Although Dante does not mention this original naming in *De Vulgari Eloquentia*, he more than makes up for the omission elsewhere in his work. Beatrice's first word in the Earthly Paradise is "Dante" (*Purg.* 30.55), the name's sole appearance in the poem[145]; and we are reminded that place names such as Gaeta (*Inf.* 26.92–93) and Mantua (*Inf.* 20.91–93) are human impositions, in a "process by which man memorializes the world."[146] Although the Fall has frayed the primeval connection of name and thing, for Dante it is still true, often enough, that *nomina sunt consequentia rerum* (*Vita Nuova* 13.4) [names are the consequences of things].[147] In the names our parents give us at birth, the hidden significance must appear by the grace of God[148]: Beatrice's parents said more than they knew when they named their daughter (*Vita Nuova* 2.1).[149] Dante's own name is so interpreted by his commentators, and perhaps also by himself.[150] Dante may implicitly compare himself with the prophet Nathan, whose name Isidore and Huguccio explain as "*Natan dedit, sive dantis*" [*Nathan* he gave, or is giving][151]; and there may even be a reference to the winged soul in "Dante 'Aliger'."[152] In any case, Dante plays with other people's names at several points in the *Commedia*. Ciacco (*Inferno* 6.52), as Singleton's Commentary notes, has a name that, fittingly, means "hog" as well as "Giacomo." Sapia in turn comments: "Savia non fui, avvegna che Sapìa/ fossi chiamata" (*Purg.* 13.109–10) [Sapient I was not, although Sapia was my name]; and Sts. Francis and Dominic are blessed with names available for etymological unfolding (*Paradiso* 11–12).[153]

Our names are, obviously, the shorthand by which we are known; and fame has the ability to preserve, not people, but these abbreviated notations of them. This possibility loads names with extra weight in the *Commedia*. Cacciaguida tells Dante that he has been shown only those souls "che son di fama note" (*Par.* 17.138) [known of fame],[154] because his listeners on earth would otherwise not pay attention to the promise or threat of such examples. Under such circumstances, the use or withholding of a name has a supercharged quality to it, which in Hell extends even to the names of the rare passers-through. Dante and Virgil never name each other there; in the *Purgatorio*, by contrast, Virgil's name comes up with some frequency until, as he is about to depart, Dante repeats his name almost obsessively (*Purgatorio* 30.46–55).[155] Christ himself is never named in the infernal reaches; indeed, even when his name appears in the *Paradiso*, it can – set apart from any other name or, for that matter, any other word – rhyme only with itself (*Paradiso* 12.71–75, 14.104–8, 19.104–8, 32.83–87).

Among the souls of the dead, the desire for name and fame changes markedly as the pilgrim poet descends. In upper Hell, the travelers' promise to keep a soul's name alive on earth is a standard *captatio benev-olentiae*. In lower Hell, there is a striking reversal[156]: the worse the sin, the less the sinner wants any continuing memorial of himself. The most notorious seeker of oblivion is Guido da Montefeltro, the liter-ary ancestor of J. Alfred Prufrock: only because he thinks that Dante must not be alive, he gives an account of his sin "sanza tema d'infamia" (*Inf.* 27.66) [without fear of infamy]. Similarly, Caiaphas writhes at his visitor's entrance (*Inf.* 23.112), presumably because Dante can report what he has seen to the world above. Bocca's desire for anonymity, in vehemently refusing to name himself to Dante, is frustrated by the malicious glee of another in naming him (*Inf.* 32.91–108). The souls in *Purgatorio*, on the other hand, as Greene observes, "tend to regard their very names as relics, outworn appendages, symbols of brief renown gained by achievements no longer worth the praise." They name them-selves in the past tense, and "the repetition of the participle 'chiamato' in each case seems to imply that naming was an arbitrary habit of the world which failed to reach the essence of the individual."[157] Even so, the souls who purge themselves by a penitential fast "del nomar parean tutti contenti" (*Purg.* 24.26) [at their naming all appeared content]: their distorted features justify their being named (24.17–18), so that the prayers of the living can expedite their progress.

These varying attitudes toward names express the normal medieval ambivalence about the meaning and value of earthly fame. The *Pur-gatorio* powerfully expresses the traditional Christian distrust of fame as human pride, in the famous passage beginning "Oh vana gloria de l'umane posse!" (11.91) [O empty glory of human powers!]. Just as Giotto has supplanted Cimabue as the most famous painter, so perhaps a poet is born who will supplant the two Guidos:

Non è il mondan romore altro ch'un fiato
  di vento, ch'or vien quinci e or vien quindi,
  e muta nome perché muta lato.
Che voce avrai tu più, se vecchia scindi
  da te la carne, che se fossi morto
  anzi che tu lasciassi il 'pappo' e 'l 'dindi,'
pria che passin mill' anni?
(*Purg.* 11.100–6)

[Earthly fame is naught but a breath of wind, which now comes hence
and now goes thence, changing its name because it changes quarter.
What greater fame will you have if you strip off your flesh when it is
old than if you had died before giving up *pappo* and *dindi*, when a
thousand years shall have passed . . .?]

Since Dante himself is presumably the poet who "forse è nato" (98), he
takes away with one hand what he gives himself with the other. This
same ambiguous modesty appears three cantos later, when he refuses
to tell his name: "dirvi ch'i' sia, saria parlare indarno, / ché 'l nome
mio ancor molto non suona" (*Purg.* 14.20–21) [To tell you who I am
would be to speak in vain, for my name as yet makes no great sound].[158]
But if Dante must take the lesson of "vana gloria" to heart, the poet's
vocation, as much as in the *House of Fame*, necessarily involves him in
Fame's work. Indeed, Guido da Pisa gives this task as one of the three
ends of the *Commedia*: the reviving of the almost forgotten books of the
poets.[159] A writer lives on in his work, as Brunetto Latini knows (*Inf.*
15.119–20); and a poet keeps alive the names of other poets, and of all
those worthy of fame.

   In this respect, the desire for fame is a good, as Virgil admonishes
Dante:

"Omai convien che tu così ti spoltre,"
  disse 'l maestro; "ché, seggendo in piuma,
  in fama non si vien, né sotto coltre;
sanza la qual chi sua vita consuma,
  cotal vestigio in terra di sé lascia,
  qual fummo in aere e in acqua la schiuma."
(*Inf.* 24.46–51)

143

["Now it behooves you thus to cast off sloth," said my master, "for sitting on down or under coverlet, no one comes to fame, without which whoso consumes his life leaves such vestige of himself on earth as smoke in air or foam on water."]

Appropriately, the indecisive – "l'anime triste di coloro/ che visser sanza 'nfamia e sanza lodo" (*Inf.* 3.35–36) [the sorry souls of those who lived without infamy and without praise] – are punished by having no fame after their deaths: "Fama di loro il mondo esser non lassa" (49) [The world does not suffer that report of them shall live]. Beatrice uses Virgil's fame, which will last as long as the world, as the foremost point in her *captatio benevolentiae* (*Inf.* 2.59–60). And Virgil himself tells Dante that the fame of the pagan poets sets them apart from the other virtuous souls in Limbo (much as fame, by arousing the prayers of the living, helps the penitent in Purgatory):

> E quelli a me: "L'onrata nominanza
> che di lor suona sù ne la tua vita,
> grazïa acquista in ciel che sì li avanza."
> (*Inf.* 4.76–78)

[And he to me, "Their honored fame, which resounds in your life above, wins grace in Heaven, which thus advances them."]

Like Chaucer, Dante exercises his power as a poet to dispense or withhold fame. The avaricious and the profligate, because of their "sconoscente vita" (*Inf.* 7.53) [undiscerning life], are now "ad ogne conoscenza . . . bruni" (54) [dim to all discernment]. Even in the lowest depth of Hell, Dante uses this preeminently evocative power to persuade Ugolino to speak:

> "dimmi 'l perché," diss' io, "per tal convegno,
> che se tu a ragion di lui ti piangi,
> sappiendo chi voi siete e la sua pecca,
> nel mondo suso ancora io te ne cangi,
> se quella con ch'io parlo non si secca."
> (32.135–39)

["tell me the wherefore," I said, "on this condition, that if you with reason complain of him, I, knowing who you are and his offense, may yet requite you in the world above, if that with which I speak does not dry up."]

The poet can thus use his own power of naming to reward virtue and punish sin. Alternatively, like Chaucer in the *House of Fame*, where the Eagle calls him by name (558, 729), he can claim to have no interest in renown when he refuses to say his name (1871–77); the dreamer cannot even name the man of great authority who appears just as the poem breaks off (2156). In this contingent world the goddess Fame takes the place of Adam as name-giver, and the name she gives to "every tydynge" is emphatically *ad placitum*, "After hir disposicioun," and of limited "duracioun" (2111–14).

The *House of Fame* also reveals Chaucer's strong interest in problems of language, signification, and the poet's function in a confusing world of multivalent words and ambiguous meaning. A fuller exposition of these issues appears in some of the *Canterbury Tales*, but Chaucer's earliest extended treatment of them reveals his awareness of and response to Dante's concerns, when he declares that he is adopting simplicity, a version of the *sermo humilis*, as his poetic style. His declaration may at first seem less self-conscious than Dante's careful working through the needs of decorum; but his conventional modesty trope appears at exactly the point where he follows Dante rather closely but also with radical differences:

> O God of science and of lyght,
> Appollo, thurgh thy grete myght,
> This lytel laste bok thou gye!
> Nat that I wilne, for maistrye,
> Here art poetical be shewed,
> But for the rym ys lyght and lewed,
> Yit make hyt sumwhat agreable,
> Though som vers fayle in a sillable;
> And that I do no diligence
> To shewe craft, but o sentence.
>
> (1091–100)

This invocation half translates but wholly inverts Dante's request for the gift of sublime expression at the beginning of *Paradiso* 1: instead of hoping, with Dante, to crown himself with Apollo's laurel, Chaucer

promises to pay homage to the god by kissing the next laurel tree he sees
(1108). Such comic self-deprecation is typically Chaucerian. One thinks
of his nervousness about finding a rhetoric lofty enough to describe
Troilus' first night with Criseyde (*Troilus* 3.43–49 and 1191–97), and of
his comic refusal, earlier in the *House of Fame*, to wax eloquent and
lengthen his poem by talking about love, of which he knows little:

> What shulde I speke more queynte,
> Or peyne me my wordes peynte
> To speke of love? Hyt wol not be;
> I kan not of that faculte.
>
> (245–48)

Instead, his summary of the Dido and Aeneas story "shortly" (239, 242)
will, he says, have to suffice. But in the *House of Fame* this stylistic
modesty, this claim for colorless verse, is comically at variance with the
pretense that Chaucer's vision is prophetic; it undercuts his claim to
be another Joseph or Paul. Even more interestingly, it is at variance
with the way in which structures of thought and expression, even words
themselves, keep proliferating – despite the narrator's claim of modest
simplicity.

The most important statement of this problem is the Eagle's memorable conclusion to his argument on the physics of sound:

> "Telle me this now feythfully,
> Have y not preved thus symply,
> Withoute any subtilite
> Of speche, or gret prolixite
> Of termes of philosophie,
> Of figures of poetrie,
> Or colours of rethorike?
> Pardee, hit oughte the to lyke,
> For hard langage and hard matere
> Ys encombrous for to here
> Attones; wost thou not wel this?"
> And y answered and seyde, "Yis."
>
> (853–64)

The Eagle accurately describes the didactic virtues of the *sermo humilis*,
just as Chaucer's reply illustrates its possibilities for terseness; but the

Eagle's description is phrased so as to turn the conventional justification inside out.[160] The reason for plain style in Scripture is to assist our understanding; God's word requires simple, easily understood language to reach more than a few erudite people. But the Eagle turns this explanation of divine condescension to human abilities into a version of intellectual slumming:

> "A ha," quod he, "lo, so I can
> Lewedly to a lewed man
> Speke, and shew hym swyche skiles
> That he may shake hem be the biles,
> So palpable they shulden be."
>
> (865–69)

Unfortunately, this explanation is irrelevant to the central problems of the poem, and reduces its complexities simplemindedly.[161] The Eagle explains nothing that is worth explaining, and he makes us see, despite himself, that the real issues are too complicated for a simple exposition.[162]

The evident disjunction here between form and elusive content recapitulates the hidden lesson of the Eagle's proof. His argument that speech, like all other sound, has its home and fitting resting place in the House of Fame, depends on emptying speech of meaning by reducing it to its physical properties; and however terse and pregnant with meaning the Eagle's own speech is (in his opinion, at least), it adds to the cacophony.[163] From the Eagle's perspective, as I have argued elsewhere, "the *Aeneid* and flatus are essentially the same thing."[164] Chaucer's joke rehearses a traditional distinction in medieval grammar between sound and meaning – in Abelard's terms, between *vox* and *sermo*.[165] The grammarian Donatus' definition of *vox* is the standard one: "Speech sound is struck air perceptible to hearing [*Vox est aer ictus sensibilis auditu*], in so far as it is in itself. Every spoken sound is either articulate or confused. Articulated is what can be comprehended in letters; confused is what cannot be written." And *verbum*, according to Isidore's *Etymologiae* 1.9.1, gets its name from reverberated air [*verberato aere*].[166] Abelard clarifies these definitions by distinguishing between mere sound and meaning. His account of the physical properties of sound is strikingly like the Eagle's: "air strikes air and conveys to it a like sound"; "it meets exterior airs which it beats and forces back, and, to the very ones that it forces back, it confers the same sound form."[167] For Abelard, that is to say, "*Vox* is . . . the spoken word regarded as physical sound and as something natural in origin; *sermo*, on the other hand, is the word in regard to the meaning imposed upon it by human choice." And he specifically attacks an opponent, perhaps William of Champeaux, for stating "that meaningful sound is nothing but the striking of air."[168]

Swift's mad projectors the Aeolists make exactly this argument: "Words are but Wind: and Learning is nothing but Words; *Ergo*, Learning is nothing but Wind."[169] And Pope's satiric version of the same point – "Since Man from beast by Words is known, / Words are Man's province, Words we teach alone" (*Dunciad* 4.149–50) – attacks modern efforts, by the Ramists and the Royal Society, "to drive a wedge between words and thought."[170] There are analogous jokes in these eighteenth-century versions of the *reductio ad absurdum* and in the Eagle's pretense of stylistic humility. In the *Commedia* one function of the *sermo humilis* is to hold out the possibility of a redeemed speech, to allow poetry, through humility and a cautious handling of poetic ornament, to attain the clarity, purity, and authoritative power of Scriptural language. In the *House of Fame*, by contrast, such a promise is held out only to be proved illusory. Just as Chaucer's vision, with all its grandiose claims, turns out to be very much an earthbound affair, so his expressions of stylistic simplicity belie the fogginess of the vision, and comically oversimplify its quandaries of meaning.

The Eagle's reductiveness, which erases categories of meaning and levels of style to no purpose, also extends to the issue of signification itself. This issue comes up primarily in a running joke about the stars and constellations as the mysterious signs of our fates, marked out in the heavens. Chaucer first raises the question with his alarm "Wher Joves wol me stellyfye, / Or what thing may this sygnifye?" (586–87). The mind-reading Eagle relieves Chaucer's doubts with the assurance, humiliating enough, that he is too insignificant:

> Thow demest of thyself amys,
> For Joves ys not theraboute –
> I dar wel putte the out of doute –
> To make of the as yet a sterre.
>
> (596–99)

As the vision unfolds, its bookishness supplants the physical actuality of the heavens, and makes us question the reality of any such apotheosis. Just as, according to the Eagle, the placing of the House of Fame verifies Ovid's description in *Metamorphoses* 13, so the constellations are apparently in heaven primarily to establish the veracity of myth. Phaethon on his ill-fated journey, which the Eagle recounts, saw "the Scorpioun, / Which that in heven a sygne is yit" (948–49). Language usurps the proper territory of the astronomer; and external, physical signs come to seem dependent on words for their proof, even for their very existence. In this poem words are prior to, not the consequences of, things: though the narrator says that he can now, having seen the heavens, believe Martianus Capella and Anticlaudianus, the poem implies that his vision simply recapitulates the terms of their descriptions.

The climax, such as it is, comes when the Eagle interrupts Chaucer's reverie:

> "Wilt thou lere of sterres aught?"
> "Nay, certeynly," quod y, "ryght naught."
> "And why?" "For y am now to old."
> "Elles I wolde the have told,"
> Quod he, "the sterres names, lo,
> And al the hevenes sygnes therto,
> And which they ben."
>
> (993–99)

As the Eagle goes on to argue, when Chaucer reads "poetrie, / How goddes gonne stellifye/ Bridd, fissh, best, or him or here" (1001–3), he does not know where these constellations are located: "For though thou have hem ofte on honde, / Yet nostow not wher that they stonde" (1009–10). Chaucer responds that he willingly believes

> Hem that write of this matere,
> As though I knew her places here;
> And eke they shynen here so bryghte,
> Hyt shulde shenden al my syghte,
> To loke on hem.
>
> (1013–17)

This exchange shows that for Chaucer's eager travel guide, a name is simply a notation, a shorthand for nothing important, a synecdoche for a fiction.

In this respect, the Eagle's disquisition on sound parallels the issue the goddess Fame herself brings up: what's in a name? At great length, Book Three of the poem works out a conventional moral: that Fame's judgments are arbitrary, that she awards renown to the undeserving as well as the deserving, and lets the names of still others, good and bad alike, vanish forever. To the extent that his vision of her court is meant to teach Chaucer's narrator anything new, its lesson is comically anticlimactic. As Chaucer tells us, he already knew that people desired fame (1896–1900); and he himself is indifferent to its rewards, as he responds to the Friend's question:

> "Frend, what is thy name?
> Artow come hider to han fame?"
> "Nay, for sothe, frend," quod y;
> "I cam noght hyder, graunt mercy,
> For no such cause, by my hed!
> Sufficeth me, as I were ded,
> That no wight have my name in honde."
> (1871–77)

His lack of curiosity about what the stars are named and where they are located extends here to a modest self-sufficiency: he is, as he goes on to say, content with his own valuation of himself, "As fer forth as I kan myn art" (1882). The two disclaimers are versions of a single realization, that language implicates its users in its possibilities for corruption. Though the tendencies to logorrhea that the *House of Fame* makes so manifest are impossible entirely to resist – one form of resistance, using names as shorthand, can itself multiply madly, as the Canon's Yeoman will show – the wise course is to use language with a temperate caution. After all, as Proverbs teaches, sin inevitably appears in a "multitude of words"; "but he that refraineth his lips is most wise" (Proverbs 10.19).[171] For this reason certainly, as much as for a certain tongue-in-cheek coyness, Chaucer refuses to pass on the one tiding he knows (2136). And his refusal to join Fame's suitors – except in the relatively austere and relatively honorable company of the poets and historians – expresses a strong awareness of the mutability of all things, including the names that Fame sees fit to perpetuate, for a time.

But the workings of Fame have to do with the workings of language itself. Towards the end of the poem the dreamer says that every tiding went

> . . . fro mouth to mouth,
> And that encresing ever moo,
> As fyr ys wont to quyke and goo
> From a sparke spronge amys,
> Til al a citee brent up ys.
> (2076–80)

This seems likely to be an allusion to James 3.5–6: "Even so the tongue is indeed a little member and boasteth great things. Behold how small a fire kindleth a great wood. And the tongue is a fire, a world of iniquity. The tongue is placed among our members, which defileth the whole body and inflameth the wheel of our nativity, being set on fire by hell."[172] The tongue's power for fiery conflagration – the *locus classicus* for which is the account of *Fama* in *Aeneid* 4 – has a close analogue in the Eagle's discourse on the "multiplicacioun" of sound (784), which itself sounds close to Holkot's explanation for echo: "if a pebble is thrown out into water, there come into being many circular ripples where the pebble fell, and a smaller circle when set in motion causes a bigger, and that one another; and thus one after another, until the power of the first one set in motion fails . . . In the same fashion, when on account of striking and being struck there is a sound in air, the sound is multiplied [*multiplicatur*], and that sound generates another and that one another, in circles, as long as the power of the first striking lasts."[173] Like echo, and for that matter sound itself, Fame has a magnifying, illusionistic power: "And made wel more than hit was/ To semen every thing, ywis, / As kynde thing of Fames is" (1290–92).

We become very much aware of the ways in which language and Fame, working together and in fact dependent on each other, expand, multiply, and distort. Dante describes the effects of amplification in the transmission of fame or infamy, specifically about how "a good reputation" results from its birth in the mind of a friend:

That mind which first gives birth to it, both to make its gift more fair [*ornato*] and for the love of the friend who receives it, does not confine itself within the limits of the truth, but oversteps them . . . The second mind which receives what is said is content not only with the amplification [*dilatazione*] supplied by the first but seeks to embellish it by transmitting it further . . . The third mind that receives it does the same, and the fourth, and hence it is inflated infinitely [*in infinito si dilata*]. And so, by reversing the above-mentioned motives to the contrary, one can perceive the reason for infamy, which increases in the same manner. Thus Vergil says in the fourth book of the *Aeneid* that 'Fame thrives on movement and acquires greatness by going about.' Anyone who wishes, then, can clearly see that the image generated by fame alone is always greater, no matter what kind it is, than the thing imagined is in its true state.[174]

Symkyn the miller, in turn, makes a joke about the multiplying powers of speech:

> Myn hous is streit, but ye han lerned art;
> Ye konne by argumentes make a place
> A myle brood of twenty foot of space.
> Lat se now if this place may suffise,
> Or make it rowm with speche, as is youre gise.
> (*Reeve's Tale* 4122–26)

For the poet, who must rely on speech and who is, willy-nilly, the servant of Fame, the implications of the poetic calling are not altogether pleasant ones.

Chaucer comically inverts the pretensions of the *Commedia*: like Dante, he is rewarded with "Unkouthe syghtes and tydynges" (*House of Fame* 2010). But if Dante's vision is of the upper bounds of language, which force a redefinition of poetry and eventually its transcendence into a wordless realm, Chaucer's is in some respects of the other extreme, the foul rag and bone shop from which the poet, like all other human beings, takes his terms of discourse.[175] What he sees is a simulacrum, a representation of language, as it works in the fallen world. Its source is uncertainty, its value ambiguous; its terms are subject to arbitrary multiplication and distortion. The House of Rumor turns "as swyft as thought" (1924); indeed, it is in some sense thought itself (just as the pillars in Fame's hall recall the places of an art of memory, such as in John of Garland's *Poetria Parisiana*).[176] We learn that Aventure is "the moder of tydynges" (1983), and that tidings accordingly tend to be haphazard: "Thus saugh I fals and soth compouned/ Togeder fle for oo tydynge" (2108–9). As Hanning says, "The interaction of Ovid, Vergil, and the narrator in transmitting Dido's story constitutes a poetic exemplum of Ovid's (and later Chaucer's) doctrine about how all tidings grow, relentlessly and uncontrollably."[177] Inside Fame's hall "there is a sudden quiet space, when the poets and historians are about to make their presence known"[178] – and indeed the pillars on which they are clustered may contain a distant reminiscence of the first two pillars of memory in human history, the ones that Josephus says were built to preserve the arts and sciences during the Flood. But the relative quiet gives way, quickly, to ambiguity and confusion.

At the center of the confusion are the various forms of *multiply* and *multiplication*, which appear here for the first time in Chaucer's poetry, to describe the amplification and dissemination of sound (784, 801, 820). In *Boece* (2.pr.7.69 and 104) the word reappears in Philosophy's dismissal of human efforts to amplify fame, and her injunction that Boethius must recognize its evanescence. In the *Canterbury Tales* it appears, predictably, in reference to God's command, "in the estaat of innocence, to multiplye mankynde to the service of God" (*Parson's Tale* 883) – this "gentil text," as the Wife of Bath calls it (*Wife of Bath's Prologue* 28–29).[179] Augustine directly links the Genesis command with verbal multiplication: "In all these things we find multitude, and fertility, and increase. But the special kind of increase and multiplication whereby one meaning is expressed in many ways, and one mode of expression is understood in many meanings, we find only in signs made corporeally, and in the concepts of the intellect."[180] This Genesis setting is so familiar and powerful that it hovers in the background when more questionable usages appear, especially because it raises the problem of when innocent multiplication turns to mad proliferation. Roger Bacon uses optics to illustrate the operations of grace: "Since the infusion of grace is very clearly illustrated through the multiplication of light, it is in every way expedient that through the corporeal multiplication of light there should be manifested to us the properties of grace in the good, and the rejection of it in the wicked."[181] In the *Melibee*, quoting the Solomon of Proverbs and Ecclesiasticus, slowly accumulating riches can multiply (1580), and "sweete wordes multiplien and encreescen freendes" (1740). God's mercy multiplies (*Prioress' Tale* 689), but so do venial sins (*Parson's Tale* 365) and deceit: the *Pardoner's Prologue* praises the magic mitten that will bestow upon its wearer "multipliying of his grayn" (374).[182] Above all, its most memorable appearance is in the *Canon's Yeoman's Prologue* and *Tale*, where variations of the word appear eight times, and the multiplication of words, money, and metals form a single nexus of deception, self-deception, fog, and confusion.

For Augustine, as for Plotinus, or so Robert J. O'Connell has argued, "being in time is, for the soul, a fallen condition," and "the origin of artistic activity, indeed of all man's symbolic activity, . . . emerges from the soul's 'fallen' state."[183] Fame and poetry are linked together as sound, and Aquinas says, in his commentary on Aristotle's *De Anima*: "But as sound is caused by change and has no fixed and stable existence, but actually *consists in* a movement or change, therefore it can be considered at one and the same time in its objective origin and in its effect on the senses."[184] Poetry and alchemy are linked by the multiplication of words and their potential for deception, and by their efforts – seemingly futile in the end – to retrieve or imagine a world before multiplication of words, languages, and metals took place. The *House of Fame* ends with "A man of gret auctorite" (2158) who does not get to speak and, even if he were to do so, would be highly unlikely in this poem to be the source of anything authoritative. The effect of all this is a pervasive, and in the end deeply pessimistic, skepticism. One way out might be for Chaucer "to extricate himself from the logocentric vicious circle by turning toward realities beyond language and fiction," at the endings of *Troilus* and the *Canterbury Tales*, "where speech and things said are superseded by silence in the apprehension of realities not subject to human discourse."[185] I am not persuaded that this escape fully works; to the extent that it does, its tone is at least notably more skeptical than Dante's hope that poetry itself can be redeemed and redemptive. In place of silence, the *House of Fame* (and as I will argue in the next chapter, the *Canon's Yeoman's Tale* even more) celebrates, in a backhanded fashion, the generative powers of fallen language itself, the cacophony that perpetually underlies and undermines human efforts to impose unity, clarity, and order on the evanescent works of human memory and art. This is a language that is itself the very essence of energy and ceaseless flux.[186]

4

The prison-house of language

"Back out of all this now too much for us, / Back in a time made simple by the loss/ Of detail . . ."[1] Robert Frost's half-ironic "Directive" to an unclouded past sums up the confusions of our complicated present in the tangled syntax of its first line; but the second implies the potential self-delusion in our universal impulse to nostalgia, since the "loss of detail" is evidently as much in our wishful perceptions as in the erosions worked by time. (As Randall Jarrell observed, "The people who live in a Golden Age usually go around complaining how yellow everything looks.")[2] These two impulses – playing with language to define historical process, and exploring the sentimental or potentially self-serving motives in nostalgia – are topics of central importance in the *Canterbury Tales*. The sentimental or self-serving are particularly evident in the sequence of tales most concerned with Paradise, the Golden Age, rhetoric, and style: Clerk, Merchant, Squire, and Franklin. The clearest because most extreme presentation of the first of these impulses, defining historical process, comes later, in the *Second Nun's Tale* and *Canon's Yeoman's Tale*.

The relationship of the declining world, language, and rhetoric is – as earlier chapters in this book have shown – the subject of a great deal of discussion in both classical and Christian writers. Chaucer uses the conventional perceptions of this relationship, not so much by specific allusion as by his general dependence on a background of discussion and commentary. There are essentially three headings under which such discussion habitually takes place, and I have already discussed them at length: their points of view are congruent and in practice they blur together. First are the commentaries on Genesis, with their accounts of the Creation and Fall, Adam's naming of the animals and of Eve, the fall of language after the Fall, and its culminating dispersion at the Tower of Babel. Second is the Ovidian association of plain speaking and innocent discourse with the Golden Age, and of rhetorical artifice with the decadent present – a historical division that Ovid posits at the same time that he undercuts the possibility of there ever having been an innocent discourse. Third are the attitudes of the early Church toward rhetoric and poetry, which have a long afterlife in medieval ideas about rhetoric, fiction, and secular literature.

Even as late as the eighteenth century, when the Biblical paradigm has lost much of its force, the ethical dimensions of human history dictate the reasons for exploring the history of words. Lord Monboddo's *Origin and Progress of Language* is characteristic, as K. K. Ruthven points out, in finding a moral lesson within changing language: "The earliest discernible meaning of a word is taken to be its 'true' meaning, and the vicissitudes of things account for all subsequent changes: to use a word in its original sense is to restore the etymon to its pristine purity."[3] The search through etymology for an untainted language is, of course, a theme of some importance in English poetry. Spenser, who praises Chaucer as the "well of English vndefyled" (*Faerie Queene* 4.2.32), tries by his characteristic indulgence in wordplay "to purify words by restoring them to their true, original meanings."[4] And Milton, as Christopher Ricks has shown, attempts "to re-create something of the pre-lapsarian state of language" by his startling use of such words as "error," "luxurious," and "wanton" in Edenic, innocent contexts.[5] He defines Edenic innocence linguistically, "by assuming that the etymon is radically innocent, and that conversely, contemporary usage reflects 'fallen' experience (semantic change being the inevitable product of a calamity which brought death into the word)."[6]

Such exercises belong to the sixteenth and seventeenth centuries, not the fourteenth; and Chaucer is not attuned to these particular subtleties. But the background of commentary on Genesis, which lies behind the verbal reconstructions attempted by Spenser and Milton, is of equal importance in Chaucer's poetry. From the beginning of his career, he uses Lamech and his children as markers for the corrupting effects of civilization, and the potentially sophistical artifices of rhetoric. In "The

Former Age," Nimrod joins Jupiter as the agents of the world's fall from its primitive purity. Nimrod's descendants are hard at work in the *Canon's Yeoman's Tale*; in the *Second Nun's*, Chaucer undertakes his own exercise in etymology as recuperation.

These two tales – with the *Manciple's Tale*, *Parson's Tale*, and *Retraction* – form a coda to the *Canterbury Tales*, in which Chaucer takes us out of the realm of language and all other human things, to the silence of death and eternity. The end of the work, as I have argued, "transcends words and a delight in poetic artifice by moving beyond them – first by an ironic disintegration, then with utter seriousness – to the absolute simplicity of supernatural truth, where no words are necessary and human language cannot follow."[7] The details of this ironic disintegration are most fully described by James Dean, in his essay "Dismantling the Canterbury Book"; Donald Howard had previously sketched out its contours. In Howard's words, "The movement of this sequence, like that of Fragment I, is degenerative"; the *Manciple's Tale* "lets language itself fall beneath corrupt human nature. The rest, or at least the end, is silence."[8] After the Manciple has shown that stories and proverbs apparently teach us nothing, after the Parson has rejected the powers of poetical rhetoric to edify, the only recourse is to brush away the web of words altogether.

The process of linguistic degeneration in fact begins a little earlier, in Fragment VIII.[9] Chaucer uses the tales of the Second Nun and Canon's Yeoman to recapitulate the history of human language, which serves as a metonymy for the larger issues of our history on earth and our salvation. In these tales we see the alpha and omega of language, the extremes before and after Babel, as it nears its termination. For its beginnings, Chaucer alludes to the opening of Genesis, but also to extra-Biblical commentarial traditions. As Beryl Smalley has shown, especially in her study of Andrew of St. Victor, later medieval commentaries often rely on rabbinical exegesis – particularly Rashi – and Jewish tradition, the *Hebraica veritas*, to explain the literal meaning of the Old Testament.[10] The various strands of exegesis – Augustine, Josephus, the apocrypha and pseudepigrapha, rabbinical tradition – all come together very interestingly in the medieval accounts of the Tower of Babel; and I think that these accounts illuminate the end of the *Canterbury Tales*, as they flesh out the narrative of Genesis 10–11.

The thematic links between the two tales in Fragment VIII are all the more startling because the Canon's Yeoman has not heard the Second Nun and cannot consciously be responding to her tale; he and the Canon rush to join the company only after an emphatic gap in time and space: "Whan ended was the lyf of Seinte Cecile, / Er we hadde riden fully fyve mile" (*Canon's Yeoman's Prologue* 554–55). Nonetheless, as we move from one tale to the other, we move from the Golden Age to the Iron, from the heavenly suffusion and clarity of outline in the primitive Church to a demonic present, from spiritual generation to cancerous multiplication,[11] from the bodiless to the vividly embodied,[12] from the sweet odor of sanctity in St. Cecilia's tale, the roses and lilies of the two invisible crowns (246–59), to the alchemist's world, in which man must indeed eat bread in the sweat of his face, and horses too sweat profusely (560, 563).[13] (Four of the thirteen Chaucerian instances of the word "sweat," which almost invariably has broadly comic overtones in his poetry, are in this tale; Cecilia, notably, does not sweat a drop in her fiery torture [522].) The Canon's Yeoman's account of the suburban alchemists, "Lurkynge in hernes and in lanes blynde" (658), uses a word that appears only once elsewhere in the *Canterbury Tales*, when the Nun's Priest berates the fox as a "false mordrour, lurkynge in thy den!" (*Nun's Priest's Tale* 3226). But the word appears as well in the ballade "The Former Age," where secrecy and sweating effectively comment on the Yeoman's fallen vocation as a modern gold-grubber:

> But cursed was the tyme, I dare wel seye,
> That men first dide hir swety bysinesse
> To grobbe up metal, lurkinge in derknesse,
> And in the riveres first gemmes soghte.
>
> (27–30)[14]

The *Prologue* to the *Second Nun's Tale* immediately announces that we inhabit a fallen world, in which Idleness, "That porter of the gate is of delices" (3) – identical with the gatekeeper of the ersatz paradise of Myrthe (*Romaunt* 593) and the porter of Venus (*Knight's Tale* 1940) – must be countered by its "contrarie," the "leveful bisynesse" that requires us to "werche" (4–5, 14), and for the Second Nun, validates the work of translation.[15] Indeed, she models her "bisynesse" after the saint whose life she tells; Cecilia herself exemplifies the "bisy bee" (195), in an English phrase that Chaucer may have coined,[16] who serves God as an assiduously laboring "thral" (196) in the vineyard of conversion. The Nun's *Prologue* copies the saint's activity even as it gestures towards a time before the modern "confusioun" of which idleness is cause and symptom (23). For in it words are translucent, as well as perfectly translatable from Latin to English: impossibly, the translator claims to take her words as well as *sentence* directly from her male Latin source, while she emphasizes several times that these words are indeed "in Englissh" (2, 87, 106).[17]

The etymological delving into Cecilia's name (85–119) assumes a meaningful correspondence of sign and thing: one can pierce through the verbal shell, in whatever language, to the reality it signifies,[18] just as in the acrostic of "An ABC" in praise of the Virgin Mary (Riverside ed., pp. 637–40), the "carmen secundum ordinem litterarum alphabeti" [poem following the order of the letters of the alphabet], all the letters conjoin to offer luminous access to the Virgin as divine intercessor.[19] Even significations that would appear to be mutually contradictory can nonetheless all be true: "hevenes lilie" (87); "the wey to blynde" (92); "hevene" and Leah "for hire lastynge bisynesse" (96); "wantynge of blyndnesse" (100); "hevene" and "leos," that is to say, "the hevene of peple" (104). This multiplication of meanings is contagious: an "unworthy sone of Eve" (62), female or male,[20] can describe Mary "the sonne of excellence" (52) and her "Sone," who is also her Father (36). And in this etymological dance literal and figurative, the saint and the qualities she metaphorically represents – the whiteness of honesty and green of conscience (89–90) – as well as the meaning of her name "in figurynge" (96), with its amalgamation of Latin, Hebrew, and Greek, and their translations "in Englissh": all fuse together into a single, transparent light, into Cecilia's name and beyond the name, the saint herself. In this woman who is a "heaven of people" we may see "goostly" (109) the spiritual meanings of the sun (the magnanimity of faith), moon (the clearness of wisdom), and stars (the bright excellence of the saint's works):

> And right so as thise philosophres write
> That hevene is swift and round and eek brennynge,
> Right so was faire Cecilie the white
> Ful swift and bisy evere in good werkynge,

And round and hool in good perseverynge,
And brennynge evere in charite ful brighte.
Now have I yow declared what she highte.
                                    (113–19)

Later in the tale Cecilia explains the Trinity by the Augustinian analogy
of the three human "sapiences" (338–41).[21] Here a flawless microcosmic
mirroring of the macrocosm verges on identity: we can see the starry
heavens in the person of Cecilia. In both instances we move from human
to heavenly realities, in Augustine's formulation from the invisible workings of the mind to the heavenly paradox at the heart of all things, but
in the Second Nun's from visible charitable works to the visible cosmos.
As woman and saint, Cecilia is a transparent sign of the macrocosm.

The humble narrative voice – weighed down "by the contagioun/ Of
my body, and also by the wighte/ Of erthely lust and fals affeccioun" (72–
74) – forswears any effort at poetic subtlety. Chaucer has several other
versions of the modesty *topos*, notably at the end of *Troilus and Criseyde*,
but it seems particularly apposite in this tale in which we are made so
aware of clear speech, the irrelevance of rhetoric, and the proximity of the
divine. The intimacy of invocation – the reverent "thou" with which the
narrator addresses both Cecilia and Mary, "the flour of virgines" (29) –
prefaces the series of paradoxes, with their dizzying shifts in perspective,
that define the Virgin: "Thow Mayde and Mooder, doghter of thy Sone"
(36); "Thow humble, and heigh over every creature" (39); "Withinne
the cloistre blisful of thy sydis/ Took mannes shap the eterneel love and
pees" (43–44); "thou, Virgine wemmelees, / Baar of thy body – and
dweltest mayden pure – / The Creatour of every creature" (47–49).

Except for the last, these paradoxes are all translated, nearly word for
word, from Bernard's hymn to the Virgin at the opening of *Paradiso* 33.
Dante struggles with the inadequacy of language to revelatory vision in
this final canto of the *Commedia*; and Chaucer evidently has Dante in
mind as he constructs his own very different ending. Bernard's hymn
also lies behind the *Prologue* to the *Prioress' Tale*. Indeed, at one point the
Prioress and the Second Nun translate the very same lines, and putting
the two translations side by side offers an instructive comparison of the
two nuns:

> Lady, thy bountee, thy magnificence,
> Thy vertu and thy grete humylitee
> Ther may no tonge expresse in no science;
> For somtyme, Lady, er men praye to thee,
> Thou goost biforn of thy benyngnytee,
> And getest us the lyght, of thy preyere,
> To gyden us unto thy Sone so deere.
>
> *(Prioress, 474–80)*

> Assembled is in thee magnificence
> With mercy, goodnesse, and with swich pitee
> That thou, that art the sonne of excellence
> Nat oonly helpest hem that preyen thee,
> But often tyme of thy benygnytee
> Ful freely, er that men thyn help biseche,
> Thou goost biforn and art hir lyves leche.
>
> *(Second Nun, 50–56)*

Both prologues take "magnificence" directly from Dante's "magnificenza" (*Paradiso* 33.20), and "benygnytee" from the verses they directly adapt:

> La tua benignità non pur soccorre
> a chi domanda, ma molte fiate
> liberamente al dimandar precorre.
>
> *(Paradiso 33.16–18)*

> [Thy loving-kindness not only succors him who asks, but oftentimes freely foreruns the asking.]

But although "magnificence" appears at several other points in the *Canterbury Tales*, usually to describe a ruler's power, the kindred noble quality, "magnanymytee," appears only twice, both times in close proximity to "magnificence" – in the *Second Nun's Prologue* (110) and, tellingly, in the *Parson's Tale*, where the two qualities are linked (732, 735) as branches of the *fortitudo* needed to combat *accidie* with good works.

The Nun's emphasis, stated and implicit, on good works suggests a subtle difference from the ethos and vision of her superior, a difference that appears even in these translations of Dante: the Prioress' Virgin is the beseecher of the light necessary to lead us to her "Son," the Second Nun's the "sun of excellence" herself, who offers us medicine for our salvation.[22] For the Second Nun, prayer to the Virgin becomes an occasion for parsing and piercing through language; but for the Prioress, it proclaims a retreat to the inarticulate state of the *infans*, the "child of twelf month oold, or lesse, / That kan unnethes any word expresse" (484–85). She makes herself an analogue to the "litel clergeon" who does not understand the words he sings, but whose words have a luminosity and significance not dependent on his understanding, and can by themselves call forth the Virgin's power for the miracle of speech even beyond death.[23]

In both the *Prioress' Tale* and the *Second Nun's Tale*, the central female characters perform an *imitatio Mariae*, an imitation adopted by their narrators as well; but these imitations are markedly different. The *mater dolorosa* of the *piéta* fits the Prioress' own sentimentality and indulgence in the pathetic. In the *Second Nun's Tale*, Cecilia's life has one striking point of comparison with the Virgin's, as recounted in the apocrypha and the mystery plays (and alluded to in the *Miller's Tale*): when Valerian voices his suspicions of the angel Cecilia claims is the ever-present guarantor of her chastity (163–68), he replicates Joseph's doubting of Mary's innocence. But Cecilia quickly adopts a more vigorous role: she is indeed a "mulier fortis" (Proverbs 31.17), a characterization that, as Florence Ridley notes, Bernard uses to praise the Virgin.[24] She proclaims for herself an aggressive sanctity, from the hairshirt she wears under her golden wedding robe (132–33) to her confident preaching,[25] her accompanying the priests who baptize her converts (380), and her quotation of Paul to "Cristes owene knyghtes leeve and deere" (383), those same converts who are about to face their martyrdom. Tiburce is earlier called "Goddes knyght" (353) after his baptism, and Cecilia aptly quotes Paul's exhortations concerning the armor of the warfaring Christian and fighting the good fight (Romans 13.12 and 2 Timothy 4.7–8). She is, in the conventional terms of medieval hagiography, a manly woman. Even if Chaucer had not changed a word in his earlier "lyf . . . of Seynt Cecile," mentioned in the *Prologue* to the *Legend of Good Women* (F 426; G 416), his assigning the tale to a female religious narrator changes its meaning. Cecilia is the only "iron virgin" (to use Blamires' witty term) among the heroines in the so-called religious tales; and the Second Nun, so unlike her superior, aligns herself with her martyred heroine.[26]

Her tale stands in contrast to the *Man of Law's Tale* as well as the *Prioress'*; patterns of verbal reminiscence as much as plot highlight the differences between them, and also the singularity of the Second Nun's vision. Chaucer altered his source for the *Man of Law's Tale*, the *Chroniques* of Nicholas Trivet, to change Custance from an "iron virgin" to a "demure virgin," and two details in the *Second Nun's Tale* directly counterpoint this revised chronicle, in which the conventions of saint's life and romance coexist uneasily. On Cecilia's wedding night, wearing her hair shirt, "to bedde moste she gon/ With hire housbonde, as ofte is the manere" (141–42), a slightly odd phrasing that recalls the Man of Law's even odder and certainly more prurient account:

> They goon to bedde, as it was skile and right;
> For thogh that wyves be ful hooly thynges,
> They moste take in pacience at nyght
> Swiche manere necessaries as been plesynges
> To folk that han ywedded hem with rynges,
> And leye a lite hir hoolynesse aside,
> As for the tyme – it may no bet bitide.
> (*Man of Law's Tale* 708–14)

By her forceful advocacy (and the threat of her guardian angel), Cecilia can achieve her prayer that she remain "unwemmed" (137), and in reward the angel gives to Cecilia and Valerian the two crowns of roses and lilies, for them to keep "With body clene and with unwemmed thoght" (225). The adjective "unwemmed" appears only once elsewhere in the *Canterbury Tales*, when the would-be rapist in the *Man of Law's Tale* falls overboard and drowns: "And thus hath Crist unwemmed kept Custance" (924). The word is conspicuous here, if only because in the *Second Nun's Tale* it properly describes spotless virginity, not chastity or honor, and all the more so because of the Man of Law's earlier comments on Custance's wedding night subjugation. Trivet's Constaunce, by contrast, is very much an "iron virgin," who tricks the rapist into looking elsewhere and pushes him overboard herself.

The *Man of Law's Tale* is set several centuries after the *Second Nun's*, in an age of migration and conversion; and even Custance's speech, "a maner Latyn corrupt" (519), implies a falling off from the clarity of the early Christian era. Both tales celebrate conversion, but Custance is an unwitting and even unwilling evangelist, at the mercy of others' speech. The Second Nun owes her story, "wordes and sentence" both, to a single authoritative source. The Man of Law thanks a merchant for being his source, and rich merchants in general for being "fadres of tidynges/ And tales, bothe of pees and of debaat" (129–30); but tidings, the *House of Fame* and the *Manciple's Tale* both argue, are at best a version of *Fama*, gossip, a corrupted communication mixing false and true. The tale begins with rich Syrian merchants carrying news of Custance's beauty and goodness to the Sultan, and their tidings set the tale, and Custance, in motion.[27]

The points of contact between the *Second Nun's Tale* and the *Prioress'* are at least as striking.[28] The tales start in parallel fashion: the "clergeon" sings his song "wel and boldely" (546), and Cecilia answers the doubting Tiburce "boldely" (319). But they quickly diverge, as rudimentary learning in the *Prioress' Tale*, "This litel child, his litel book lernynge" (516), contrasts with accomplished learning in Fragment VIII: Valerian is "taught by his lernynge" where to find Pope Urban (184); Urban christens Tiburce and makes him "Parfit in his lernynge, Goddes knyght" (353); and the would-be alchemist sits "at his book bothe day and nyght/ In lernyng of this elvysshe nyce loore" (*Canon's Yeoman's Tale* 841–42).[29] (The only other appearance of the word in the *Canterbury Tales* is in the *General Prologue*, describing the Clerk, "On bookes and on lernynge he it spente" [300], though there are of course many instances of the verb *lerne*.)

The largest contrast is of style: the world of St. Cecilia, like the style of its narrator, is one in which outlines are clear. Augustine's *De Doctrina Christiana* 4.2 recommends rhetorical training, so that the Christian teacher may compete on an equal footing with the teachers of evil. Cecilia obviously does not need any such training. She persuades her husband, who is "corrected" by her talk (162), to live in a celibate marriage, and persuades her jailer to become a Christian (372–78) with the righteous assurance of plain speech. Paul appears in a vision, with "a book with lettre of gold in honde" (202), to reinforce her message, and his words, a paraphrase of Ephesians 4.5–6, stress unity – the unity of faith, of God, and of Christendom; her own words are as luminous as the apostle's, which as the narrator repeats, "al with gold ywriten were" (210). She need say little more than "Believe," and her word is sufficient to evoke a fervent unity of faith and voice:

> But they, converted at hir wise loore,
> Wepten ful soore, and yaven ful credence
> Unto hire word, and cryden moore and moore,
> "Crist, Goddes Sone, withouten difference,
> Is verray God – this is al oure sentence –
> That hath so good a servant hym to serve.
> This with o voys we trowen, thogh we sterve!"
>
> (414–20)

Indeed, the verbal abruptness of both the saint and her tormentor – "Whoso wol nat sacrifise, / Swape of his heed; this my sentence heer" (365–66) – captures perfectly the dominant tone in the *Acta Martyrum*.[30]

The plain-spoken confrontation between Cecilia and Almachius brings to the forefront an earlier interplay between the formal and informal second-person pronoun. When Cecilia warns Valerian not to touch her on their wedding night, she addresses him as "ye"; when he answers skeptically but with a willingness to believe, he responds with "thou," the favored pronoun within the community of the Church in the tale. This relatively mild confrontation with and victory over husbandly authority – mild even though Urban says that Cecilia has miraculously turned a "fiers leoun" of a husband into a meek lamb (198–99) – foreshadows her much harsher meeting with Almachius. He consistently addresses her in court with the informal and in this context condescending "thou" (424–92), while she begins by answering him with the formal "ye." That "ye," of course, masks an absolute unwillingness to cede to his authority or even perspicacity:

> "What maner womman artow?" tho quod he.
> "I am a gentil womman born," quod she.
> "I axe thee," quod he, "though it thee greeve,
> Of thy religioun and of thy bileeve."
>
> "Ye han bigonne youre questioun folily,"
> Quod she, "that wolden two answeres conclude
> In o demande; ye axed lewedly."
> Almache answerde unto that similitude,

"Of whennes comth thyn answeryng so rude?"
"Of whennes?" quod she, whan that she was freyned,
"Of conscience and of good feith unfeyned."

(424–34)

Once again here, as in the translation from Ephesians 4.5–6, "O Lord, o faith, o God" (in 207–9), and in the converts' belief in Father and Son, without difference (417), Cecilia reduces doubleness, confusion, and the worship of many gods (emphasized again by Almachius [492]), to singleness of purpose and meaning, and the worship of the one true God.[31]

Her answer, by its attack on Almachius' "questioun," proclaims that she is at ease in the world of philosophical discourse.[32] After several such exchanges she drops the pretense of formality, this time not for the intimacy suitable for fellow Christians but with a contempt that matches Almachius' condescension[33]:

Almache answerde, "Chees oon of thise two:
Do sacrifice, or Cristendom reneye,
That thow mowe now escapen by that weye."
At which the hooly blisful faire mayde
Gan for to laughe, and to the juge sayde:

"O juge, confus in thy nycetee,
Woltow that I reneye innocence,
To make me a wikked wight?" quod shee.
"Lo, he dissymuleth heere in audience;
He stareth, and woodeth in his advertence!"
To whom Almachius, "Unsely wrecche,
Ne woostow nat how fer my myght may strecche?"

(458–69)

Choosing "oon of thise two," indeed, even admitting that there is more than one choice possible, is not something that Cecilia is willing to do. If her gentility of birth gives her license to speak to Almachius as an equal,[34] unabashed, her name as Christian (as in a similar scene in the *Passio Sanctis Perpetuae*), when added to the power inherent in her own proper name, gives her even greater force:

"For as muche as we doon a reverence
To Crist, and for we bere a Cristen name,
Ye putte on us a cryme and eek a blame.

"But we that knowen thilke name so
For vertuous, we may it nat withseye."

(453–57)

This courtroom scene is conspicuously different from the one in the *Man of Law's Tale*, which emphasizes Custance's passivity; and in Cecilia's most powerful rejoinder, that Almachius has the power, not of life and death as he claims (470–72), but only to be the "ministre of deeth" (485), she readies herself for her martyrdom.

Almachius says he can resist her boldness, "For I kan suffre it as a philosophre" (490), and her response to him as "A lewed officer and a veyn justise" (497) ties the word he chooses even more explicitly to the *Canon's Yeoman's Tale*, which is soon to follow:

"Ther lakketh no thyng to thyne outter yen
That thou n'art blynd; for thyng that we seen alle
That it is stoon – that men may wel espyen –
That ilke stoon a god thow wolt it calle.
I rede thee, lat thyn hand upon it falle
And taste it wel, and stoon thou shalt it fynde,
Syn that thou seest nat with thyne eyen blynde."

(498–504)

Her first punishment, to be burned to death in "a bath of flambes rede" (515), "made hire nat a drope for to sweete" (522); and despite the three sword strokes she suffers, her executioner "myght noght smyte al hir nekke atwo" (528). She preserves her cool integrity, bodily and spiritual, until a time of death of her own choosing.

Cecilia's world, then, has the fresh clarity of a spring morning, with the savor of invisible roses and lilies, of garlands that can never rot or wither (228), and an awakening to the humble simplicity of the Truth:

Tiburce answerde, "Seistow this to me
In soothnesse, or in dreem I herkne this?"
"In dremes," quod Valerian, "han we be
Unto this tyme, brother myn, ywis.
But now at erst in trouthe oure dwellyng is."

(260–64)

In this tale the search for the "primordial substance" and primordial unity, which will be the alchemists' obsessive, sweaty, and murky pursuit

in the *Canon's Yeoman's Tale*, appears in its pellucid, unearthly original.[35]
When Tiburce visits his brother and smells the invisible flowers of his
crown, he exclaims: "The sweete smel that in myn herte I fynde/ Hath
chaunged me al in another kynde" (251–52) – in effect, he has experienced
a kind of divine alchemy, in which dreams have become waking truth,
and the invisible has brought into being the martyr's insertion of self
into history as a witness.[36] And when Cecilia converts Tiburce and is
"ful glad he koude trouthe espye" (291), she alludes to the corruption of
divine alchemy into an idolatrous worldly pursuit:

> Tho shewed hym Cecile al open and pleyn
> That alle ydoles nys but a thyng in veyn,
> For they been dombe, and therto they been deve,
> And charged hym his ydoles for to leve.
>
> (284–87)

Similar settings obscure essential differences: Pope Urban, who is to
baptize Tiburce, is in fact suburban, like the alchemists of the following
tale. He is hiding under sentence of death in the catacombs just outside
Rome, as Tiburce anxiously says:

> "Men sholde hym brennen in a fyr so reed
> If he were founde, or that men myghte hym spye,
> And we also, to bere hym compaignye;
>
> "And whil we seken thilke divinitee
> That is yhid in hevene pryvely,
> Algate ybrend in this world shul we be!"
> To whom Cecile answerde boldely,
> "Men myghten dreden wel and skilfully
> This lyf to lese, myn owene deere brother,
> If this were lyvynge oonly and noon oother."
>
> (313–22)

The *Canon's Yeoman's Tale*, by contrast, searches for a false divinity
hidden in earth, and for a unity that has been long lost. It is full of
sweat (for the victim of the confidence trick [1186] as much as the con-
man himself), fire, suburbs as *banlieues*, and idols. The Golden Age
has given way to grubbers for gold, the golden letters of Paul's book to
the Yeoman's crass boast that his Canon "koude al clene turnen" the
road to Canterbury "up-so-doun, / And pave it al of silver and of gold"

(625–26). Chaucer's use of alchemy to point his moral adds a further irony: if by an Ovidian paradigm flux has replaced the original stability of the cosmos, the alchemist in effect tries to metamorphose things backwards, to find the gold beneath the superficies of baser metals in the decaying world, to – as Jean de Meun says – reduce them to their primordial matter ["les ramaine/ a leur matire prumeraine"] (*Roman de la Rose* 16039–40).[37] But in the search for primordial unity, the alchemist has to move vehemently in the opposite direction; and the only unity he will find is a unanimity of confusion: "And konne he letterure or konne he noon, / As in effect, he shal fynde it al oon," since "bothe two" merely "concluden in multiplicacioun" (846–49).[38]

The fact of the world's decline is apparent in the alchemist's method; the quest for the singular through "multiplying" requires the deception of borrowing gold in the attempt to find it:

> To muchel folk we doon illusioun,
> And borwe gold, be it a pound or two,
> Or ten, or twelve, or manye sommes mo,
> And make hem wenen, at the leeste weye,
> That of a pound we koude make tweye.
>
> (673–77)

Twelve pounds, or more, borrowed for the illusion of making two is hardly a profitable investment; and in fact, multiplication is most likely to end in nothing: "A man may lightly lerne, if he have aught, / To multiplie, and brynge his good to naught!" (1400–1).[39] The supply of gold in the fallen world is, paradoxically, devoured by the very process of searching for gold:

> Considereth, sires, how that, in ech estaat,
> Bitwixe men and gold ther is debaat
> So ferforth that unnethes is ther noon.
> This multiplying blent so many oon
> That in good feith I trowe that it bee
> The cause grettest of swich scarsetee.
>
> (1388–93)

The Second Nun's "leveful bisynesse" (5) has turned into a hectic frenzy (576): the Canon, to make his sudden entrance, "hadde ay priked as he were wood" (576). Philosophical "philosophres" (*Second Nun's Tale*

113 and 490) have become merely alchemical "philosophres" (the word occurs eight times in the *Canon's Yeoman's Tale*). In an alchemist's version of the Tower of Babel, a broken pot provokes hellish dissension (906–61, especially 916–17: "Though that the feend noght in oure sighte hym shewe, / I trowe he with us be, that ilke shrewe!"). Indeed, the Canon's Yeoman's world has many demonic associations. It is a world of goatish stench (886) and brimstone, mentioned four times in the tale. The proper object of worship has been subverted: the Second Nun refers five times to the "Lord," while of the fifteen occurrences of "lord" in the *Canon's Yeoman's Tale*, one names the Devil, and the other fourteen the Canon whom the Yeoman serves. This is a world in which we half expect to meet Mephostophilis:

> Of alle thise names now wol I me reste,
> For, as I trowe, I have yow toold ynowe
> To reyse a feend, al looke he never so rowe.
>
> (859–61)

But the obsessive search goes on, in part simply because misery loves company (746–47), and the adepts of multiplying search for converts – just as Cecilia does – as much as for gulls. One can hardly forget Cecilia's scornful charge that the pagans take a stone and call it a god (500–1): the alchemist does the same thing with his "philosophres stoon, / Elixer clept" (862–63), as he does with the object of his quest: "The idols of the Gentiles are silver and gold [*simulacra gentium argentum et aurum*], the works of the hands of men" (Psalm 113B:4).

Yet the Canon's Yeoman reminds us of the lost purity of Eden and the Golden Age, buried within the flat proverbiality of a maxim:

> But al thyng which that shineth as the gold
> Nis nat gold, as that I have herd told;
> Ne every appul that is fair at eye
> Ne is nat good, what so men clappe or crye.
> Right so, lo, fareth it amonges us:
> He that semeth the wiseste, by Jhesus,
> Is moost fool, whan it cometh to the preef;
> And he that semeth trewest is a theef.
>
> (962–69)

Apples and gold are no longer to be taken at face value. And people too have undergone a comparable doubling, evident even in the narration of the two tales: the nearly anonymous narrator of the *Second Nun's Tale*, whose "neutral stylized manner" obscures nothing in the narrative,[40] contrasts with the entirely self-defined Canon's Yeoman, whose personality is centrally at issue in the psychology of his performance. A violent disjunction between pretense and sordid reality – fool's gold and rotten apples – is evident in the Yeoman's own appearance and his general obliviousness to it, even though the alchemists claim that their threadbare array is meant to disguise them from potential murderers (890–96) who are after their secret knowledge (also see 1372–74). Unlike Pope Urban, who "woneth in halkes alwey to and fro, / And dar nat ones putte forth his heed" (*Second Nun's Tale* 311–12), the alchemists lurk in the "suburbes" with thieves who "Holden hir pryvee fereful residence, / As they that dar nat shewen hir presence" (660–61).[41] Hiding from others becomes a more devastating hiding from oneself. The Yeoman is unaware that his face is discolored: "I am nat wont in no mirour to prie, / But swynke soore and lerne multiplie" (668–69); and his fogginess defines him as a narrator. In a near-parody of the miraculous ease of conversion in the *Second Nun's Tale*, when dreams give way to reality, a word from Harry Bailly is enough to move the Yeoman to confession by awakening him to his and his master's condition – "Why artow so discoloured of thy face?" (664); "Why is thy lord so sluttissh, I the preye?" (636), that lord whom the Yeoman had just described as "a passyng man" (614) and who, Harry Bailly says, should be able to buy better cloth "If that his dede accorde with thy speche" (638). The Yeoman's face itself has undergone a metamorphosis, going through the alchemical colors of transformation in reverse order (727–28);[42] since the alchemical transformations are meant to get back to the primitive state of things, the Yeoman's transformations in reverse have put him right back in the muddy present, where he is capable of joking ruefully about his plight: "For shame of hym my chekes wexen rede. / Algates they bigynnen for to glowe, / For reednesse have I noon, right wel I knowe" (1095–97). The Yeoman is a postlapsarian naïf, whose attempts at slight duplicity are scarcely less transparent than his newly found candor; his stage aside, "I wol nat avowe that I seye" (642), is as clumsy as the unlikely vehemence of his protest that he is not attacking canons in general (992–98) or describing his own former employer (1088–101). But he also displays the compulsiveness of the addict. Despite his apologia, he is still consumed by his obsession: lines 712–14 are in the past tense, but there is every evidence that his obsession is ongoing. The game of alchemy continues to be, as it has been, earnest to him (708–10).[43] Despite the momentary clarity evoked by the Host's catechism, with a verbal confessional that brings inner depths to light, the Yeoman's account of alchemical practices quickly returns to a helter-skelter murkiness.

The fogginess of the Yeoman's mind, and of the world he describes, is summed up by Chaucer's jokes on the word "multiplying."[44] Its primary meaning in the *Canon's Yeoman's Tale* is "to practice alchemy." But words also "multiply," as one of the entries for *multiplien* in the *Middle English Dictionary* corroborates, and as the Eagle in the *House of Fame* explains (817–21). "Multiplicacioun," whether of metals or of words, exemplifies the fragmentation and confusion of human experience.[45] In the *House of Fame*, rapidly multiplying words seek their proper resting place in the turbulent air. In the *Canon's Yeoman's Tale* the proliferation of words and of alchemy are analogous if not related processes; the great jokes of this tale are primarily linguistic ones. For if words in the *Second Nun's Tale* are translucent, in the Yeoman's world they are opaque. Jargon and technical vocabulary are self-consciously and deliberately obfuscatory – counters in a shell game. The false canon of the tale can "so wynde" himself in his "termes" (980) that he can fool anyone; and the Yeoman describes the practice of his master and himself in much the same fashion:

> Whan we been there as we shul exercise
> Oure elvysshe craft, we semen wonder wise,
> Oure termes been so clergial and so queynte.
> (750–52)

Here as always in Chaucer's poetry, the word "termes" implies a specialist's argot; and the *General Prologue* had offered several examples of how such an argot can be used for self-promotion and the deception of others.

Yet in the *Canon's Yeoman's Tale*, the confidence man himself becomes the gull. The opacity of jargon prevents even its users from achieving any clear sight:

Philosophres speken so mystily
In this craft that men kan nat come therby,
For any wit that men han now-a-dayes.
They mowe wel chiteren as doon jayes,
And in hir termes sette hir lust and peyne,
But to hir purpos shul they nevere atteyne.

(1394–99)

Just as Chaucer in the *General Prologue* describes the Physician by a list of names, the authors of his medical textbooks, so the Canon's Yeoman gives us a comically rebarbative list of terms, out of order, "as they come to mynde," and not set "in hir kynde" (788–89). His case of logorrhea lasts for forty lines before it abates. But then, having returned to his narration, the Yeoman interrupts himself once again: "Yet forgat I to maken rehersaille" (852) of another seven terms, also out of order and incoherently presented.[46]

The final joke in the tale epitomizes Chaucer's perception of language in the fallen world. In the *Second Nun's Tale* the word "name" appears five times, twice to emphasize the virtuous power of the name "Christian" (454, 456), and three times in the etymology of Cecilia's own name (85, 91, 102), which points us to the realities it signifies. In the *Canon's Yeoman's Tale* the memorable occurrences of the word come at the end, when it becomes apparent that the philosopher's stone is, by God's decree, beyond the reach either of alchemists or of the signifying power of words. No one, we are told, should become an alchemist "But if that he th'entencioun and speche/ Of philosophres understonde kan" (1443–44); but we discover immediately, when Plato refuses to tell what he knows, that such understanding is not attainable:

"Telle me the name of the privee stoon."
    And Plato answerde unto hym anoon,
"Take the stoon that Titanos men name."
    "Which is that?" quod he. "Magnasia is the same,"
Seyde Plato. "Ye, sire, and is it thus?
This is *ignotum per ignocius*.
What is Magnasia, good sire, I yow preye?"
    "It is a water that is maad, I seye,
Of elementes foure," quod Plato.
    "Telle me the roote, good sire," quod he tho,

"Of that water, if it be youre wil."
   "Nay, nay," quod Plato, "certein, that I nyl.
The philosophres sworn were everychoon
That they sholden discovere it unto noon,
Ne in no book it write in no manere.
For unto Crist it is so lief and deere
That he wol nat that it discovered bee,
But where it liketh to his deitee
Men for t'enspire, and eek for to deffende
Whom that hym liketh; lo, this is the ende."
                                    (1452–71)

Here language, itself manifesting the fallen state of the world and of alchemy as "slidynge science" (732), stands as an impermeable veil, as if illustrating Isidore's dictum, "Nisi enim nomen scieris, cognitio rerum perit" [For unless you know the name, the understanding of things perishes].[47] The alchemist's (and poet's) only recourse, or at least his best one, must be a version of Johnson's comic resignation before the limits of our human powers to master our terms of discourse: "I am not yet so lost in lexicography, as to forget that words are the daughters of earth, and that things are the sons of heaven."[48]

Johnson's singular image, with its reminiscence of the sons of God and the daughters of men – and the "giants in the earth in those days" (Genesis 6:4) – is peculiarly apt in the context of the *Canon's Yeoman's Tale* because Chaucer is, I think, making his own allusion to the most notorious of the giants, Nimrod. The alchemist's confusion punishes his presumptuous effort to find gold.[49] Such presumption is exactly what God punished at Babel; and Nimrod, the tower's builder, is associated with forbidden knowledge as well as tyranny and pride, and habitually associated with heretics, magicians, and astrologers. Indeed, the *Bible Moralisée* comments on Babel as the vainglory of "astronomers and philosophers" "reduced to nothing."[50]

Even more important for Chaucer's purposes is another accretion to the Biblical narrative of Babel: the tradition that Nimrod was the first fire-worshipper, and that he compelled the Chaldaeans to worship fire.[51] Many medieval accounts (listed in Chapter 1) describe this aspect of Nimrod's tyranny; and the Canon and his Yeoman are, as fire-worshippers, direct descendants of Nimrod's Chaldaeans. Their connection with their ancestors is, I think, yet more startling, in the context of an especially striking addition to the Biblical narrative of Genesis. Peter Comestor habitually interrupts his textbook of Biblical history with what his manuscripts term "additiones," "incidentia," "glose," or to use Stephen Langton's description, "glosa extrinseca." These "additions" are in effect footnotes or expansions of material corollary to Old Testament history; and when Peter describes Nimrod's tyranny, idolatry, and fire-worship, he adds this little story:

> The Chaldaeans worshipped fire, and compelled others to do the same, burning up other idols. The priests of Canopus, hearing this, because they had fashioned a great idol in honor of Bel, after removing its golden crown attached an earthen vessel [*vas fictile*] in the manner of a crown, perforated by holes stopped up with wax. When the Chaldaeans arrived they set a fire against it, and after the wax liquefied, the water that was in the crown, flowing down, put out the fire, and the idols of Canopus prevailed. (*PL* 198:1088–89)

Peter takes this story from Rufinus,[52] but his retelling gives it a very wide currency. Although, like the other *additiones*, it does not appear in every copy of the *Historia Scholastica*, Chaucer would almost certainly have seen it when he read the work.[53] Of the sixteen manuscripts of Peter Comestor in the British Library dating from the fourteenth century or before, nine include the story. (Most of the others include none of the *additiones* at all.) Like all the *additiones*, this one is especially conspicuous – highlighted either as an inset or as a gloss in the margin – and would catch the eye of any reader of this standard textbook.

It certainly caught the eye of Peter's imitators, who often move the story from the margin to the body of the text. In the 1290s Guyart Desmoulins made a French translation of the *Historia Scholastica*. The story of the Chaldaeans and the priests of Canopus appears in each of the nine copies of this work in the British Library. (The most interesting of these, for extra-literary reasons, is no doubt MS Royal 19.D.II, captured at the battle of Poitiers.[54]) Moreover, Guido da Pisa quotes this story – citing Comestor as the compiler of the history Moses wrote in Genesis – in his commentary on canto 31 of the *Inferno*; there, indeed, he makes it an integral part of his account of Nimrod and the tower of Babel. Nimrod compelled men to worship fire; the Chaldaeans followed his example and got their comeuppance with the wax trick; Nimrod gathered together all the sons of Noah, that is to say, the whole human race, and they began to build the Tower of Babel:

> Nimrod was the son of Chus, the son of Cham, who was the son of Noah. And so this Nimrod began to be a mighty one on the earth, and a mighty hunter of men on the earth in the presence of the Lord, that is a destroyer and oppressor, with a love of domineering. And he compelled men to worship fire. Following him, the Chaldaeans worshipped fire, and compelled others to the same, burning up other idols. The priests of Canopus, hearing this, because they had fashioned a great idol in honor of Bel, after removing its golden crown attached an earthen vessel made in the manner of a crown, perforated on all sides by holes filled with water and stopped up with wax. The Chaldaeans in truth set a fire; but after the wax liquefied, the water that was in the crown, flowing down, put out the fire. And so Nimrod, inflamed by a love of domineering, gathered together all the sons of Noah, that is the entire human race, into one place in the field of Senaar, and they began to build the tower that would stretch all the way to the heavens, having bricks for stones and bitumen for cement. But God descended so that he might see the tower, that is, he took notice of it so that he might punish, and said to the angels: "Come, let us confound their tongue, so that everyone may not understand the speech of his neighbor."[55]

Now this trick of the priests of Canopus is of course precisely the trick the alchemist twice uses to gull his victim, with silver instead of water behind the wax seal (1159–64; 1265–69); and the source of this part of the *Canon's Yeoman's Tale* has never been identified. There are other more indirect indications that when Chaucer wrote the *Canon's Yeoman's Tale*, he had in mind the story of Babel – describing as it does the fall of language and the origins of idolatry. But it seems quite plausible to me that his rumination on Comestor's narrative, including this "addition," provoked his thinking. Indeed, although I cannot prove it, I like to think that this little narrative gave Chaucer the idea for his own particular version of idolatry confounded.[56]

These two stories, one concerning a trick to gull the gullible, the other using essentially the same trick to debunk idolatry, use trickery to opposite ends, but they have in common a delight in artifice itself; and this essentially poetic delight has broader implications for the *Canon's*

Yeoman's Tale. For if the Yeoman's chaotic, jumbled list of terms suggests the plight of fallen language as it decays into impenetrable jargon, it also manifests a version, however comic and debased, of poetic pleasure.[57] Chaucer is drawing here on the quintessential features of the alchemical vocabulary, as Michel Butor aptly summarizes them:

> The texts pile up challenges to the principle of contradiction. One knows the famous aphorism cited by Khunrath: "If the stone was a stone, one would not have named it 'stone.'" I pick in *Artephius* this phrase which is no less surprising: "And this quicksilver is called fire, because it is nothing but fire, and non-fire, because it is nothing but sulphur, and non-sulphur, because it is nothing but quicksilver." A term is often endowed with a multitude of appellations, of which several find themselves in the litanies joined to other terms. It is forbidden to prepare a dictionary of simple equivalences, because numerous words of the first column seem able to apply to the quasi-totality of those in the second, and even to their negations. At the extreme limit, anything could refer to anything [*n'importe quoi pourrait désigner n'importe quoi*].[58]

Under the guise of the alchemist's need for hermetic secrecy and obscurity – the "numerous 'cover names'" required "to guard its holiness from the profane"[59] – the meaning of words imposed *ad placitum* has become a referential free-for-all[60]; Butor's quotations from the alchemists sound remarkably like the stories in which a workman on the Tower of Babel suddenly fails to understand the meaning of another's request for "stone."

The *Canon's Yeoman's Tale* comes across as play at the very heart of desolation, with something of the characteristic effect of Samuel Beckett, though arrived at by verbal excess rather than spareness.[61] Throughout this final sequence of tales, the counterexample of Dante is barely below the surface. In the Yeoman's hands, poetry is hardly redeemed – this is not a place, as at the beginning of *Purgatorio*, where dead poetry rises again; but even in this degraded, half-demonic context, there is verbal delight. The terms of alchemy, listed in a long, breathless *occupatio*, are not particularly opaque in themselves; they become so because they appear in no order or sequence. In Chaucer's other notable lists, the trees and birds of the *Parliament of Fowls* suggest by their variety the plenum of Nature's realm; the trees felled for Arcite's funeral pyre, within the irony of an *occupatio*, point to the destruction of the natural world for the sake of human ritual.[62] The lists in the *Canon's Yeoman's Tale*, however, are closest in spirit to the dream categories, or lists of tidings, in the *House of Fame*, another version of verbal artifice in the midst of great confusion, a welter of categories to match the plenum of Nature.[63]

The Canon's Yeoman uses the congeries of words and things to search for the single thing that lurks behind its many names, the philosopher's stone that can in turn be the key to finding the single primordial substance lurking within the multiplicity of the material world; but at the end of this futile search, the clutter of words remains our only possession, whether to decry or celebrate. The opening lines of the *General Prologue* offer a sunnier analogy: the simplicity of Nature following God's plan gives way to human multiplicity and complexity of motive, a multiplicity that marks a moral decline but also a vital and quintessentially human exuberance.[64] Such exuberance in its poetic form appears triumphantly in the Nun's Priest's celebration of human consciousness, where Chaucer proclaims, in an almost Nabokovian fashion, the power of the human mind to assert connections, even in the face of an intractable reality. Surprisingly, the anticlimactic conclusion to the *Canterbury Tales*, which contrasts with the *Nun's Priest's Tale* by stripping away the powers of rhetoric and language, is not entirely its opposite. At the beginning of the work, the Miller "quites" the *Knight's Tale* by allusion and direct quotation; the tales following the Wife of Bath respond to her directly and by allusion; the Nun's Priest quotes and incorporates the morally or poetically impoverished tales that immediately precede his own. But since the Canon's Yeoman has emphatically not heard the *Second Nun's Tale*, the conspicuous patterns of image and meaning that unite his tale to hers have been put there by some other agency – either by the mind of the poet, or within the terms of the fiction, by the Creator who gives pattern to earthly things. In their deployment of art and language, poet and alchemist are themselves connected, in the first instance by verbal echo: the Yeoman refers twice to "Oure elvysshe craft" (751) and "this elvysshe nyce loore" (842), and the only other appearance of the word in Chaucer's poetry is when Harry Bailly remarks on Chaucer's own "elvyssh" countenance (*Prologue to Sir Thopas*, 703).[65] Like the would-be alchemist, who sits "at his book bothe day and nyght" (841), the poet spends every night as a non-lover writing love poetry, and poring over one book after another in his quest for knowledge (*House of Fame* 632–40, 655–58).[66]

Claude-Gilbert Dubois, in a book on myth and language in the sixteenth century, notes that the searches of the alchemist and linguistic antiquarians, "ces alchimistes du verbe," are similar, all of them looking for "their philosopher's stone – the lost formula that will permit giving to the word again the essential content that it had at its origin – and in naming an object, to know it."[67] The alchemist of the *Canon's Yeoman's Tale* is much like the poet of the *House of Fame*: each lives in a world in which language has lost its moorings, as terms proliferate, and fog and confusion multiply. Elsewhere in the *Canterbury Tales* – notably in Fragments IV and V, the tales of the Clerk, Merchant, Squire, and Franklin – Chaucer explores the dimensions of nostalgia in the search for a world of unity beyond or behind multiplicity and alienating categories. The final sequence of tales, in a darker register, shows his skepticism about the possibility for a successful outcome, even if he must be sympathetic to the urgencies behind the search itself.[68]

COUSIN TO THE DEED

At both the beginning and the end of the *Canterbury Tales*, Chaucer quotes a proverb that he himself almost certainly introduced into English: that the word should be cousin to the deed.[69] The maxim is particularly significant for the tension it contains between natural and conventional understandings of language, and by implication, between unfallen and fallen instances of how language works. In the lyric "Lak of Stedfastnesse," Chaucer laments that the world, which "hath mad a permutacioun/ Fro right to wrong, fro trouthe to fikelnesse" (19–20) and where once "mannes word was obligacioun," has now become "so fals and deceivable/ That word and deed, as in conclusioun, / Ben nothing lyk" (2–5). Similarly, Gower complains, in the *Prologue* to the *Confessio Amantis*, that the connection of language to thought has decayed: formerly, "The word was lich to the conceite/ Withoute semblant of deceite" (113–14). The gap between word and deed blurs together, somewhat confusingly, with the analogous but not identical gaps between word and intent, and word and thought. The Parson defines lies, "lesynges, which generally is fals signyficaunce of word, in entente to deceyven his evene-Cristene" (607), and "the synne of double tonge," when a pretended "good entencioun," or speech supposedly "in game and pley," covers up an actual "wikked entente" (644). Intention evidently pertains to will, not language; but the corrupted intent of the fallen will infects the capacity of language itself to be "cousin to the deed." The original innate congruence of language and reality has been vitiated.[70]

Chaucer's proverb differs noticeably from the Boethian passage that is its ultimate source. Book 3, prose 12 of the *Consolation* begins with the narrator's acknowledgment that he now accepts what Plato had said: knowledge is in fact remembrance, the recollection of what in some sense we already know. Since Philosophy had just argued in prose 11 that everything in the universe desires unity, which equals the goodness on which being itself depends,[71] he can now understand, by the analogous process of retrieving memory and thought from behind obscuring sorrow and "the contagious conjunccioun of the body with the soule" (3.pr 12.4–6), that there must be a unity at the heart of multiplicity:

> This world ... of so manye diverse and contraryous parties, ne myghte nevere han ben assembled in o forme, but yif ther ne were oon that conjoyned so manye diverse thinges ... Ne the certein ordre of nature ne schulde not brynge forth so ordene moevynges by places, by tymes, by doynges, by spaces, by qualites, yif ther ne were on, that were ay stedfaste duellynge, that ordeynide and disponyde thise diversites of moevynges. And thilke thing, whatsoevere it be, by whiche that alle things ben ymaked and ilad, Y clepe hym 'God,' that is a word that is used to alle folk. (30–47)

But he worries, when Philosophy then expounds the seeming paradox that evil has no being, that she is trapping him within "the hous of Didalus, so entrelaced that it is unable to ben unlaced" (156–57): "Ne fooldist thou nat togidre by replicacioun of wordes a manere wondirful sercle or envirounynge of the simplicite devyne?" (160–62); she is using many words to get at the definition of the One. He continues: "And thise thinges ne schewedest thou naught with noone resouns ytaken fro withouten, but by proeves in cercles and homliche knowen, the

whiche proeves drawen to hemself heer feyth and here accord everiche
of hem of othir" (179–84) – that is to say, her proofs are internal to the
system whose existence she is proving. Her reply, that the divine essence
is self-contained, hence does not need outside proofs and is indeed
impermeable to them – derives from a similar statement in *Timaeus*
29B:

> And in speaking of the copy and the original we may assume that
> words are akin to the matter which they describe; when they relate to
> the lasting and permanent and intelligible, they ought to be lasting
> and unalterable, and as far as their nature allows, irrefutable and
> invincible – nothing less. But when they express only the copy or
> likeness and not the eternal things themselves, they need only be
> likely and analogous to the former words.[72]

But Boethius concludes Philosophy's argument with the crucial
phrasing:

> But natheles, yif I have styred resouns that ne ben nat taken from
> withouten the compas of the thing of whiche we treten, but resouns
> that ben bystowyd withinne that compas, ther nys nat why that thou
> schuldest merveillen, sith thow hast lernyd by the sentence of Plato
> that nedes the wordis moot be cosynes to the thinges of whiche thei
> speken. (200–7)

Saying that the word should be cousin to the thing is here, then, not
a Cratylist argument, as it is implicitly in the *Timaeus*, or in Dante's
invention of *I* as the true name of God. Instead, Philosophy says that
words must be within the same realm of discourse as the things they
describe – a stipulation made more difficult when those things are ineffable and divine. We know that Chaucer paid particular attention to
this passage, for Book Three then concludes with Meter 12, "Felix qui
potuit," which tells the story of Eurydice and Orpheus, whose failure
at self-control is summed up by the question, "But what is he that may
yeven a lawe to loverys?" (52–53), the question that Arcite quotes as "the
olde clerkes sawe": "who shal yeve a lovere any lawe?" (*Knight's Tale*
1163–64). The "fable" of Orpheus marks out those who willfully turn
against the search for the "sovereyn good" (3.m 12.63) in favor of the
earthly and partial; and Boethius has just noted, as he worries about

Philosophy's circular argument, that she has defined "the simplicite devyne" as "sovereyn good," that is to say, "that God himself is sovereyn good" (3. pr 12.162–66).

In Chaucer's hands, though, Philosophy's argument devolves into simply a concern for stylistic decorum and reportorial accuracy. The divine is beyond the reach of language, and the perfect language of Adam has been lost beyond recovery; what remains is a diminished thing, and "cousin to the deed" must have a narrower meaning.[73] The phrase first appears in the *Canterbury Tales* toward the end of the *General Prologue* in a familiar passage that upon examination rapidly seems less familiar:

> But first I pray yow, of youre curteisye,
> That ye n'arette it nat my vileynye,
> Thogh that I pleynly speke in this mateere,
> To telle yow hir wordes and hir cheere,
> Ne thogh I speke hir wordes proprely.
> For this ye knowen al so wel as I:
> Whoso shal telle a tale after a man,
> He moot reherce as ny as evere he kan
> Everich a word, if it be in his charge,
> Al speke he never so rudeliche and large,
> Or ellis he moot telle his tale untrewe,
> Or feyne thyng, or fynde wordes newe.
> He may nat spare, althogh he were his brother;
> He moot as wel seye o word as another.
> Crist spak hymself ful brode in hooly writ,
> And wel ye woot no vileynye is it.
> Eek Plato seith, whoso kan hym rede,
> The wordes moote be cosyn to the dede.
> Also I prey yow to foryeve it me,
> Al have I nat set folk in hir degree
> Heere in this tale, as that they sholde stonde.
> My wit is short, ye may wel understonde.
>   (*General Prologue* 725–46)

This passage unravels itself, starting with its ending, since we are hardly likely to accuse the narrator of ignoring degree, and even if we were inclined to do so, the *General Prologue* has proved that class rankings are a complicated matter, with numerous overlaps and inconsistencies. If reportorial accuracy cannot be achieved in description, its possibility in memorial retelling is still more chimerical; even the most gifted memorizer may make mistakes and inadvertently use new words in the effort to recall what others have said. After all, in the House of Rumor tidings change their content even when they are transmitted instantaneously to the next teller (*House of Fame* 2060–75). Chaucer is also, of course, feigning when he claims that he is not someone to "feyne thyng." And as Hanning points out, the narrator uses this Platonic dictum "in order to justify using (or repeating) vulgar language. Needless to say, neither Lady Philosophy nor Timaeus ever intended any such license"; the poet hopes "to breach decorum without paying the price."[74]

Not very far below the surface of this passage is the notorious quarrel between Reason and the Lover in Jean de Meun's *Roman de la Rose*: it also has some interesting points of contact with Boccaccio's Epilogue to the *Decameron*. Certainly the Chaucerian narrator's defense of plain speech, of factual reportage, of one word being as good as any other, pretends that the fiction of the *Canterbury Tales* is not what it self-evidently is, a fiction in which all the things the narrator wants to defend against – untrue tales, feigned things, new words found, improper words in both senses – are already present and present on his own authority. The accurate reporter must, he says, speak "pleynly," must speak others' words "proprely" even when those words are themselves improper, must rehearse exactly "everich a word." Much the same defense occurs in the prologue to the *Miller's Tale*, where Chaucer asks "every gentil wight" to forgive him, since "I moot reherce/ Hir tales alle, be they bettre or werse, / Or elles falsen som of my mateere" (3173–75). These are defensive apologies that resonate in the context of medieval theories about translation, interpretation, and the imposition of meaning; but they become ironic in this poem in which ventriloquism, the "art of impersonation,"[75] means that this multiplicity of voices all comes from the single mind of the poet. Minnis points out that Chaucer "is personalizing language theory": "For him 'propre' speech is speech belonging to certain individuals, rather than a quality which belongs to the speech, and speaking plainly is something which people do rather than something relating to the spoken word itself."[76] The Canterbury pilgrims have something in common, then, with the embodied sounds in the *House of Fame*, where every speech

> . . . wexeth lyk the same wight
> Which that the word in erthe spak,
> Be hyt clothed red or blak;
> And hath so verray hys lyknesse
> That spak the word, that thou wilt gesse
> That it the same body be,
> Man or woman, he or she.
>
> (1076–82)

Interestingly, the red or black clothing of these embodied sounds suggests that they take shape as written letters, or as books, as much as in human form; but here as well speech is defined by its speakers.

In the *Roman de la Rose* Reason talks of the interchangeability, inside a world of language *ad placitum*, of "balls" and "relics"; in the *Canterbury Tales*, according to its narrator, the reporter of others' speech "moot as wel seye o word as another," and Christ himself spoke "broadly." The reference here might be to the parables, "as fictions or *fabulae*,"[77] though the context appears to restrict the meaning of speaking "broadly" to plain and even coarse speech. In a wider Biblical context, Augustine defends such passages "which seem like wickedness to the unenlightened, whether just spoken or actually performed," when he argues that they must be understood figuratively.[78] Yet parables present their own problems. For Alexander of Hales and Aquinas, a parable is contained in the literal sense, but instructs "in an apparently fictional manner and through a sort of concealment": "Developing Aquinas's theory of the *modus parabolicus*, Nicholas Trivet argued that a parable expresses one idea on the surface of the words, which is the sign and outer rind, and another in the inward understanding, which is the thing signified and inner pith."[79] Thus for parables too, the word is not exactly cousin to the deed.

Moreover, as Cooper says, this argument for decorum and affinity collapses since "the words are interchangeable while the deed stays the same."[80] In this context the desire for words to be cousin to the deed turns into merely stylistic decorum, and not at a very elevated level. It is fitting to "A woful wight to han a drery feere, / And to a sorwful tale, a sory chere" (*Troilus and Criseyde* 1.13–14), just as it is for an elegant speaker to be decorous: "Accordant to his wordes was his cheere, / As techeth art of speche hem that it leere" (*Squire's Tale* 103–4). By extension, debased or morally problematic deeds in the fallen world require similarly debased words: the *Legend of Philomela* says that the "dede" of Tereus was so "grisely" "That, whan that I his foule storye rede, / Myne eyen wexe foule and sore also," infected by "the venym of so longe ago" (*LGW* 2238–41). Even the word "cosyn" itself can designate trickery as well as connection.[81] In a world in which words in a proper moral sense are not cousins to the deed, glossing, which can as "glosyng" itself be a form of trickery, becomes the order of the day.[82] And when the maxim is attributed to Plato, "whoso kan hym rede" (*GP* 741), Chaucer complicates matters still further, because the uncertainty of translation, and of the text itself, undermines the possibility of close relation between text and text, let alone word and deed.[83]

The *Manciple's Tale* repeats the proverb, but in a notably cynical context:

> And so bifel, whan Phebus was absent,
> His wyf anon hath for hir lemman sent.
> Hir lemman? Certes, this is a knavyssh speche!
> Foryeveth it me, and that I yow biseche.
>   The wise Plato seith, as ye may rede,
> The word moot nede accorde with the dede.
> If men shal telle proprely a thyng,
> The word moot cosyn be to the werkyng.
> I am a boystous man, right thus seye I:
> Ther nys no difference, trewely,
> Bitwixe a wyf that is of heigh degree,
> If of hir body dishonest she bee,
> And a povre wenche, oother than this –
> If it so be they werke bothe amys –
> But that the gentile, in estaat above,
> She shal be cleped his lady, as in love;
> And for that oother is a povre womman,
> She shal be cleped his wenche or his lemman.
> And, God it woot, myn owene deere brother,
> Men leyn that oon as lowe as lith that oother.
>   (203–22)

Likewise, the only difference between "a titlelees tiraunt/ And an outlawe or a theef erraunt" (223–24) is that the former has enough power of sheer force to insist on being called "capitayn" (230). This passage, which at first seems to be a bracing call to tell it like it is, to call a spade a spade, in a parody of Adamic language, is itself undermined by its context. Instead of "When Adam delved and Eve span, / Who was then the gentleman?", the dream of an egalitarian state before the fall, this flattening of social and stylistic distinction becomes a call to reduce everything to the baseness of the lowest common denominator.[84] (The Manciple, after all, makes no corresponding call to name a "lemman" or "wench" a "lady" when she deserves the dignity of the more elevated term.) The *Manciple's Tale* is in effect a parodic recapitulation of the movement from the Second Nun to the Canon's Yeoman, from plain-spoken truth to chattering jargon. His confrontation with the Cook shows that plain speech is not always prudent, which is the point of his tale about the crow; and he garrulously enjoins silence, repeating the advice of his garrulous mother: "My sone, be war, and be noon auctour newe/ Of tidynges, wheither they been false or trewe" (359–60).[85] This is a tale in which the snow-white crow should have remained content with his ability to "countrefete the speche of every man/ . . . , whan he sholde telle a tale" (134–35), the faithful transcription that the narrator claims for himself in the *General Prologue*; the caged bird gets into trouble when he freelances with a vulgar comment imitated from another bird, "Cokkow!", on the freelancing of the caged wife. His intemperate speech provokes Phebus himself – in a detail that Chaucer adds to his Ovidian source – to destroy his poetic instruments (267–68).[86] The poet's anxiety in the *House of Fame*, in which he learns that his sources, tidings, are almost inevitably of "fals and soth compouned" (2108), has become the Manciple's cynical and apparently unworkable injunction that speechlessness is the best solution.

Whatever hope Chaucer expresses for verbal rectitude and plain reference, he also continuously undermines the possibility that the word can ever truly be cousin to the deed in this fallen world. His final work concludes with gestures toward the transcendence of language, accomplished paradoxically by verbal flattening – the Parson's rejection of fable, and of verse itself (*Parson's Prologue* 31, 43–44), and the "essentially denotative" quality of his prose,[87] under the urgent pressure of confession: "Thow shalt nat eek peynte thy confessioun by faire subtile wordes, to covere the moore thy synne; for thanne bigilestow thyself, and nat the preest. Thow most tellen it platly, be it nevere so foul ne so horrible"

(*Parson's Tale* 1022).[88] Chaucer presents himself as a mere "compiler," a version of the crow who can counterfeit the speech of others, until as "makere" he takes authority for and leave of his book.[89] But even in this final renunciatory gesture, he complicates the Parson's insistence on the univocal,[90] even by the resistant detail of including a perfect iambic pentameter line – "many a song and many a lecherous lay" – within this retraction in prose.[91]

Most poignant of all is the contrast between the end of the *Canterbury Tales* and the end of the *Commedia*, the final canto in *Paradiso* that Chaucer had used three times previously for its hymn to the Virgin. Dante moves beyond speech, as he sees the Eternal Light:

> Nel suo profondo vidi che s'interna,
>   legato con amore in un volume,
>   ciò che per l'universo si squaderna.
> (*Par.* 33.85–87)

[In its depth I saw ingathered, bound by love in one single volume, that which is dispersed in leaves throughout the universe.][92]

The intact volume of God's authorship compares with the audacious frailty of Dante's own:

> Da quinci innanzi il mio veder fu maggio
>   che 'l parlar mostra, ch'a tal vista cede,
>   e cede la memoria a tanto oltraggio.
> Qual è colüi che sognando vede,
>   che dopo 'l sogno la passione impressa
>   rimane, e l'altro a la mente non riede,
> cotal son io, ché quasi tutta cessa
>   mia visïone, e ancor mi distilla
>   nel core il dolce che nacque da essa.
> Così la neve al sol si disigilla;
>   così al vento ne le foglie levi
>   si perdea la sentenza di Sibilla.
> (*Par.* 33.55–66)

[Thenceforward my vision was greater than speech can show, which fails at such a sight, and at such excess memory fails. As is he who dreaming sees, and after the dream the passion remains imprinted and the rest returns not to the mind; such am I, for my vision almost

wholly fades away, yet does the sweetness that was born of it still drop
within my heart. Thus is the snow unsealed by the sun; thus in the
wind, on the light leaves, the Sibyl's oracle was lost.]

Chaucer at his ending is very different. Unlike Machaut and Froissart,
who carefully construct their anthologies, binding together the totality
of their poetic *œuvres* into a single volume,[93] he adopts a notably careless
pose, with three diffident catalogues of his literary career. He leaves us
lists of his poetic works only as they are put into the mouths of an inept
reader and critic (the Man of Law), a hesitant defense attorney (Alceste
in the *Prologue* to the *Legend of Good Women*), or *in propria persona*, in
a list of vanities the poet hopes, as he contemplates his death, will not
be held against him at the Day of Doom.[94] Thus he prepares himself,
with a gesture more of sybilline dispersion than of collection, more of
expectant hope than of fading vision, for the refining purgatorial fire:
"*Quando fiam uti chelidon* . . . These fragments I have shored against
my ruins."[95]

Notes

1. An earlier version of these opening pages appeared in Fyler, "St. Augustine." See Jameson on the relation of structuralism to the "prison-house of language." Almond recounts the lively seventeenth-century interest in Genesis as a scientific, historical, and literary text, as well as its gradual loss of a "mythological role" (pp. 213–14); see esp. pp. 126–42, on "The Language of Adam" and "Undoing Babel." Pagden, pp. 118–40, describes the linguistic theme in early modern European responses to the New World.

2. Stam, p. 255, quotes the bylaws of the Société. Gans argues that language began with human sacrifice, when the victim's body was named as "the other." Sommerfelt offers an overview of theories on language origin, categorizing them as pre- or post-Darwinian. The question has recently attracted the serious attention of evolutionary linguists: see *Language Evolution*, and Jackendoff, pp. 231–64.

3. Forsyth, p. 425. Jager, *Tempter's Voice*, which appeared after I had finished the corresponding sections of this chapter, outlines patristic ideas on language and the Fall, especially Augustine's influential description of the human soul as "a repository of God's word" (p. 36), in *De Trin.* 13.20, par. 26. Todorov, pp. 36–59, analyzes Augustine's thinking on signification.

4. Murdoch also recounts many interesting details in the medieval elaborations on Genesis.

5. The Latin Biblical quotations are from the Biblia Vulgata, the English from the Douay-Rheims translation. Sidebottom, esp. pp. 26–49, analyzes the Logos in John's Gospel. Cave, p. 86n., explores the implications of Erasmus' "notorious rendering of *logos* as *sermo*" instead of *verbum*, which "destroys the unity of the original utterance and initiates a movement beyond the scriptural circle into the fallen language of man." For a fuller account, see Bainton, p. 140.

6. Wyclif, p. 496; see Weiss on the 1311 Council of Vienne. Pico della Mirandola argues that only Hebrew words can have magical power, because they "were taught to Adam and Eve by God himself" (Kieckhefer, p. 148); and there are various seventeenth-century proposals for a "restored Hebrew" (Almond, p. 130), associated in particular with the Kabbalah. Francis Bacon argues that knowledge seeks "a restitution and reinvesting (in great part) of man to the sovereignty and power (for whensoever he shall be able to call the creatures by their true names he shall again command them) which he had in his first state of creation." (Quoted by Hamilton, p. 121; for the seventeenth-century context, see Almond, pp. 114–18.) Richard Rolle is careful to distinguish the cult of the Holy Name, which he helped to popularize in England, from such magic (Bennett, *Middle English Literature*, p. 307).

7. See Almond.

8. Derrida, *Grammatology*, p. 283; Jager, *Tempter's Voice*, p. 57, notes a similar viewpoint in patristic writers. Céard, p. 579, points out that a number of Renaissance texts give writing preeminence over speech because of a "density of which speech is incapable"; so too, medieval "*grammatica* was primarily a textual discipline that privileged writing over speech" (Irvine, *Making*, p. 4).

9. *Abbreuiatio* 3.47 (p. 463) (see Dronke, "Thierry," p. 365); cf. Aquinas, *ST* 1a.13,3. Ziolkowski, *Grammar of Sex*, pp. 120–27, has assembled a number of such metaphors.

10. *De Gen. ad Litt.* 1.2.4–6 (*PL* 34:248; trans. 1:21). Cf. Isidore, *Etym.* 9.1.11. Also see *Confessions* 11.6–7, and *De Gen. ad Litt.* 6.8, which differentiates between the words of God spoken in time by Christ or the prophets, and God's words of Creation, "spoken before there were any sound vibrations in air and before any voice coming from man or from cloud existed . . . They were not like sounds that strike human ears, but they implanted in things made the causes of things yet to be made" (*PL* 34:344; trans. 1:186–87). Basil (trans. Eustathius, p. 27) makes similar remarks. Augustine's account is copied by Bede, *Hex.*, p. 8, and Vincent of Beauvais, *Speculum Historiale* 1.17 (p. 7). Lonergan analyzes Aquinas' extensive treatment of *Verbum*.

11. Compare Luther's comment: "God's works are his words . . . his doing is identical with his speaking" [*idem est facere et dicere Dei*] (quoted by Schwartz, p. 64). Dragonetti, "Dante face à Nemrod," p. 388, notes that Jean de Meun's Reason, by using *cria*, the *passé simple* of the verb *créer*, enacts a wordplay on the *cri* and the Creation of God: "quant il prumierement cria/ tout le monde et quan qu'il i a" (*Roman de la Rose* 7059–60) [when he first created (or cried) the whole world and everything in it].

12. *De Gen. ad Litt.* 4.23.40 (*PL* 34:312; trans. 1:131).

13. *Confessions* 9.10; trans. p. 200.

14. *De Trin.* 15.10, par. 19 (trans. p. 409). Also see *Confessions* 10.2, on the difference between bodily words and the words of the soul, and especially *Enarr. in Psalmos* 9.7 (p. 61; trans. 1:76–77), which uses the inner and uttered words as an analogy for "*the world's world*," the eternal world "whose image and shadow, as it were, this world possesses": "As a verse in the mind, and a verse in the voice: the former is understood, the latter heard; and the former fashions the latter: and hence the former works in art and abides, the latter sounds in the air and passes away."

15. *De Trin.* 15.11, par. 20 (trans. p. 410) and 15.16, par. 26 (p. 417). On our promised equality with angels, see *De Gen. ad Litt.* 4.24, which quotes Matthew 22.30.

16. See, e.g., *De Gen. ad Litt.* 9.2 and 11.33.

17. "Aquinas," p. 15.

18. *De Gen. contra Man.* 2.4 (*PL* 34:198–99). Also see *De Gen. ad Litt.* 8.18 and 8.27, on the manner in which God spoke to Adam; and for a general discussion, Duchrow, and Evans, *Augustine on Evil*, pp. 53–90. Aquinas, similarly, argues that "Hearing came in the original state, not from a man speaking from without, but from God inspiring from within" (*ST* 2a2ae.5,1, ad. 3).

19. See Ong, pp. 316–17. Ong also discusses Augustine's play on *Verbum infans*, referring both to the infant Jesus and to the paradox of the unspeaking Word. Hugh of St. Victor, *De Archa Noe*, pp. 51–52, presents a particularly elegant version of such wordplay.

20. Dante, *DVE* 1.1.1.

21. The first quotation is from Justin Martyr's *Dialogue with Trypho*, the second from Tertullian's *De Carne Christi* (trans. Phillips, pp. 133–34). Cf. Jager, *Tempter's Voice*, pp. 14 and 74–75.

22. Colish, *Mirror of Language*, pp. 7–54. Also see Evans, *Language and Logic: Earlier Middle Ages*, pp. 1–5.

23. The *Vetus Latina* and the Vulgate are identical here: Augustine uses and quotes the earlier translation in *De Gen. contra Man.* 1.17 (*PL* 34:186). Chaucer's paraphrase in the *Franklin's Tale* (879–80) reads: "Which mankynde is so fair part of thy werk/ That thou it madest lyk to thyn owene merk."

24. *Confessions* 7.10. See Gilson, esp. p. 126, and Ferguson; also see O'Donnell's note on Augustine's text, 2:443–44. For the uses of "in regione dissimilitudinis," especially in the twelfth century, see Javelet, 1:266–85; and for its sources as well as twelfth-century uses, Courcelle, "Tradition."

25. Calvin, p. 43. Milton appears to occlude the distinction between *image* and *similitude* in his paraphrase of Genesis 1.26, which implies that they are synonyms: see *Paradise Lost* 7.519–20, with Fowler's note.
26. Ladner, "Physical Anthropology," p. 64; also see Floeri.
27. Cf. *De Gen. Imperf. Liber* (*PL* 34:242), and Evans, *Language and Logic: Earlier Middle Ages*, p. 101. Ladner, *Idea of Reform*, surveys the developing distinction between *image* and *similitude*, in Paul (pp. 58–59), the Greek Fathers (83–88), and Augustine (185–203); also see Ladner, *Ad Imaginem Dei*, pp. 12–13 and p. 70, n. 2.
28. Aquinas, *ST* 1.a.93,1, and 93,9. Cf. Grosseteste's *Hexaëmeron*, p. 217 (with commentary by Southern, *Robert Grosseteste*, pp. 212–13), and more generally, Javelet.
29. One example among many is Abelard, *Introductio ad Theologiam* 1.9 (*PL* 178:991); Horowitz provides a fuller discussion.
30. Jerome, *Adv. Jov.* 1.16 (*PL* 23:236). For analogues in the Jewish commentarial tradition, see Dahan, pp. 136 and 144. Fowler, p. 5, notes that Pythagorean number theory identifies the dyad with the "only feminine." Burke talks with his usual incisiveness about the "fall" implied by all division, hence by the idea of Creation itself (pp. 174, 203, 266, and 279).
31. *Opera de Temporibus*, p. 201. For Bede's interpretation of uneven numbers as good and even numbers as bad, see Jones, "Some Introductory Remarks," p. 169: "Two is evil, as the first step from unity to multiplicity." Also see Peter Lombard, *Sentences* 2.14.4 (*PL* 192:680); Evans, *Old Arts*, p. 132, explores the implications of mathematical unity and plurality for Thierry of Chartres, for whom two is "the beginning of all otherness" (*Tractatus*, p. 568).
32. Guibert: *PL* 156:31–33. The quoted paraphrase of Philo is Baer's (p. 37); the original appears in the Loeb edition, 1:118–21. Ambrose interprets woman in the Creation narrative as the senses, and man as mind: *De Paradiso* 15.73 (*PL* 14:311), cited by Blamires, *Woman Defamed*, p. 3, n. 10. For a more general discussion, see Lloyd.
33. For the literary implications of these two versions, see Nyquist, esp. pp. 153–55, and Froula, p. 345. Alter (*Art*, pp. 141–46) discusses why and how the two Creation narratives are conflated but do not entirely cohere; Forsyth, p. 149, summarizes recent arguments about their dating and designation.
34. Boccaccio uses Genesis 2 for a misogynistic moral: Eve rebels against Adam's dominion and naming of her, repaying with disobedience the first "man made in the image and semblance of God, a perfect creature, born to

govern and not to be governed" (*Corbaccio*, p. 35). The Chester *Adam* play, less stridently, emphasizes Adam's sovereign prerogative: "Ryse, Adam, and awake./ Heare have I formed the a make;/ hir to thee thou shalt take, / and name hir as thee liste" (141–44). In Willet's early seventeenth-century commentary, "Hee giueth the woman her name, to shew the authoritie of man ouer the woman" (p. 39). Also see Bloch, *Etymologies*, pp. 37–44, and "Invention," pp. 289–91.

35. *The Woman's Bible*, Part 1, p. 20.

36. *The Tablet* for 1 October 1988 summarizes the Pope's letter. Bal, p. 116, makes a feminist argument for the semiotic congruence of the two stories; cf. Pardes' response (pp. 26–31).

37. Meeks, p. 185, mentions a rabbinical text of Genesis 1.27 that reads "male and female he created *him*"; for the apocryphal legends behind such a reading, see *Hebrew Myths*, pp. 66–67; also see Willet's *Hexapla* (1608), p. 16, which mentions the androgyne in Plato's *Symposium*. In *De Gen. ad Litt.* 3.22, Augustine rejects the idea of an original hermaphrodite, proclaiming that woman too is created in God's image, though he also paraphrases this passage as "fecit illum masculum et feminam" [He made him male and female].

38. See Børresen, pp. 20–21, and Nyquist, p. 168, for discussion. Cf. "The Life of Adam and Eue," p. 365 (from B. L. MS Harley 4775): "Adam in that daie in the whiche god made mane of nought to the ymage and liknesse of god and he made of hem both male and ffemale and he made hem of nought and than he blessid hem and clepid the name of hym Adam."

39. Andrew of St. Victor, *CCCM* 53:21. John Scotus Erigena frames his argument in much the same way (*Periphyseon* 4, p. 107).

40. Cf. *De Civ. Dei* 14.22.

41. *PL* 191:1632–33; cf. Augustine, *De Trin.* 12.7, par. 10 (trans. p. 329). There are similar remarks in Hugh of Amiens (p. 260), and earlier, in John Scotus Erigena, *Periphyseon* 2, p. 19. The commentaries on Paul (especially on Romans 8.29 and Ephesians 4.13) also contain injunctions that women should "become male" to be redeemed as *homo*: see Vogt, and such texts as Jerome's commentary on Ephesians (*PL* 26:533) and Ambrose's on Luke (*PL* 15:1844) (both discussed by Salisbury, p. 280); for the broader medieval context, see Newman.

42.   car Dex an leur conmancemant
         les aime touz ouniemant
         et donne resonables ames
         ausinc aus homes conme aus fames.
                                       (19581–84)

[When they are first created, God has the same love for all, and gives rational souls to men as well as to women.]

The Prologue to the second Wycliffite Bible (c. 1396) expands on "the ymage maad of Goodis hondis, that is, a cristen man, either a cristen womman" (ch. 10, p. 34) (discussed by Aston, p. 160).

43. Buc, esp. pp. 57–66. For Augustine's view, see Markus, *Saeculum*, pp. 202–6; and for Luther's ambivalence, see Almond, p. 149.

44. *Hist. Schol.* (*PL* 198:1074), quoting nearly exactly from Peter the Chanter's *Glossae super Genesim* (p. 73); also see Hugh of St. Victor's *Notulae* (*PL* 175:43), and Buc's discussion, pp. 75 and 105.

45. Buc, p. 103.

46. Andrew of St. Victor, *CCCM* 53:37.

47. Buc, pp. 103–4, offers the relevant quotations, and d'Alverny, pp. 137–40, useful comments on these readings of Gen. 1.27.

48. Stegmüller provides an indispensable index to the medieval Biblical commentaries, to which I am deeply indebted; Smalley, "L'Exégèse Biblique," Courtenay, "Bible," and Spicq are also quite helpful.

49. In the *Vetus Latina*, Augustine's source, this phrase in Gen. 2.18 appears as "secundum ipsum"; but "similis ipsi" appears at the end of Gen. 2.20 (for the Vulgate's "similis eius").

50. Bede, *Hex.*, p. 53, notes that God says this with internal, not audible words.

51. Skinner, p. 67. Rosenberg, "Garden Story," p. 7, notes the analogue to this scene in *Gilgamesh*.

52. See Augustine, *De Gen. contra Man.* 2.11 (*PL* 34:205) (copied by Bede, *Hex.*, p. 56): Adam shows his superiority to the animals by displaying his reason in the very act of naming them. Evans, "*Paradise Lost*," p. 95, quotes a similar passage in John Chrysostom. Also see Alcuin, *Interrogationes* (*PL* 100:522); Comestor (*PL* 198:1070); and Stephen Langton, *Expositio moralis*, fol. 116ᵛ.

53. Ambrose, *De Paradiso*, PL 14:299, and cf. Rashi's commentary. In *Paradise Lost*, Raphael explains to Adam the difference between God's perfect Oneness and oneness as "single imperfection" in man, a "unity defective, which requires/ Collateral love, and dearest amity" (8.424–26).

54. Caxton's *Legenda*, 1:170; Aquinas, *ST* 1a.99,2. Cf. Chaucer's *Tale of Melibee* (1102–5) and the *Norwich Grocers' Play* (p. 8, 3–4):

> Yt ys not semely for man, *sine adjutorio*,
> To be allone, nor very convenyent.
> Let us make an adjutory of our formacion
> To hys symylutude, lyke in plasmacion.

55. Rashi 1:25. Aquinas discusses the particularities of Adam's universal "scientia," specifically in the context of his naming the birds and animals (*ST* 1a.94,3); cf. Philo's very interesting remarks (1:119) on the details of Adam's cognition and naming.

56. Augustine, *De Gen. contra Man.*, *PL* 34:180. His remarks are copied by Bede, *Hex.*, p. 9, and Rabanus, *PL* 107:448.

57. Abelard, *Expositio*, pp. 97–101, and Buytaert, ed., pp. 176–77. For early Christian and medieval images of Adam naming the animals, see Klingender, Maguire, and Muratova; an especially fine fourteenth-century example is in a Bohun Psalter, Bodl. MS Auct. D. 4.4, fol. 1. Also see d'Alverny, p. 144, and "Naming of the Animals" in Jeffrey, pp. 537–38.

58. Alcuin, *PL* 100:523; Augustine, *De Gen. ad litt.* 11.28.35; Evans, *Language and Logic: Earlier Middle Ages*, p. 72, notes the "gap between *intellectus* and *vox*" in Alcuin's serpent. Also see Ambrosiaster, pp. 59–60, and Honorius, *Elucidarium* 1.85, p. 376, and for further discussion, Kelly, "Metamorphoses."

59. Jerome, *Liber Interpr.*, p. 60. This etymology is standard in Biblical commentaries: Isidore, *Etym.* 7.6.4 (copied by Bede, *Hex.*, pp. 92–93, which compares the etymologies of *adam* and the Latin *homo*); Gregory, *Moralia* 18.47; Gregory of Tours, 1:1:386–87 (Bk. 8, ch. 20); and Comestor, *PL* 198:1071. The stage directions of the *Jeu d'Adam* give Adam a *tunica rubea* (9). See Clark, "Heresy, Asceticism."

60. Bede makes the standard comparison between the creations of Eve and the Church, emphasizing its grammatical aspect (*Hex.*, p. 57): just as Adam "wished the woman created from his flesh to become the sharer of his own name [*nominis sui participem*]," so Christ offered the partaking of his own name [*participium sui nominis*] so that the Christian might be named after Him. Hugh of St. Cher's gloss on Colossians 3.10 points out that the name of woman, like her material body, is taken from man; Peter the Chanter notes (p. 62) that *Christianus* is thus derived from *Christus* (see Isidore, *Quaestiones* [*PL* 83:217–18]).

61. Rashi 1:26–27.

62. *De Gen. contra Man.* 2.13 (*PL* 34:206); also see Pseudo-Eucherius, *PL* 50:909. Isidore comments on the differences in meaning between *virgo* and *virago*, in his *Differentiae* (*PL* 83:68) and *Etym.* 11.2.22. His remarks are copied in the later medieval dictionaries of Papias (fol. 196) and Joannes Balbus (fol. 313). Remigius, p. 50, notes that "We call a strong woman [*mulierem fortem*], imitating manly works [*uirilia opera*], a *Virago*" – echoing Isidore's etymology, and pointing to the congruence here of Latin and Hebrew: just as "*uirago* is derived from *uir*," so the Hebrew word for

mulier, issa, comes from the Hebrew word for *uir, is*. "Whence as well *Israel* means a man [*uir*] seeing God."

63. Cf. Jerome's comments in *Hebraicae Quaestiones*, p. 5 (trans. p. 32 and 113–14).

64. Comestor, *PL* 198:1071; Guilelmus Brito, fol. 191 (ed. Daly, 2:837). Also see Trivet, *Chronicles*, B. L. MS Arundel 56, fol. 2ᵛ; and Caxton's *Legenda Aurea*, 1:172: "Adam gave her a name like as her lord, and said she should be called virago, which is as much as to say as made of a man, and is a name taken of a man." Milton recalls this argument in *Paradise Lost*: "woman is her name, of man/ Extracted" (8.496–97).

65. "In quacumque . . . ," ed. Buytaert, p. 180 (also ed. Hauréau, 5:243).

66. Wycliffite Genesis: Forshall-Madden, p. 83. Also see the "Life of Adam and Eue," ed. Horstmann, p. 355; *Mistére du Viel Testament*, 1:34; the Chester *Adam* play (150); and the *Norwich Grocers' Play*: "And *virago* I call hyr in thy presens/ Lyke onto me in natural preemynens" (p. 8, 20–21). The *Bible de la Macé de la Charité* sustains such wordplay in French with "baron" and "barone" (lines 354–56; pp. 16–17), unlike the thirteenth-century *Bible Française* (*virago* from man, *home*) (p. 108) or the twelfth-century translation by Evrat (*virago* from *baron*) (lines 777–78).

67. Isidore, *Differentiae*, *PL* 83:68; Geoffrey le Baker, p. 29.

68. Gerson accordingly praises Christine de Pizan as a "virilis femina" and a "virago" (*Débat*, p. 168); and Christine herself praises Dido, whose name "is the equivalent of saying *virago* in Latin, which means 'the woman who has the strength and force of a man'" (*Cité des Dames*, p. 775; trans. p. 95).

69. Corpus MS 30, fol. 7 (*CCCM* 53, p. 34).

70. *Etym.* 11.2.23. As Klinck, p. 76, notes, such etymological pursuits attempt to "link Latin and Hebrew word-derivation with one another."

71. *ST* 1a.98,1.

72. Alter, *Art*, pp. 142–43, notes the "orderliness of P's vision," with its series of a "balancing of opposites" or "bifurcation producing difference."

73. *Elucidarium* 1.30–31, p. 366.

74. Greene, *Descent*, pp. 380–87, gives a succinct account of the "divergent conceptions of language" at work in Milton's style.

75. One version of the *Cursor Mundi* also registers Satan's name change: see Leonard, p. 89.

76. *Paradise Lost* 9.510–14. This acrostic was discovered by Klemp, p. 91; I learned of his remarkable argument from Leonard, p. 136. Schnapp, "Virgin Words," p. 280, argues that for Dante in the *Commedia*, "acrostic writing reaches backward towards Eden and forward towards Apocalypse," by signalling the "iconic power of the word."

77. Comestor, *PL* 198:1071. Willet's *Hexapla* notes that before the Fall, "Adam called her *Ishah*, as if you would say, Mannesse, as a name of the whole sexe, but here hee calleth her Heuah, as by her proper name" (p. 54). Peter the Chanter comments that *issa* and *Adam* were originally the proper names for the first woman and man, but are now *commune* (p. 58). But the *Histoire Ancienne* (ed. Joslin, p. 82) collapses the two namings into one.

78. Comestor (*PL* 198:1072), naming Bede as his authority, gives this idea great prominence; it derives from the apocryphal legends of Adam (Trapp, p. 262; also see Flores, and Réau, 2:1:84). (Bonnell had argued for an origin in mystery play performances.) The serpent with a maiden's face has many pictorial representations, including the *St. Omer Psalter*, the *Holkham Bible Picture Book*, the *Speculum Humanae Salvationis*, and the *Tres Riches Heures* of the Duc de Berry; in one manuscript, Veronica Sekules notes, "it is wearing the kind of fashionable headdress that would have been worn by a bourgeois lady" (*Age of Chivalry*, p. 41). The image also appears in the Chapter House of Salisbury Cathedral, and a fifteenth-century roof boss in Norwich Cathedral. The *Man of Law's Tale* describes the Sowdanesse as a "serpent under femynynytee" (360); also see *Piers Plowman* 18.337–38 (B text): "Thus ylik a Lusard wiþ a lady visage/ Thefliche þow me robbedest."

79. Guibert of Nogent thus comments on the singular "man" and plural "male and female" of Gen. 1.27, as marking a shift because of sin from identity to "diversity, as humanity was divided in two" (*PL* 156:57). See Javelet, 1:241–43. Milton's modern critics have pointed out that he uses punning and etymological wordplay, "scoffing in ambiguous words" (*Paradise Lost* 6.568), to demarcate the Fall: see Stein, pp. 66–67, on "error"; Fowler's note on *Paradise Lost* 6.566, which quotes Landor: "the first overt crime of the refractory angels was *punning*"; Ricks; Fish; and for the fullest discussion, Leonard. Jager, *Tempter's Voice*, pp. 1 and 3, quotes a Pentateuch commentary attributed to Bede in the *PL*: "The Serpent asked the first question in the world" (*PL* 91:212).

80. Bede says that Adam names her Eve "by divine instinct" (*Hex.*, p. 69), connecting her creation with the creation of Ecclesia, the gate to life, from the side of the crucified Christ (for this Augustinian reading of John 19.34, see for example *De Civ. Dei* 22.17).

81. *De Gen. ad litt.* 11.1.1 (*PL* 34:430).

82. Augustine, *PL* 34:212; Jerome, *Liber Interpr.*, p. 65. Hayward (Jerome, *Hebrew Questions*, pp. 18–19) notes that Jerome, wanting to correct some possibly "inaccurate and misleading" entries in his *Liber Interpretationis*, deleted "calamity or woe" when he discussed Eve's name in the *Hebrew Questions* (*Hebraicae Quaestiones*, p. 6; trans. p. 33 and pp. 117–18).

83. *Middle English Genesis*, p. 60.
84. Luther, fol. 52^v.
85. This sentence could equally well be translated as "calamity took its name from her falling"; or "calamity assumed her name because of its ending"; or "the noun 'calamity' derived from the word 'falling.'" Isidore had used exactly the same sentence to explain the orthographical substitution of "calamitas" for the earlier word "cadamitas" (1.27.14). And he so explains grammatical case [*casus*]: "Casus a cadendo dicti; per eos enim inflexa nomina variantur et cadunt" [Cases are named from "falling" or "ending"; for by them inflected nouns are changed and terminate] (1.7.31).
86. Isidore, *Etym.* 7.6.5–6; copied by Huguccio, fol. 38^v, and Joannes Balbus, fol. 136^v; also see Pseudo-Eucherius, *Interpretationes*, fol. 87^v, and *Commentarii* (*PL* 50:909). Jerome's gloss has wide currency in the later Middle Ages because of these dictionaries and such glossaries as Remigius' *Interpretationes*: "Eua ue uel uita seu calamitas" [*Eva* woe or life or calamity] (fol. 412).
87. Rabanus, *PL* 111:31; Lehmann, p. 53 and p. 108. Alford gives an extensive catalogue of such metaphors. The *De Planctu Naturae* is of course the *locus classicus* for grammatical wordplay: see Ziolkowski, *Grammar of Sex*.
88. Hirn, pp. 520–21, lists many examples of this wordplay on "Eva" and "Ave." Also see Guldan, and Woolf, pp. 115–16. In the famous hymn "Ave, maris stella," the *Ave* from the mouth of Gabriel offers redemption to us, "changing the name of Eve" [*mutans nomen Evae*] (*Oxford Book*, ed. Raby, p. 94). Also see the *Bible de la Macé de la Charité*, lines 360–68 (p. 17), in which *Eve* as the "interjection" woe [*vé*] is broken to pieces [*depeciez*] by *avé*.
89. *In Librum Sapientiae*, lectio CXCV, p. 642.
90. *De Miseria Condicionis Humanae*, pp. 102–3. This explanation of babies' cries comes from Comestor (*PL* 198:1071), who is quoted by Guilelmus Brito, fol. 1^v. Also see Peter the Chanter, p. 74; Stephen Langton, fol. 116^v; and the late thirteenth-century translation of Comestor by Guyart Desmoulins (B. L. MS Harley 4381, fol. 8; B. L. MS Royal 17.E.VII, fols. 7^v–8).
91. Peter Riga, *Aurora*, 1:39 (lines 321–28).
92. I have discussed this issue at greater length in "Man, Men, and Women." Almond, p. 143, quotes William Austin's *Haec Homo*:

> How ill did hee his *Grammar* skan
> that call'd a *Woman woe* to man?
> For (*contrary*) who doth not know,
> *Women* from *men* receive their *woe*?

93. *DVE* 1.4.4.

94. See Genette's discussion of Cratylism, but also the caveats expressed by Robinson, *Essays*, pp. 120–21. Colish, "Stoic Theory," esp. pp. 19–20, discusses Stoic influences on the medieval Plato. Coudert outlines some later speculations on a "natural language."
95. Aristotle, *On Interpretation*, p. 117. McKusick, pp. 34–38, compares Plato's "etymological reduction of nouns to verbs" with Aristotle's opposing view, "that verbs are in fact reducible to nouns," which "must be historically as well as logically prior to verbs" (p. 35). Medieval discussions of Genesis are noun-centered, in part because they inevitably focus on Adam naming the animals.
96. *Noctes Atticae* 10.4 (1:345); Allen, "Ancient Ideas," esp. pp. 40–53, discusses the classical theories; Manetti offers a general overview, as does Robins, pp. 7–8. Boethius' first commentary on *De Interpretatione (Peri Hermeneias)* is especially important (see pp. 45–46, 50, and 59); Engels, "Origine," and Marenbon, pp. 80–83, describe its dissemination. Engels, "Portée," discusses Isidore's meaning, and Curtius, pp. 495–500, his pervasive influence. Rotta's account is still useful; Kretzmann, "History," outlines medieval semantics in detail.
97. I am summarizing Jolivet's account of Abelard's ideas (*Arts du langage*, pp. 72–73).
98. Reynolds, p. 82.
99. Courtenay, "Force of Words," p. 109, n. 8.
100. *De Dialectica* 6, pp. 94–95: quoted and discussed by Pagliaro, "Dottrina linguistica," p. 488.
101. *Metalogicon* 1.14, p. 33; trans. pp. 38–39.
102. Minnis, *Magister Amoris*, p. 142, n. 57, commenting on Bloch's *Etymologies*; also see Zeeman, p. 161, and Myles, pp. 10–11.
103. Vance, *Mervelous Signals*, p. 258.
104. See Reynolds, pp. 45–60.
105. Bloch, *Etymologies*, p. 44.
106. *ST* 1.a.94,3. This reading of Adam's naming of the animals can be traced back ultimately to Philo Judaeus: Dronke, "Creazione," pp. 810–13.
107. Also see Hugh of St. Cher's gloss on Gen. 2.19.
108. Meister Eckhart, 1:336; the editor notes similar passages in John Scotus Erigena and Aquinas.
109. *De Doctrina Christiana* 3.25.
110. Williams, *Common Expositor*, p. 228, records how sixteenth-century commentaries on Genesis note this shift; also see Padley, p. 139.
111. Comestor, *PL* 198:1070. Peter the Chanter, p. 56, makes a nearly identical argument. Cf. Bede (*Hex.*, p. 55); Remigius, p. 48; and Andrew of St. Victor, Corpus MS 30, fol. 6ᵛ (*CCCM* 53:33). Sylvester's *Du Bartas*

(1:433) imagines, wonderfully, Adam's analogous invention of the parts of speech other than nouns: first verbs and then "Small particles, which stand in lieu of strings/ The master members fitly to combine," like plumes on helmets or "Frenges to mantles: eares, and rings to vessels:/ To marble statues; bases, feet, and tressels."

112. *Etym.* 12.6.4. His account is copied by Papias, fol. 114, and "Thomas Aquinas," p. 15.

113. *De Gen. ad Litt.* 9.12 (trans. 2:83–85; *PL* 34:400–1). Abelard addresses this issue in the fortieth of the *Problemata Heloissae* (*PL* 178:721–22), and in "In quacumque," ed. Buytaert, pp. 177–78.

114. Adelard of Bath, *De Eodem et Diverso*, pp. 35–37; the quoted description is from Reynolds, pp. 46–48. Adelard's remarks are very close in spirit to much later texts such as Wilson's preface to his *Arte of Rhetorique*.

115. Cf. Eco, *Search*, pp. 34–52.

116. *DVE* 1.9.6.

117. An eloquent later statement of the mutability of language and instability of the human mind appears in Johnson's "Preface to the *Dictionary*," as he gives up the illusory hope that his work might give fixity to the English language in a sublunary world of "corruption and decay" (pp. 293–94). Even so, "It remains that we retard what we cannot repel, that we palliate what we cannot cure. Life may be lengthened by care, though death cannot be ultimately defeated: tongues, like governments, have a natural tendency to degeneration; we have long preserved our constitution, let us make some struggles for our language" (p. 296).

118. *De Cat. Rudibus* 2.3; p. 122. Rist, p. 37, summarizes Augustine's view of our self-division and lack of self-knowledge: "Since our linguistic signs convey ambiguous beliefs, for that reason alone they must be less than fully effective."

119. See Marenbon, pp. 128–30, and Chenu, "Un cas," pp. 666–68.

120. Priscian, *Institutiones* 2.18 and 2.22, in *Grammatici Latini*, 2:1:55–57; Anselm, *Monologion* 31 (p. 126). Robinson, *Essays*, p. 106, notes that "the *Cratylus* deals only with the relation of the name to the thing, and never discusses or even mentions the relation of the name to the thought."

121. *De Interpretatione* 1.16a. Derrida, *Grammatology*, p. 11, discusses the implications of this passage; also see McKeon's articles on "Aristotle's Conception," and the clarifications by Broadie, pp. 6–7. The second version of Boethius' *Commentary* (ed. 1880), pp. 20–43, translates *De Interpr.* 1.16a; but Kretzmann, "Aristotle," p. 5, argues that Boethius, by translating both "symbol" and "sign" as *notae*, obscures a significant terminological distinction in Aristotle's text. Cf. Aquinas' translation: "voces sunt signa

intellectuum, et intellectus sunt rerum similitudines" [words are signs for thoughts and thoughts are likenesses of things] (*ST* 1.a.13,1).

122. Augustine makes a similar point: that the impressions (*uestigia*) of intellect upon the memory, which are themselves universally human, may form intelligible signs that are unique to particular languages (*De Cat. Rudibus* 2.3; p. 122).

123. Arthur, p. 11, mentions the fourteenth-century debate on whether words signify things directly or their mental images; for the details, see Maurer and Tabarroni. Pinborg describes the shift in English logic from a modistic approach, which assumes "that language, thought, and things are isomorphic with one another" (p. 21), to a sense that *suppositio*, "propositional knowledge alone, in a world of changing objects, has the properties of necessity and unchangeability required for the objects of science" (p. 36). On Ockham in particular, see Spade, p. 47, and especially Maurer, p. 796: concepts for Ockham are "the primary and natural signs of things," whereas words, both written and spoken, "are only secondary signs," with written words inferior to spoken. Elsky's first chapter surveys these issues as they impinge on sixteenth and seventeenth-century concerns.

124. Augustine, *De Ordine*, 2.12.35 (pp. 138–39), and 1.9.27 (pp. 52–53). Also see Isidore, *Etym.* 1.3.1; Ziolkowski, *Grammar of Sex*, p. 143, cites a twelfth-century statement on the civilizing effect of writing.

125. As in the *Phaedrus*: see Friedländer, pp. 110–15. Southern, *Platonism*, p. 19n., quotes "a striking expression of the superior authority of the living presence to the written word," in the *Sententiae* of Robert of Melun: "For what else is writing than a certain image and obscure figure of the will of its writer?" For the Latin text see Southern, *Saint Anselm*, p. 334n.

126. Kirwan, p. 54, comments on *De Dialectica* 5 (pp. 88–89), *De Magistro* 4.8 (in *Augustine: Earlier Writings*, p. 75), and *De Doctrina Christiana* 2.4. In *Enarr. in Psalmos* 44.4–7 (A.V. 45) (pp. 496–99), the difference between speech and writing serves as an analogy for the difference between God's Word and man's. (See Irvine, *Making*, pp. 172–89, and Colish, "Rhetoric of Silence," pp. 19–20.) Kretzmann, "Aristotle," p. 12, notes that convention is more clearly evident in "written marks than spoken sounds," citing Aquinas: "It is not only that the principle of their signifying is by imposition, but also that the formation of them is a production of art. Spoken sounds, on the other hand, are formed naturally, and so some men have raised the question as to whether they signify naturally" (*In Aristotelis Libros Peri Hermeneias . . . Expositio*, p. 11). Unsurprisingly, as Jager notes (*Tempter's Voice*, p. 61), in patristic commentary "the Fall marked a transition from the spoken to the written," and writing is thus "a

phenomenon of the fallen world." Also see his "Did Eve Invent Writing?,"
and Householder.

127. Vincent of Beauvais, *Speculum Naturale*, 25.57, in *Speculum Quadruplex*,
1:1811.

128. *DVE* 1.3. I will quote this passage in full in Chapter 3.

129. Augustine, *Enarr. in Psalmos* 38.7 (p. 409; trans. 2:106). In a similar vein,
see *Confessions* 4.10–11 and the other relevant quotations collected by
Vance, "Saint Augustine." Abelard notes that we can understand a phrase
only when it is finished, by using a sort of immediate memory, for "a
phrase has meaning only when all of its parts have disappeared" (Jolivet,
Arts du langage, p. 26).

130. *De Cat. Rudibus* 2.3.

131. Jackson, p. 27; Rist, p. 37. Hugh of St. Victor will argue that language is
in fact a consequence of the Fall: *De Archa Noe*, pp. 95–96. Cf. Nichols,
"Prophetic Discourse," pp. 54–58, for Augustine's account of carnal, material language in the Old Testament. In *De Civ. Dei* 13.11, Augustine finds
it significant that the verb *moritur* [he dies] is indeclinable, though with
the help of divine Grace we may "decline . . . that second death."

132. *De Civ. Dei* 22.29; see Jager, *Tempter's Voice*, p. 54.

133. *In Ecclesiasten Homiliae*, no. 13 (*PL* 175:204); quoted by Lubac, 2:1:187–
88, as part of his discussion of the *Verbum Abbreviatum*, the conventional
idea that the multiplicity of human words collapses into the one Word
of Christ. Also see the end of Augustine's *De Trin.* (15.28, par. 51; trans.
pp. 436–37), which meditates on Proverbs 10.19, "In the multitude of
words there shall not want sin."

134. *Confessions* 13.23; trans. p. 342. Such multiplicity has its good effects, as
Augustine hastens to affirm (13.24): "For example, the single idea of love
of God and our neighbor is expressed in countless symbols and countless
tongues, and in each tongue by innumerable modes of speech" (trans.
Sheed, pp. 328–29). On these issues of language and communication see
Alici, pp. 126–37.

135. Augustine, *Enarr. in Psalmos* 93.6 (pp. 1305–6; trans. 4:349). See Mazzeo,
"Rhetoric of Silence," esp. p. 9: "This movement from words to silence,
from signs to realities, is the fundamental presupposition of Augustinian
allegorical exegesis"; but Colish, "Rhetoric of Silence," pp. 15–16, expresses
some hesitations about this argument.

136. *Sermones de Diversis, PL* 183:736. Trans. by Gallacher, p. 25.

137. Bonaventure, *Expositio in Quatuor Libros Sententiarum*, lib. I, Dist. XXII,
quaest. II; quoted by Rotta, p. 248.

138. For references in Augustine's works, see Marrou, *Saint Augustin*, p. 349;
and Johnson, p. 31. See especially *De Magistro* 10.33, 11.36, and 9.25–27:

"the knowledge of things is preferable to knowledge of their signs" (trans. p. 89). In *De Doctrina Christiana* 2.13, Augustine argues that solecisms and barbarisms are not especially important, because things are more important than signs (pp. 77–79). Jager, *Tempter's Voice*, p. 58, notes that his frequent reference to words as "vessels" for ideas suggests "that verbal signs should be mediating instruments rather than ends in themselves."

139. *Didascalicon* 5.3, p. 121.

140. Jolivet, *Arts du langage*, p. 76 and p. 32.

141. *Policraticus*, 2:41.

142. *De Magistro* 11.36; trans. pp. 94–95. See Markus, "St. Augustine," and Marrou, *Saint Augustin*, p. 292; also see *Confessions* 10.11.

143. *Tractatus*, p. 574.

144. *De Libero Arbitrio* 3.20; trans. p. 202.

145. *Confessions* 13.25; trans. p. 345.

146. Jager, *Tempter's Voice*, p. 89, comments: "Making feelings intelligible requires making them 'sensible' in the form of signs, and the signs crossing the gap between inside [*intus*] and outside [*foris*] reflect the various kinds of alienation – of soul from body, of will from desire, of knowledge from intellect – that are among the most divisive legacies of the Fall."

147. Mazzeo, "Rhetoric of Silence," p. 21, notes the significance of Augustine's silent reading; Augustine of course coined the word "soliloquy." The authoritative discussion of this episode is Courcelle, *Confessions*, pp. 137–63.

148. Augustine is echoing such warnings as Cicero's, at the beginning of *De Inventione*, on the dangers of eloquence without wisdom – quoted by Holkot, *In Librum Sapientiae*, lectio C, p. 340. Holkot cites Augustine, Cicero, and Seneca (*Epistle* 112) on this point. McKeon, "Rhetoric," pp. 6–7, comments on Augustine's "dialectical doubling" of Cicero's terms, with the effect that "the wisdom and eloquence of the world are to be contrasted with the eternal wisdom and eloquence."

149. William of Conches rehearses the frequent argument that the *divina pagina* "is not subject to the rules of grammar" (Jeauneau, "Deux rédactions," p. 240).

150. *Epistola* 22.29, in *Jerome: Select Letters*, p. 124. Jerome's famous dream immediately follows, in which he is confronted with the charge: "You are a Ciceronian, not a Christian" [*Ciceronianus es, non Christianus*]. For a general discussion of this issue, see Marrou, *Saint Augustin*, pp. 469–77.

151. Cassirer, pp. 81–82.

152. The *Compendium Historiae* is meant to accompany and sum up the *Historia Scholastica*; it often appears independently. See Moore, pp. 97–110,

and Monroe. The clarity and visual force of the summary are apparent in B. L. MS Royal 8.C.IX, fol. 3, and B. L. MS Cott. Faust. B.VII, fol. 45. The *Compendium* often appears in the form of a roll: see B. L. MSS Royal 14.B.IX, Add. 14819, and Add. 24025.

153. Philo, 2:94–97.
154. Shereshevsky, p. 274.
155. Philo, 2:354–57; also see 4:76–79, on the descent of the Tower's builders "from the depravity which is ever dying and never dead, whose name is Cain"; see Quinones, pp. 28–33.
156. E.g., Milton's *Of Education*, pp. 366–67.
157. *Didascalicon* 2.1, p. 61 (also see 1.5, p. 52); the preface to Huguccio's dictionary makes a similar claim. Peter Lombard is quoted by Curtius, p. 556. Du Bartas particularly praises Adam's mastery of eloquence (Fowler's notes to *Paradise Lost*, p. 262). Also see John Cassian, *Conferences* 8.21.
158. Southern, *Scholastic Humanism*, p. 10. The passage from Remigius is quoted by Copeland, *Rhetoric, Hermeneutics, and Translation*, p. 74.
159. Wyclif, p. 495.
160. *Didascalicon* 1.8–9, p. 55; see Chenu, "Civilisation," and for Hugh's views on "the growth of the human sciences," Southern, "Aspects," pp. 170–72. As Camille, *Gothic Idol*, p. 40, observes, these aprons are "the very first art objects in human existence." See Ovitt, and O'Connell, p. 72: "the origin of artistic activity, indeed of all man's symbolic activity . . . emerges from the soul's 'fallen' state." Galloway discusses Chaucer's "*Former Age*" within the later fourteenth-century context for these ideas.
161. Comestor, *PL* 198:1078.
162. I quote with permission from Harvard, fMS Eng 938, p. 2. For the French text, see B. L. MS Arundel 56, fol. 2ᵛ; and cf. *Middle English Genesis*, lines 433–40. Caxton's *Legenda Aurea*, 1:178, offers an explanation for Cain's walls: "dreading them that he hurted, for surety he brought his people into the towns." See Dean's entries on "Cain" and "Mark of Cain," which is "sometimes interpreted as writing," in Jeffrey's *Dictionary*.
163. *Jewish Antiquities* 1.2.2; for the Latin text see *The Latin Josephus*. This account of Cain also appears in the *Polychronicon* (2:227), where it immediately precedes the story of Lamech and his children. Augustine, *De Civ. Dei* 15.5 and 15.8, discusses Cain as the first city-builder. One of the Bohun Psalters, Exeter College, Oxford, MS 47, contains a miniature [Plate I (b) in James & Millar] of Cain inventing weights and measures. Williams, *Cain and Beowulf*, p. 22, argues persuasively that these are considered evil because, like boundaries and cities, they exemplify division: all "define by negation and exclusion and introduce self-consciousness, the very evil experienced by Adam and Eve when they chose 'to know.'" Cf. Lucretius,

5.1440–57, where city walls and the parcelling out of land are among the arts of civilization.

164. Copeland, *Rhetoric, Hermeneutics, and Translation*, esp. p. 215 and pp. 219–20. Also see Lusignan, *Parler Vulgairement*, p. 52, and Stillinger, pp. 74–79.

165. Borst, II/2, pp. 931–52, reproduces several lists of the seventy-two languages, from the third century to the seventeenth. Weigand focuses on such lists in medieval German literature.

166. The two Lamechs are sometimes confused, as in chapter 13 of *Mandeville's Travels*, p. 77. *John Capgrave's Abbreuiacion of Cronicles*, p. 17, distinguishes between them: "on was of þe kynrod of Cayn and he broute in first bigamie; the oþir was of þe kynrod of Seth and he was fader to Noe."

167. Goulburn, p. 22, cites this as "the only extant specimen of Antediluvian Poetry."

168. Jerome mentions the story, citing "a certain Hebrew book," in a letter to Pope Damasus (*Epistola* 36; *PL* 22:455); and it also appears in Isidore (*Etym.* 7.6.14), who offers the standard etymological explanation of Lamech's name: *percutiens* [striking down], "For he struck down and killed Cain." (Cf. Jerome, *Liber Interpr.*, p. 68.) The legend appears in early Jewish and Christian apocryphal writings: e.g., *The Book of Adam and Eve*, p. 122; *The Book of the Cave of Treasures*, pp. 78–79; *Hebrew Myths*, pp. 108–10; and Ginzberg, 1:116–17 and 5:146–47. These works were not well known in the medieval West; but see Kaske, and also Day's introduction to EETS o.s. 155 (1921), pp. xxii–xxxiii, on Latin and Middle English versions. Ambrosiaster, writing about the same time as Jerome, says that the story cannot be true because Lamech lived five generations later than Cain (pp. 29–30).

169. *Commentarie*, pp. 152–53. Luther, pp. 67–68, and "Thomas Aquinas," p. 28, have similar reactions to the story. Not all late responses are skeptical: see Kircher, *Arca Noë*, p. 13.

170. Among them Pseudo-Methodius, in the work translated by John Trevisa as "þe Bygynnyng of þe World . . . ," p. 96; Bede (*Hex.*, pp. 86 and 90); Alcuin (*PL* 100:526); Honorius Augustodunensis, *Imago Mundi* 3.1, p. 125; and Andrew of St. Victor, fol. 9 (*CCCM* 53:43). Several of these works copy Jerome in mentioning the Jewish tradition: Haimo of Auxerre (*PL* 131:72); Bruno de Segni (*PL* 164:175); Gilbertus Universalis, fol. 14; and the *Glossa Ordinaria* (*PL* 113:101). When Hugh of St. Victor refers in his *Notulae* (*PL* 175:44) to the "ancient opinion of the Jews," he may in fact be referring to Rashi (Smalley, *Study of the Bible*, p. 104).

171. *PL* 198:1079; see Morey, "Peter Comestor," pp. 13–14. Comestor adds the detail (perhaps from Jewish tradition, according to Shereshevsky, pp. 273–74) that Lamech was hunting for delight, and to obtain fur, since human

beings were not carnivorous before the Flood. Among the offshoots of his narrative are Peter Riga, 1:46–47; Vincent of Beauvais, *Speculum Historiale* 1.56; Nicholas de Gorran, fol. 18; the *Middle English Genesis*, lines 471–84, and *Cursor Mundi*, lines 1513–14; Caxton's *Legenda Aurea*, 1:179; Boccaccio, *De Casibus* 1.1 (pp. 16–17); and Trevisa's *Polychronicon*, 2:229. The story also appears in the glosses of Hugh of St. Cher and Nicholas of Lyra, the Cornish *Creacion of the World*, and a play in the *N-Town* cycle: see Emerson, pp. 874–77; Reiss, "Lamech"; and Spector's note to his edition of the play (2:424).

172. *Holkham Bible Picture Book*, pp. 70–71; Egerton 1894, fol. 3; Cockerell gives further references. Also see the *St. Omer Psalter*; *Bohun Psalter*, fol. 40; and *Omne Bonum*, 2:82. There are a number of Continental examples, listed by Mâle, and Réau, 2:1, plate 6 and pp. 99–100.

173. On Lamech's relation to Cain and Cain's city, see, for example, Pseudo-Eucherius, *PL* 50:923. The seventy-seven fold curse is glossed by Isidore, *Allegoriae* (*PL* 83:101); Bede, *In Lucae Evangelium*, pp. 90–93; and the *Glossa*, *PL* 113:101.

174. Alcuin, *PL* 100:523.

175. *De Civ. Dei* 15.17 and 15.20; Isidore, *Quaestiones* (*PL* 83:229); Bede, *Hex.*, pp. 88–89; Guibert of Nogent, *PL* 156:84; and the *Glossa*, *PL* 113:101–2.

176. *De Civ. Dei* 15.17; Isidore, *Quaestiones* (*PL* 83:227).

177. Jerome, *Adv. Jov.* 1.14 (*PL* 23:233) (paraphrased in a Latin marginal gloss to the *Wife of Bath's Prologue* 54–56), comments on Lamech's bigamy: "At the beginning one rib was turned into one wife . . . Lamech, a bloody and homicidal man, was the first who divided one flesh into two wives. The same punishment of the cataclysm abolished fratricide and digamy." Also see Comestor (*PL* 198:1078), Vincent of Beauvais, *Speculum Historiale* 1.57, and Caxton's *Legenda*, 1:178 (all of which say that Lamech's bigamy was also the first adultery); Nicholas de Gorran, fol. 17ᵛ; and Nicholas of Lyra's gloss. Stephen Langton, fol. 117, excuses Jacob's bigamy and differentiates it from Lamech's. In *Mistére du Viel Testament*, 1:190, Lamech realizes that he will never again have any rest, because his two wives will constantly remind him of his double homicide (lines 4961–69). Cf. Stanton's mordant comments in *The Woman's Bible*, Part 1, pp. 29–30.

178. Chaucer's epithet "shrewed" is very close to Trevisa's phrasing in *Polychronicon* 2:227: "Lamech, þe seuenþe from Adam and most schrewe, was þe firste þat brouȝte yn bygamye, and so spousebreche aȝenst þe lawe of God and of kynde, and aȝenst Goddis owne dome."

179. In Leach's structuralist sketch of Genesis, "the Tree of Death is called the 'Tree of Knowledge of Good and Evil' which might also be called the 'knowledge of sexual difference,' or the 'knowledge of logical categories.'"

The theme is repeated: isolated unitary categories such as man alone, life alone, one river, occur only in ideal Paradise; in the real world things are multiple and divided; man needs a partner, woman; life has a partner, death" (p. 394). Williams, *Cain and Beowulf*, pp. 28–35, and Dean, *World Grown Old*, pp. 127–34, discuss Lamech's children, the confusion of Ham and Cain, and the line of descent to Nimrod. Hugh of St. Victor, *Didascalicon* 3.2, pp. 83–86, provides a more general view of the "Authors of the Arts," pagan as well as Biblical.

180. Egerton 1894, fol. 2ᵛ. Skinner, p. 119, in a reading that is at odds with early commentaries, suggests that the children of Adah [meaning the Dawn?] invent the better side of civilization, represented by music and shepherds, while Zillah [the shadow] is the mother of the more sinister, or at least more ambiguous Tubalcain and Naamah.

181. Comestor, *PL* 198:1079; *Middle English Genesis*, line 458; Jerome, *Liber Interpr.*, p. 67.

182. Comestor, *PL* 198:1079; Jerome, *Liber Interpr.*, p. 67. In the *Legenda Aurea*, Jubal is "the finder of music, that is to say of consonants of accord, such as shepherds use in their delights and sports" (1:178).

183. *Polychronicon*, 2:229; Comestor, *PL* 198:1079. Peter Comestor in fact appropriates the story of Pythagoras' discovery and assigns it to Jubal (Young, p. 301). Also see Beichner, *Jubal or Tubalcain?*, pp. 10–15.

184. Young, p. 300, notes that Chaucer's details here owe more to Comestor or Vincent of Beauvais than to the *Aurora*.

185. *Jewish Antiquities*, 1.2.3; *Polychronicon*, trans. Trevisa, 2:223–25. Also see *Cursor Mundi* 1469, and Honorius Augustodunensis, *Imago Mundi* 3.1, p. 124. Otto of Freising, quoting Josephus, assigns the work of pillar-building to the Sethites: see *The Two Cities* (1.2), p. 124 (and Josephus 1.68–71; LCL, p. 33); so does the Cornish *Creacion* play, 2182ff., and Sylvester's *Du Bartas* 1:468–69.

186. Jubal constructs the two pillars, according to the *Glossa*, *PL* 113:101, copying Isidore's *Chronica*, pp. 17–18; Comestor (*PL* 198:1079); Peter of Poitiers, B. L. MS Royal 8.C.IX, fol. 3; Peter Riga, *Aurora* 469–76; Stephen Langton, fol. 117; Matthew Paris, *Chronica* 1:4; Trivet's *Annales*, fol. 3ᵛ; and the *Golden Legend* (1:179). (The story also appears in the metrical translation of Methodius' *Revelations*, lines 167–98.) In the *Middle English Genesis*, the "pillars" are called "tables" (461), as they also are in a late fourteenth-century English version of the apocryphal "Life of Adam and Eve" (ed. Horstmann, p. 135; also see EETS o.s. 155, pp. 97–98). In the *Cursor Mundi*, they are the work of Lamech's sons (1533–40); in *Mistére du Viel Testament*, 1:221–22, specifically Tubal (i.e., Tubalcain) and Jubal.

187. *Second Conference of Abbot Serenus* in *Conférences*, 2.30–31; trans. Williams, *Cain and Beowulf*, p. 35. Also see Arnaud of Bonneval's preface to his *Hexameron*, which describes the invention and corruption of the arts, and the disappearance of almost all earlier writing in the Flood, to preface a discussion of Moses as the author of the Pentateuch.

188. See Pseudo-Methodius, trans. Trevisa, p. 96, and Beichner, *Jubal or Tubalcain?* The confusion is understandable: in the *Latin Josephus*, Jabel, Jubal, and Tubalcain are all named "Iobel." In the Cornish *Creacion* play, Jabel and Tubal mock Noah for his piety (2295–409).

189. Ed. D'Evelyn, lines 153–54 (p. 160).

190. See *The Book of the Cave of Treasures*, pp. 87–91, which castigates the devilish powers of music; Philo is less severe (2:388–89).

191. Josephus, *Jewish Antiquities* 1.2.2 (also see Philo, 2:392–97); *Glossa*, PL 113:101; Comestor, PL 198:1079; Peter Riga, *Aurora* 477–80.

192. Jerome, *Liber Interpr.*, p. 73; Rashi 1:45. Alter, *Genesis*, p. 16, notes that "Cain" literally means "smith," which "Tubal" also means in Sumerian and Akkadian. Lord notes that in an illustration for the *Ovide Moralisé*, Tubalcain takes part in forging the Cross, and that in the *Speculum Humanae Salvationis* he makes nails for the Cross.

193. Comestor (PL 198:1079); Caxton's *Legenda*, 1:179; also see Higden's *Polychronicon*, 2:227.

194. Jerome, *Liber Interpr.*, p. 69, says that "Noema" means "beauty, or pleasure, or faith" [*decus siue uoluptas uel fides*].

195. There is a late reference to this story in Charles Churchill's *The Ghost* (*Poetical Works*, p. 118):

> For, from the time that JUBAL first
> Sweet ditties to the harp rehears'd,
> *Poets* have always been suspected
> Of having Truth in Rhime neglected.
> (3.495–98)

196. *Glossa*, PL 113:101; Bede, *Hex.*, p. 87.

197. *Book of the Knight of the Tower*, p. 70; also see p. 73.

198. *Mistére du Viel Testament* identifies Noema, Sella, and Ada as the "daughters of men" who fornicate with the "sons of God," i.e., the descendants of Seth: 1:203–15; also see the *Glossa*, PL 113:104; Comestor, PL 198:1081–82; and *Polychronicon*, 2:231. The *Mistére* also describes (1:226–28) the deaths of Ada, Sella, Noema, Tubal, and Jubal in the Flood, in which Lamech himself, in some accounts, also died (Honorius Augustodunensis, *De Imagine Mundi*, PL 172:165). On sexual license as the primary cause of God's wrath, see *Cleanness*, lines 250–83, and the *Parson's Tale*

838. Some of the rabbinical texts, including Rashi's, confusingly identify Noema as Noah's wife (Mellinkoff, pp. 190–91). In one apocryphal myth, from Adam's union with Lilith the "demoness, and with another like her named Naamah, Tubal Cain's sister, sprang Asmodeus and innumerable demons that still plague mankind" (*Hebrew Myths*, p. 65).

199. Hugh of St. Victor, *Selected Spiritual Writings*, p. 47 (*De Archa Noe*, p. 5). Cf. Milton, *Paradise Lost* 11:609–12: "studious they appear/ Of arts that polish life, inventors rare, / Unmindful of their maker, though his Spirit/ Taught them, but they his gifts acknowledged none."

200. *Speculum Historiale* 1.57. See esp. Gregory the Great, *Moralia* 9.11.12 (trans. 1:503), on "spoiling the Egyptians" as a model for appropriating the arts: he glosses Job 9.9 – which names Arcturus, Orion, and the Hyades – as an example of how Scripture makes use of names "invented by the votaries of carnal wisdom. . . Thus in Holy Writ the wise ones of God derive their speech from the wise ones of the world, in like sort as therein God the very Creator of man, for man's benefit, takes in Himself the tones of human passion," as happens in Genesis 6.

201. Bede, *Hex.,* pp. 87–88.

202. For Chaucer's relation to medieval Biblical exegesis, see Besserman, *Chaucer and the Bible*, and also his *Biblical Poetics*.

203. *Ecloga Theoduli*, lines 85–92; see Dronke, *Dante*, p. 136, n. 48. Nimrod the giant, as in *Inferno* 31, comes from the phrasing of the Septuagint and Vetus Latina versions of Genesis: Jerome substitutes "potens" and "robustus" for their "gigans." See Jerome, *Hebraicae Quaestiones*, p. 13 (trans. pp. 40–41 and 142); and also Menner, p. 122; Bede, *Hex.,* pp. 144–45; Comestor, *PL* 198:1088; Dronke, *Dante*, p. 39; and Stephens, pp. 67–84. The Hereford Mappamundi has a caption "Babilonia a *nembroth* gigante fundata" [Babylon founded by Nimrod the giant], and Ælfric's sermon "In Die Sancto Pentecosten," p. 358, describes how *entas* [giants] built the Tower.

204. Cf. Derrida's amusing pirouette around the proper name Babel ("Des Tours de Babel," pp. 166–67; French text, pp. 210–11).

205. Augustine, *De Doctrina Christiana* 2.4, pp. 60–61. Boccaccio's chapter on Nimrod in his *De Casibus* describes the alienation of minds that accompanied the confusion of tongues (1.3; pp. 22–23).

206. See, for example, Josephus, *Jewish Antiquities* 1.4.2, Augustine, *De Civ. Dei* 16.4, and Isidore, *Etym.* 7.6.22. Dean, *World Grown Old*, pp. 134–39, summarizes the commentaries on Nimrod's hunting and tyranny.

207. In the metrical commentary on Genesis by Donizo of Canossa, Nimrod as hunter lures human minds "to the punishments of the abyss" (lines

253–54; p. 32). Cf. Rabanus Maurus (*PL* 107:528) on the term "hunter": "What is meant by this name, if not a deceiver of earth-born beings, and one catching men towards their death?"

208. *Etym.* 15.1.3–4.

209. Friedman, *Monstrous Races*, p. 100, and Mellinkoff, pp. 194–95. The *Parson's Tale* 766 says that "the name of thraldom" was never known before Ham's time (Genesis 9). Otto of Freising revises the Biblical account to emphasize the continuity of the "two cities," from Seth to Noah's line and from Cain to Ham's (Friedman, *Monstrous Races*, p. 236, n. 55); also see Bede, *Hex.*, p. 144, and Honorius Augustodunensis, *Speculum Ecclesiae*, *PL* 172:1094. In the *Ovide Moralisé* 2408–24 (15:113), copying Comestor (*PL* 198:1090) and Vincent of Beauvais (*Speculum Historiale* 1.101, p. 37), the pillars of marble and clay, meant to survive flood and fire, which are attributed to Jubal in most accounts, are described as Cham's work; and Cham is identified with Zoroaster. Lutz comments on the origins of the story, which also appears in Hugh of St. Victor's *Notulae* (*PL* 175:49), and the confusion of these columns with Jubal's.

210. Osbern of Gloucester, fol. 13.

211. *Collation* 15.1–2 (pp. 217–18).

212. Jerome, *Liber Interpr.*, p. 69; his etymology is copied by Isidore, *Etym.* 7.6.22, and explained at length by Bede (*Hex.*, p. 146).

213. Rupert of Deutz (*PL* 167:366), in part copied from Isidore, *Etym.* 7.6.22. Also see Hugh of St. Victor (*PL* 175:49); John of Salisbury, *Policraticus* 1.4 (1:27); and Trevisa's *Polychronicon* (2:251): "Nemprot, a stronge huntere of men, þat is, a tyraunt vppon men." Tyranny itself, in one apocryphal account, becomes subject to fragmentation after the division of tongues: "And when they were thus divided, they had over them seventy-two rulers, one to every tongue, and to every country, by way of a king" (*The Book of Adam and Eve*, p. 173).

214. Isidore, *Etym.* 18.1.1; and Hugh of St. Victor, *Didascalicon*, p. 85.

215. Philippe de Mézières, *Letter to King Richard II*, pp. 56–59 and 129–33.

216. Leonard, p. 54, notes Milton's irony: that Nimrod, who with the other builders of the Tower hopes "to make our name famous" (Gen. 11.4), is pointedly not referred to by name.

217. *Sibyllinische Texte*, pp. 63–65; John Trevisa's English translation (EETS o.s. 167, pp. 97–99) names Ionithus as Nimrod's father. The much more obscure *Liber Nimrod* is discussed at length by Livesey & Rouse; also see Haskins, pp. 336–45, and the excursus in Dronke, *Dante*, pp. 112–17. According to the *Histoire Ancienne* (ed. Joslin, p. 104), Ionitus devised the first astrolabe. See Smithers' extensive note (pp. 155–56).

218. See James, *Illustrations*, pp. 7–8 and 31. Réau, 2:1:120–23, lists other visual representations of the tower.

219. Holkot, *In Librum Sapientiae*, lectio CXXVII, p. 427, citing Comestor (*PL* 198:1088), discusses Ionithus as the inventor of astronomy, though not in connection with Nimrod. The two of them both appear in Vincent of Beauvais, *Speculum Historiale* 1.61 (p. 24).

220. *Didascalicon*, p. 84. Gower, *Confessio Amantis*, 2:272 (7.1451–53), names "Ychonithon" as Nembrot's disciple.

221. Dronke, *Dante*, p. 46, describes Comestor's version of the story, in which astrology "is not pure research," but a look into the future for a prospective "world-conqueror. Ionithus outlines the future empires of the world to Nimrod, and thus the giant, prepared, sets about acquiring kingdoms by trickery." Isidore, *Quaestiones*, *PL* 83:237, compares Nimrod's presumption to Satan's. Also see the *Glossa*, *PL* 113:113; Peter Riga, *Aurora*, lines 689–706; and John of Salisbury, *Policraticus* 7.2 (vol. 2:94).

222. *Histoire Universelle*, fol. 12ᵛ: "Il parla caldeu lengage qui auant auoit parle ebreu" [He spoke the Chaldaean language who before had spoken Hebrew]; and Brunetto Latini, *Li Livres dou Tresor*, p. 35: "Nembrot meismes mua sa langhe de ebreu en caldeu" [This same Nimrod changed his tongue from Hebrew to Chaldaean].

223. Haimo of Auxerre names Nimrod as the first fire-worshipper (*PL* 131:80). The story has apocryphal origins: see *The Book of the Cave of Treasures*, pp. 142–43, and Ginzberg, 5:200–1. One of Gower's Latin notes to the *Confessio Amantis*, Book Five, states: "And note that Nimrod the fourth from Noah first decreed that fire be worshipped as a God in Chaldaea" (Gower 1:423). On the origins of idolatry in Babel, where Nimrod and then Ninus ruled, see Honorius' *Elucidarium* 2.75–76, pp. 433–34. According to Isidore's *Chronica*, p. 29, Ninus also invented war and armaments.

224. *Recognitions* 1.30 (*PG* 1:1224–25); *Chronica*, p. 24.

225. *Notulae* (*PL* 175:49). Many medieval texts describe Nimrod's compelling other men to worship fire. See Comestor (*PL* 198:1088); Peter of Poitiers' *Compendium* (as in the roll B. L. MS Royal 14.B.IX); *Histoire Universelle*, fol. 12ᵛ; Vincent of Beauvais, *Speculum Historiale* 1.100 (p. 37); Brunetto Latini, *Li Livres dou Tresor*, p. 35; Egerton 1894, fol. 5, which shows Nimrod the giant tyrannizing over other men, and compelling them to worship fire; Trevisa's *Polychronicon*, p. 251; Guido da Pisa, p. 639.

226. For Ninus' idolatrous images of Belus, see Isidore, *Etym.* 8.11.23 and *Chronica*, p. 28, which notes that some people identified Belus with Saturn; *Middle English Genesis*, lines 675–97; *Histoire Ancienne* (ed. Joslin,

p. 127); Trivet, *Chronicles*, fol. 4; Gower, *Confessio Amantis* 5.1541–58 (in *Works* 1:444); and Trevisa's *Polychronicon*, p. 279.

227. *Recognitions, PG* 1:1327.

228. *Mandeville's Travels*, p. 25 (also see p. 146). The confusion of Nimrod with Ninus also appears in *Cursor Mundi*, lines 2289–90. The *Legenda Aurea* (1:187) describes Nimrod as "the first man that found mawmetry and idolatry, which endured long and yet doth."

229. *Glossa* (*PL* 113:115): "freed by the aid of God, he escaped from the idolatry of fire." See Rappoport, 1:246–53; and Rupert of Deutz, *PL* 167:368. Nicholas of Lyra specifically names Nimrod as the Chaldaean leader who orders Abraham's death. According to Livesey and Rouse, p. 234, he takes this embellishment "from the Midrash on Gen. 11.28, which he has taken from Rashi." Also see *Mistére du Viel Testament*, 1:280.

230. Boccaccio, *De Mulieribus Claris* (p. 126; trans. p. 60).

231. The first translation of *Polychronicon*, 2:278–79 is Trevisa's; the second is from B. L. MS Harley 2261.

232. *De Genealogia Deorum* 14.8 (trans. Osgood, p. 43).

233. Deschamps, *Balade DCCCCLXI*, line 25, in *Œuvres Complètes* 5:189.

234. Augustine argues in *De Musica* 6.41 that even apart from the confusion of tongues at Babel, God has limited the powers of human tyranny by allowing human beings to communicate with each other only indirectly, that is, by signs; see Jackson, p. 27, and Rist, p. 36.

235. The most exhaustive treatment of the story is in Borst; there is also much of interest in Steiner, and Eco, *Search*.

236. Moir, p. 13. Toynbee, p. 111, notes that Dante's understanding of the name Babel (in *De Vulgari Eloquentia* and *Epistola* 7.8) apparently comes from Huguccio: "*Babel* means 'confusion,' whence Babylon or Babylonia the city from the confusion of tongues."

237. See the facsimile of the *Speculum Humanae Salvationis*, chapter XXXIV; and cf. James, "Pictor," p. 164.

238. *Glossa, PL* 114:430–31.

239. *Glossa, PL* 113:114. This gloss copies Isidore's *Quaestiones* (*PL* 83:237–38). The primary source for these ideas is Augustine, *De Civ. Dei* 16.4; also see *In Ioannis Evangelium* 6.10 (*PL* 35:1429–30). (See "Babel," in Jeffrey, p. 67.) Bede, *Hex.*, pp. 152 and 161, describes division as manifested by heretics and schismatics; also see Dante, *DVE* 1.7.

240. *Book of the Cave of Treasures*, p. 132. The *Book of Jubilees*, p. 28, summarizes early Jewish arguments in favor of Hebrew, and others in favor of Syriac or Greek, as the first language.

241. *A Restitution of Decayed Intelligence*, p. 191.

242. Herodotus, *Histories* II.2 (recounted in Sylvester's *Du Bartas* 1:429). Salimbene, trans. McLaughlin, in *Portable Medieval Reader*, p. 366. According to the *Histoire Ancienne*, a child raised until age fifteen without human conversation, would speak Hebrew naturally (ed. Joslin, p. 82).

243. Vincent of Beauvais, *Speculum Historiale* 1.62, p. 24; Augustine, *De Civ. Dei* 16.11. One of the marginal glosses to the "Prologus" of Gower's *Confessio Amantis* (1:33) notes Nimrod's contempt of God, and the confusion of tongues in which "the former language, Hebrew, was divided into diverse languages by heavenly punishment." Katz shows the persistence of this idea in the seventeenth century.

244. *Etym.* 9.1.1 and 12.1.1–2.

245. E.g., *Cursor Mundi*, lines 2281–82. According to Hugh of St. Victor's *Notulae* (*PL* 175:49), Heber, Sem, and other good men did work on building the Tower, but under compulsion; also see Dante, *DVE* 1.7.8. Comestor notes (*PL* 198:1090) that Peleg's name means "division" in Hebrew, because in his days languages and nations were divided. (This argument, Shereshevsky, p. 277, believes, "leans strongly" on *Genesis Rabba*. It also appears, however, in Josephus 1.146; LCL, p. 71.)

246. Also see Alcuin, *PL* 100:533. Haimo's comment (*PL* 131:81) is duplicated by the twelfth-century commentary of Rainaldus de sancto Eligio, fol. 54.

247. *DVE* 1.6.5–6; also see Comestor, *PL* 198:1070.

248. Augustine, *In Ioannis Evangelium* 117.4 (p. 653). Brunetto Latini, *Trésor* 3.1, p. 317.

249. *De Grammatica*, p. 79. Hugh notes (p. 70) that Hebrew is the mother of all languages and letters, as is evident in the progression from aleph to alpha to A; he is paraphrasing Isidore, who refers to the "tres linguae sacrae" (*Etym.* 9.1.3). McNally, and Amsler, p. 53, discuss the chronological "unfolding of God's truth of salvation" as Greek follows Hebrew, and Latin Greek. (Also see Lusignan, *Parler Vulgairement*, p. 42 and pp. 44–45.) Smalley, "*Postilla*," p. 279 and p. 291, cites Wyclif on this issue; and Holkot, *In Librum Sapientiae*, lectio CXXVII, p. 427, discusses these three "principal" languages (citing Augustine, *De mirabilibus*, ch. 15).

250. For a summary of the views of Jerome and Gregory the Great, see Evans, *Language and Logic: Earlier Middle Ages*, pp. 6–7.

251. See Schwarz, pp. 18–21, for the ancient Jewish accounts of the Septuagint: the Aristeas Letter (c. 100 BC) and Philo.

252. Quoted by Thurot, p. 131.

253. *De Civ. Dei* 19.7. Nicole Oresme quotes these lines in the commentary to his translation of Aristotle's *Politics* (Lusignan, *Parler Vulgairement*, p. 109). Oresme adds that when Jesus Christ wished to unite the world

in the faith, he made the apostles to be understood by all peoples; hence it is unnatural for a man to rule over a people "who do not understand his mother tongue."

254. *In Librum Sapientiae*, lectio CXXVII, p. 427. Aristotle also provides the context for Holkot, *In Librum Sapientiae*, lectio X, p. 36: "The tongue is fitting for two works: that is to say, taste and speech," the first common to all animals, the second particular to human beings. "For man is a political animal: that is, naturally social with respect to communications, thoughts, and affections, and desiring to love and be loved." Hence God gave us a tongue, the "natural office" of which "is to multiply love and benevolence among men." Willet notes that the confusion was less thoroughgoing than it might have been: "Not euery mans language was confounded, for then all societie would haue been taken away euen in families, but the speech of certane kindreds and companies was changed" (p. 128).

255. *A Restitution of Decayed Intelligence*, p. 6.

256. *Histoire Universelle*, fol. 11ᵛ. Among the early Dante commentaries, see Jacopo della Lana, 1:480; *Commento . . . d'Anonimo Fiorentino*, p. 658; and *Ottimo Commento*, p. 539. The story also appears in Sylvester's *Du Bartas*, 1:427, in the *Speculum Historiale* of Vincent of Beauvais (1.62, p. 24), and as Corti, "Torre di Babele," p. 254, notes, in the thirteenth-century *General Estoria* of Alfonso X the Wise. The story of this sudden failure of communication goes back at least to Fulgentius (pp. 138–41; trans., pp. 193–95), and is alluded to in Remigius' *Expositio*, p. 102, and in Ælfric's sermon "In Die Sancto Pentecosten," p. 358: "there were afterwards as many languages [*gereord*] as there were workers."

257. *Mistére*, 1:269–72; *Hebrew Myths*, p. 126.

258. *DVE* 1.7.7. Antony of Padua, p. 471, adds: "From this pride by which everyone wants to rule over another, language was confused. For one speaks of the oppression of a neighbor, another of usuries, another of false contracts. Truly indeed the tongue was confused, because one cannot understand another: they speak and tell, who rush to the courts where their causes are put forward."

259. *De Civ. Dei* 16.4; quoted in the *Glossa Ordinaria*, *PL* 113:115.

260. *Confessio Amantis*, Prologus 849–55.

261. *Prologue* 975–78, 1018–24, and 1005. Anderson, p. 214, notes the "revealing correspondence between Chaucer's treatment of Theban fraternal strife in the Knight's Tale and Gower's analysis."

262. Haimo of Auxerre, *PL* 131:62–63; also see Bede, *Hex.*, p. 55.

263. Alcuin, *PL* 100:533–34; *Glossa*, *PL* 113:115; Remigius (p. 103), and Comestor (*PL* 198:1089). Haimo, *PL* 131:81, notes that "the same words are found with different meanings among different peoples," and gives examples of

homonyms from Hebrew and Latin, and from Greek and Latin; so do later commentators, such as Hugh of St. Cher and Nicholas of Lyra.

264. In Chaucer's source, Trivet, Constance is fluent in several languages. Burrow analyzes the context and meaning of the phrase "a maner Latyn corrupt," which appears in the preface to the Wycliffite Bible as the speech of "the comoun puple in Italie," and in the *Alliterative Morte Arthure* as the language of the king of Rome (3477–78) (*King Arthur's Death*, p. 214), presumably Italian. Cf. Rothwell, pp. 53–54, arguing that "Latin corrupt" denotes the macaronic lingua franca used "over a wide area of western Europe" (repeating Chaytor's argument, p. 28).

265. *Polychronicon* 2.156–62; trans. and discussed by Taylor, "*Universal Chronicle*," p. 169. Trevisa expands Higden's Latin phrasing, "boatus et garritus," into "straunge wlafferynge, chiterynge, harrynge, and garrynge grisbaytyng" (*RS* 41.2:159). Higden blames the "present debasement of the native language" on the teaching of French instead of English to children, and the emulative efforts of peasants "to Frenchify [*francigenare*] their speech" (*RS* 41.2:159–60). Richter, pp. 160–61 discusses this passage. Thomas Lodge, in his 1621 excursus on "Babylon" (pp. 174–75), agrees with du Bartas and others that Hebrew "is the first Language of the world": "But whereas this first language hath neither letter, nor word, which is not full of mysteries, after the dissipation of *Babel*, a man may say of euery other language, that it is but a corrupt, effeminate, and inconstant gibridge, and which changeth from age to age, as diuers haue already declared heretofore."

266. Gellrich, pp. 98–101, discusses this view of grammar as a necessity after Babel. Sidney wittily praises English as a language that does not need grammar, "being so easy of itself, and so void of those cumbersome differences of cases, genders, moods, and tenses, which I think was a piece of the Tower of Babylon's curse, that a man should be put to school to learn his mother-tongue" (*An Apology for Poetry*, p. 140). Erasmus' *Praise of Folly* imagines the Golden Age as a time before grammar was necessary; and Wyclif, p. 495, notes that humans in Paradise (speaking Hebrew) as well as beasts would have had *voces naturales*. In that state there would have been no need for grammar, dialectic, or rhetoric, "when truth of locution without duplicity and propriety without ugliness" [*veritas locucionis sine duplicitate et decencia sine difformitate*] would have been naturally congenial to innocent human beings (p. 497).

267. "Two Infinites," p. 185.

268. Sprat, p. 113; for the historical context, see Markley and Salmon. Padley, pp. 132–42, discusses the characteristic seventeenth-century distinction between *res* and *verba*; and Wellek, pp. 83–94, summarizes seventeenth and eighteenth-century views of language. There is an extensive literature on

this topic: I have already cited Stam, Leonard, and De Grazia, "Language," and would add Foucault, Cohen, and Allen, "Some Theories." Dubois, Demonet, and De Grazia, "Shakespeare's View," discuss sixteenth-century theories. Knowlson, p. 40, quotes Hobbes, that one must be careful with words, "for words are wise mens counters, they do but reckon by them; but they are the mony of fooles, that value them by the authority of an Aristotle, a Cicero, or a Thomas, or any other doctor whatever, if but a man."

269. Smalley, *Study of the Bible*, p. 362, is summarizing a letter, c. 1080, "by a monk to an anchoress, describing the joys of heaven."

270. Jerome, *Epistola* XVIII, *PL* 22:365; John of Salisbury, *Metalogicon* 1.8 (p. 25; trans. p. 28).

271. Ambrose uses this passage to extol Moses as the divinely inspired author of Genesis (*Hexameron* 1.2; *PL* 14:125). Southern, *Scholastic Humanism*, pp. 116–18, describes God's use of *figura*, an unchanging "language of events" that is subject to no linguistic barriers, as a powerful means to instruct fallen human beings. He also cites Peter Lombard's account of David, whose prophecies came directly from the Holy Spirit while other prophets had to rely on dreams and visions, and on "a cloak of images and words" [*quasdam rerum imagines atque verborum integumenta*] (*Commentarium in Psalmos; PL* 191:55). David thus foreshadows Paul, in "a compendium of the whole divine plan: what the Psalmist foresaw and expressed symbolically, Paul interpreted and declared as historical events." Strubel discusses the medieval distinction between "allegoria in factis" and "allegoria in verbis."

272. Bruno de Segni, *Expositio in Numeros*, *PL* 164:480. Brinkmann, pp. 166–67, summarizes medieval definitions of parable.

273. See Hugh of St. Victor, *De Archa Noe*, pp. 95–98 (*Selected Spiritual Writings*, p. 134) on why "God speaks darkly and in secret."

274. Ambrose, *PL* 14:1180. Cf. the opening of Hugh of St. Victor's short treatise *De Verbo Dei* (p. 60): "'God has spoken once' because he has brought forth one Word through which he has made everything. This Word is his discourse [*Hoc Verbum est sermo eius*]. There is thus a single discourse of God, because there is a single Word of God. A single one truly, because one and of one, which is not encompassed in multiple utterances, but brought to perfection in a single and simple word."

275. *De Doctrina Christiana* 2.6; p. 61 (discussed by Smith, pp. 227–28).

276. For the iconography of Pentecost, see Réau, 2:2:591–96.

277. *N-Town Play*, pp. 165–66. The shepherds in the York and Chester plays likewise try ineptly to imitate the angel's words.

278. Cf. Camille, in *Age of Chivalry*, pp. 38–39.

279. Short, p. 476.
280. See the essays by Levitan and Levy, and also Hanning, "Roasting," p. 14: "the Summoner depicts friars as the devil's fart," that is, "as a cosmic inversion and perversion of the *Verbum Dei*."
281. Fyler, *Chaucer and Ovid*, p. 54.
282. *Enarr. in Psalmos* 64.2 (p. 823; trans. 3.251).
283. *Enarr. in Psalmos* 147.19 (p. 2156; trans. 6.404); discussed by Travers, pp. 27–29. Also see Wolff, pp. 113–14, and Origen's similar comment, on prayers in various languages being "one utterance" to "the Lord of every language": "For the supreme God is not one of those that have been allotted a particular language, barbarian or Greek, who no longer understand the rest or are no longer willing to pay heed to those who speak in other languages" (*Contra Celsum* VIII.37, p. 479).
284. *Enarr. in Psalmos* 54.11 (p. 665; trans. 3:39). His comments are largely repeated by Bede, *Hex.*, p. 152. Cf. Augustine, *In Ioannis Evangelium* 6.10, in which "Christ's humility" is the unifier of tongues: "Now what that tower pulled apart, the Church has collected together. Of one tongue were made many; do not wonder, pride caused this; of many tongues was made one; do not wonder, charity caused this" (pp. 58–59).
285. Augustine, *De Gen. ad Litt.* 12.8 (trans. 2:189), comments: "Hence, in view of the fact that signs of things and not the things themselves are given forth by the tongue, the member of the body which is moved in the mouth in speech, St. Paul, using a metaphor, designated as tongue any production of signs before they are understood."
286. Aquinas, *ST* 3a.7,7.
287. *De Sacramentis* 1.9.2 (*PL* 176:317); cited by Brusegan, p. 79, who notes that Hugh's distinction between visible and invisible is analogous to the division between body and soul in human beings, and literal and allegorical in Scripture. Also see De Grazia, "Language," p. 153: Christ "both signifies and is God's Word. The sacraments he instituted are also both – signs of grace and grace itself."
288. There is a vivid and succinct connection of Pentecost with Babel in Ælfric's sermon "In Die Sancto Pentecosten," pp. 358–59. Also see Gregory, *Hom. 30* (*PL* 76:1222).
289. *Enarr. in Psalmos* 18.4 (p. 102; trans. 1:125–26). Also see his *Sermo CCLXIX*, for Pentecost (*PL* 38:1234–37); and *De Trin.* 4.20, par. 29. Peter Lombard, *Commentarium in Psalmos* (*PL* 191:208), glosses the word *sermones* as: "id est genera dicendi, scilicet humile, mediocre, altum" [that is, kinds of speech, i.e. humble, middle, high].
290. James, "Pictor," prints the list of types and antitypes in the *Pictor in Carmine*, meant as a guide for artists (cxviii): "*The apostles speak in various*

tongues brought together from every nation to the Jews. After the tongues were confused at the tower of Babel the builders were dispersed."

291. *ST* 2a2æ.176,1.

292. *Sermo* 271. De Grazia, "Language," pp. 146–47, points out that in Augustine's view, Pentecost resolves the confusion of multiple statements within a particular language as well as between different languages: "That they ultimately expressed God's Word . . . dispelled all contradiction and inconsistency, just as it could resolve the confusion of tongues."

293. Bede's commentary on Acts 2.4 (p. 16). His *Hexaemeron*, p. 156, says that the answer to Babel is in Jerusalem, which recalls the people of diverse tongues to the single-minded construction of the holy city. Céard, p. 581, notes that in Renaissance accounts the confusion of tongues, "which is certainly a punishment, is also an aspect of the ordered variety of the world. This is why certain authors prefer the expression, usefully equivocal, of '*linguarum varietas*.'"

294. Jerome, in his *Commentarii in Sophoniam* 3.8.9 (p. 700), notes that the prophet implies Jewish hopes for the Messiah, with Hebrew once again the only tongue.

295. *Enarr. in Psalmos* 136.17 (pp. 1974–75; trans. 6.172). Travers, p. 35, argues that "tongue" and "speech" are too prosaic for "the city of the elect. It is rather of song or hymn that one must speak."

296. *Elucidarium* 3.63, p. 459. Jesus compares the separation of the saved from the damned to a shepherd's separating sheep from goats (Matthew 25.32). Peter Comestor almost certainly has this prophecy in mind when he describes Jabel the son of Lamech making the first such separation (*PL* 198:1079): thus Christ's final, judging act of separation and division counters the alienating divisions at the start of human history.

297. Jager, *Tempter's Voice*, pp. 70–71, discusses the implications of this phrasing and its relation to the skin garments of Adam and Eve. Also see Smith, p. 223: the Incarnation, "this enfleshing, was real in the straightforward sense of the animal flesh which made up" the medieval book. "Turning the pages of a codex is a constant reminder of the intimate relation between word and flesh."

298. *Confessions* 13.15; trans. pp. 331–32. Jager, *Tempter's Voice*, p. 96, sums up Augustine's argument in an evocatively Augustinian fashion (also see p. 61). Also see Rist's comment, p. 38, on the end of *De Civ. Dei*: "There would be silence in heaven because language (the *verbum vocis*), at least human language, would often necessarily fall short of the requirements of the speakers, even though the speakers' will was always to speak the uncorrupted truth."

299. Frye, p. 54.
300. Hart, p. 22.
301. Cf. Parker's comments on Milton (p. 137): "The 'to come' dimension of the figure is the mark of its insufficiency but it is also, paradoxically, its hope, the promise of continued movement rather than the Satanic reduction of meaning, the premature collapse of words and things . . . Ambiguity and metaphor are, like the 'degrees' to be traversed by Adam and Eve, part of an intervening space of trial, and process rather than elimination becomes the crucial focus."
302. *Breviloquium* IV, 1, conclusio (*Opera* 5.242a; trans. p. 111). I owe this reference to Rudd, p. 3, who discusses the passage.
303. Benson, "Alliterative *Morte Arthure*," p. 75; also see Muscatine, *French Tradition*; Brewer, "Gothic Chaucer"; and Justman. Leicester, "Harmony," effectively applies such ideas to the *Parliament of Fowls*, and Wetherbee, "*Romance of the Rose*," p. 334, to the influence of the *Roman* on Chaucer (also see Wetherbee, "Latin Structure," p. 8).
304. See McGerr; there are also pertinent remarks on inconclusiveness and lack of closure in Chaucer's poetry in Sklute and in Grudin, pp. 164–82. Reiss, "Ambiguous Realities," discusses inconclusiveness in other fourteenth-century works. Engle and McClellan discuss the relevance of Bakhtin, especially "dialogism," to Chaucer; also see the more extended discussion in Ganim, and Rigby, pp. 18–77.
305. The phrase is Leff's (p. 10).
306. Jordan, *Chaucer and the Shape of Creation*, describes a Chaucerian "poetics of uncertainty" grounded in rhetoric, although I am not wholly persuaded by his theory of "inorganic form." The final chapter of his *Chaucer's Poetics* compellingly evokes the pull in Chaucer's poetry towards fragmentation and multiplicity, and to "distinctly contingent and occasional" truths (p. 104, and esp. pp. 164–74). Also see Gellrich, e.g. p. 27.
307. Mazzotta, *World at Play*, p. 6, notes "the overt narrative disjunctions, fragmentary viewpoints, overlapping narrators, shifty symbolic patterns" of the *Decameron*. Kiser, *Truth*, p. 112, sets Boccaccio and Chaucer against Dante's "realist poetics," by their recognition of "the tendency of signifiers to drift away from the signifieds when language is in actual use and because of the unpredictable social and personal agendas of individual readers, who will always do with texts whatever they wish." For Petrarch's ambivalence on these issues, see Menocal, pp. 37 and 49. Nolan, p. 197, describes Chaucer's contrast with Boccaccio, in his use of the *roman antique* and its pagan setting: "His ethical questions remain incompletely resolved and his poetic coverings intransitive. His fictions bind both his pagan characters and his readers to fallen human language, leaving

them for the most part in the realm of images, metaphors, dreams, and possibilities."

308. Cf. Jordan, *Chaucer's Poetics*, p. 20: "Today's writers and readers share with Chaucer this ambiguous orientation toward the relation of words and things, language and 'life.' 'Postmodern' writers – Barth, Calvino, Beckett, and a host of others – have reconditioned us to a poetics of uncertainty, where the givens are not unity and coherence but multiplicity and contingency."

309. Freccero, "Fig Tree," p. 36. Parker, p. 221, makes much the same point about the "veil" of language: "The modern figure is separated from the earlier one by the prospect of a perpetual regression, the impossibility of any final unveiling."

310. Boas, pp. 204–5, argues that Christian dogma was anti-primitivistic because the New Testament "made it impossible for Christians to maintain that in all respects men should turn back to earlier times." Auden's comments (pp. 409–13) on Eden and the New Jerusalem are also of great interest.

311. Lawler, p. 15. He elaborates on this statement by arguing that "The major source of diversity in the poem is sex. The major source of unity is order" (p. 24).

312. Myles, p. 58; also see Peck's comments in "Public Dreams."

313. Burlin expresses some of the same hesitations in his review of Lawler's book.

314. The Augustinian readings of the *Canterbury Tales* often seem overstated, as in Shoaf, *Currency of the Word*, pp. 13–15. The same shortcoming appears in several discussions of *Troilus*, such as Pulsiano or Vance, *Mervelous Signals*, p. 335, which argues for a sequence at the poem's end to "coax the believing reader to find the unmediated presence of the 'uncircumscript' illuminating word by prayer," what Haidu, p. 885, calls "the real or serious use of language, still full, still directed toward God." See Wetherbee's summation, in "Convention and Authority," of these "reductive" readings: "On the one side, the inevitably corrupt language of human art; on the other, language informed by the Word."

315. E.g., Baldwin, Nitzsche, and Taylor, "Alchemy of Spring." Nims, p. 227, analogously frames the work as moving from the *Knight's Tale* to the *Parson's*, "from myth to unadorned truth, from the philosophic circle and the unmoved mover to the one true way and a God incarnate." Thus Lawler's final sentence: "The Trinity is the only absolute marriage of one and many Chaucer knew, and the whole thrust of the poem toward balance of these terms leads inevitably to it" (p. 172).

316. See Machan, "Chaucer as Translator."

317. Rudd, p. 9, characterizes the Incarnate Word as "a meeting point of two different languages – the pure, divine *logos* and the human *verbum*," an "act of translation" that "necessarily involves some degree of approximation, since man is incapable of understanding the Divine Word in its transparent state, and so any exact translation which encompassed all that the *logos* signified would be equally incomprehensible." She also notes (pp. 199–200) Joannes Balbus' definition of the translator as a mediator between different languages or discourses.

318. Pearsall, *Life*, p. 215.

319. Machan, *Techniques*, p. 130.

320. See Fyler, "Fabrications," and Fyler, "*Auctoritee* and Allusion."

321. Fyler, *Chaucer and Ovid*, pp. 33–39, and more generally the studies by Desmond and Baswell.

322. Beer, p. 4, quotes a prologue by the thirteenth-century writer Nicolas de Senlis, claiming that "no rhymed story is true."

323. Hanna, "*Compilatio*," pp. 10–11.

324. *Philobiblon*, pp. 48–49.

325. *Riverside Chaucer*, p. 650. On Adam as a scribe, see Jager, *Tempter's Voice*, p. 73, and more generally, on Adam and "Adam Scriveyn," see Dinshaw, pp. 3–10.

326. There is a particularly vivid illustration of such transcription problems in *Troilus and Criseyde*, where the *fownes* [fawns] of desire (1.465) become, in various fifteenth-century manuscripts of the poem, *foules, fode, fantasie,* and *sownes*.

327. Interestingly, *Li Ars d'Amours* (1:15) of Jehan le Bel (the editor in a revised attribution assigns the work to Jean d'Arckel) says that *amours* is an equivocal name [*nons equivokes*]: just as a *chiens de mer* [sea dog], though a dog, does not have four feet and bark, so "one must ask of all names that signify several things," including *amours*, which possible meaning is to be understood. Chaucer's dream visions, and indeed his poetry as a whole, examine these equivocal and paradoxical meanings of Love.

328. Evans, *Language and Logic: Road to Reformation*, pp. 114–15.

329. Evans, *Language and Logic: Road to Reformation*, p. 116, quoting Bonaventure, *In John*, 12, Q.1 (*Opera Omnia*, 6.415). Also see Evans, "Wyclif," pp. 262–63, for the view, in his *De Civili Dominio*, that words in Scripture are always "*proprie vera*; they take their 'propriety' not from their signification, but from the intention of the author (*iuxta sensum proprisime loquentis*). Were we ourselves to follow the same usage in talking of our own human affairs we should be using the words improperly; human language must always in that sense be improper (*locuciones nostre sunt improprie*), because we cannot speak with God's intention."

330. Copeland, "Rhetoric," pp. 1 and 14. Nims, p. 220, quotes a stanza from the *Rithmus de Incarnatione Domini* of Alain of Lille, in which *Rhetorica* describes the Incarnate Word as at once the supreme violation and supreme fulfillment of the rules of discourse.
331. *Confessions* 5.6; trans. p. 89.
332. Mystical writers, by contrast, distrust rhetoric and language, as Gillespie, p. 153, argues: "*The Cloud of Unknowing* recommends short words, ideally of one syllable only. The single, uninflected, syntactically uninhibited word aspires to escape from referentiality and from the chains of signification of earthly discourse. It resists interpretation."
333. *Etym.* 1.37.24. Unlike irony, Isidore adds, "antiphrasis in fact does not signify the contrary by the voice of the one speaking, but only by the words themselves, whose origin is contradictory" (*Etym.* 1.37.24–25). Schibanoff, pp. 105–6, notes a marginal notation, "antiphrasis," in the *Manciple's Tale*: "Alle thise ensamples speke I by thise men/ That been untrewe, and nothyng by women" (187–88).
334. See Casagrande and Vecchio, and Craun. Huppé, pp. 41–43, discusses "manner of speech" as a characterizing device in the *General Prologue*. Bloch, "Medieval Misogyny," pp. 18–20, discusses the relation of the poet, rhetoric, and the misogynistic construction of woman.
335. Patterson, "Parson's Tale," pp. 375–76.
336. *De Planctu Naturae* 10.142–44; trans. p. 164.
337. William of Conches, in his glosses on Priscian (Jeauneau, "Deux rédactions," p. 246), cites this definition from Isidore – where it is phrased somewhat differently (*Etym.* 1.35.7) – to distinguish figures, or metaplasms, from barbarisms and solecisms. John of Salisbury, who is evidently copying William of Conches, is quoted by Zeeman, p. 160. On this issue of tropes as "deviant forms of expression – the *vitia* or 'faults' of style," see Irvine, *Making*, pp. 104–7; Coletti, p. 62, notes "the potential for transgression . . . inherent in all tropes."
338. *Metalogicon* 1.16 (p. 41; trans. p. 50).
339. *De Oratore* 3.37.149, cited by Ginsberg, "Ovid," p. 13; also see Bloch, *Etymologies*, p. 40.
340. Haidu, pp. 884–85.
341. The conclusion of Paul's sentence, in the earlier Wycliffite translation. As Sisam, p. 58, 675n., says: "The quotation in its context is hardly so sweeping" as it is in the *Nun's Priest's Tale*.
342. Furrow, p. 249, outlines the commonplace fourteenth-century misuse of Paul's words to mean "reading is good for you." Also see Hanning, "Roasting," p. 6, who ascribes this Pauline sentiment to 2 Timothy 3:16,

"co-opted to become, by a feat of verbal legerdemain, an excuse for bad but well-intentioned poetry" in the *Retraction*, but not to be understood as the key to Chaucer's meaning.

343. Lanham, p. 5.
344. Zeeman, p. 161. She adds: "Figuration, then, is the unstable site where the grammarians negotiate and hold in play a series of extreme polarizations" between "correct" and "incorrect" usage.

CHAPTER 2

1. *Elucidarium* 1.76 (p. 374).
2. Bloch, *Scandal*, pp. 90 and 102.
3. *De Trin.* 9.7–8, par. 12–13 (trans. p. 278). Cave, discussing Erasmus, explores the implications of Augustine's argument: "the opacity and ambiguity of fallen language are not simply an inert barrier: they are the means by which desire is aroused, appetite provoked, and the pursuit set in motion. Self-evidence is stasis: a premature arrival at an empty place. It is only through the awareness of not-having, of not-seeing, that the movement towards possession and insight (true evidence) may be released" (pp. 101–2).
4. Evans, "*Paradise Lost*," pp. 114–21.
5. "Balade MCCCLXXXI," in *Œuvres Complètes*, 7:230–31. (Also see his Balades 936–937: *Œuvres* 5:147–50.) This section of Chapter Two is an adaptation of Fyler, "Love and the Declining World"; cf. Schmidt, "Chaucer's *Nembrot*." Honorius Augustodunensis describes the time from Adam to Noah as a Golden Age, with no rain, no rainbow, no meat-eating, and no wine: "the entire time was a sort of springtime mildness and there was an abundance of everything, which all were changed afterwards because of the sins of men" (*Elucidarium* 1.93, p. 377). The *Glossa Ordinaria* says that meat-eating was allowed after the Flood "because of the barrenness of the earth and the fragility of man" (*PL* 113:111; this detail is quoted from Alcuin, *PL* 100:531). The invention of meat-eating is also described by Isidore, *De Eccles. Off.* 1.45, and Andrew of St. Victor, in his gloss on Gen. 9.4 (*CCCM* 53:52).
6. See Ladner, *Idea of Reform*, p. 40, on Lactantius, for whom the Golden Age "was a postparadisiac era in which man still worshipped the true God and was just toward his fellow man" (citing the *Divinae Institutiones* 5.5.19.413ff.). Singleton, *Dante Studies 2*, pp. 184–203, notes Dante's fusion of Adam and Eve with the human beings of the Golden Age as the *prima gente* [first people].

7. I have used Kenney's edition of Ovid's elegiac works; the translations, with some changes, are by Mozley. Cf. Myerowitz's remarks on Ovid's excursus (pp. 50–57).

   Ovid's comments on the month of April, which "kindly Venus" claims, are similar: "She drew rude-minded men together and taught them to pair each with his mate" (*Fasti* 4.97–78). She is the force that unites human beings and beasts, taming the "savage ram" and the "dread" bull, and teaching men "decent attire and personal cleanliness [*cultus mundaque cura*]." She teaches lovers to be eloquent: "This goddess has been the mother of a thousand arts; the wish to please has given birth to many inventions that were unknown before" (4.105–14).

8. See *De Rerum Natura* 5.962–65: "Venus coupled the bodies of lovers in the greenwood. Mutual desire brought them together, or the male's mastering might and overriding lust, or a payment of acorns or arbutus berries or choice pears." Later in the book Lucretius argues that the discovery of fire, and the softening influence of Venus, led to monogamy and the beginnings of family life (5.1011–18). Ovid provides another version of this primal shift from chaos to order (and specifically to *Maiestas*) at the opening of *Fasti* 5.

9. *De Inventione* 1.2.2. Otto of Freising, p. 130, connects this description and a similar one in Eusebius with the era of Ninus, who could succeed as tyrant and conqueror "the more readily because men were as yet simple and rustic." Also see the commentary by Thierry of Chartres (*Latin Rhetorical Commentaries*, p. 62). Cf. Lucretius (5.1041–45): "To suppose that someone on some particular occasion allotted names to objects, and that by this means men learnt their first words, is stark madness. Why should we suppose that one man had this power of indicating everything by vocal utterances and emitting the various sounds of speech when others could not do it?"

10. Brown, "Sexuality and Society," p. 64. Also see his comments on pp. 52–53: "Augustine drove a wedge between society and sexuality in the present condition of man"; fallen sexuality constitutes "a profoundly asocial element in the human person . . . , an ineradicable and indiscriminate drive, contrary to order, even within marriage."

11. As Jacoff has shown, Statius' treatment of Parthenopaeus in the *Thebaid*, which emphasizes the hero's Arcadian origins, associates the Golden Age with "primitive undifferentiated (ungendered, presexual) origins" (Jacoff, pp. 139–40), i.e., with "an Edenic condition of nondifferentiation, forever lost, but worthy of semiliturgical reminiscence" (p. 142).

12. Plato, *Symposium*, p. 544. Philo (*De Opificio Mundi* [LCL ed., 1:151], quoted by Aspegren, p. 88) uses this Platonic language of divided halves

desiring union to characterize the Fall: Love begets a desire for fellowship, which in turn begets the evils of bodily pleasure. Also see Freud's
remarks in *Beyond the Pleasure Principle*, pp. 51–52, and *Civilization and
Its Discontents*, pp. 310–14.

13. Dante, *Inferno* 12.40–43; see Singleton's Commentary, pp. 189–90.
14. Cf. Milton's *Doctrine and Discipline of Divorce* (quoted by Leonard, p. 172):
"by his divorcing command the world rose out of Chaos, nor can be
renewed again out of confusion but by the separating of unmeet con-
sorts." Ovid may also have in mind Lucretius' comments on death as a
process of separating out the elements of an old conjunction [*coetum*] and
recombining them (*De Rerum Natura* 2.1002–9).
15. Fyler, *Chaucer and Ovid*, pp. 10–11. Chaucer shows his awareness of this
idiom in *Boece* 2.pr.3.62–65: "Tho yave thow woordes to Fortune, as I
trowe, (*that is to seyn, tho feffedestow Fortune with glosynge wordes and
desceyvedest hir*)."
16. Trans. pp. 12–13. Bergin, p. 254, uses this passage to show "how far Boccaccio has come since the *Decameron*," comparing it with the story of
Cymon (day 5, story 1), who is changed "from an insensate beast into a
man through the keen stimulus of Love" (*Decameron*, p. 414). The tone
of the story, though, seems more than a little ironic.
17. Blamires, *Case for Women*, p. 222. "Adapting materials from Boccaccio's
De Mulieribus Claris, she identifies women as inventors not only of the
Latin language but also of numeracy, cloth-making, body armour, literary
forms, agriculture, nets, and silk, to name but a few." Quilligan, *Allegory
of Female Authority*, provides an extended discussion. Brown-Grant compares Christine and Boccaccio.
18. See Boucher, and also Peck, "Nominalist Questions," and Watts and Utz.
19. Hult describes the paradox in Jean de Meun's account of fallen language,
in terms that apply almost as well to Chaucer: set against a regret for
the lost "fullness of an originary language" is the vitality of a "release,"
"itself positive insofar as it makes possible figuration in all of its forms"
("Language and Dismemberment," p. 122). Cf. Poirion, "Signification,"
pp. 179–81.
20. *Roman de la Rose*, and *Reason and the Lover*.
21. Badel, *Roman au XIVᵉ Siècle*, pp. 486–89, recounts the early fifteenth-
century French assessments of Dante's debt to the *Roman*.
22. George, p. 37, tentatively adopts Gunn's position.
23. The first two quotations are from Fleming, *Reason and the Lover*, p. 3, the
third from Fleming, *Roman de la Rose*, p. 107.
24. *Débat*, pp. 94–95.
25. Robertson, p. 199.

26. Ferrante, *Woman as Image*, p. 114; Nykrog, p. 320.
27. Among the studies I have particularly learned from are Wetherbee, "Literal and Allegorical," and *Platonism and Poetry*; Hill; Bloch, *Etymologies*; Rowe; Hult, "Language and Dismemberment"; Huot, *"Romance" and Medieval Readers*; and Kay, *Romance of the Rose*.
28. For Jean's inconclusiveness see, e.g., Hicks, "Sous les pavés."
29. *ST* 1a.94,4.
30. *ST* 1a.94,1.
31. ST 1a.101,2.
32. Hult, "Language and Dismemberment," p. 123.
33. Zink, p. 106, comments on Macrobius' view of the *somnium*, "in itself the figurative or indirect representation of a meaning which only the decipherment resulting from interpretation is able to make apparent."
34. *ST* 1a.95,3.
35. William of St. Thierry's *De Natura et Dignitate Amoris* adopts an Ovidian paradigm of love's history even as it attacks Ovid. He begins with the aphorism "Ars est artium ars amoris" [The art of arts is the art of love], true love being the force of specific gravity in the universe, a force that by Nature and Nature's Creator makes all things desire to return to their proper place (*PL* 184:379). In the fallen world, love is improperly taught as a "filthy carnal love" by the "doctor of the *ars amatoria*" (381). This is a fallen love of labor and sweat (expressed in the language of Ovid's Vergilian parody): "this is the labor, this the task; a labor of many sweaty exertions, a work of many labors." By contrast, the love that God requires, which is charity, insists that *ratio* and *amor* be allied, and complement each other's insufficiencies (393).
36. *Débat*, pp. 14–15; Baird and Kane, p. 49: "Reason denied her heavenly father in that teaching, for He taught an entirely different doctrine. If you hold one of these two to be better than the other, it would follow that both are good, and this cannot be. I hold a contrary opinion: it is far less evil, clearly, to be deceived than to deceive [*Et je tiens par oppinion contraire que mains est mal, a realement parler, estre deceu que decevoir*]." Hicks, "Querelle de la Rose," discusses the implications of this debate for the *Roman*.
37. Fyler, *"Omnia Vincit Amor,"* revised in *Chaucer and Ovid*, pp. 2–17.
38. Rudd, p. 53, quotes Aquinas in the *De Regimine Principum*: "so, in a certain sense, reason is to man what God is to the universe." Augustine says in *De Trin.* 12.7, par. 12 (trans. pp. 328–29): "After all, the authority of the apostle as well as plain reason [*ueracissima ratio*] assures us that man was not made to the image of God as regards the shape of his body, but as regards his rational mind [*sed secundum rationalem mentem*]." Hence

Badel, *Roman au XIVe Siècle*, p. 48 (and also in "Raison 'Fille de Dieu'"), makes no distinction between unfallen and fallen Reason in the *Roman*.

39. Hult, "Language and Dismemberment," p. 109, aligning himself with Hill. Also see Wetherbee, *Platonism and Poetry*, pp. 258–59. Tuve, p. 267, argues that Jean's irony prevents our seeing Reason as "an easy answer" (p. 267); Cherniss, p. 230, echoes her argument. Marc-René Jung, in the post-lecture discussion of Ineichen, p. 252, argues that "Reason is limited because she is Reason." Also see Jung, p. 34, and especially Hult, "Language and Dismemberment," p. 119.

40. Rudd, p. 55. Wetherbee, "Literal and Allegorical," p. 271, n. 32, likewise argues that after the Fall, Reason can be "God's daughter and at the same time ignorant of Grace."

41. Kay, "Women's Body of Knowledge," p. 223; see the *Somme "Quoniam Homines,"* p. 121.

42. Rudd, p. 48.

43. Rudd, p. 59.

44. *De Planctu Naturae* 6.154–55; trans., p. 125. See Rowe, p. 104.

45. See William Calin's review of Fleming's *Roman de la Rose* (*Speculum* 47 [1972], p. 312), responding specifically to Fleming's argument on pp. 132–35; also see Hill, p. 421, and Allen, *Art of Love*, p. 85. Wetherbee, "Some Implications," p. 47, aptly cites Richard of St. Victor's *Benjamin Major* (*PL* 196.82), on the cloudiness of reason after the Fall [*rationis oculus peccati nube obductus*]. Rudd, p. 59, cites the same passage.

46. Gower, *Confessio Amantis* 5.854–55; *Ovide Moralisé*, 1.651–52. John Lydgate uses the euphemism "membres of engendrure" (*Reson and Sensuallyte*, 1300). Kay, "Birth of Venus," pp. 29–37, appends a useful anthology of texts from Isidore and the mythographers, in which "genitalia" and "virilia" (though in one text "testicula" and "pudenda") are the words of choice. Kelly, *Internal Difference*, pp. 46–47, singles out Macrobius' use of "pudenda," and Christine de Pizan's use of "genitaires" in the *Epistre Othea*; Reason, as he notes, could easily have chosen the latter as a more polite word than "coilles" (p. 49). Dronke, *Fabula*, p. 29, notes that William of Conches discusses Saturn's castration, arguing that it needs to be read metaphorically; if not, "the truth of this fable . . . is hidden and covered over by dishonourable words, unworthy of the gods [*verba inhonesta et indigna numinibus*]." William himself uses the word "testiculos."

47. Cicero, *De Officiis* 1.35.127. For Gerson, see *Débat*, p. 82; Baird and Kane, p. 87; for Pierre Col, see *Débat*, p. 96; Baird and Kane, p. 99.

48. Cf. Dragonetti, "Une métaphore": he argues that Reason employs "the innocent language of the earthly paradise. The speech of this Lady is a pure speech that names directly things as they are" (p. 386), unlike

metaphorical language, which does not name things as they are and is merely "sanctioned by foul custom" (p. 390). But as Patterson, *Subject of History*, p. 408, n. 109, says, we must question Reason's assertion of "the natural fitness of words and things," "precisely the assumption that her discussion of *reliques* and *coilles* shows to be unwarranted."

49. Poirion, "Signification," pp. 168–71, argues that for Amor, "language controls morals," and that since the castration of Saturn symbolizes "censure and repression that are directed simultaneously at language and at morals," Jean is trying to effect a "double rehabilitation," both of sexuality and of "direct and crude" language. Pearcy, p. 164, points out the sometimes confusing conflation of ontological and stylistic arguments, when modern critics discuss obscenity in the *Roman* and the fabliaux.

50. Jean de Meun here seems to be thinking of such texts as the *Roman de Renart*, which celebrates *cons* as the "most noble name" in the world and as "li plus sovereigns mire" [the best physician of all] for love's malady (VII.438 and 448); *Renart*, 1:253). (I owe this reference to Muscatine, *French Tradition*, p. 78.)

51. On courtly euphemism and verbal taboo, see Muscatine, "Courtly Literature," *Old French Fabliaux*, and "(Re)Invention of Vulgarity"; Benson, "Chaucer and Courtly Speech," esp. pp. 20–30; and Leupin, pp. 78–119. Hult, "Words and Deeds," p. 353, points out the latent paradox in a prurient response, by Jean's "rather perverse logic": because Shame, "the enforcer of obscenity restrictions, . . . is also the sign of (or even punishment for) original sin," would-be censors reveal themselves to be "the most marked by the condition of the Fall."

52. *Débat*, p. 125; Baird and Kane, pp. 124–25. Early on in the debate, she complains about Genius' "sophistical words" [*mots sophistez*]: "the 'sermon' is superfluous, for a work which is of the very order of Nature cannot, obviously, fail. If it were not so, then it would be good for the maintenance of human generation to invent and say exciting and inflaming words and terms [*mos et termes actisans et enflammans*] in order to stimulate man to continue that work" (*Débat*, p. 16; Baird and Kane, p. 50).

53. Tuve, p. 262. There are a number of useful accounts of the crucial Pygmalion episode, especially Dragonetti, "Pygmalion"; Brownlee, "Pygmalion"; Huot, "Medusa Interpolation"; and Stakel, pp. 109–21. Barney, *Allegories*, p. 209, effectively counters Robertson's interpretation.

Kay, *Romance of the Rose*, p. 47, argues that the Pygmalion story mocks "the inadequacy of masculine art, and masculine fantasy, when they join forces to confine women in the role of object" (also see Minnis, *Magister Amoris*, p. 197); but cf. Brownlee, "Pygmalion," p. 207, who argues for "the actantial reciprocity of Pygmalion's and Galatea's mutual desire." In either reading, Venus' role is crucial, as the embodiment of a necessary feminine desire (Poirion, "Narcisse," p. 159); that necessity undermines Cahoon's argument that the final scene describes a rape, even though by any reading, the language of assault, of storming the castle, is purposely upsetting and dehumanizing.

54. Gaunt, p. 282; also see Moi, and Bloch, "Modest Maids," p. 300. Appositely, one of Augustine's letters talks about the spiritual seductiveness of allegorical imagery, more alluring than openly expressed proper terms (*Ep.* 55 [*PL* 33:214], cited by Pépin, p. 254).

55. The poem appears in Swift, *Poetical Works*, pp. 519–27.

56. Buxton, p. 69, summarizes Hesiod's two versions of the Kronos myth and the historical placement of the Golden Age.

57. Huot, *"Romance" and Medieval Readers*, pp. 275–77, discusses castration as a recurring motif in the poem, and mentions a detail from the bestiary tradition, illustrated in London B. L. MS Stowe 947, of a beaver castrating itself.

58. Cf. George, p. 34, on the castration of Saturn as "the end of the age of love," an end that "made justice, law and government necessary, with the consequent loss of human freedom."

59. La Vieille describes "the bath in which Venus makes women bathe" (12721–22). Also see 15800–7, in which Venus takes responsibility for enflaming women, and asks her son Amor to do the same for men. Genius throws down his candle, "not made of virgin wax" (19460); "and its smoky flame spread throughout the world. It was so effectively spread by Venus that no lady could protect herself from it, and so fanned by the wind that the bodies, hearts, and thoughts of every lady alive were permeated by its odour" (20641–48).

60. Pelen, p. 118, notes the "playful juxtaposition" of Jupiter and Virginius as cutters-off, and the implicit "silent authorial mockery" here of Reason's supposed "abilities in 'philosophical' teaching."

61. *Commentary on the Dream of Scipio* 1.2.17; quoted and discussed by Dronke, *Fabula*, p. 47. There are useful remarks on *integumentum* scattered throughout Minnis and Scott; and see Jeauneau, "L'usage." Chenu discusses the related term *"Involucrum."*

62. Macrobius, *Commentary on the Dream of Scipio* 1.2.11. See Mann, p. 319; Huot, *"Romance" and Medieval Readers*, p. 108; and Rowe, p. 105.

63. Dronke, *Fabula*, p. 47.

64. The two words are *coillon* and *vit*. I am grateful to David Hult for helping me with the complexities of this passage.

65. Josephus says that Cain "was the first to think of ploughing the soil" (*Jewish Antiquities* 1.2.1)(LCL ed., 4:25).

66. Friend expatiates further (9557–634) on the beginnings of private property and boundaries, the divisions of the earth, the newly urgent need for a prince and lord, and the symptomatic appearance of taxation, wealth, and war. For the Augustinian and medieval political theory behind these lines, and Jean's conflation of Genesis and the Golden Age myth, see Dean, *World Grown Old*, p. 151. Also see Huot, *"Romance" and Medieval Readers*, pp. 148–50.
67. *Rethinking the "Romance of the Rose,"* p. 9.
68. Fleming, *Reason and the Lover*, p. 79, n. 24, lists me – in the good company of Langlois, Lecoy, and Marc-René Jung – as among the "naïve readers of this passage," which I quoted in connection with the *Book of the Duchess* (*Chaucer and Ovid*, pp. 71–72).
69. Deschamps, *Œuvres* 1.225–26.
70. Also see Walther, pp. 101–2, who finds here Jean de Meun's serious reply – offering the Golden Age as a contrafactum [*Kontrafaktur*] – to Aquinas' argument that Adam had sovereignty over Eve even before the Fall.
71. See Friedman, "Jean and Ethelred," pp. 138–41.
72. Aelred 1.57–59; *PL* 195:667–68; trans. p. 39.
73. See Kooper; Rist, pp. 197 and 246–47, summarizes the source of this idea in Augustine.
74. Fleming, *Reason and the Lover*, p. 93, somewhat oversimplifies Aelred's meaning, and hence its implications for the *Roman*, by defining *amor sauvage* as Christian friendship and equating them both with charity: "In saying that he knows nothing of *amor sauvage*, the Lover is saying no more and no less than that he knows nothing of *caritas*." But Aelred explicitly distinguishes *caritas*, to be bestowed on good and bad alike, from the even higher demands of virtuous friendship in the fallen world.

    For a fascinating and more literal version of *amor sauvage*, see the *Dialogues curieux* of Baron de Lahontan (1703), in which the Huron Adario, the supposed *sauvage*, has much to teach the European about Golden Age virtues and the meaning of love (pp. 224–29).
75. See George, p. 35, on the Vieille's imagining of the Golden Age and of "a kind of caveman period, presumably after Saturn's reign had come to an end, when men loved women and left them as they pleased and the resultant strife and bloodshed was halted only when the institution of marriage was ordained."
76. Kay, *Romance of the Rose*, pp. 64–65, is very good on the ironies here, in Jean's "perverse and playful refusal to commit himself to any unambiguous position." In Friend's speech, the Golden Age ideal frames Vilain Jalous' desire for mastery; in Vieille's, "'real-life' sexual behaviour" frames the Golden Age, which is as if "now only a memory, or a myth, well beyond

the reach of contemporary sexual-political experience. Yet the 'digression' (or content of the frame) can also be read in each case as undermining the frame."

77. Wetherbee, "Some Implications," p. 58.

78. Jean may also be thinking of Noah's sons viewing their father's genitals, as an analogous dividing point between innocent and fallen world. See, for example, the Beatus page of the *St. Omer Psalter* (described by Camille, *Image on the Edge*, p. 153).

79. Fleming, *Reason and the Lover*, p. 120.

80. Kay, "Birth of Venus," p. 7, discusses this gendering of qualities. Wetherbee, "Some Implications," p. 47, discusses a similar gendering in "the allegories of *Natura*."

81. There are other jokes at her expense: when personified abstractions are fleshed out as allegorical characters, comedy can result (Kay, *Romance of the Rose*, p. 30) – as in the psychomachia in which Franchise and her company of female allegorical qualities go into battle against Daunger and his allies. When Reason offers to be the Lover's *amie*, he prudishly accuses her of being promiscuous; but we have already been told by Guillaume de Lorris that Reason has a daughter, Honte [Shame], who was conceived when she merely looked at Malfet [Misdeed or Fiend] (2821–28).

82. Chaucer, interestingly, reserves the word and notion of "labour" almost exclusively for jokes about sexual activity in the fallen world. Even in the *Miller's Tale*, in which the real-world labor of John the carpenter and Gerveys the blacksmith is set against clerical idleness, Absolon sets off, hot plowshare in hand, almost as if a parodic version of Piers Plowman.

83. Rowe's comments (pp. 119–20) are useful here.

84. Jolivet, "Quelques cas," and Chenu, "Un cas."

85. Dronke, *Women Writers*, p. 5 and p. 45. Also see Chenu, "Grammaire et théologie."

86. *In Aristotelis Libros Peri Hermeneias . . . Expositio*, p. 21; quoted by Arthur, pp. 29–30. The *Logica* of Lambert of Auxerre tries to reconcile naming *ad placitum* with etymology; see Arthur, pp. 27–29. (But note Minnis' important *caveat* in his review of Arthur's book: *Speculum* 65 [1990], p. 247.)

87. "Commentary on Boethius' *De Trinitate*," p. 292.

88. Thierry, "Lectures," pp. 170–71. This passage owes much to, and at several points directly quotes, Augustine's *De Genesi ad Litteram* 9.12.20 (*PL* 34:400). See Evans, *Language and Logic: Earlier Middle Ages*, p. 76, who sums up Thierry's view: "the union of word and thing is ultimately an absolute one."

89. Letter 4, Epistola 5; *PL* 178:207; trans. Radice, p. 148. Cf. Nichols, "Sociology," p. 68.

90. Andrew, *In Genesim*, CCCM 53, pp. 34–35.

91. Clark, "Adam's Only Companion," discusses the place of *De Civ. Dei*, Book 14, in Augustine's evolving views on sexuality. Ziolkowski, "Obscenity," pp. 46–47, describes Augustine's solution to an "unresolved stumbling block in the rhetorical tradition," that words are conventional signs and thus "inherently harmless" but a few are nonetheless obscene: "the 'parts of shame' acquired their shamefulness as a result of the fall," and their rebellions against the will "generate shame" and "cause obscenity in speech."

92. *De Civ. Dei* 14.21; trans. p. 583.

93. *De Civ. Dei* 14.23; trans. pp. 586–87.

94. *De Civ. Dei* 14.23; trans. p. 587.

95. *De Civ. Dei* 14.26; trans. p. 591.

96. *De Planctu Naturae*, trans. pp. 143–44. Fleming, *Reason and the Lover*, p. 106, discusses this passage, as does Ziolkowski, *Grammar of Sex*, p. 47. Immediately following is Alain's account of the Creation "by, so to speak, a material word" (p. 144) [*uelut materiali uerbo* (8.201–2)].

97. *De Planctu Naturae* 10. pr. 5; trans. p. 156.

98. Quilligan, "Words and Sex," p. 196.

99. *Ars versificatoria* 79–80, in Faral, p. 27.

100. Dinshaw, p. 169. The first translation is Bloch's ("Modest Maids," p. 303), the second Hult's ("Language and Dismemberment," p. 116). See Ziolkowski, "Obscenities of Old Women," p. 80, for almost identical phrasing in a thirteenth-century Latin commentary on Joseph of Exeter's Troy poem.

101. See Hult, "Language and Dismemberment," p. 128n., for a critique of Fleming, *Reason and the Lover*, pp. 110–11, and the passage from Augustine's *De Dialectica* that Fleming cites. Minnis, *Magister Amoris*, p. 92, relates Jean's "naked text" of plain speech to the generic demands of satire.

102. As Huot, *"Romance" and Medieval Readers*, p. 108, points out, "The Lover shares Natura's preference for the 'cloak of euphonious speech' while ignoring her concern for the truth; Reason shares her belief that poetic figures must express truths, but denies the need for euphemism."

103. Quilligan, "Words and Sex," pp. 198–200. Also see her "Allegory, Allegoresis."

104. John of Trevisa, *On the Properties of Things* 5.48 (p. 261).

105. See, for example, Dinshaw, p. 168.
106. Kelly, *Internal Difference*, pp. 49–50, notes "that the metaphor *andoilles* has been improper from Old French until today," as a euphemism for "penis," and cites similarly indecorous conjunctions of the two words in Villon's *Testament* and the *Roman de Renart*.
107. Fleming, *Reason and the Lover*, p. 37, argues that Jean takes this "idea that Reason is the inventress of language," which is "not a general commonplace," from Augustine's *De ordine* 2.12: "Reason recognized the need to put names to things, that is, to establish sounds that might have signification" [*uidit esse inponenda rebus uocabula, id est significantes quosdam sonos*].
108. Dragonetti, "Une métaphore," pp. 388–89, argues that since proper names come uniquely from God, a name that Reason produces as "proper" is in fact nothing "but a metaphor of the thing." Wetherbee, "Literal and Allegorical," p. 266, demonstrates that for Alain de Lille, the words of postlapsarian man "are barren of legitimate *significatio*, his actions wilful and self-destructive."
109. Kelly, *Internal Difference*, p. 49.
110. *Débat*, p. 117; Baird and Kane, pp. 117–18. For a different reading of this passage, see Benson, "Chaucer and Courtly Speech," pp. 18–19.
111. *Débat*, p. 123; Baird and Kane, p. 123.
112. The Manciple offers a mock-apology for his "knavyssh speche," going on to say that "a wyf that is of heigh degree" is called a "lady," while "a povre wenche" has the sobriquet "lemman," but there is no difference between them "If it so be they werke bothe amys" (205–22). Cf. Walther von der Vogelweide (cited by Dronke, *Medieval Lyric*, p. 137), on the inherent dignity of plain speech, set against fashionable usage. "'Woman' [*wip*] will always be woman's highest name – it honours her more than 'lady' [*frouwe*]."
113. Fleming, *Reason and the Lover*, p. 106.
114. See Kelly, *Internal Difference*, p. 47. Minnis, *Magister Amoris*, pp. 122–23n., argues "that such language would indeed have been regarded as 'talking dirty' in Jean de Meun's day," and sensibly adds: "as used by Raison, the words in question *had* to appear shocking, or else the fuss made of them in the *Rose* would have seemed inexplicable."
115. Dinshaw, pp. 167–75, discusses this passage and its connections to the *Pardoner's Tale*: "human language was seen, by many medieval thinkers, to be *essentially* partial. This is why Reason's narration of castration leads to a discussion of language and relics: 'coilles,' 'reliques,' 'paroles,' they're *all* fragments" (p. 171).

116. C. S. Lewis' point is germane here, in his brief note on "Four-Letter Words" (Lewis, p. 121): "Reason defies (and thus gives evidence for) traditional linguistic behaviour."
117. Fleming, *Reason and the Lover*, pp. 118–19; also see Tuve, p. 254n.: "As in Tasso, prelapsarian 'freedoms' are selected, admired and praised for the most grossly wrong and postlapsarian reasons."
118. *Mutacion de Fortune* 2.137; line 8163.
119. *Débat*, p. 13; Baird & Kane, p. 48. Christine, interestingly, is not fastidiously delicate about all words or bodily functions, for she can respond to Pierre Col with: "la matiere en est tres deshonneste, ainssy come aucuns arguemistes qui cuident fere de fiens or" [the matter is very dishonorable, much like certain alchemists who think they can transmute dung into gold] (*Débat*, p. 126; Baird & Kane, p. 125).
120. *Débat*, p. 13; Baird and Kane, p. 48.
121. *Débat*, pp. 13–14; Baird and Kane, p. 48.
122. *Débat*, p. 14; Baird and Kane, p. 49.
123. Quoted by Kelly, *Internal Difference*, p. 45.
124. See Minnis, "*De Impedimento Sexus*," and Minnis, *Magister Amoris*, p. 124: Boethius may have intended "cousin to the thing" as "a catch-all *sententia* on the desirability of suiting style to subject." But for Jean "to adapt it for a defence of bawdy or foolish words on the grounds that the subject may require such expression is to take an extraordinary liberty with his authoritative source."
125. Minnis, *Magister Amoris*, p. 158.
126. Wyclif, p. 495.
127. Kay, *Romance of the Rose*, p. 18.
128. Roy, p. 157.
129. See Muscatine, *Old French Fabliaux*, pp. 145–46.
130. Hult, "Language and Dismemberment," pp. 119–21.
131. Cf. Bloch, *Scandal*, p. 101, on "the ubiquitous theme of bodily dismemberment" and its significance in the medieval comic tale.
132. Lori Walters catalogues *Roman* manuscripts with author portraits, particularly at the midpoint when Jean de Meun takes over. She singles out Paris B.N. fr. 1569, "apparently the only example of its kind," in which "Guillaume de Lorris is shown passing the *Romance of the Rose* to Jean de Meun" (Walters, p. 362). I would also call attention to London, B.L. MS Stowe 947, fol. 30ᵛ, on which Guillaume and Jean are portrayed seated, facing each other, and each of them writing as if on the same bench, though as the divider emphasizes, in different rooms (Jean's room has a golden wall).

133. See Kay, *Romance of the Rose*, p. 41, on the multiple ironies here. Also see Hult, "Closed Quotations," pp. 267–68.
134. Hult, "Language and Dismemberment," p. 118, mentions "an interpolated passage, found nonetheless in a surprising number of manuscripts" of the *Roman*: "And if you had heard me provide the name *coilles* for *reliques* you would take the word for such a beautiful one and would so prize it that you would everywhere venerate *coilles* and would kiss them in churches, enshrined in gold and in silver" [trans. Hult].

    Also see Kay, *Romance of the Rose*, p. 70, for a witty summary of the problem here, expanding on Poirion, "Mots et choses," p. 9: "Derrière le mot, le doute atteint la parole": "not only are the notions of the genital and the sacred now irremediably (and comically) associated with one another, but any mention of the sacred which could possibly be attracted into the orbit of obscene meaning is so instantly."
135. Harry Bailly seems to get this joke, in his sally at the Pardoner:

    > "I wolde I hadde thy coillons in myn hond
    > In stide of relikes or of seintuarie.
    > Lat kutte hem of, I wol thee helpe hem carie;
    > They shul be shryned in an hogges toord!"
    > (*Pardoner's Tale* 952–55)

    Even so, as Dinshaw, p. 168, says, "The Host may not know, any better than the others do, whether the relics, as it were, signify castration or suggest plenitude. 'I wolde I hadde' suggests primarily that the Host doesn't have the balls in hand but wishes he did, but secondarily it suggests that he doesn't because he *can't*: they don't exist." Also see Patterson, *Subject of History*, pp. 407–10.

CHAPTER 3

1. Aquinas, *Politicorum Aristotelis Expositio*, Lectio 1, 1.1.36 (p. 11), describes the distinction between *vox* and *locutio*: "For we see that although some other animals have voice, man alone over other animals has speech. For even if some animals bring forth human speech, they are not in a proper sense speaking, because they do not understand what they say, but bring forth voices from a kind of practice." Also see Cicero, *De Officiis* 1.4 – "Nature likewise by the power of reason associates man with man in the common bonds of speech and life" – and especially 1.16, where he says that "ratio et oratio" [reason and speech] are the bond of connection [*vinculum*] among human beings. Much the same view appears in Isocrates (quoted by Marrou, *History of Education*, p. 122). Ray, pp. 63–64, notes that John

of Salisbury's *Metalogicon* "begins with the claim that eloquence gave rise
to civilization." But in the *Policraticus* John stresses "the destructive power
of language" and later in the *Metalogicon* "goes on to warn that the tongue
unchecked can all but dismantle society."

2. The page references for the *Convivio* are to Richard Lansing's translation.
Also see *DVE* 1.2–3.

3. See Singleton, Commentary on *Purgatorio*, p. 606; and Mazzotta, *Poet
of the Desert*, p. 214, who notes that the word "fante" "connects language
indissolubly with the creation of the soul."

4. Barański, pp. 123–24. Cf. Pagliaro, "I 'primissima signa,'" p. 224: "significare ad placitum" is, because of human reason, an attribute of freedom;
the animals, by contrast, understand sounds only in a univocal fashion.
Eco et al. discuss "Animal Language" in the context of medieval sign
theory.

5. See Casagrande and Vecchio.

6. In Mandelbaum et al., *Lectura Dantis*, p. 303. Likewise Vallone notes
that silence in the *Inferno* marks distance from God, but in the *Paradiso*
manifests the insufficiency of language.

7. Ferrante, "Relation of Speech to Sin," p. 34; also see the extended discussion in Colish, *Mirror of Language*, which catalogues examples of perverted
speech (p. 208).

8. Ferrante, "Relation of Speech to Sin," p. 39.

9. Hollander, "Babytalk," p. 79, n. 19, notes the tongues of flame at
Pentecost, described in Acts 2 and parodied here. Also see Olson, "*Inferno*
27."

10. See Rupert of Deutz, *In Genesim* (*PL* 167:366–67), on Nimrod, who is
to be understood as standing for everyone "who lifts up on high his own
horn, who speaks iniquity against God," quoting Psalm 74.5–6.

11. See Hollander, *Allegory*, pp. 115–16, on the comparison of Dante and
Ulysses as rhetoricians: *Inferno* 26.19–24 serves as "a sort of 'There but for
the Grace of God go I' passage." Nencioni provides a general discussion
of Dante and the rhetorical tradition.

12. Commentary on *Inferno*, p. 326.

13. See Freccero, *Poetics of Conversion*, pp. 152–66, and Yowell.

14. *DVE* 1.3. Dante's remarks here are in accord with Aquinas' commentary
on *Peri hermeneias*, pp. 9–17: see Arens, pp. 402–3 and 439–40. Also see *ST*
1a.107,1, on the question of whether angels speak, especially Responsio 2:
"We have to make use of an outward, vocalized communication because of
the interference of the body. Hence among the angels there is no place for
outward, but only for inward speech; this includes not only a conversing
with self in an inner thought, but also the thought's being directed by

the will towards communicating with another. Accordingly, the *tongues of angels* is a metaphor for the power they have to make their thoughts known." Lo Piparo, p. 14, summarizes Dante's argument on why animals within a species do not need to speak: "Since they all have the same instincts and passions, each animal knows the psychic world of the others through its own"; and different species of animals cannot communicate with each other. By contrast, according to Dante, "human *ratio* . . . is so varied – and its variety seems so natural in man – that each man seems to possess his specific *ratio*."

15. Ferrante, "Relation of Speech to Sin," p. 37, points out that "coins, like words, are a basic medium of exchange in a civilized state – the misuse of either can disrupt the social order. Indeed, Dante often associates sinners with words and sinners with coins": the "usurers and blasphemers," and the "falsifiers of coins and words." For further meditations on this topic, see Chapter 6, "Exchange and Communication, Commerce and Language in the *Comedy*," in Ferrante, *Political Vision*, pp. 311–79; also see Shoaf, *Currency of the Word*, and Vance, *Mervelous Signals* (as well as Vance, "Chaucer's *House of Fame*," p. 23, which describes "an art of inflation").

16. Singleton, *Dante Studies 1*, p. 62.

17. See Ferrante, "Relation of Speech to Sin," p. 42, on the self-deceptions and unwitting self-revelations of Francesca, Farinata, and Brunetto Latini.

18. See Mazzotta, *Poet of the Desert*, p. 73, on Babel as "the symbolic interaction of city and language."

19. Ferrante, "Relation of Speech to Sin," p. 42.

20. Hollander, "Babytalk," p. 78, n. 17, echoes Sarolli's observation that Plutus' speech "is 'rectified' in Justinian's similar (but now sacrosanct) linguistically mingled utterance in the opening lines of *Par.* VII."

21. Barański, p. 132, observes that the final word of Nimrod's gibberish, "almi" (*Inferno* 31.67), is also an Italian word, which can rhyme with "salmi," making "the familiar unfamiliar." Also see Dragonetti, "Dante face à Nemrod," and especially the interesting argument of Nohrnberg, p. 11n., that Nimrod gives "a distorted rendition of the words from the cross" (Matt. 27.46). John Ahern (in Mandelbaum et al., *Lectura Dantis*, pp. 416 and 420) describes the elaboration on "bocca" *mouth*, in *Inferno* 32 and the succeeding cantos, especially in the "traitor named 'Mouth' (Bocca degli Abati)," Ugolino of Pisa, and Satan, who "uses his three mouths not for speech but to devour three traitors."

22. See Ferrante, "Relation of Speech to Sin," p. 37: "effective communication is essential to the proper working of any society"; hence, "Dante uses the most blatant examples of non-communication, the gibberish

of Plutus and Nimrod, to enclose the sins that threaten the social order." For other helpful accounts of Nimrod in *Inferno* 31, see Jacob and especially Dronke, *Dante*, p. 39, pp. 134–35, and passim. Schnapp, "Virgin Words," p. 279, notes "Dante's participation in the pervasive medieval practice of associating imaginary alien tongues with transgressive forms of discourse such as magical incantation, malediction and sacred parody."

23. Hollander, "Babytalk," p. 79. Barański, pp. 130–32, convincingly shows how the details of *Inferno* 31 make a sustained parody of 1 Corinthians 14, especially 14.4: "He that speaketh in a tongue edifieth himself."

24. See Remo Ceserani's comment on *Inferno* 34 (in Mandelbaum et al., *Lectura Dantis*, p. 436).

25. Barański, pp. 113–14, points out that *De Vulgari Eloquentia* omits any mention of Adam naming the animals, or of God naming Day and Night and speaking to Adam and Eve after their eating of the forbidden fruit, or of Pentecost and the gift of tongues; these episodes that Dante "ignores could have potentially undermined the logic of his account." Also see the accounts of Adamic language in Castaldo and in Terracini, and of the *De Vulgari Eloquentia* in Pagani.

26. Singleton's commentary, p. 118, notes that Aquinas appositely "cites Gregory of Nyssa's view that 'acedia est tristitia vocem amputans.' ('Torpor is sorrow depriving of speech.')"

27. Singleton's Commentary on *Purgatorio*, p. 96. Barański, p. 110, argues that in Purgatory "physical speech reaches its most perfect results," and in contrite prayers as "in the pilgrim's conversations about poetry, also suggests how language can best be deployed."

28. Wilkins and Bergin, *Concordance*. To be exact, there are six forms of the verb *cantare* in the *Inferno*, 38 in the *Purgatorio*, and 25 in the *Paradiso*; the proportion for the noun *canto* is 3:11:17. The proportions for *inno* and *salmo* are similar; that is to say, 1:4:1 and 1:2:1.

29. See Ferrante, "Relation of Speech to Sin," p. 34.

30. Ahern (in Mandelbaum et al., *Lectura Dantis*, pp. 413–14) comments interestingly on Dante as Orpheus and as Amphion (*Inferno* 32.11), whom Horace and Brunetto Latini link together as civilizing poets.

31. Mazzotta, *Poet of the Desert*, p. 169, discusses the Augustinian echoes in Dante's exploration of author as go-between, "as part of the unavoidable ambiguities of the language of desire."

32. As Mazzeo, *Medieval Cultural Tradition*, p. 8, says: "There is a sense in which Dante always remained a poet and therefore a 'sinner' . . . The blessed in heaven have no more need of literature than of food and drink." But cf. Mazzotta, in Mandelbaum et al., *Lectura Dantis*, p. 355, on the

ways in which "Dante draws a sharp distinction between himself and Ulysses."

33. See Poggioli, p. 318, on the cranes' *lai* in the context of this wailing and complaint.

34. Ferrante, "Relation of Speech to Sin," p. 34, cites Old Testament examples of such advice, and some similar passages from Gregory's *Moralia*.

35. Also see *Paradiso* 9.4, for Charles' advice: "Taci e lascia muover li anni" [Keep silence, and let the years revolve].

36. Singleton's Commentary on *Purgatorio*, p. 633.

37. See Kirkpatrick, p. 30.

38. See Cassata for an extended discussion of the puzzling "per lungo silenzio . . . fioco" (1.63), and more recently, Casagrande. Hollander, *Virgilio dantesco*, pp. 23–79, argues that "fioco" marks visual rather than aural faintness, and "lungo" spatial rather than temporal distance – so that the verse might be paraphrased: "who appeared indistinct in the vast silence." Durling and Martinez suggest in their note to *Inferno* 1.63 that "Virgil" might be taken to mean the codex of Virgil's poetry, precisely where the visual and the audible merge, and "fioco" might thus mean both "faint" and "hoarse."

39. Whitfield, p. 96, compares Dante and Aeneas as exiles.

40. On Beatrice's naming of Dante, see Cervigni.

41. Among the useful comments on this line, see Mazzotta, *Poet of the Desert*, pp. 186–87; Singleton's Commentary on *Purgatorio*, pp. 734–35; and Hollander, ed., *Purgatorio*, p. 630.

42. Hollander, ed., *Purgatorio*, pp. 631–32.

43. Leo, pp. 59–60.

44. Greene, "Dramas of Selfhood," pp. 128–29.

45. Mazzotta, *Poet of the Desert*, pp. 220–21, quotes Paul, speaking of the Jew as "a guide to the blind, a light of them who are in blindness" (Romans 2:19), and Augustine's address to the Jews as the ones who "carried in your hands the lamp of the law in order to show the way to others while you remained in darkness" (*De Symbolo ad Catechumenos* 4.4).

46. See Ferrante, "Words and Images," and Ferrante, "Relation of Speech to Sin," p. 34, on Dante's coinage of new words "to describe mystic concepts, 's'india,' 'intrea,' 's'inluia,' etc." She notes ("Words and Images," p. 119) that most of Dante's coinages are verbs, which he "creates from nouns, adjectives, and pronouns, to extend or violate our sense of time and place, and to suggest the fusion of separate beings." Also see Hawkins, *Dante's Testaments*, pp. 214–18.

Schnapp, "*Paradiso*," p. 677, describes how Dante places *Paradiso* within the context of Western mysticism by "stretching the expressive capabilities of language" and simultaneously "emphasizing language's breakdown through repeated assertions of incapacity and ineffability."

47. See Hollander, *Allegory*, pp. 297–98, for the connections between this "visible speech" and two other instances of the same thing: the inscription on the gate of Hell (*Inf.* 3.1–9), and the sky writing of *Par.* 18.91–93 – each of the three concerned with God's justice.

48. Schnapp, "Virgin Words," p. 281, argues that "the miraculous alien tongue" of this hymn "serves to anoint the speaker as well as the spoken. Justinian's Hebraeo-Latin marks him as the legitimate heir of the Hebrew kings and attests to the divinely sanctioned character of his vision of salvation history."

49. Ferrante, "Words and Images," p. 116. The particular soundplays that Ferrante comments on – "the repetition of the same sounds for different shades of meaning, particularly different grammatical forms," "or the same sound for totally different meanings, e.g., homonym rhymes" – are especially interesting as efforts, from within the essential equivocation of fallen language, to rehabilitate its potential.

50. See Mazzeo, "Dante's Three Communities," p. 73, and Mazzotta, *Poet of the Desert*, p. 316.

51. See Marigo, pp. lxii–lxiii. Pagliaro, "I 'primissima signa,'" argues that Dante's view of the fixed grammatical language probably derives in part from the idea of *latinitas*, as expressed by Varro and by Cicero's *De Oratore* 3.44.

52. Pagliaro, "Dialetti e lingue," p. 452, notes that Dante marks Cacciaguida's nobility and antiquity by his first speaking in Latin (*Par.* 15.28–30), then with Latinisms in his antique dialect. Also see Pézard, "Trois langues."

53. Letter to Cangrande (29), trans. Haller, p. 110. On the "imageless vision," see Chiarenza.

54. Cf., e.g., Mazzotta, "Virtues of Exile," p. 667: "Poetic language – and from Adam's speech we can infer all language – is the allegory of exile, the figure of man's displacement into an alien world."

55. Singleton, *Dante Studies 2*, pp. 26–27; also see Schnapp, "Lectura Dantis," p. 84, n.8, on neologism as part of Dante's effort to redeem language.

56. Singleton's commentary on *Par.* 18.1 quotes Aquinas, *ST* 1.34, a. 1, resp.: "Wherefore the exterior vocal sound is called a word from the fact that it signifies the interior concept of the mind. Therefore it follows that, first and chiefly, the interior concept of the mind is called a word." Anthony Oldcorn (in Mandelbaum et al., *Lectura Dantis*, p. 334) notes that *Inferno* 25.16 is the only appearance of the word *verbo* in the *Commedia* outside of *Paradiso*.

57. Ascoli argues persuasively for a connection between the play on *actor, auctor, autor* and the "vowels of authority" in *Convivio* 4.6.3–4 and the end of *Paradiso*.
58. Ferrante, "Relation of Speech to Sin," p. 34.
59. Greene, *Light in Troy*, p. 13, focuses on the verb *abbella*, "evidently coined . . . from the Provençal," and its very interesting implications within Dante's account of linguistic instability. Also cf. his remarks on p. 7, on Dante's change of mind from *De Vulgari Eloquentia* to *Paradiso* 26, which Palmieri also discusses.
60. *ST* 2a2ae.85,1. For commentary see, e.g., Mazzocco, pp. 163–64. A closely similar and derivative comment appears in the *De regimine principum* of Egidio Romano, which quotes Aristotle's *Peri hermeneias*: see Mazzocco, p. 255, and Guerrieri Crocetti, p. 374.
61. *ST* 1a.96,1,3. Cf. *Paradise Lost* 8.352–54: "I named them, as they passed, and understood/ Their nature, with such knowledge God endued/ My sudden apprehension."
62. Nardi, "Due capitoli." Also see Nardi, *Dante*, p. 245; Damon; and Rizzo, esp. p. 73 and pp. 80–81.
63. Rizzo, pp. 80–81, argues persuasively that "I" is a sign signifying unity. Also see d'Ovidio, p. 317.
64. The first quotation is from Cremona, "Paradiso XXVI," pp. 188–89, the second from Brownlee, "Angels Speak Italian," p. 600, n. 8. Also see Cremona, "Dante's Views"; Benfell, p. 86; and Mengaldo, "Appunti," p. 245.

    Corti, "Les notions," pp. 32–33, argues that for Dante in *De Vulgari Eloquentia*, the *forma locutionis*, created by God at the same time as the soul (1.6.4), "is not a concrete language," but its formal cause and generating principle, distinct from the *voces* that Adam uses to give birth to the first natural and universal language. Dante does, however, explicitly postulate: "I say 'form' with reference both to the words used for things, and to the construction of words, and to the arrangement of the construction"; in Barański's paraphrase, "God had bestowed on Adam both the ability to speak and a completely formed tongue" (p. 107). Cremona, "*Paradiso* XXVI," p. 187, makes the same point, but argues that in *Paradiso* 26 "it is only the faculty of language that God has given man."
65. Arbery, p. 38.
66. *Ars Poetica* 60–72. Dante also cites this passage in *Convivio* 2.13, when he discusses the appropriateness of Grammar to the heaven of the Moon. Greene, *Light in Troy*, p. 14, discusses *Paradiso* 26 in this Horatian context.

67. Colish, *Mirror of Language*, p. 213.
68. So Schildgen, p. 108, also argues: by Dante's change of mind in *Paradiso* 26, he "restricts the first language of Adam to Eden, insisting that language since the Fall is occasional and ruled by historical circumstance and time." Also see Eco, *Search*, p. 45.
69. *Historia Scholastica* (PL 198:1075); *Elucidarium* 1.90–91 (p. 377): PL 172:1119.
70. See, for example, Brownlee, "XXVI," p. 397: "This depriveleging of Hebrew means that all human languages are 'equal' with regard to their potential, both for expressing theological truth and for grammatico-poetic enrichment." Also see Contini, p. 343; Mengaldo, "Gramatica," p. 264; and Hawkins, "Adam," pp. 4–5.
71. Mazzotta, *Poet of the Desert*, p. 215, notes that the three cantos 26 in the *Commedia* share a focus on language, "as caught in the spirals of a temporal instability."
72. Brownlee, "Angels Speak Italian," p. 599.
73. Guerri, pp. 63 and 69.
74. Damon, pp. 61–62. He argues that "The language spoken in the state of innocence, here represented by its word for the Supreme Good, was superior not, as Dante had once thought, because it was extra-human, but rather because it reflected a superior mode of human apprehension."
75. Mazzocco, p. 179. Cf. Arbery, pp. 38–39, who notes, as Singleton had, that "*I* is both the first letter of the later names of God and the Roman numeral for one," and that "the name becomes a number only when it is written," implying that "speech enjoys no privilege over writing."
76. Damon, p. 61, argues persuasively that Dante "had taken *primum* . . . to mean 'in the beginning' instead of 'first of all.'"
77. *Etym.* 14.3.12.
78. Cited in Singleton's Commentary on *Paradiso*, p. 248.
79. Hollander, ed., *Purgatorio*, p. 269.
80. Medici, p. 345.
81. Singleton substitutes 1 for the *i* of other editions, and explains why in his note to line 100: "The *Anonimo fiorentino* comments: . . . 'These two letters, *O* and *I*, are written with one stroke of the pen; and therefore they can be written faster than the others.' But for this to be so, the *i* must be undotted." Ferrante comments on *o* and *i* in *Inferno* 24: the circle and line are the basic components "on which all construction and writing rely"; in reverse, the two letters together form *io*, the pronoun *I*, the marker of selfhood and "individual existence" (in Mandelbaum et al., *Lectura Dantis*, p. 324).

82. Heilbronn-Gaines, p. 269.
83. Cited by Medici, p. 345. Barański, p. 126, points out that "the *signum* 'I' was a perfect synthetic example of the instability of human linguistic creations," since in these cantos of *Paradiso* it can be "a letter, a numeral and a proper noun."
84. See Medici, p. 345.
85. Vincent, p. 12. On p. 13, he notes the horror implicit in the word *Peccato* and its mark by *P* in the *Purgatorio*, emphasized by patterns of alliteration (e.g., *Purgatorio* 9.109–14): "In many of the relevant passages we have what we can only call a crepitation of P's." Barolini argues that "the acrostic spelling UOM, a form of visual poetry signifying man's sinful tendency toward pride, is also an example of the very pride it condemns," by conflating the poet's visual art with God's (*Undivine "Comedy,"* p. 141).
86. Mazzotta, *Poet of the Desert*, p. 129, cites Macrobius as another source of this passage.
87. Mazzotta, *Poet of the Desert*, p. 11; also see Greene, *Light in Troy*, p. 12.
88. Mazzotta, *Poet of the Desert*, offers the fullest exploration of this pattern.
89. Cambon, p. 39.
90. Corti, "Les notions," p. 36; also see her *Dante a un nuovo crocevia*, pp. 56–60 and 70–76.
91. Corti, "Torre di Babele," p. 255.
92. The thirteenth-century grammarian Henri de Crissey (quoted by Mengaldo, "Gramatica," p. 260) elaborates on the distinction between the lay idioms of the Latin peoples, imposed *ad placitum* and taught to children by their mothers and fathers, and the clerical idiom, the same for everyone and taught to children in schools by teachers. Mengaldo cites a number of thirteenth and fourteenth-century examples of *gramatica* meaning something written in Latin. Also see Copeland, *Rhetoric, Hermeneutics, and Translation*, p. 104, for Giles of Rome's view that the philosophers invented Latin as a literary language, "so profound and rich that they could adequately express all their meanings through it" (also cited by Lusignan, "Le français et le latin," pp. 958–59).
93. See Cremona, "*Paradiso* XXVI," pp. 188–89. Benfell, p. 83, describes the *Commedia* and Dante, attempting the work of linguistic reparation, as *in bono* versions of the Tower of Babel and Nimrod.
94. *Convivio* 1.5. Among several efforts to resolve the contradiction between the *Convivio* and the *De Vulgari Eloquentia* – the latter arguing that the vernacular is nobler than "grammatical" language, the former the reverse – see Grayson and also Dragonetti, "Conception du langage," esp. p. 29.

95. At several other points, Dante's Tuscan identity is revealed by or associated with his speech (catalogued by Pagliaro, "Dialetti e lingue," p. 454): four in the *Inferno*, three in *Purgatorio*, and one in *Paradiso*.
96. See Barolini, *Dante's Poets*, p. 229, and Freccero, "Dante's Ulysses," p. 109. Interestingly, Horace's comments on the Homeric high style, appropriate for "the exploits of kings and captains and the sorrows of war" (*Ars Poetica* 73–74), come directly after the remarks on linguistic change that Dante adapts in *Paradiso* 26.
97. See Pagliaro, "Dialetti et lingue," p. 449. Florentine mythology traced the city's origin to Troy: see Rubinstein. Dante's *Epistola* 5.11–12 argues that the Lombards were originally Scandinavian.
98. Rizzo, pp. 81–82. Barolini, *Dante's Poets*, p. 232n., suggests that Virgil's Lombard is in effect ancient Lombard, "a vernacular form of the *gramatica* in which he wrote, i.e. a vernacular form of Latin." And *DVE* 1.9.7 implies enough continuity between ancient and modern Pavians for dialectal differences to be noticeable.
99. See *DVE* 1.15.2, on why Sordello, "this man of unusual eloquence abandoned the vernacular of his home town not only when writing poetry but on every other occasion." On this episode in *Purgatorio* see Barolini, *Dante's Poets*, pp. 161–63.
100. See Mengaldo, "Gramatica," and Lo Piparo, p. 6. Dante does evidently think that Latin was always a learned language, distinct from the vernacular: see the *Vita Nuova* 25:3 and 25:6. Herren provides a general discussion of Latin and the vernaculars.
101. Lusignan, "La topique," p. 14 (also see Lusignan, "Langue maternelle"). Oresme's introduction to his translation of Aristotle's *Ethics* and *Politics*, pp. 100–1, argues that Greek was in the same relation to classical Latin as Latin is now in relation to French: the language that students had to learn in order to gain access to a storehouse of knowledge. And for the Romans, "le langage commun et maternel, c'estoit latin" [the common and maternal language was Latin]. (See Lusignan, "La topique," p. 13 and pp. 156–57).
102. Schwarz, p. 157, thus characterizes Jerome's opinion.
103. Cf. Tyndale's justification for his translation of the Bible into "the mother tongue": "Saint Jerome also translated the Bible into his mother tongue. Why may not we also?" (quoted by Daniell, p. 229). Hanna, "Difficulty," p. 321, discusses the Lollard view "that, at least *vis-à-vis* Hebrew, Latin is like English – simply another secondary vernacular"; also see Hudson, "Wyclif," p. 90, for Wyclif's "amazingly nonchalant" view of every language as a mere *habitus* – "almost an 'accident' as opposed to the 'substance' of the gospel message."

104. *Four English Political Tracts*, p. 5. John of Trevisa, "Prefaces on Translation," p. 292, lines 130–35, makes a similar statement.
105. Hollander, "Babytalk," expands on the implications of this paradox.
106. Earlier in the *Inferno*, there was mention of Plutus' "voce chioccia" (7.2) [clucking voice].
107. For this account of Francis' style, see Auerbach, *Mimesis*, p. 162.
108. Benvenuto's comment on Dante's title explores its paradoxes (quoted by Auerbach, *Mimesis*, p. 188): "But perhaps, reader, you will say: Why do you want to rebaptize the book for me, when the author called it a Comedy? I say that the author wished to call it a comedy because of its low and vernacular style [*a stylo infimo et vulgari*], and in fact, speaking literally, it is low in style, but in its kind is sublime and exalted [*humilis respectu litteralis, quamvis in genere suo sit sublimis et excellens*]." (See Benvenuto, p. 19, for the original text.) On the issue of "comedy" generally, see the note on the poem's title by Mariani, pp. 79–81.
109. See the discussion in Jenaro-MacLennan, pp. 92–104 (and the review by Scott, pp. 933–34), and more recently, Kelly, *Tragedy*. The Epistle to Cangrande makes a series of comments on comedy as "rustic song" (10.28), characterized by a relaxed and humble style (10.30) and by its use of the vernacular, the language "in which even women communicate" (10.31) (*Epistola XIII*, trans. Haller, p. 101). Cf. Boccaccio's preface to the fourth day of the *Decameron*, his long work disarmingly "senza titolo" [without a title]; interestingly, Coluccio Salutati's epitaph for Boccaccio reads: "Inclyte cur vates, humili sermone locutus, / de te pertransis?" ["Celebrated bard, why do you who have spoken in humble voice pass on?] (quoted by Branca, p. 290).
110. *Convivio*, trans. pp. 12 and 14.
111. Pagliaro, "Teoria e prassi," p. 530; also see Singleton's Commentary on the *Inferno*, p. 363, and Barolini's comment in Mandelbaum et al., *Lectura Dantis*, p. 281. Singleton makes a similar point in his comment on the word "rogna" [itch] in *Paradiso* 17.129.
112. Cambon, p. 199, n. 17.
113. Hollander, *Virgilio dantesco*. Jacoff & Stephany, pp. 15–17, analyze this canto in the context of Dante's larger linguistic concerns about *parola ornate* and *sermo humilis*.
114. For the *sermo humilis* in Augustine and Biblical commentary more generally, see Auerbach, "Sermo humilis," and his *Literary Language*, esp. pp. 44–66. Augustine records his shift from embarrassment to pride in the humble style of the Bible, "compared with the majesty of Cicero" (*Confessions* 3.5), and praises the Bible's holy simplicity (*Confessions* 6.5). Marrou, *Saint Augustin*, pp. 473ff., Pézard, *Pluie de feu*, pp. 153–63, and

Murphy, pp. 46 and 51, summarize the attacks by the Church Fathers on classical literature and the grammarians.

But see Dronke's important caveat (*Women Writers*, p. 16), that "Augustine did not, as Auerbach claimed, exalt the lowly style over other ways of writing, or 'see the style of Scripture as *humilis* throughout.'"

115. Goldstein, p. 326, n. 36, discusses *Inferno* 26 as an anti-epic. Also see Mazzotta, *Poet of the Desert*, pp. 88–91; Barolini, "Dante's Ulysses"; and Kirkpatrick, p. 71: "'Ulysses' is what Dante himself might have been if he had not read the *Aeneid*, or responded to the influence of Beatrice."

116. See Singleton's Commentary on *Purgatorio*, p. 77, on the "homely simile" of *Purg.* 4.21 (translating Benvenuto da Imola's phrase for this *comparatio domestica*); and his Commentary on *Paradiso*, p. 556, for the image of the "buon sartore" [good tailor] at *Par.* 32.140–41. (For further discussion, see Mengaldo, "L'elegia 'umile.'")

117. Quoted by Auerbach, *Literary Language*, p. 66.

118. Botterill, p. 173.

119. Giovanni Villani's *Cronica* 8.10, translated by Davis, p. 168. On the complicated issue of Brunetto's place in the *Inferno*, see Pézard, *Pluie de feu*; Kay, *Dante's Swift and Strong*; and Vance, *Mervelous Signals*, pp. 230–55.

120. See Singleton's Commentary on *Inferno* 13.67–72 (p. 213). Spitzer, "Speech and Language," p. 92, remarks on Dante's remarkable use here of onomatopoeia, specifically of "harsh-sounding, consonant-ridden words," and the horrifying fact "that we have to do with speech of a non-human order, with speech that is a matter of bodily discharges" (p. 89).

121. Alain, *Theologiae regulae* 34 (*PL* 210:637); quoted in Taylor's notes to Hugh of St. Victor's *Didascalicon*, p. 183.

122. Salter, pp. 222–23, gives an account of such arguments in favor of prose by Roger Bacon, Wyclif, Usk, and John of Trevisa.

123. *Convivio*, trans. p. 25.

124. Dante does, however, approvingly use the verbs *carminare* and *induere*, with their connotations of weaving and putting on clothes, in *DVE* 2.1.1 and 2.1.4.

125. Guido da Pisa, *Prooemium*, ed. Jenaro-MacLennan, p. 128; also see Cioffari and Mazzoni, p. 132. One of the manuscripts of Guido reads *ornate* for *ordinate*; see Jenaro-MacLennan's extended note on the "technical distinction . . . between 'ornare' and 'ordinare'" (p. 124).

126. Quoted by Jenaro-MacLennan, p. 121. There is an equivalent oxymoron when Guido da Pisa refers in his *Prooemium* to the "altissima Comedia" [most lofty *Comedy*] (quoted by Jenaro-MacLennan, p. 125) and explicates Dante's title: "Incipit profundissima et altissima Comedia Dantis

excellentissimi poete" [Here begins the most profound and lofty *Commedia* of Dante the most excellent poet] (Jenaro-MacLennan, p. 128).

127. Mazzotta, *Poet of the Desert*, p. 158, and Jacoff and Stephany, p. 17.

128. One of the most interesting cruxes appears early in the poem, in *Inf.* 3.10, immediately following the inscription on the gate of hell: "Queste parole di colore oscuro" [These words of obscure color]. Is color rhetorical here, as verse 12 seems to suggest: "Maestro, il senso lor m'è duro" [Master, their meaning is hard for me]? Or are the words literally hard to read, because dim in color?

129. The word *latin* is, interestingly, used by Chrétien de Troyes and William IX of Aquitaine for language more generally, specifically the language of birds.

130. See Hollander, "Babytalk," p. 79, on the *femmina balba*.

131. Singleton's Commentary on *Inferno* 18.25 (p. 313).

132. Winthrop Wetherbee has reminded me that although I was a careful enough reader when I reviewed his *Chaucer and the Poets* to notice an index entry for Carleton Fisk, I had managed to forget since then that he makes a similar point about "making" and "poesye" (*Chaucer and the Poets*, pp. 226–27). He also knows what I had entirely forgotten, that we were both anticipated by Tatlock, p. 631, n. 8. Also see Olson, "Making and Poetry," and cf. Middleton, "Chaucer's 'New Men,'" pp. 35–37.

133. Wetherbee, *Chaucer and the Poets*, p. 227, makes the intriguing and indeed persuasive suggestion that Chaucer's "poesie" may recall "Dante's sole use of *poesi*" in *Purg.* 1.7.

134. Fyler, "*Auctoritee* and Allusion," p. 77.

135. For Dante's self-naming as "vernacular *poeta*," see Brownlee, "Angels Speak Italian," esp. pp. 602–3.

136. For the amalgam of different styles in *Troilus and Criseyde*, see above all Muscatine, *French Tradition*, pp. 124–65.

137. See my general note to the *House of Fame* in the *Riverside Chaucer*, p. 977.

138. For the idea that the *House of Fame* parodies Dante, see Rambeau and also Chiarini; their arguments are convincingly refuted by Robinson, "Chaucer and Dante." For the poem as a replica of Dante, see Koonce. Schless, pp. 29–76, summarizes the various debates, and examines the allusions in detail.

139. *Riverside Chaucer*, p. 348. See Kiser, "Eschatological Poetics"; Taylor, *Chaucer Reads 'The Divine Comedy,'* pp. 20–49; and also Cooper, "Four Last Things," which argues that Chaucer, "fascinated and appalled, in roughly equal measure" (p. 42), proceeds "to mount a direct challenge to Dante and the world he constructs" (p. 41).

140. Riverside Chaucer note to lines 499–508 (pp. 981–82).
141. There is also an echo, noted in the *Riverside Chaucer* (p. 982), of *Paradiso* 1.61–63 in lines 504–6. The note to lines 888–89 (p. 984) notes an evident reminiscence of *Paradiso* 22.128–29; and in line 1803, "beloweth" echoes the "mugghia" of *Inferno* 5.29.
142. The *Riverside* note to line 734 (p. 983) gives specific source references.
143. The *Riverside* note to lines 1871–72 (p. 989) cites the details in the *Commedia*.
144. Clemen, p. 93 and p. 97.
145. Dante's son Pietro etymologizes the name *Dante* as "he was giving" or "he gave," in a commentary on this verse (Hollander, ed., *Purgatorio*, p. 632).
146. The phrase is Mazzotta's (*Poet of the Desert*, p. 89).
147. "The name of Love is so sweet to hear that it seems impossible that in most instances its own operations can be other than sweet, for names are consequent upon the things named, just as it is written: 'Nomina sunt consequentia rerum'" (*Vita Nuova* 13.4). Guerrieri Crocetti, p. 376, cites a contrary medieval opinion (Marino da Caramanico), which argues that common names are immutable and tied to things, whereas proper names – decent or indecent – are imposed by the individual will, with no apparent connection to the person named.
148. Pézard, *Pluie de feu*, pp. 355–64, discusses some Patristic and medieval views on the prophetic quality of certain names.
149. See Pézard, *Pluie de feu*, p. 101, and Singleton, "*Vita Nuova*," p. 119. Cf. Dante's name play in *Par.* 7.14: "per *Be* e per *ice*."
150. Guido da Pisa's *Prooemium*, ed. Jenaro-MacLennan, p. 125: Dante is so named, according to Guido, because "from Dante is given to us [*a Dante datur nobis*] this most noble work." Guido compares Dante to the hand writing on the wall in Daniel 5: "Hand, then, that is, Dante; for by hand we mean Dante. Indeed *manus* (hand) comes from *mano, manas* (to pour forth), and Dante comes from *do, das* (to give); because just as from the hand comes forth a gift, so from Dante there is given to us this most lofty work" (Cioffari and Mazzoni, pp. 126–27). Also see Benvenuto, pp. 11–12: Dante is so named for "*dans se ad multa*" [giving himself to many things], specifically to the pursuit of all knowledge, and especially of poetry; or for "*dans theos*," "that is, the knowledge of God and divine things." Hollander, *Allegory*, pp. 128–29, notes that *Aeneid* 8.670, which mentions Cato as a just lawgiver [*his dantem iura*] may explain Cato's appearance in Purgatorio 1, along with "one further touch in Virgil which must have made Dante start and smile: the line contains his own name."

Chaucer, of course, never calls himself a shoemaker.

151. Whitfield, p. 99; Sarolli, pp. 414–22, also discusses the Nathan/Dante wordplay. Isidore's *Etym.* 7.7 discusses the predestination inherent in certain Patriarchs' names.

152. Shankland, esp. pp. 773–76. Also see Tambling, p. 147, and for a more general exploration of "Etymology as a Category of Thought," Curtius, pp. 495–500.

153. See Vincent, pp. 7–8, and Mazzotta, *Poet of the Desert*, pp. 299–300, which argues that this etymologizing canto 12 appropriately ends with Donatus, the master of "the first art" (12.138), grammar, "the ground in which the split between words and things, which characterizes the language of the fallen world, is healed and correct interpretation is envisioned."

154. Auerbach, *Mimesis*, p. 184, and Barolini, *Undivine "Comedy,"* p. 18, point out that this assertion is not true: most owe their fame to the *Commedia* itself.

155. See Jacoff, and also Greene, "Dramas of Selfhood," pp. 128–29.

156. Singleton's Commentary on the *Inferno*, pp. 302–3.

157. Greene, "Dramas of Selfhood," p. 123. He adds (p. 133): "In the *Paradiso*, as nowhere else, Dante is extraordinarily reticent with names . . . The soul's earthly designation seems to be considered increasingly a mere linguistic accident."

158. Cf. the Eagle's jocular comment to Geffrey in the *House of Fame*, that Jove has no plans to stellify him "as yet" (597–99). On the relation of *vox* and *vanitas* in canto 11, see Marks.

159. Ed. Jenaro-MacLennan, p. 128.

160. But see the interesting discussion of this passage by Brewer, "Chaucer's Poetic Style," p. 240, as "a good example of the fusion of orality with more learned elements," combining a "plain and ordinary" vocabulary with "a number of learned words," occurring in English for the first, or almost the first time: *subtilite, prolixite, poetrie, rhetorike, encombrous, palpable, figure* and *colour* as stylistic terms, and for that matter *term* itself.

161. Fyler, *Chaucer and Ovid*, pp. 53–55.

162. Cf. Vance, "Chaucer's *House of Fame*," p. 27: he argues that the Eagle fallaciously accepts "certain 'Cratylistic' doctrines," in claiming "that the word materially conserves either the person who utters it about himself or who is named in the utterance." Taylor, *Chaucer Reads 'The Divine Comedy,'* pp. 24–25, sees here an allusion to God's *visibile parlare* (*Purgatorio* 10.95), in order "to portray a problematic poetry of the imagination." For Edwards, *Dream of Chaucer*, p. 117, the account of Fame illustrates "a radical separation of words from things."

163. Cf. the Flood narrative in the epic of *Gilgamesh*: "In those days the world teemed, the people multiplied, the world bellowed like a wild bull, and

the great god was aroused by the clamour. Enlil heard the clamour and he said to the gods in council, 'The uproar of mankind is intolerable and sleep is no longer possible by reason of the babel.' So the gods agreed to exterminate mankind" (p. 108).

164. Fyler, *Chaucer and Ovid*, p. 54.

165. For the broader implications of grammar in relation to the poem, see Irvine, "Medieval Grammatical Theory," and Boitani, "Chaucer's Labyrinth," pp. 212–15.

166. Donatus, p. 367; translated by Irvine, *Making*, p. 92 (I have altered his translation slightly). Cf. Isidore, *Etym.* 3.20.2: "Voice [*vox*] is air reverberated [*verberatus*] by breath, from which indeed words [*verba*] are named. Properly, however, a voice is of men, or of irrational animals." *Vox* is used improperly, Isidore adds, in other contexts such as "the voice of the trumpet roared." Also see Servius' *Commentarius in Artem Donati* (p. 405) on *verbum*, and the discussion in Aquinas, *Politicorum Aristotelis Expositio*, Lectio 1, 1.1.36 (p. 11), quoted above in note 1, on the distinction between voice and speech.

167. Quoted by Jolivet, *Arts du langage*, p. 25. The first quotation is from the *Glossae super Praedicamenta Aristotelis*, the second from the *Dialectica*.

168. The quotation on *vox* and *sermo* is from Sikes, p. 104. Also see Luscombe, p. 284: because the Latin word *vox* is ambiguous, designating either meaningful or empty sound, Abelard complements it with the term *sermo*: "*Sermo* represents the second meaning of *vox*, its *sensus*." The dispute with an unnamed opponent is described by Stock, p. 374.

169. *A Tale of a Tub*, p. 153.

170. Williams, *Pope's Dunciad*, p. 114. For the connections between the *House of Fame* and Pope's youthful imitation, the *Temple of Fame*, see Fyler, "Chaucer, Pope, and the *House of Fame*."

171. Though Benjamin Franklin counters, in the 1738 *Poor Richard's Almanack*: "As we must account for every idle word, so we must for every idle silence."

172. Also see *Paradiso* 1.34: "Poca favilla gran fiamma seconda" [A great flame follows a little spark]. For the importance of James's epistle in *Inferno* 26, see Cornish.

173. *In Librum Sapientiae*, lectio CXCIIII, p. 638. There are, he says, in fact two explanations for Echo: "one is natural, the other fabulous." The fabulous one comes from *Metamorphoses* 3, the natural by analogy with what Aristotle says in "de Lumine" about "light multiplied in air."

174. *Convivio* 1.3 (pp. 9–10). Boitani discusses this passage in *Imaginary World of Fame*, pp. 74–75.

175. Hanning, "Chaucer's First Ovid," aptly describes the House of Rumour as having "a distinctly vulgar, plebian quality," indeed, "as Chaucer's version

of the grimy kitchen beneath the fancy restaurant in George Orwell's *Down and Out in Paris and London*" (pp. 148–49).

176. On this topic see Carruthers.
177. Hanning, "Chaucer's First Ovid," p. 152.
178. Fyler, *Chaucer and Ovid*, p. 62.
179. The Wife's exuberance in fulfilling the task set by this command stands in contrast to Zenobia's rejection of sexual intercourse, except "To have a child, the world to multiplye" (*Monk's Tale* 2282), which is itself paired with Chauntecleer's self-indulgent service to Venus, "Moore for delit than world to multiplye" (*Nun's Priest's Tale* 3345).
180. *Confessions* 13.24; trans. p. 344.
181. *Opus Majus*, part 4, pp. 238–39. Quoted and discussed by Lindberg, pp. 19–20. On optics as an organizing principle in the *Roman de la Rose*, see Eberle.
182. Appropriately, Malory defines the "inchaunter" as "a multiplier of wordis" (*Works*, p. 548).
183. O'Connell, pp. 72 and 80. See his very interesting remarks (pp. 76–83) on these issues in Augustine's *De Musica*.
184. Lectio 16, pp. 279–80. This passage is quoted and discussed by Bennett, *Chaucer's "Book of Fame,"* p. 147.
185. Irvine, "Medieval Grammatical Theory," p. 876.
186. Cf. the interesting comments on the poem's ending by Baswell, p. 248.

CHAPTER 4

1. Frost, p. 377. Some of the following remarks, and indeed the germinal idea for this book, derive from a paper I gave at the Medieval Institute, Kalamazoo, in 1980 on "The Decay of Language in Fragment VIII of the *Canterbury Tales*."
2. Jarrell, p. 17.
3. Ruthven, pp. 11–12; also see Borchardt.
4. Hamilton, p. 121.
5. Ricks, pp. 110–12.
6. Ruthven, p. 14. I assume that "word" here is, as frequently happens, a typographical error for "world."
7. Fyler, *Chaucer and Ovid*, p. 155.
8. Howard, p. 304. Also see Lawler, pp. 145–46.
9. For interpretations of Fragment VIII as a unified whole, see Grennen, "Chemical Wedding," and Rosenberg, "Contrary Tales." Grennen, p. 480, argues plausibly that Chaucer must have modified the *Second Nun's Tale* from an earlier version of his "lyf of Seinte Cecile" by adding

specific allusions to the alchemical literature, preparing for the tale about alchemy that is to follow.

10. See Smalley, "Andrew of St. Victor." She discusses her findings again in *Study of the Bible.* The phrase "Hebraica veritas" is Jerome's coinage, in his *Hebrew Questions on Genesis.*

11. Kolve, pp. 150–52, describes Cecilia's "spiritual procreation, spiritual fecundity" (p. 151). Fleming points out that the early Franciscan literature, with its emphasis on the power of the Word and on "rhetorical simplicity" (*Introduction*, p. 116), offers a more recent model than the *Acta Martyrum.*

12. See Brown, *Body and Society*, for a fascinating account of body and bodilessness in early Christian thought, including the alchemical image in a fifth-century letter "extolling the power of God. God would 'make our nature translucent.' At the resurrection, human flesh would 'turn molten to regain its lost solidity,' as base metal flowered into gold in the alchemist's crucible" (pp. 441–42).

13. As the Riverside note to 583–86 points out, the narrative's precision about distances (555, 561) shows that there is no need for such a sweaty rush: "Chaucer clearly wishes to have them make a dramatic and striking entrance." Its abruptness is also marked by the narrator's interjection of himself, as the "I" (569–70) who deduces that one of the new arrivals is a canon. On "sweetness and sweat" in Fragment VIII, see Cowgill.

14. Olson, "Chaucer, Dante," p. 224, points out the ambiguous syntax of "lurkinge in derknesse," which could describe the gold-grubbers as well as the gold they seek. Dean, *World Grown Old*, pp. 94–95, notes the association of the declining world with a list of ten metals, in the Vulgate commentary on the *Metamorphoses*, suggesting "a slowly evolving decline leading inexorably to the basest metal, a process akin to alchemy in reverse." Calabrese discusses the collocation of the base with the golden, specifically with "aurifying dung," in *De medicamina faciei* and in the fourteenth-century poem *Antiovidianus.*

15. The word "werche" is repeated several times over the course of the tale (see the Riverside note to 14). Peck notes that both Cecilia and the Canon's Yeoman are translators, "concerned with transforming base into pure," and "with multiplying the fruits of their labor. But the effects of their labors are antithetical: Cecilia conceives and begets a multitude of fruitful transformations; the Yeoman's pains always prove abortive and bring him only increased frustration, a multiplication of woes" ("'Entente' and Translation," pp. 34–35). They are also both "bisy," as Olson notes ("Chaucer, Dante," pp. 222–23).

16. See the Riverside note to 195.

17. See Patterson "Perpetual Motion," pp. 32–33, on her "belief in the unbreakable connection between words and their significance."
18. On the significance of names, see Clogan, p. 232, and especially Hanning, "Uses of Names," and Robinson, "Significance of Names."
19. In the *Prologue* to the *Legend of Good Women*, Chaucer's variation on the French marguerite poem, Alceste the daisy, the "dayes ye," enacts the etymology of her name as heliotrope and, in Cupid's religion, as the redeeming Sun.
20. See the Riverside note to 62.
21. For a more nearly contemporaneous instance of this widely influential Augustinian argument, see Bonaventure, *Itinerarium* III. 5 (p. 68).
22. Cf. Pearsall, *Canterbury Tales*, pp. 253–54, Benson, *Drama of Style*, pp. 133–35, and Martin, p. 151. Pratt, p. 257, argues that Chaucer adapts the Prioress' prayer from his own earlier version, the Second Nun's, "without recourse to the text of the *Paradiso*"; Schless, p. 207, counters, I think correctly, that these "are two separate borrowings from *Par.* 33, one affected by the precedence of the other." Chaucer also mines the opening of *Paradiso* 33 for *Troilus and Criseyde* 3.1261–67, Troilus' hymn to "Benigne Love."
23. Sherman, p. 144: "By identifying both with the Mother and the child, by playing the role both of *infans* and bearer of the Word, the Prioress veils the knowledge of the split process of language."
24. Riverside note to 437.
25. See Blamires, "Women and Preaching," esp. p. 151.
26. Blamires, *Case for Women*, p. 133, n. 26, quotes Augustine's Sermon 281, on Perpetua and Felicity: "the crown is all the more glorious when the sex is weaker, and the soul shows itself assuredly more virile in women [*uirilis animus in feminas maius aliquid fecit*] when they do not succumb to the weight of their fragility."
27. Cf. Shoaf, "'Unwemmed Custance.'"
28. Brody outlines the points of comparison in the three tales.
29. See Benson, *Drama of Style*, p. 141.
30. See Musurillo, pp. liii and 179. Beichner, "Confrontation," p. 204, points out that Chaucer "intensified the clash between Almachius and Cecilia . . . ; Cecilia had never before been quite so contentious or belligerent, nor had Almachius been so obtuse or stupid."
31. Cf. Hirsh, pp. 163–66.
32. Cecilia thus makes a striking exception to the general rule that "The scholastic *quaestio*, as a method of argumentation employed in a system of higher education open only to men, is in this sense masculine" (Riddy, p. 67, n. 11).

33. See Walcutt, p. 283.
34. Hirsh, pp. 165–66.
35. Ridley summarizes (Riverside note to 490) the various links between the tales of the Second Nun and Canon's Yeoman: "images of the philosopher's stone and stone idols; night and blindness; the bath of flames and the tempering of metals; sweat and coolness; failure to multiply metals, and the multiplication of converts." See Manzalaoui, pp. 256–58, for Chaucer's attitude toward alchemy and its meaning in the *Canon's Yeoman's Tale*.
36. The notion of "divine alchemy" is strengthened by the characteristic ironies in alchemical mysticism, pointed out by Grennen, "Commonplaces of Alchemy," p. 307, undermining "a theory which spoke of sweet-smelling flowers, heavenly essences, and weddings of Sun and Moon" with "the fetid air of the chemical laboratory."
37. "Gold, after all, is prized precisely because it functions as a palpable sign of the incorruptible." It rises "above the processes of corruption and generation that govern our world" as "a prelapsarian metal: the uncontaminated trace of the Golden Age and/or of Eden" (Schnapp, "Lectura Dantis," p. 79).
38. See Grennen, "Commonplaces of Alchemy," p. 318, on the debt of the alchemists to "the Gnostic belief" that "'All things are one, they arose from the One and will return to the One,' a "'unity' topic" that "is blandly mouthed amidst the most confusing welter of terms and processes." He also notes the "oft-recurring invective against the foolish workers who 'multiply' the number of things they work with instead of confining themselves to the 'one substance, one vessel, one process' demanded by the unity topic" – ironically, since "multiply" is also the standard term for the final alchemical transformation (p. 320).
39. See Grennen, "Cosmic Furnace," p. 227.
40. The description comes from Howard, p. 291. As Leicester says, "This narrator aspires to perfect transparency . . ." (*Disenchanted Self*, p. 199).
41. Scattergood discusses suburbs as they appear in these two tales, and especially as they represent "the subversion of the value systems and ideologies which sustain these cities [Rome and London], and which they represent" (p. 130).
42. See John Reidy's note in the Riverside ed., p. 947.
43. On this point see Donaldson, pp. 1100–11.
44. See the Riverside note to line 669. Rosenberg, "Contrary Tales," p. 284, n. 17, notes the analogy with the *Pardoner's Prologue* (365), where supposedly numinous relics produce resolutely non-spiritual "multiplying" of cattle and possessions.

45. See Grennen, "Commonplaces of Alchemy," pp. 332–33, and Patterson, "Perpetual Motion," p. 34. Bloch, *Etymologies*, p. 35, paraphrases Augustine's view that "A single thing stated multiply, or a single statement understood multiply, participate in the degeneration of signification that accompanied the multiplication of mankind."

46. Cf. Grennen, "Commonplaces of Alchemy," pp. 323–25, and Muscatine, *French Tradition*, p. 219: "The technical imagery of the poem is very powerful in evoking the feeling of matter as matter . . . Nowhere else in Chaucer is there such a solid, unspiritual mass of 'realism.'" John of Salisbury, *Metalogicon* 1.4 (trans., p. 18) attacks the "strange terms" of physicians, and professional jargon more generally. The Canon's Yeoman anticipates Rabelais, where "Language is freed from the burden of signification and communication; words are piled up and played with for no reason at all, 'for the hell of it,' to use Spitzer's felicitous expression" (Berry, p. 51, quoting Spitzer, "Works of Rabelais," p. 145).

47. *Etym.* 1.7.1.

48. Samuel Johnson, "Preface to the *Dictionary*," in *Selected Poetry and Prose*, p. 280.

49. Cf. Leicester, "Piety and Resistance," p. 157, on the *Canon's Yeoman's Tale* as a tale of "gnostic religiosity" in search of the secret "which would transform not only the world but the adept, and bring them both to wholeness."

50. Oxford MS Bodl. 270b, fol. 11ᵛ. *Piers Plowman* 15.349–76, catalogues modern woes as *lussheburghes* (given a bawdy double meaning in the *Monk's Prologue* 1962), counterfeit coins that look like sterling but are made of "feble" metal (*Piers* 15.349–50): "Boþe lettred and lewed beþ alayed now wiþ synne" (354). Among other examples, including Grammar and the inability of clerks to construe authors and master languages, Langland attacks astronomers who "alday in hir Art faillen/ That whilom warned bifore what sholde falle after" (359–60); "Astronomyens also aren at hir wittes ende;/ Of þat was calculed of þe element þe contrarie þei fynde" (370–71). Gower discusses alchemy as a remedy for sloth, along with letters and the other invented arts. The unretrievable philosopher's stone would have the power to purify metals into gold and silver, cleansing them "Of rust, of stink and of hardnesse" (*Confessio Amantis* 4.2557).

51. An earlier version of the following pages appeared as Fyler, "Nimrod."

52. Rufinus, *Historia Ecclesiastica, PL* 21:535.

53. Chaucer's knowledge of the *Historia Scholastica* may be reflected in an odd marginal note, "Comestor," in the *Nun's Priest's Tale*, presumably written in response to the word *cronycle* in line 3208. In the *Monk's*

Tale, Chaucer evidently made use of Guyart Desmoulins' translation. For further discussion see Morey, "Petrus Comestor."

54. In this manuscript the gloss appears on fol. 16 as "glose incidens." For a list of these British Library manuscripts, see Fyler, "Nimrod," pp. 206–7.

55. Guido da Pisa, p. 639, gives the Latin text.

56. Travis argues that "The Second Nun's Tale is a saint's-life variant of the Christian archetype of spiritual alchemy, the story in *Daniel 3* of Shadrach, Meschack, and Abednigo, who for their refusal to worship Nebuchadnezzar's golden idol, were cast into a burning cauldron; rather than perish, they prospered and multiplied, and a fourth figure, symbolizing the Son of Man, was seen accompanying them." Nicholas of Lyra, as I mentioned in Chapter 1, says that Nimrod cast Abraham into the fire because he refused to become a fire-worshipper.

57. Raybin, pp. 204–5, notes "the strangely poetic lists" in the tale, the sense "of Chaucer poring over the words and mysteries that are as much the matter of the artist's craft as of the alchemist's."

58. Butor, p. 17.

59. John Reidy, in the *Riverside* notes (p. 947).

60. Cf. Patterson's astute remarks on this passage ("Perpetual Motion," pp. 44–45).

61. Schmidt's edition, p. 39, argues that the Yeoman sounds like Pinter or Beckett. Jordan, *Chaucer's Poetics*, pp. 28–29, also thinks of Beckett, though in a discussion of the *House of Fame*. Leicester, "Piety and Resistance," p. 158, comments on "the music of the names of things" here, and describes the list of terms as "a genuine lyric"; also see Hilberry.

62. See Barney, "Chaucer's Lists," especially pp. 214–15.

63. Not surprisingly, Jonson's play *The Alchemist* centers on the same paradoxes, the gulling use of terms but also "the joy in wit that the play expresses" (Steane's introduction to *The Alchemist*, p. 22). Most notable is Jonson's reprise, in II.3, 182–207 (*The Alchemist*, pp. 67–68), of the issues raised by the *Canon's Yeoman's Tale*: a helter-skelter list of terms – summed up as "all these, named, intending but one thing, which art our writers used to obscure their art" – that is meant to warn off the "simple idiot" who would profane the mystery. Alchemical terms are compared here to the "mystic symbols" of the Egyptians, Biblical parables, and the "choicest fables of the poets," "wrapped in perplexed allegories."

64. Fyler, *Chaucer and Ovid*, p. 150.

65. Travis points out these connections in an unpublished paper, as does Patterson, "Perpetual Motion," p. 55. Cf. Green, "Changing Chaucer."

66. See Chism, p. 354, and especially Hanning, "Theme of Art and Life," p. 36, on Chaucer's "audacious comparison of alchemy and his own art.

For if alchemists degrade themselves into examples of the rubble amidst which they work, Chaucer the poet transforms the rubble, the 'poudres diverse, asshes, donge, pisse and cley,' of pseudoscience into art that is both didactic and pleasurable."

67. Dubois, p. 28.
68. Cf. Patterson "Perpetual Motion," p. 31, on the modernity, "endowed with both urgency and belatedness," of alchemy and of Chaucer himself.
69. Taylor, "*Cosyn to the Dede*," p. 321, points out that Chaucer's word "cosyn" comes directly from Jean de Meun's translation of Boethius, and is the word Jean uses in the *Roman* (15160–62): in the former, words are cousins to *chosez*, in the latter to *fez*. As Taylor says, "The shift of the Boethian *choses* to *faiz* intimates that the *Roman* passage is the likely source for Chaucer, where *dede* contrasts with his use of *thinges* for Boethius's *res*."
70. See Purdon, but cf. Myles, p. 26, who maintains that for Chaucer, lack of steadfastness characterizes "the will of the speaking subject," not language itself; "it is not language that has changed; language was and always has been conventional."
71. For Chaucer's comic use of this passage in the *House of Fame*, see Fyler, *Chaucer and Ovid*, p. 54.
72. *Timaeus* 29B (p. 1162). Chadwick, p. 239, notes that *Timaeus* 29B has a significant role in efforts to reconcile Aristotle's conventional theory of language with Plato's view that there is something in names "which corresponds to reality and is therefore 'nature.'"
73. Reiss, "Chaucer's Fiction," p. 97, states the evident corollary to the argument in the *Timaeus*: "when the matter concerns the mutable world, then the words are likewise imperfect."
74. Hanning, "Roasting," p. 7. Also see Minnis, *Magister Amoris*, p. 124.
75. The phrase is from Leicester, *Disenchanted Self*; the book offers a brilliant demonstration of its implications in practice.
76. Minnis, *Magister Amoris*, pp. 131–32; also see his "*A leur fez cousines*."
77. Taylor, "*Cosyn to the Dede*," p. 320; but cf. Besserman, *Biblical Poetics*, p. 46. Perhaps "ful brode" responds more generally to the perceived rhetorical inelegance of the New Testament, an issue addressed by Jerome and Augustine: see Kamesar, pp. 46–49.
78. *De Doctrina Christiana* 3.12.18; ed. Green, p. 151. Besserman, *Biblical Poetics*, pp. 58–59, notes that the use of Romans 15.4 at the end of the *Nun's Priest's Tale* and in the *Retraction* makes such a claim for Chaucer's secular poetry.
79. Minnis, *Medieval Theory of Authorship*, p. 131.

80. Cooper, *Oxford Guide*, p. 60: "The General Prologue has already demonstrated a further principle: that deeds cannot necessarily be identified at all when they are shifted into the medium of language."

81. Taylor, "*Cosyn to the Dede*," p. 324.

82. For late fourteenth-century anxieties about "glosyng" in both senses, see Hudson, *Premature Reformation*, pp. 274–77; Hanning, "Roasting," p. 10; and Besserman, *Biblical Poetics*, pp. 145–57.

83. As Taylor points out (*Cosyn to the Dede*, p. 320), the phrase "alludes simultaneously to ignorance of Greek, inability to comprehend his philosophy, and the inaccessibility of Plato's works." A close analogue appears in *Troilus and Criseyde*, where the narrator refers to the "Troian gestes, as they felle, / In Omer, or in Dares, or in Dite, / Whoso that kan may rede hem as they write" (1.145–47); here too, the untranslatability of Greek seems more at issue than the lack of a good library.

84. Ginsberg, *Italian Tradition*, p. 74, notes that "the Manciple turns all similarity into alternate forms of emptiness." For him, "black and white are contraries only in illusion; in truth, the difference between them means nothing."

85. This advice reads almost as if a parody of Gower's *Mirour de l'Omme*, which says that silence is preferable to foolish speech, whether about friend or foe [*Ou soit d'amy ou d'adversaire*] (12781–83), and that *mesure* in speech is all-important (12792). Reiss, "Chaucer's Fiction," p. 109, describes the Manciple as "the jangler jangling while speaking against false speaking"; also see Ginsberg, *Italian Tradition*, p. 89: "with the Manciple, truth-telling becomes a way to maintain a lie; confession an accessory of obfuscation."

86. Grudin, p. 152, notes that Apollo, Amphion (to whom he is compared), and the snow-white crow all "suggest a golden age of speech and song," now metamorphosed into "a world in which discourse is fallen." Christine de Pizan, in the *Epistre Othéa*, specifically links the white raven with the first age of the world, "that was pure and later blackened by the sins of creatures" (quoted by Hindman, p. 79).

87. Patterson, "Parson's Tale," p. 361, arguing that for the Parson, unlike the other pilgrims, homiletic language "functions symbolically, in its order and coherence invoking and delineating the larger order and coherence of a divine reality." Cf. Taylor, "Parson's Amyable Tongue," p. 403, which claims that the Parson tries to reconstitute "linguistic Realism."

88. Cf. the *Confessio Amantis* 1.281–84:

> For what a man schal axe or sein
> Touchende of schrifte, it mot be plein,
> It nedeth noght to make it queinte,
> For trowthe hise wordes wol noght peinte.

89. Minnis, *Medieval Theory of Authorship*, pp. 206–10; also see Galloway, "Authority," p. 28.

90. See Ginsberg, *Italian Tradition*, pp. 99–100. Travis discusses the "hermeneutic double bind" of this ending: "Deconstructing Chaucer's Retraction," p. 147.

91. Kane, p. 116, who points out this buried iambic pentameter line, calls it a gesture of "unconscious poignancy."

92. See Ahern on "Binding the Book."

93. Huot, *From Song to Book*, pp. 238–41, 303–5; Brownlee, "1342?," pp. 112–13. See Dean, "Dismantling," p. 755, on "knitting up" at the end of the *Canterbury Tales*, set against "Chaucer's inability, or unwillingness, to finish" the work (p. 757); for a similar view from a different perspective, see Strohm, p. 181.

94. Fyler, "Froissart and Chaucer," p. 200.

95. Eliot, "The Waste Land," lines 429 and 431.

Primary sources

Abelard. *Expositio in Hexaemeron. CCCM* 15 (2004).

——. "In quacumque . . ."; fragment in Paris B.N. ms. lat. 17251. Transcribed in Jean Barthélémy Hauréau, *Notices et Extraits de Quelques Manuscrits Latins de la Bibliothèque Nationale.* 5:237–44. Paris: C. Klincksieck, 1892. Now superseded by E. M. Buytaert, "Abelard's Expositio in Hexaemeron," *Antonianum* 43 (1968), 163–94 (the fragment appears on pp. 174–81).

——. *Introductio ad Theologiam. PL* 178:979–1114.

——. *Problemata Heloissae. PL* 178:677–730.

——. *The Letters of Abelard and Heloise.* Trans. Betty Radice. Harmondsworth: Penguin, 1974.

Adelard of Bath. *De Eodem et Diverso [On the Same and the Different].* In *Adelard of Bath, Conversations with his Nephew.* Trans. Charles Burnett. Cambridge Medieval Classics 9. Cambridge University Press, 1998.

Ælfric. "In Die Sancto Pentecosten." *Ælfric's Catholic Homilies: The First Series,* XXII, pp. 354–64. Ed. Peter Clemoes. EETS S.S. 17. Oxford University Press, 1997.

Aelred of Rievaulx. *De spirituali amicitia. PL* 195:659–702. *Spiritual Friendship.* Trans. Mark F. Williams. Scranton: University of Scranton Press; London and Toronto: Associated University Presses, 1994.

Alain of Lille (Alanus de Insulis). *De Planctu Naturae.* Ed. Nikolaus M. Häring. *Studi Mediaevali,* 3rd ser., 19 (1978), 797–879. Trans. James J. Sheridan. Mediaeval Sources in Translation 26. Toronto: Pontifical Institute of Mediaeval Studies, 1980.

——. *La Somme "Quoniam Homines" d'Alain de Lille.* Ed. P. Glorieux. *AHDLMA* 20 (1953), 113–364.

Alcuin. *Interrogationes et Responsiones in Genesin. PL* 100:515–66.

Ambrose. *De Paradiso. PL* 14:275–314. *Hexameron, Paradise, and Cain and Abel.* Trans. John J. Savage. The Fathers of the Church 42. Washington, DC: Catholic University of America Press, 1961.

—— *Expositio Evangelii Secundum Lucam. CCSL* 14:1–400 (1957) (*PL* 15:1527–850).

——. *Hexameron. PL* 14:123–274.

—— *In Psalmum LXI Enarratio. PL* 14:1165–80.

Ambrosiaster. *Quaestiones Veteris et Novi Testamenti CXXVII*. Ed. Alexander Souter. *CSEL* 50. 1908; rpt. New York: Johnson Reprint Corporation, 1963.

Andrew of St. Victor. *In Heptateuchum et XII Prophetas*. Corpus Christi College, Cambridge, MS 30, fols. 1–118b. *Andreae de Sancto Victore Opera, I: Expositio super Heptateuchum*. *CCCM* 53 (1986).

Anselm. *Monologion*. Ed. F. S. Schmitt. Stuttgart-Bad Cannstatt: Friedrich Frommann Verlag, 1964.

Antony of Padua. *Expositio Mystica, in Genesim*. Paris, 1641.

Aquinas, Thomas. *Aristotle's De Anima in the Version of William of Moerbeke and the Commentary of St. Thomas Aquinas*. Trans. Kenelm Foster, O. P., and Silvester Humphries, O. P. London: Routledge and Kegan Paul, 1951.

— *In Aristotelis Libros Peri Hermeneias et Posteriorum Analyticorum Expositio*. Ed. Raimondo M. Spiazzi, O. P. 2nd edn. Turin: Marietti, 1964.

— *In Octo Libros Politicorum Aristotelis Expositio*. Ed. Spiazzi. Turin: Marietti, 1966.

— *Summa Theologiae*. Latin text and English translation. 60 vols. New York: McGraw-Hill, 1964–76.

"Aquinas, Thomas." *Complectens Expositionem in Genesim . . .* Paris: D. Moreau, 1640.

Aristotle. *On Interpretation*. Ed. Harold P. Cook. LCL. 1938; rpt. Cambridge, MA.: Harvard University Press, 1973.

Arnaud of Bonneval. Preface to *Hexameron*: see Jean Leclercq, "Écrits Monastiques sur la Bible aux XIᵉ–XIIIᵉ Siècles," *MS* 15 (1953): 95–106 (Arnaud's text appears on 96–98). The *Hexameron*, lacking its preface, appears in *PL* 189:1515–70.

Augustine. *De Catechezandis Rudibus*. *CCSL* 46:121–78 (1969). *On the Catechizing of the Uninstructed*. Trans. S. D. F. Salmond. Library of Nicene and Post-Nicene Fathers. 3:282–314. Buffalo: Christian Literature Co., 1887.

—. *De Civitate Dei*. *CCSL* 47–48 (1955). Trans. Henry Bettenson. Harmondsworth: Penguin Books, 1972.

—. *Confessiones*. Ed. James J. O'Donnell. 3 vols. Oxford: Clarendon Press, 1992. Trans. F. J. Sheed. New York: Sheed & Ward, 1943.

—. *De Dialectica*. Ed. Jan Pinborg; trans. B. Darrell Jackson. Dordrecht & Boston: D. Reidel, 1975.

—. *De diuersis quaestionibus LXXXIII*. *CCSL* 44 (1970). *Eighty-three Different Questions*. Trans. David L. Mosher. The Fathers of the Church 70. Washington, DC: Catholic University of America Press, 1982.

—. *De Doctrina Christiana*. Ed. and trans. R. P. H. Green. Oxford Early Christian Texts. Oxford: Clarendon Press, 1995.

—. *Enarrationes in Psalmos*. *CCSL* 38–40 (1956). *Expositions on the Book of Psalms*. Trans. J. Tweed et al. Oxford: J. H. Parker, 1847–57.

—. *Expositio epistolae ad Galatas*. *PL* 35:2105–48.

—. *De Genesi contra Manichaeos*. *PL* 34:173–220.

—. *De Genesi . . . Imperfectus Liber*. *PL* 34:219–46.

—. *De Genesi ad Litteram*. *PL* 34:245–486. *The Literal Meaning of Genesis*. Ed. John Hammond Taylor, S. J. Ancient Christian Writers 41–42. New York: Newman Press, 1982.

—. *In Ioannis Evangelium Tractatus CXXIV. CCSL* 36 (1954) (*PL* 35:1379–976).

—. *De Libero Arbitrio. CCSL* 29:205–321 (1970).

—. *De Magistro. CCSL* 29:151–203 (1970). *Augustine: Earlier Writings.* Trans. John H. S. Burleigh. Library of Christian Classics 6. Philadelphia: Westminster Press, 1953.

—. *De Ordine. CCSL* 29:87–137 (1970). Trans. Robert P. Russell, O. S. A. New York: Cosmopolitan Science and Art Service Co., 1942.

—. *De Sermone Domini in Monte Libri Duos. CCSL* 35 (1967).

—. *Sermones. CCSL* 41 (1961). *Sermons: 273–305A: On the Saints.* Trans. Edmund Hill, O. P. *The Works of Saint Augustine.* Pt. 3, vol. 8. Hyde Park, NY: New City Press, 1994.

—. *De Trinitate. CCSL* 50 (1968). Trans. Edmund Hill, O. P. *The Works of Saint Augustine.* Pt. 1, vol. 5. Brooklyn: New City Press, 1991.

Aulus Gellius. *Noctes Atticae.* Ed. Carl Hosius. 1903; rpt. Stuttgart: Teubner, 1967.

Bacon, Roger. *The "Opus majus" of Roger Bacon.* Trans. Robert Belle Burke. 2 vols. Philadelphia: University of Pennsylvania Press, 1928.

Baker, Geoffrey le. *Chronicon Galfridi le Baker de Swynebroke.* Ed. Edward Maunde Thompson. Oxford: Clarendon Press, 1889.

Basil of Caesarea. *Ancienne Version Latine des Neuf Homélies sur l'Hexaéméron de Basile de Césarée.* Ed. Emmanuel Amand de Mendieta and Stig Y. Rudberg. Texte und Untersuchungen zur Geschichte der Altchristlichen Literatur 66. Berlin: Akademie-Verlag, 1958.

Bede. *Hexaemeron [Libri quatuor in principium Genesis]. CCSL* 118A (1967).

—. *Expositio Actuum Apostolorum et Retractatio.* Ed. M. L. W. Laistner. Cambridge, MA.: Mediaeval Academy of America, 1939.

—. *In Lucae Evangelium Expositio. CCSL* 120 (1970).

—. *Opera de Temporibus.* Ed. Charles W. Jones. Cambridge, MA.: Mediaeval Academy of America, 1943.

Benvenuto da Imola. *Comentum super Dantis Comoediam.* Vol. 1. Florence: G. Barbera, 1887.

Bernard of Clairvaux. *Sermones de Diversis. PL* 183:537–748.

Bible. *Biblia Vulgata.* Ed. Alberto Colunga, O. P., and Laurentio Turrado. Madrid: La Editorial Catolica, 1965. English translation: Douay-Rheims version. London: Catholic Truth Society, 1956.

—. *La Bible de Macé de la Charité. I: Genèse, Exode.* Ed. J. R. Smeets. Leiden: Universitaire Pers Leiden, 1967.

—. *La Bible Française du XIIIᵉ Siècle: Edition critique de la Genèse.* Ed. Michel Quereuil. Geneva: Droz, 1988.

The Holy Bible . . . Made from the Latin Vulgate by John Wycliffe and His Followers. Ed. Rev. Josiah Forshall and Sir Frederic Madden. Vol. 1. Oxford University Press, 1850.

Biblia Latina cum Glossa Ordinaria: Facsimile Reprint of the Editio Princeps Adolph Rusch of Strassburg 1480/81. Introduction by Karlfried Froehlich and Margaret T. Gibson. 4 vols. Turnhout: Brepols, 1992.

Bible Moralisée. Oxford Bodleian MS 270b.

Boccaccio, Giovanni. *Corbaccio.* Trans. Anthony K. Cassell. 2nd, rev. ed. Binghamton, NY: Medieval and Renaissance Texts and Studies, 1993.

—. *Decameron.* Trans. G. H. McWilliam. Harmondsworth: Penguin Books, 1972.

—. *De Casibus Illustrium Virorum.* Ed. Pier Giorgio Ricci and Vittorio Zaccaria. Vol. 9 of *Opere.* Ed. Vittore Branca. Milan: Mondadori, 1983.

—. *De Genealogia Deorum*, Books 14–15. *Boccaccio on Poetry.* Trans. Charles G. Osgood. Princeton University Press, 1930.

—. *De Mulieribus Claris.* Ed. Vittorio Zaccaria. Vol. 10 of *Opere.* Ed. Vittore Branca. Milan: Mondadori, 1970. *Concerning Famous Women.* Trans. Guido A. Guarino. New Brunswick: Rutgers University Press, 1963.

Boethius. *Commentarii in librum Aristotelis "Peri Hermeneias."* Ed. Carolus Meiser. Leipzig: Teubner, 1877–80.

Bohun Psalter. Oxford Bodleian MS. Auct. D.4.4.

Bonaventure. *Breviloquium.* In *S. Bonaventurae Opera Omnia*, 5.201–91. 10 vols. Quaracci: Collegium S. Bonaventurae, 1882–1902. Trans. Erwin Esser Nemmers. St. Louis and London: B. Herder Book Co., 1946.

—. *Collations on the Six Days [Collationes in Hexaëmeron].* *The Works of Bonaventure*, vol. 5. Trans. José de Vinck. Paterson, NJ: St. Anthony Guild Press, 1970.

—. *Expositio in Quatuor Libros Sententiarum.* Freiburg: Kilianus Piscator, 1493.

—. *Itinerarium Mentis in Deum.* Ed. Philotheus Boehner, O.F.M. St. Bonaventure, NY: The Franciscan Institute, St. Bonaventure University, 1956.

The Book of Adam and Eve. Trans. S. C. Malan. London: Williams and Norgate, 1882.

The Book of Jubilees. Trans. R. H. Charles. London: Adam and Charles Black, 1902.

The Book of the Cave of Treasures. Trans. Sir E. A. Wallis Budge. London: The Religious Tract Society, 1927.

The Book of the Knight of the Tower. Ed. M. Y. Offord. EETS S. S. 2. Oxford University Press, 1971.

Brunetto Latini. *Li Livres dou Tresor.* Ed. Francis J. Carmody. University of California Publications in Modern Philology 22. Berkeley and Los Angeles: University of California Press, 1948.

Bruno de Segni (Bruno of Asti). *Expositio in Genesim.* PL 164:147–234.

—. *Expositio in Numeros.* PL 164:463–508.

Calvin, John. *A Commentarie of John Calvine, upon the first booke of Moses called Genesis.* Trans. Thomas Tymme. London: [by Henry Middleton] for John Harison and George Bishop, 1578.

Capgrave, John. *John Capgrave's Abbreuiacion of Cronicles.* Ed. Peter J. Lucas. EETS o.s. 285. Oxford University Press, 1983.

Cassian, John. *Conférences.* Ed. Dom E. Pichery. Sources Chrétiennes 42, 54, 64. Paris: Éditions de Cerf, 1955–59.

Caxton, William, trans. (of Jacobus de Voragine). *Legenda Aurea. The Golden Legend.* 7 vols. London: Dent, 1900.

Chaucer, Geoffrey. *The Riverside Chaucer.* Larry D. Benson, gen. ed. Boston: Houghton Mifflin, 1987.

The Chester Mystery Cycle. Ed. R. M. Lumiansky and David Mills. EETS S. S. 3. London: Oxford University Press, 1974.

Christine de Pizan. "The *Livre de la Cité des Dames* of Christine de Pisan: A Critical Edition." Ed. Maureen Cheney Curnow. Diss. Vanderbilt University, 1975. *The Book of the City of Ladies.* Trans. Earl Jeffrey Richards. New York: Persea Books, 1982.

——. *Le Livre de la Mutacion de Fortune.* Ed. Suzanne Solente. SATF. 4 vols. Paris: A. & J. Picard, 1959–1966. Trans. Kevin Brownlee, in *The Selected Writings of Christine de Pizan.* Trans. Renate Blumenfeld-Kosinski and Kevin Brownlee. New York and London: W. W. Norton, 1997.

Churchill, Charles. *The Poetical Works of Charles Churchill.* Ed. Douglas Grant. Oxford: Clarendon Press, 1956.

Cicero. *De Inventione.* In *De Inventione; De Optimo Genere Oratorum; Topica.* Ed. H. M. Hubbell. LCL. Cambridge, MA.: Harvard University Press, 1949.

——. *De Officiis.* Ed. Walter Miller. LCL. 1913; rpt. Cambridge, MA.: Harvard University Press, 1968.

——. *De Oratore,* Book III. Ed. H. Rackham. LCL. 1942; rpt. Cambridge, MA.: Harvard University Press, 1968.

Cleanness. In *The Poems of the Pearl Manuscript.* Ed. Malcolm Andrew and Ronald Waldron. Berkeley and Los Angeles: University of California Press, 1978.

Commento alla Divina Commedia d'Anonimo Fiorentino del Secolo XIV. Ed. Pietro Fanfani. Bologna: G. Romagnoli, 1866.

The Creacion of the World [Gwreans an bys]. Ed. and trans. Paula Neuss. Garland Medieval Texts 3. New York and London: Garland Publishing, 1983.

Cursor Mundi. Ed. Richard Morris. EETS o.s. 57. London: Kegan Paul, Trench, Trübner & Co., 1874.

Dante Alighieri. *Commedia.* Ed. and trans. with commentary, Charles Singleton. Princeton University Press, 1970–75. Robert M. Durling and Ronald L. Martinez, eds. *Inferno.* New York: Oxford University Press, 1996. Robert Hollander, ed. *Purgatorio.* New York, London: Doubleday, 2003.

——. *Il Convivio (The Banquet).* Ed. Giorgio Inglese. Milan: Rizzoli, 1993. Trans. Richard H. Lansing. Garland Library of Medieval Literature, vol. 65, series B. New York and London: Garland Publishing, 1990.

——. *Vita Nuova.* Ed. and trans. Dino S. Cervigni and Edward Vasta. University of Notre Dame Press, 1995.

——. *De Vulgari Eloquentia.* Ed. and trans. Steven Botterill. Cambridge Medieval Classics 5. Cambridge University Press, 1996.

——. *Literary Criticism of Dante Alighieri.* Trans. Robert S. Haller. Lincoln: University of Nebraska Press, 1973.

Le Débat sur le Roman de la Rose. Ed. Eric Hicks. Bibliothèque du XVᵉ Siècle 43. Paris: Honoré Champion, 1977. Baird, Joseph L., and John R. Kane, eds. "*La Querelle de la Rose*": *Letters and Documents.* North Carolina Studies in the Romance Languages and Literatures 199. Chapel Hill, 1978.

Primary sources

Deschamps, Eustache. *Œuvres Complètes de Eustache Deschamps*. Ed. le marquis de Queux de Saint-Hilaire and Gaston Raynaud. SATF. 11 vols. Paris: Firmin Didot, 1878–1903.

Donatus. *Ars Grammatica*. In *Grammatici Latini*, vol. 4. Ed. Heinrich Keil. Leipzig: Teubner, 1864.

Donizo of Canossa. "The Metrical Commentary on Genesis of Donizo of Canossa." Ed. I. S. Robinson. *RTAM* 41 (1974), 5–37.

Meister Eckhart. *Die Lateinische Werke*. Ed. Konrad Weiss. Stuttgart: W. Kohlhammer, 1964.

Ecloga Theoduli. Ed. Johann Osternacher. Urfahr: Collegium Petrinum, 1902. Now superseded by *Seven Versions of Carolingian Pastoral*, pp. 26–35. Ed. R. P. H. Green. Reading University Medieval and Renaissance Texts. Dept. of Classics, University of Reading, 1980.

Egerton Genesis. London BL. MS Egerton 1894.

Eliot, T. S. *The Complete Poems and Plays: 1909–1950*. New York: Harcourt, Brace & World, 1958.

Pseudo-Eucherius (Claude of Turin). *Commentarii in Genesim*. PL 50:893–1048.

—. *Interpretationes . . . de nominibus Hebraicis, ac uariis uocabulis . . . atque expositione diversarum rerum*. Oxford Bodleian MS 186, fol. 87v–96.

Evrat. "Genesis." Reinhold R. Grimm, *Schöpfung und Sündenfall in der altfranzösischen Genesisdichtung des Evrat*. Europäische Hochschulschriften, ser. 13: Französische Sprache und Literatur 39. Bern: Herbert Lang, 1976.

Four English Political Tracts of the Later Middle Ages. Ed. Jean-Philippe Genet. Camden Fourth Series, vol. 18. London: Offices of the Royal Historical Society, University College London, 1977.

Frost, Robert. *The Poetry of Robert Frost*. Ed. Edward Connery Lathem. New York: Holt, Rinehart and Winston, 1969.

Fulgentius, Fabius Planciades. "De Aetatibus Mundi et Hominis." In *Opera*, ed. Rudolf Helm. Leipzig: Teubner, 1898. *Fulgentius the Mythographer*. Trans. Leslie George Whitbread. Columbus: Ohio State University Press, 1971.

Gilbertus Universalis. *Commentary on Genesis*. London B. L. MS Royal 2.E.VIII, fols. 10–28.

The Epic of Gilgamesh. Trans. N. K. Sandars. Rev. ed. London: Penguin, 1972.

Glossa Ordinaria. PL 113–14:752.

Gower, John. *Confessio Amantis*. Ed. G. C. Macaulay. 2 vols. EETS e.s. 81–82. London: Oxford University Press, 1900–1.

—. *Mirour de l'Omme. The Complete Works of John Gower*. Ed. G. C. Macaulay. Vol 1: *The French Works*. Oxford: Clarendon Press, 1899.

Gregory the Great. *Homiliae XL in Euangelia*. PL 76:1075–312.

—. *Moralia in Job*. CCSL 173–173A (1979–85). Trans. James Bliss. Oxford: John Henry Parker, 1844–50.

Gregory of Tours. *Libri Historiarum X*. Ed. Bruno Krusch and Wilhelm Levison. Monumenta Germaniae Historica: Scriptores Rerum Merovingicarum. Hannover: Hahn, 1942.

Guibert of Nogent. *Moralia in Genesin. PL* 156:31–338.

Guido da Pisa. *Expositiones et Glose super Comediam Dantis.* Ed. Vincenzo Cioffari. Albany: State University of New York Press, 1974.

Guilelmus Brito. *Vocabularium Biblicum.* London B. L. MS Additional 10350. *Summa Britonis: sive Guillelmi Britonis Expositiones vocabulorum Biblie.* Ed. Lloyd William and Bernadine A. Daly. 2 vols. Thesaurus Mundi 15–16. Padua: In dibus Antenoreis, 1975.

Guillaume de Lorris and Jean de Meun. *Le Roman de la Rose.* Ed. Félix Lecoy. *CFMA* 92, 95, 98. Paris: Honoré Champion, 1966–70. Trans. Frances Horgan. Oxford University Press, 1994.

Guyart Desmoulins. *Bible Historiale.* London B. L. MS Harley 4381 and 4382; London B. L. MS Royal 17.E.VII.

Haimo of Auxerre ("Remigius of Auxerre"). *Commentarius in Genesim. PL* 131:53–134.

Hebrew Myths: The Book of Genesis. Ed. Robert Graves and Raphael Patai. Garden City, NY: Doubleday, 1964.

Higden, Ranulf. *Polychronicon . . . together with the English Translations of John Trevisa and of an Unknown Writer of the Fifteenth Century.* Ed. Churchill Babington and J. R. Lumby. *RS* 41. 9 vols. London, 1865–86. A second trans. in London B. L. MS Harley 2261.

Histoire Universelle. London B. L. MS Additional 15268. *The Heard Word: A Moralized History: The Genesis Section of the "Histoire Ancienne" in a Text from Saint-Jean D'Acre.* Ed. Mary Coker Joslin. University, MS: Romance Monographs, 1986.

Holkham Bible Picture Book. London B. L. MS Additional 47682. Ed. W. O. Hassall. London: Dropmore Press, 1954. F. P. Pickering, ed. *The Anglo-Norman Text of the "Holkham Bible Picture Book."* Anglo-Norman Texts 23. Oxford: Basil Blackwell (for the Anglo-Norman Text Society), 1971.

Holkot, Robert, O. P. *In Librum Sapientiae Regis Salomonis Praelectiones CCXIII.* Basel, 1586.

Honorius Augustodunensis. *Elucidarium. L'Elucidarium et les Lucidaires,* pp. 361–477. Ed. Yves Lefèvre. *Bibliothèque des Écoles Françaises d'Athènes et de Rome,* 180. Paris, 1954.

—. *Imago Mundi.* Ed. V. I. J. Flint. *AHDLMA* 49 (1982), pp. 7–153.

—. *Speculum Ecclesiae. PL* 172:807–1108.

Horace. *Satires, Epistles and Ars Poetica.* Ed. and trans. H. Rushton Fairclough. LCL. 1926; rpt. Cambridge, MA.: Harvard University Press, 1978.

Hugh of Amiens. "Un Commentaire Scripturaire du XIIe Siècle: Le 'Tractatus in Hexaemeron' de Hugues d'Amiens (*Archevêque de Rouen 1130–1164*)." Ed. F. Lecomte. *AHDLMA* 25 (1958), pp. 227–94.

Hugh of St. Cher, O. P. Biblical *Postilla. Biblia . . . cum postilla domini Hugonis Cardinalis . . .* Basel: Johann Amerbach: 1498–1502.

Hugh of St. Victor. *De Archa Noe. CCCM* 176 (2001).

—. *Didascalicon.* Trans. Jerome Taylor. Records of Civilization: Sources and Studies, 64. New York: Columbia University Press, 1961.

—. *De Grammatica*. In *Opera Propaedutica*. Ed. Roger Baron. University of Notre Dame Publications in Medieval Studies 20. Notre Dame, 1966. 75–163.

—. *In Ecclesiasten Homiliae XIX*. *PL* 175:113–256.

—. *Notulae [= Adnotationes Elucidatoriae in Pentateuchon]*. *PL* 175:29–86.

—. *De Sacramentis Christianae Fidei*. *PL* 176:173–618.

—. *De Verbo Dei*. In *Six Opuscules Spirituels*. Ed. Roger Baron. Sources Chrétiennes, 155. Paris: Les Éditions du Cerf, 1969.

—. *Selected Spiritual Writings*. Ed. Aelred Squire, O. P. New York and Evanston: Harper & Row, 1962.

Huguccio of Pisa. *Liber Derivationum*. London B. L. MS Additional 18380.

Innocent III (Lotario dei Segni). *De Miseria Condicionis Humanae*. Ed. Robert E. Lewis. Athens: University of Georgia Press, 1978.

Isidore of Seville. *Allegoriae Quaedam Sacrae Scripturae*. *PL* 83:97–130.

—. *Chronica*. *CCSL* 112 (2003).

—. *Differentiae*. *PL* 83:9–98.

—. *De Ecclesiasticis Officiis*. *CCSL* 113 (1989).

—. *Etymologiae, sive Origines*. Ed. W. M. Lindsay. 2 vols. Oxford: Clarendon Press, 1911.

—. *Quaestiones in Ueteri et Nouo Testamento. In Genesin*. *PL* 83:207–88.

Jacopo della Lana. *"Comedia" di Dante degli Allagherii col commento di Jacopo della Lana Bolognese*. Ed. Luciano Scarabelli. 3 vols. Bologna: Tipografia Regia, 1866.

Jehan le Bel. *Li Ars d'Amour, de Vertu et de Boneurté*. Ed. Jules Petit. 2 vols. Académie Royale de Belgique. Brussels: Victor Devaux, 1867–69.

Jerome. *Adversus Jovinianum*. *PL* 23:211–338.

—. *Commentarii in Epistolam ad Ephesios*. *PL* 26:439–554.

—. *Commentarii in Sophoniam*. *CCSL* 76A (1970). 655–711.

—. *Epistolae*. *PL* 22:325–1191. *Select Letters of St. Jerome*. Ed. F. A. Wright. LCL. 1933; rpt. Cambridge, MA.: Harvard University Press, 1963.

—. *Hebraicae Quaestiones in Libro Geneseos*. *CCSL* 72 (1959). 1–56. *Saint Jerome's "Hebrew Questions on Genesis."* Trans. C. T. R. Hayward. Oxford: Clarendon Press, 1995.

—. *Liber Interpretationis Hebraicorum Nominum*. *CCSL* 72 (1959). 59–161.

Le Jeu d'Adam (Ordo representacionis Ade). Ed. Willem Noomen. *CFMA* 99. Paris: Honoré Champion, 1971.

Joannes Balbus de Janua (Giovanni Balbi of Genoa, John of Genoa). *Catholicon*. London B. L. MS Stowe 981.

John of Salisbury. *Metalogicon*. *CCCM* 98 (1991). *The Metalogicon of John of Salisbury*. Trans. Daniel D. McGarry. Berkeley: University of California Press, 1955.

—. *Policraticus*. Ed. Clement C. J. Webb. 2 vols. Oxford: Clarendon Press, 1909.

John Scotus Erigena. *Periphyseon [De Divisione Naturae]*. *CCCM* 161–65 (1996–2003).

Johnson, Samuel. "Preface to *A Dictionary of the English Language*." In *Samuel Johnson: Selected Poetry and Prose*. Ed. Frank Brady and W. K. Wimsatt. Berkeley and Los Angeles: University of California Press, 1977.

Jonson, Ben. *The Alchemist*. Ed. J. B. Steane. Cambridge University Press, 1967.

Primary sources

Josephus (Flavius Josephus). *Jewish Antiquities*. In Latin: *The Latin Josephus*. Ed. Franz Blatt. Acta Jutlandica 30 (Humanistisk Serie 44). Copenhagen: E. Munksgaard, 1958. *Jewish Antiquities, Books I–IV*. Ed. H. St. J. Thackeray. LCL ed. of Josephus, vol. 4. Cambridge, MA.: Harvard University Press, 1930.

King Arthur's Death: The Middle English "Stanzaic Morte Arthur" and the "Alliterative Morte Arthure." Ed. Larry D. Benson. The Library of Literature. Indianapolis, New York: Bobbs-Merrill, 1974.

Kircher, Athanasius. *Arca Noë*. Amsterdam: Joannes Janssonius van Waesberghe, 1675.

Lahontan, Baron de (Louis Armand de Lom d'Arce). *Dialogues curieux entre l'auteur et un sauvage de bon sens qui a voyagé*. Ed. Gilbert Chinard. Baltimore: Johns Hopkins Press, 1931.

Langland, William. *Piers Plowman: The B Version*. Ed. George Kane and E. Talbot Donaldson. 1975; rev. ed. London & Berkeley: Athlone & University of California Press, 1988.

"The Life of Adam and Eve" (Vernon MS: Oxford Bodley MS Eng. Poet. a1). Ed. Carl Horstmann. *Sammlung Altenglischer Legenden*. Heilbronn: Henninger, 1878.

"The Life of Adam and Eue" (London B. L. MS Harley 4775). In "Nachträge zu den Legenden." Ed. Ludwig Herrig. *Archiv für das Studium der Neueren Sprachen und Litteraturen* 74 (1885), pp. 353–65.

Lodge, Thomas. "Babylon," from "The Summary of the Second Day of the Second Weeke," pp. 167–95. In Simon Goulart, *A Learned Summary Upon the Famous Poeme of William of Salust Lord of Bartas*. Trans. Thomas Lodge. London: John Grismand, 1621.

Lucretius. *De Rerum Natura*. Ed. William Ellery Leonard and Stanley Barney Smith. Madison: University of Wisconsin Press, 1942. *On the Nature of the Universe*. Trans. R. E. Latham. Harmondsworth: Penguin, 1951.

Luther, Martin. *Uber das Erst Buch Mose*. Wittemberg, 1527.

Lydgate, John. *Reson and Sensuallyte*. Ed. Ernst Sieper. EETS e.s. 84. London: Kegan Paul, Trench, Trübner & Co., 1901.

Malory, Sir Thomas. *Works*. Ed. Eugène Vinaver. 2nd edn. London: Oxford University Press, 1971.

Mandeville, Sir John. *Mandeville's Travels*. Ed. P. Hamelius. EETS o.s. 153. London: Oxford University Press, 1919. *The Bodley Version of Mandeville's Travels*. Ed. M. C. Seymour. EETS o.s. 253. London: Oxford University Press, 1963. *The Travels of Sir John Mandeville*. Trans. C. W. R. D. Moseley. Harmondsworth: Penguin, 1983.

Pseudo-Methodius. *Revelationes*. In *Sibyllinische Texte und Forschungen*. Ed. Ernst Sackur. Halle a. S.: Max Niemeyer, 1898. "þe Bygynnyng of þe World and þe Ende of Worldes." Trans. John Trevisa. In *Trevisa's Dialogus inter Militem et Clericum . . .* Ed. Aaron Jenkins Perry. EETS o.s. 167. London: Oxford University Press, 1925. Also Charlotte d'Evelyn, "The Middle-English Metrical Version of the *Revelations* of Methodius," *PMLA* 33 (1918), 135–203.

The Middle English Genesis and Exodus. Ed. Olof Arngart. Lund Studies in English 36. Lund: C. W. K. Gleerup, 1968.

Milton, John. *Paradise Lost*. Ed. Alastair Fowler. London: Longman, 1971.

—. *Of Education* (1644). *Complete Prose Works of John Milton, Volume II: 1643–1648.* New Haven: Yale University Press, 1959.

Le Mistére du Viel Testament. Ed. James de Rothschild. SATF. Paris: Firmin Didot, 1878.

Nicholas de Gorran [or de Gorham], O. P. *Postillae super Pentateuchum.* Oxford Bodleian MS Laud misc. 161.

Nicholas of Lyra, O. F. M. *Expositiones librorum Veteris et Novi Testamenti.* Rome: C. Sweynheim and A. Parmartz, 1471.

The Norwich Grocers' Play. In *Non-Cycle Plays and Fragments.* Ed. Norman Davis. EETS S. S. 1. Oxford University Press, 1970.

The N-Town Play: Cotton MS Vespasian D.8. Ed. Stephen Spector. EETS S. S. 11–12. Oxford University Press, 1991.

Omne Bonum: A Fourteenth-Century Encyclopedia of Universal Knowledge; British Library MSS Royal 6 E VI–6 E VII. Ed. Lucy Freeman Sandler. London: Harvey Miller, 1996.

Origen. *Contra Celsum.* Ed. Henry Chadwick. Cambridge University Press, 1953.

Oresme, Nicole. *Le Livre de Ethiques d'Aristote.* Ed. Albert Douglas Menut. New York: G. E. Stechert & Co., 1940.

Osbern of Gloucester. *Dialogi de quaestionibus in Genesim.* London B. L. MS Royal 6.D.IX, fol. 1–72.

L'Ottimo Commento della Divina Commedia. Ed. A. Torri. Pisa: N. Capurro, 1827.

Otto of Freising. *The Two Cities.* Trans. Charles Christopher Mierow. Records of Civilization. New York: Columbia University Press, 1928.

Ovid (Publius Ovidius Naso). *Amores; Medicamina Faciei Femineae; Ars Amatoria; Remedia Amoris.* Ed. E. J. Kenney. Oxford: Clarendon Press, 1961. Trans. J. H. Mozley. LCL. London: William Heinemann, 1929.

—. *Fasti.* Ed. Sir James George Fraser. LCL. Cambridge, MA.: Harvard University Press, 1951.

Ovide Moralisé. Ed. C. de Boer. *Verhandelingen der Koninklijke Nederlandse Akademie van Wetenschappen.* New Series 15 (1915), 21 (1920), 30 (1931), 36–37 (1936), and 43 (1938).

The Oxford Book of Medieval Latin Verse. Ed. F. J. E. Raby. Oxford: Clarendon Press, 1959.

Papias. *Elementarium Doctrinae, sive Vocabularium.* London B. L. MS Harley 2735.

Paris, Matthew. *Chronica Majora.* Ed. Henry Richards Luard. *RS* 57. 7 vols. London, 1872–83.

Peter of Poitiers. *Compendium Historiae in Genealogia Christi.* London B. L. MS Royal 8.C.IX; MS Cotton Faust. B.VII; MS Royal 14.B.IX; MS Additional 14819; and MS Additional 24025.

Peter the Chanter. *Petrus Cantor, Glossae super Genesim. Prologus et Capitula 1–3.* Ed. Agneta Sylwan. Studia Graeca et Latina Gothoburgensia 55. Gotenburg, 1992.

Peter Comestor. *Historia Scholastica. PL* 198:1053–722.

Peter Lombard. *Commentaria in Epistolas D. Pauli. PL* 191:1297–192:520.

—. *Commentarium in Psalmos. PL* 191:55–1296.

—. *Libri Sententiarum. PL* 192:519–964.

Peter Riga. *Aurora.* Ed. Paul E. Beichner, C. S. C. University of Notre Dame Publications in Medieval Studies 19. Notre Dame, 1965.

Philippe de Mézières. *Letter to King Richard II.* London B. L. MS Royal 20.B.VI. Ed. G. W. Coopland. Liverpool University Press, 1975.

Plato. *Symposium.* Trans. Michael Joyce. In *The Collected Dialogues.* Ed. Edith Hamilton and Huntington Cairns. Bollingen Series LXXI. New York: Pantheon Books, 1961.

Priscian. *Institutiones.* In *Grammatici Latini,* vols. 2–3. Ed. Heinrich Keil. Leipzig: Teubner, 1855, 1859.

Rabanus Maurus. *Commentarii in Genesim. PL* 107:439–670.

—. *De Universo. PL* 111:9–614.

Rainaldus de sancto Eligio. *Commentarius in quinque libros Mosis, in Josuam, Judices, et Ruth.* Paris B. N. MS lat. 2493.

Rashi (Solomon ben Isaac). *The Pentateuch and Rashi's Commentary: A Linear Translation into English.* Trans. Rabbi Abraham Ben Isaiah and Rabbi Benjamin Sharfman. 5 vols. Brooklyn, New York: S. S. and R. Publishing Company, 1949.

Remigius of Auxerre. *Expositio super Genesim. CCCM* 136. (1999).

—. *Interpretationes Hebraicorum Nominum.* In Bible MS, dated 1254: London B. L. MS Royal 1.B.XII, fol. 399b–431.

Richard of Bury. *Philobiblon.* Text ed. and trans. E. C. Thomas; ed. Michael Maclagan. Oxford: Basil Blackwell, for the Shakespeare Head Press, 1970.

Robert Grosseteste. *Hexaëmeron.* Ed. Richard C. Dales and Servus Gieben. British Academy: Auctores Britannici Medii Aevi 6. London: Oxford University Press, 1982.

Le Roman de Renart. Ed. Mario Roques. CFMA 78. 2 vols. Paris: H. Champion, 1948–51.

Rousseau, Jean-Jacques, and Johann Gottfried Herder. *On the Origin of Language.* Trans. John H. Moran and Alexander Gode. University of Chicago Press, 1966.

Rufinus. *Historia Ecclesiastica. PL* 21:461–540.

Rupert of Deutz. *De Trinitate et Operibus Eius. In Genesim. PL* 167:199–566.

St. Omer Psalter. London B. L. MS Additional 39810.

Servius. *Commentarius in Artem Donati.* In *Grammatici Latini,* vol. 4. Ed. Heinrich Keil. Leipzig: Teubner, 1864.

Sidney, Sir Philip. *An Apology for Poetry.* Ed. Geoffrey Shepherd. Nelson's Medieval and Renaissance Library. London and Edinburgh: Thomas Nelson and Sons, 1965.

Speculum Humanae Salvationis. London B. L. MS Harley 4996. With prefaces by M. R. James and Bernhard Berenson. Oxford University Press, 1926.

Spenser, Edmund. *The Faerie Queene.* Ed. A. C. Hamilton. London and New York: Longman, 1977.

Sprat, Thomas. *The History of the Royal-Society of London, for the Improving of Natural Knowledge.* London: J. R., for J. Martyn, 1667.

Stanton, Elizabeth Cady. *The Woman's Bible.* 1895; rpt. New York: Arno Press, 1972.

Stephen Langton. *Expositio moralis.* Paris B. N. MS lat. 14414.

Swift, Jonathan. *A Tale of a Tub.* Ed. A. C. Guthkelch and D. Nichol Smith. Oxford: Clarendon Press, 1920.

Primary sources

—. *Swift: Poetical Works*. Ed. Herbert Davis. London: Oxford University Press, 1967.

Sylvester, Joshua, trans. *The Divine Weeks and Works of Guillaume de Saluste Sieur du Bartas*. Ed. Susan Snyder. 2 vols. Oxford: Clarendon Press, 1979.

Thierry of Chartres. *Abbreuiatio Monacensis contra Eutychen*. In *Commentaries on Boethius by Thierry of Chartres and His School*. Ed. Nikolaus M. Häring. Studies and Texts 20. Toronto: Pontifical Institute, 1971. 439–77.

—. Nikolaus M. Häring, "A Commentary on Boethius' *De Trinitate* by Thierry of Chartres (*Anonymus Berolinensis*)." *AHDLMA* 23 (1956), 257–325.

—. Nikolaus M. Häring, "The Lectures of Thierry of Chartres on Boethius' *De Trinitate*." *AHDLMA* 25 (1958), 113–226.

—. *The Latin Rhetorical Commentaries by Thierry of Chartres*. Ed. Karin M. Fredborg. Studies and Texts 84. Toronto: Pontifical Institute of Mediaeval Studies, 1988.

—. *Tractatus de sex dierum operibus*. In *Commentaries on Boethius . . .*, ed. Häring. 553–75.

Trevisa, John of. "Dialogus inter Militem et Clericum." EETS o.s. 167. Ed. Aaron Jenkins Perry. London: Oxford University Press, 1925.

—. *On the Properties of Things: John Trevisa's translation of "Bartholomaeus Anglicus De Proprietatibus Rerum."* Ed. M. C. Seymour et al. 3 vols. Oxford: Clarendon Press, 1975–88.

—. Waldron, Ronald. "Trevisa's Original Prefaces on Translation: A Critical Edition." *Medieval English Studies Presented to George Kane*. Ed. Edward Donald Kennedy, Ronald Waldron and Joseph S. Wittig. Woodbridge, Suffolk: D. S. Brewer, 1988. 285–99.

Trivet, Nicholas. *Annales*. London B. L. MS Royal 13.B.XVI.

—. *Chronicles*. London B. L. MS Arundel 56. Middle English translation: Harvard Houghton Library fMS Eng 938.

Verstegan, Richard. *A Restitution of Decayed Intelligence*. Antwerp: Robert Bruney, 1605.

Vincent of Beauvais. *Speculum Historiale; Speculum Naturale*. In *Speculum Quadruplex; Bibliotheca Mundi Vincenti Burgundi*. Douai, 1624; rpt. Graz: Akademische Druck- u. Verlagsanstalt, 1964–65.

The Wakefield Pageants in the Towneley Cycle. Ed. A. C. Cawley. Manchester University Press, 1958.

Willet, Andrew. *Hexapla in Genesin*. London: Thomas Creede, 1608.

William of St. Thierry. *De Natura et Dignitate Amoris*. PL 184:379–408.

Wilson, Thomas. *The Arte of Rhetorique*. London: Ihon Kingston, 1560.

Wyclif, John. *Tractatus de Statu Innocencie*. Ed. J. Loserth and F. D. Matthew. Wyclif Society 23 (1922).

Bibliography

Age of Chivalry: Art in Plantagenet England 1200–1400. Ed. Jonathan Alexander and Paul Binski. London: Royal Academy of Arts, 1987.

Ahern, John. "Binding the Book: Hermeneutics and Manuscript Production in *Paradiso* 33." *PMLA* 97 (1982): 800–9.

Alford, John A. "The Grammatical Metaphor: A Survey of Its Use in the Middle Ages." *Speculum* 57 (1982): 728–60.

Alici, Luigi. *Il linguaggio come segno e come testimonianza: una rilettura di Agostino.* Rome: Edizioni Studium, 1976.

Allen, Don Cameron. "Some Theories of the Growth and Origin of Language in Milton's Age." *PQ* 28 (1949): 5–16.

Allen, Peter L. *The Art of Love: Amatory Fiction from Ovid to the "Romance of the Rose."* Philadelphia: University of Pennsylvania Press, 1992.

Allen, W. Sidney. "Ancient Ideas on the Origin and Development of Language." *Transactions of the Philological Society* 81 (1948): 35–60.

Almond, Philip C. *Adam and Eve in Seventeenth-Century Thought.* Cambridge University Press, 1999.

Alter, Robert. *The Art of Biblical Narrative.* New York: Basic Books, 1981.

—. *Genesis: Translation and Commentary.* New York and London: W. W. Norton, 1996.

Amsler, Mark. *Etymology and Grammatical Discourse in Late Antiquity and the Early Middle Ages.* Studies in the History of the Language Sciences 44. Amsterdam & Philadelphia: John Benjamins, 1989.

Anderson, David. *Before the "Knight's Tale": Imitation of Classical Epic in Boccaccio's "Teseida."* Philadelphia: University of Pennsylvania Press, 1988.

Annotation and Its Texts. Ed. Stephen A. Barney. Oxford University Press, 1991.

Arbery, Glenn C. "Adam's First Word and the Failure of Language in *Paradiso* XXXIII." *Sign, Sentence, Discourse.* 31–44.

Archéologie du signe. Ed. Lucie Brind'Amour and Eugene Vance. Papers in Mediaeval Studies 3. Toronto: Pontifical Institute of Mediaeval Studies, 1983.

Arens, Hans. *Aristotle's Theory of Language and Its Tradition: Texts from 500 to 1750.* Studies in the History of Linguistics 29. Amsterdam & Philadelphia: John Benjamins, 1984.

Bibliography

Arthur, Ross G. *Medieval Sign Theory and "Sir Gawain and the Green Knight."* University of Toronto Press, 1987.

Ascoli, Albert Russell. "The Vowels of Authority (Dante's *Convivio* IV.vi.3–4)." *Discourses of Authority in Medieval and Renaissance Literature.* Ed. Kevin Brownlee and Walter Stephens. Hanover, NH: Dartmouth/University Press of New England, 1989. 23–46.

Aspegren, Kerstin. *The Male Woman: A Feminine Ideal in the Early Church.* Ed. René Kieffer. Acta Universitatis Upsaliensis: Uppsala Women's Studies, 1990.

Aston, Margaret. *Lollards and Reformers: Images and Literacy in Late Medieval Religion.* London: Hambledon Press, 1984.

Auden, W. H. "Dingley Dell & the Fleet." *The Dyer's Hand and Other Essays.* New York: Random House, 1962. 407–28.

Auerbach, Erich. *Literary Language and Its Public in Late Latin Antiquity and in the Middle Ages.* Trans. Ralph Manheim. Bollingen Series No. 74. New York: Pantheon, 1965.

—. *Mimesis: The Representation of Reality in Western Literature.* Trans. Willard R. Trask. 1953; rpt. Princeton University Press, 1968.

—. "Sacrae Scripturae sermo humilis." *Neuphilologische Mitteilungen* 42 (1941): 57–67.

Badel, Pierre-Yves. "Raison 'Fille de Dieu' et le rationalisme de Jean de Meun." *Mélanges de langue et de littérature du Moyen Âge et de la Renaissance offerts à Jean Frappier.* Publications romanes et françaises 112, 1:41–52. Geneva: Droz, 1970.

—. *Le Roman de la rose au XIVᵉ Siècle: Étude de la réception de l'oeuvre.* Publications romanes et françaises 153. Geneva: Droz, 1980.

Baer, Richard A., Jr. *Philo's Use of the Categories Male and Female.* Leiden: E. J. Brill, 1970.

Bainton, Roland H. *Erasmus of Christendom.* New York: Charles Scribner's Sons, 1969.

Bal, Mieke. *Lethal Love: Feminist Literary Readings of Biblical Love Stories.* Bloomington & Indianapolis: Indiana University Press, 1987.

Baldwin, Ralph. *The Unity of the "Canterbury Tales."* Anglistica 5. Copenhagen: Rosenkilde and Bagger, 1955.

Barański, Zygmunt G. "Dante's Biblical Linguistics." *Lectura Dantis* 5 (1989): 105–43.

Barney, Stephen A. *Allegories of History, Allegories of Love.* Hamden, CT: Archon Books, 1979.

—. "Chaucer's Lists." *The Wisdom of Poetry: Essays in Early English Literature in Honor of Morton W. Bloomfield.* Ed. Larry D. Benson and Siegfried Wenzel. Kalamazoo: Medieval Institute Publications, Western Michigan University, 1982. 189–223.

Barolini, Teodolinda. *Dante's Poets: Textuality and Truth in the "Comedy."* Princeton University Press, 1984.

—. "Dante's Ulysses: Narrative and Transgression." *Dante: Contemporary Perspectives.* Ed. Amilcare A. Iannucci. Toronto Italian Studies: Major Italian Authors. University of Toronto Press, 1997. 113–32.

—. *The Undivine "Comedy": Detheologizing Dante.* Princeton University Press, 1992.

Bibliography

Baswell, Christopher. *Virgil in Medieval England: Figuring the "Aeneid" from the Twelfth Century to Chaucer.* Cambridge Studies in Medieval Literature 24. Cambridge University Press, 1995.

Beer, Jeanette M. A. *Early Prose in France: Contexts of Bilingualism and Authority.* Kalamazoo: Medieval Institute Publications, Western Michigan University, 1992.

Beichner, Paul E., CSC. "Confrontation, Contempt of Court, and Chaucer's Cecilia." *ChRev* 8 (1974): 198–204.

—. *The Medieval Representative of Music, Jubal or Tubalcain?* Ed. A. L. Gabriel and J. N. Garvin. Texts and Studies in the History of Medieval Education 2. Notre Dame: The Mediaeval Institute, 1954.

Benfell, V. Stanley, III. "Nimrod, the Ascent to Heaven and Dante's 'Ovra Incon-summabile'." *DS* 110 (1992): 77–93.

Bennett, J. A. W. *Chaucer's "Book of Fame": An Exposition of 'The House of Fame.'* Oxford: Clarendon Press, 1968.

—. *Middle English Literature.* Ed. Douglas Gray. Oxford History of English Literature. Oxford: Clarendon Press, 1986.

Benson, C. David. *Chaucer's Drama of Style: Poetic Variety and Contrast in the "Canterbury Tales."* Chapel Hill and London: University of North Carolina Press, 1986.

Benson, Larry D. "The Alliterative *Morte Arthure* and Medieval Tragedy." *Tennessee Studies in Literature* 11 (1966): 75–87.

—. "Chaucer and Courtly Speech." *Genres, Themes, and Images in English Literature: From the Fourteenth to the Fifteenth Century.* Ed. Piero Boitani and Anna Torti. The J. A. W. Bennett Memorial Lectures, Perugia, 1986. Tübingen: Gunter Narr; Cambridge: D. S. Brewer, 1988. 11–30.

Bergin, Thomas G. *Boccaccio.* New York: Viking Press, 1981.

Berry, Alice Fiola. "Rabelais: Homo Logos." *JMRS* 3 (1973): 51–67.

Besserman, Lawrence. *Chaucer and the Bible: A Critical Review of Research, Indexes, and Bibliography.* New York & London: Garland, 1988.

—. *Chaucer's Biblical Poetics.* Norman: University of Oklahoma Press, 1998.

Blamires, Alcuin. *The Case for Women in Medieval Culture.* Oxford: Clarendon Press, 1997.

—. "Women and Preaching in Medieval Orthodoxy, Heresy, and Saints' Lives." *Viator* 26 (1995): 135–52.

—, ed., with Karen Pratt and C. W. Marx. *Woman Defamed and Woman Defended: An Anthology of Medieval Texts.* Oxford: Clarendon Press, 1992.

Bloch, R. Howard. *Etymologies and Genealogies: A Literary Anthropology of the French Middle Ages.* University of Chicago Press, 1983.

—. "Medieval Misogyny." *Representations* 20 (1987): 1–24.

—. "Medieval Misogyny and the Invention of Western Romantic Love." *Modernité au Moyen Âge: Le Défi du Passé.* Ed. Brigitte Cazelles and Charles Méla. Recherches et Rencontres: Publications de la Faculté des Lettres de Genève: Littérature, No. 1. Geneva: Droz, 1990. 289–313.

—. *Medieval Misogyny and the Invention of Western Romantic Love.* University of Chicago Press, 1991.

—. "Modest Maids and Modified Nouns: Obscenity in the Fabliaux." *Obscenity*. 293–307.

—. *The Scandal of the Fabliaux*. University of Chicago Press, 1986.

Boas, George. *Essays on Primitivism and Related Ideas in the Middle Ages*. Baltimore: Johns Hopkins University Press, 1948, rpt. 1997.

Boitani, Piero. *Chaucer and the Imaginary World of Fame*. Chaucer Studies X. Cambridge: D. S. Brewer, 1984.

—. "Chaucer's Labyrinth: Fourteenth-Century Literature and Language." *ChRev* 17 (1983): 197–220.

Bonnell, John K. "The Serpent with a Human Head in Art and Mystery Play." *American Journal of Archaeology* 21 (1917): 255–91.

Borchardt, Frank L. "Etymology in Tradition and in the Northern Renaissance." *Journal of the History of Ideas* 29 (1968): 415–29.

Børresen, Kari Elisabeth. *Subordination and Equivalence: The Nature and Rôle of Women in Augustine and Thomas Aquinas*. Trans. Charles H. Talbot. Washington, DC: University Press of America, 1981.

Borst, Arno. *Der Turmbau von Babel: Geschichte der Meinungen über Ursprung und Vielfalt der Sprachen und Völker*. Stuttgart: Anton Hiersemann, 1957–63.

Botterill, Steven. "Dante and the Authority of Poetic Language." *Dante: Contemporary Perspectives*. Ed. Amilcare A. Iannucci. Toronto Italian Studies: Major Italian Authors. University of Toronto Press, 1997. 167–80.

Boucher, Holly Wallace. "Nominalism: The Difference for Chaucer and Boccaccio." *ChRev* 20 (1986): 213–20.

Branca, Vittore. "The Myth of the Hero in Boccaccio." *Concepts of the Hero in the Middle Ages and the Renaissance*. Trans. John Guthrie. Ed. Norman T. Burns and Christopher J. Reagan. Albany: State University of New York Press, 1975. 268–91.

Brewer, Derek. "Chaucer's Poetic Style." *The Cambridge Chaucer Companion*. Ed. Piero Boitani and Jill Mann. Cambridge University Press, 1986. 227–42.

—. "Gothic Chaucer." *Geoffrey Chaucer*. Ed. Derek Brewer. Writers and Their Backgrounds. London: G. Bell & Son, 1975. 1–32.

Brinkmann, Hennig. *Mittelalterliche Hermeneutik*. Tübingen: Max Niemeyer Verlag, 1980.

Broadie, Alexander. *Introduction to Medieval Logic*. Oxford: Clarendon Press, 1987.

Brody, Saul Nathaniel. "Chaucer's Rhyme Royal Tales and the Secularization of the Saint." *ChRev* 20 (1985): 113–31.

Brown, Peter. *The Body and Society: Men, Women, and Sexual Renunciation in Early Christianity*. Lectures on the History of Religions n. s. 13. New York: Columbia University Press, 1988.

—. "Sexuality and Society in the Fifth Century AD: Augustine and Julian of Eclanum." *Tria Corda: Scritti in Onore di Arnaldo Momigliano*. Ed. Emilio Gabba. Como: Edizioni New Press, 1983. 49–70.

Brown-Grant, Rosalind. "Décadence ou progrès? Christine de Pizan, Boccace et la question de 'l'âge d'or'." *Revue des langues romanes* 92 (1988): 295–306.

Bibliography

Brownlee, Kevin. "Pygmalion, Mimesis, and the Multiple Endings of the *Roman de la Rose*." *YFS* 95 (1999): 193–211.

—. "1342? Lyricism in the Age of Allegory." *A New History of French Literature*. Ed. Denis Hollier. Cambridge, MA: Harvard University Press, 1989. 109–14.

—. "Why the Angels Speak Italian: Dante as Vernacular *Poeta* in *Paradiso* XXV." *Poetics Today* 5:3 (1984): 597–610.

—. "XXVI." *Lectura Dantis* 16–17 (1995): 388–401.

Brusegan, Rosanna. "Verità e finzione nel *Jeu d'Adam*." *Cultura Neolatina* 40 (1980): 79–102.

Buc, Philippe. *L'ambiguïté du Livre: prince, pouvoir, et peuple dans les commentaires de la Bible au Moyen Age*. Théologie Historique 95. Paris: Beauchesne, 1994.

Burke, Kenneth. *The Rhetoric of Religion: Studies in Logology*. Berkeley and Los Angeles: University of California Press, 1970.

Burlin, Robert R. Review of Lawler. *Speculum* 56 (1981): 630–31.

Burrow, J. A. "'A Maner Latyn Corrupt'." *Medium Aevum* 30 (1961): 33–37.

Butor, Michel. "L'Alchimie et son langage." *Répertoire: Études et conférences 1948–1959*. Paris: Éditions de Minuit, 1960. 12–19.

Buxton, Richard. *Imaginary Greece: The Contexts of Mythology*. Cambridge University Press, 1994.

Cahoon, Leslie. "Raping the Rose: Jean de Meun's Reading of Ovid's *Amores*." *Classical and Modern Literature* 6 (1986): 261–85.

Calabrese, Michael A. "Meretricious Mixtures: Gold, Dung, and the *Canon's Yeoman's Prologue and Tale*." *ChRev* 27 (1993): 277–92.

Cambon, Glauco. *Dante's Craft: Studies in Language and Style*. Minneapolis: University of Minnesota Press, 1969.

Camille, Michael. *The Gothic Idol: Ideology and Image-Making in Medieval Art*. Cambridge University Press, 1989.

—. *Image on the Edge: The Margins of Medieval Art*. Cambridge, MA: Harvard University Press, 1992.

Carruthers, Mary J. "Italy, *Ars Memorativa*, and Fame's House." *SAC: Proceedings* 2 (1987): 179–88.

Casagrande, Carla, and Silvana Vecchio. *I peccati della lingua: disciplina ed etica della parola nella cultura medievale*. Bibliotheca biographica: Sezione storico-antropologica. Rome: Istituto della Enciclopedia Italiana, 1987.

Casagrande, Gino. "Parole di Dante: Il 'lungo silenzio' di 'Inferno,' I, 63." *Giornale storico della letteratura italiana* 174 (1997): 243–54.

Cassata, Letterio. "Il lungo silenzio di Virgilio (*Inf.* I 61–63)." *SD* 47 (1970): 15–41.

Cassirer, Ernst. *Language and Myth*. Trans. Susanne K. Langer. New York and London: Harper & Brothers, 1946.

Castaldo, Dino. "L'etica del primiloquium di Adamo nel *De Vulgari Eloquentia*." *Italica* 59 (1982): 3–15.

Cave, Terence. *The Cornucopian Text: Problems of Writing in the French Renaissance*. Oxford: Clarendon Press, 1979.

Bibliography

Céard, Jean. "De Babel à la Pentecôte: La transformation du mythe de la confusion des langues au XVIe siècle." *Bibliothèque d'Humanisme et Renaissance* 42 (1980): 577–94.

Cervigni, Dino. "Beatrice's Act of Naming." *Lectura Dantis* 8 (1991): 85–99.

Chadwick, Henry. *Boethius.* Oxford: Clarendon Press, 1981.

Chaucer and the Craft of Fiction. Ed. Leigh A. Arrathoon. Rochester, MI.: Solaris Press, 1986.

Chaytor, H. J. *From Script to Print: An Introduction to Medieval Literature.* Cambridge University Press, 1945.

Chenu, Marie-Dominique. "Un cas de platonisme grammatical au XIIe siècle." *Revue des Sciences philosophiques et théologiques* 51 (1967): 666–68.

—. "Civilisation urbaine et théologie: L'École de Saint-Victor au XIIe Siècle." *Annales* 29 (1974): 1253–63.

—. "Grammaire et théologie aux XIIe et XIIIe siècles." *AHDLMA* 10 (1935–36): 5–28.

—. "*Involucrum.* Le mythe selon les théologiens médiévaux." *AHDLMA* 22 (1955): 75–79.

Cherniss, Michael D. "Irony and Authority: The Ending of the *Roman de la Rose.*" *MLQ* 36 (1975): 227–38.

Chiarenza, Marguerite Mills. "The Imageless Vision and Dante's *Paradiso.*" *DS* 90 (1972): 77–91.

Chiarini, Cino. *Di una imitazione inglese della Divina Commedia: La Casa della Fama di G. Chaucer.* Bari: Laterza, 1902.

Chism, Christine N. "I Demed Hym Som Chanoun For To Be." *Chaucer's Pilgrims: An Historical Guide to the Pilgrims in The Canterbury Tales.* Ed. Laura C. Lambdin and Robert T. Lambdin. Westport, CT; London: Greenwood Press, 1996. 340–56.

Cioffari, Vincenzo, and Francesco Mazzoni. "The Prologue to the Commentary of Guido da Pisa." *DS* 90 (1972): 125–37.

Clark, Elizabeth A. "'Adam's Only Companion': Augustine and the Early Christian Debate on Marriage." *RA* 21 (1986): 139–62.

—. "Heresy, Asceticism, Adam, and Eve: Interpretations of Genesis 1–3 in the Later Latin Fathers." *Ascetic Piety and Women's Faith: Essays on Late Ancient Christianity.* Lewiston, NY and Queenston, Ontario: Edwin Mellen Press, 1986. 353–85.

Clemen, Wolfgang. *Chaucer's Early Poetry.* 1938. Trans. C. A. M. Sym. London: Methuen, 1963.

Clogan, Paul M. "The Figural Style and Meaning of *The Second Nun's Prologue and Tale.*" *M&H* n.s. 3 (1972): 213–20.

Cockerell, S. C. *Old Testament Miniatures.* New York: Braziller, 1927, rpt. 1969.

Cohen, Murray. *Sensible Words: Linguistic Practice in England, 1640–1785.* Baltimore: Johns Hopkins University Press, 1977.

Coletti, Theresa. *Naming the Rose: Eco, Medieval Signs, and Modern Theory.* Ithaca and London: Cornell University Press, 1988.

Colish, Marcia L. *The Mirror of Language: A Study in the Medieval Theory of Knowledge.* Rev. ed. Lincoln and London: University of Nebraska Press, 1983.

—. "St. Augustine's Rhetoric of Silence Revisited." *Augustinian Studies* 9 (1978): 15–24.

—. "The Stoic Theory of Verbal Signification and the Problems of Lies and False Statements from Antiquity to St. Anselm." *Archéologie du signe*. 17–43.

Contini, Gianfranco. "Dante come personnagio-poeta della 'Commedia'." *Varianti e altra linguistica: una racolta di saggi (1938–1968)*. 1958; rpt. Turin: Einaudi, 1970. 335–61.

Cooper, Helen. "The Four Last Things in Dante and Chaucer: Ugolino in the House of Rumour." *New Medieval Literatures* 3. Ed. Wendy Scase, Rita Copeland, and David Lawton. Oxford: Clarendon Press, 1999. 39–66.

—. *Oxford Guides to Chaucer: The Canterbury Tales*. Oxford: Clarendon Press, 1989.

Copeland, Rita. "Rhetoric and the Politics of the Literal Sense in Medieval Literary Theory: Aquinas, Wyclif, and the Lollards." *Interpretation: Medieval and Modern*. 1–23.

—. *Rhetoric, Hermeneutics, and Translation in the Middle Ages: Academic Traditions and Vernacular Texts*. Cambridge Studies in Medieval Literature 11. Cambridge University Press, 1991.

Cornish, Alison. "The Epistle of James in 'Inferno' 26." *Traditio* 45 (1989–1990): 367–79.

Corti, Maria. *Dante a un nuovo crocevia*. Florence: Libreria Commissionaria Sansoni, 1982.

—. "Dante e la Torre di Babele: una nuova 'allegoria in factis'." *Il viaggio testuale: Le ideologie e le strutture semiotiche*. Turin: Einaudi, 1978. 243–56.

—. "Les notions de 'langue universelle' et de 'langue poétique' chez Dante Alighieri." *Logos Semantikos: Studia Linguistica in Honorem Eugenio Coseriu 1921–1981*. Ed. Horst Geckeler et al. Berlin and New York: Walter de Gruyter, 1981. 1:31–39.

Coudert, Allison. "Some Theories of a Natural Language from the Renaissance to the Seventeenth Century." *Magia Naturalis und die Entstehung der Modernen Naturwissenschaften*. Studia Leibnitiana Sonderheft 7 (1978): 56–114.

Courcelle, Pierre. *Les Confessions de Saint Augustin dans la tradition littéraire*. Paris: Etudes Augustiniennes, 1963.

—. "Tradition néo-platonicienne et traditions chrétiennes de la 'région de dissemblance' (Platon, Politique, 273d)." *AHDLMA* 24 (1957): 5–33.

Courtenay, William J. "The Bible in the Fourteenth Century: Some Observations." *Church History* 54 (1985): 176–87.

—. "Force of Words and Figures of Speech: The Crisis over *Virtus Sermonis* in the Fourteenth Century." *Franciscan Studies* 44 (1984): 107–28.

Cowgill, Bruce Kent. "Sweetness and Sweat: The Extraordinary Emanations in Fragment Eight of the *Canterbury Tales*." *PQ* 74 (1995): 343–57.

Craun, Edwin David. *Lies, Slander and Obscenity in Medieval English Literature: Pastoral Rhetoric and the Deviant Speaker*. Cambridge Studies in Medieval Literature 31. Cambridge University Press, 1997.

Bibliography

Cremona, Joseph. "Dante's Views on Language." *The Mind of Dante*. Ed. Uberto Limentani. Cambridge University Press, 1965. 138–62.

—. "*Paradiso* XXVI." *Cambridge Readings in Dante's Comedy*. Ed. Kenelm Foster and Patrick Boyde. Cambridge University Press, 1981. 174–90.

Curtius, Ernst Robert. *European Literature and the Latin Middle Ages*. Trans. Willard R. Trask. New York: Pantheon Books, 1953.

Dahan, Gilbert. "Les interprétations juives dans les commentaires du Pentateuque de Pierre le Chantre." *The Bible in the Medieval World: Essays in Memory of Beryl Smalley*. Ed. Katherine Walsh and Diana Wood. Oxford: Blackwell, 1985. 131–55.

d'Alverny, Marie-Thérèse. "L'homme comme symbole. Le microcosme." *Simboli e Simbologia nell'Alto Medioevo. Settimane di studio del Centro italiano di studi sull'alto Medioevo* [Spoleto] 23 (1976): 123–83.

Damon, Phillip. "Adam on the Primal Language: 'Paradiso' 26.124." *Italica* 38 (1961): 60–62.

Daniell, David. *William Tyndale: A Biography*. New Haven and London: Yale University Press, 1994.

The Dante Encyclopedia. Ed. Richard Lansing. New York and London: Garland, 2000.

Davis, Charles T. *Dante's Italy and Other Essays*. Philadelphia: University of Pennsylvania Press, 1984.

Dean, James M. "Dismantling the Canterbury Book." *PMLA* 100 (1985): 746–62.

—. "The World Grown Old and Genesis in Middle English Historical Writings." *Speculum* 57 (1982): 548–68.

—. *The World Grown Old in Later Medieval Literature*. Medieval Academy Books No. 101. Cambridge, MA: The Medieval Academy of America, 1997.

De Grazia, Margreta. "*Language in Elizabethan England: The Divine Model*." Diss. Princeton University, 1975.

—. "Shakespeare's View of Language: An Historical Perspective." *Shakespeare Quarterly* 29 (1978): 374–88.

Demonet, Marie-Luce. *Les voix du signe: nature et origine de langage à la Renaissance (1480–1580)*. Bibliothèque Littéraire de la Renaissance; Série 3:29. Paris and Geneva: Champion-Slatkine, 1992.

Derrida, Jacques. "Des Tours de Babel." *Difference in Translation*. Ed. & trans. Joseph F. Graham. Ithaca and London: Cornell University Press, 1985. 165–248.

—. *Of Grammatology*. Trans. Gayatri Chakravorty Spivak. Baltimore: Johns Hopkins University Press, 1976.

Desmond, Marilynn. *Reading Dido: Gender, Textuality, and the Medieval Aeneid*. Medieval Cultures 8. Minneapolis: University of Minnesota Press, 1994.

Dinshaw, Carolyn. *Chaucer's Sexual Poetics*. Madison: University of Wisconsin Press, 1989.

Donaldson, E. T., ed. *Chaucer's Poetry: An Anthology for the Modern Reader*. 1958; 2nd edn.: New York: John Wiley and Sons, 1975.

d'Ovidio, Francesco. "Dante e la filosofia del linguaggio." *Studii sulla Divina Commedia*. Vol. 2. Caserta: Casa Editrice Moderna, 1931. 291–325.

Dragonetti, Roger. "La Conception du langage poétique dans le 'De vulgari eloquentia' de Dante." *Aux Frontières du Langage Poétique. Romanica Gandensia* [Ghent] 9 (1961): 9–77.

—. "Dante face à Nemrod: Babel mémoire et miroir de l'Eden?" *Critique* 35, Nos. 387–88 (Aout-Septembre) (1979): 690–706.

—. "Une métaphore du sens propre dans le *Roman de la Rose.*" *La Musique et les lettres: études de littérature médiévale.* Publications romanes et françaises 171. Geneva: Droz, 1986. 381–97. (Rpt. from *Digraphe* 21 (1979): 69–85.)

—. "Pygmalion ou les pièges de la fiction dans le *Roman de la Rose.*" *Orbis Mediaevalis: Mélanges de langue et de littérature médiévales offerts à Reto Raduolf Bezzola.* Ed. Georges Güntert, Marc-René Jung and Kurt Ringger. Berne: Francke, 1978. 89–111.

Dronke, Peter. "La creazione degli animali." *L'Uomo di fronte al mondo animale nell'alto Medioevo. Settimane di studio del Centro italiano di studi sull'alto Medioevo* [Spoleto] 31 (1983): 810–13.

—. *Dante and Medieval Latin Traditions.* Cambridge University Press, 1986.

—. *Fabula: Explorations into the Uses of Myth in Medieval Platonism.* Mittellateinische Studien und Texte 9. Ed. Karl Langosch. Leiden and Cologne: E. J. Brill, 1974.

—. *The Medieval Lyric.* 1968; rpt. London: Hutchinson, 1978.

—. "Thierry of Chartres." *A History of Twelfth-Century Western Philosophy.* 358–85.

—. *Women Writers of the Middle Ages.* Cambridge University Press, 1984.

Dubois, Claude-Gilbert. *Mythe et langage au seizième siècle.* Bordeaux: Éditions Ducros, 1970.

Duchrow, Ulrich. *Sprachverständnis und Biblisches Hören bei Augustin.* Tübingen: J. C. B. Mohr (Paul Siebeck), 1965.

Eberle, Patricia J. "The Lover's Glass: Nature's Discourse on Optics and the Optical Design of the *Roman de la Rose.*" *UTQ* 46 (1977): 241–62.

Eco, Umberto. *The Search for the Perfect Language.* Trans. James Fentress. Oxford: Blackwell, 1995.

Eco, Umberto, and Roberto Lambertini, Costantino Marmo, and Andrea Tabarroni. "On Animal Language in the Medieval Classification of Signs." *On the Medieval Theory of Signs.* 3–41.

Edwards, Robert R. *The Dream of Chaucer: Representation and Reflection in the Early Narratives.* Durham and London: Duke University Press, 1989.

Elsky, Martin. *Authorizing Words: Speech, Writing, and Print in the English Renaissance.* Ithaca and London: Cornell University Press, 1989.

Emerson, Oliver F. "Legends of Cain, Especially in Old and Middle English." *PMLA* 21 (1906): 831–929.

Enciclopedia Dantesca. Ed. Umberto Bosco and Giorgio Petrocchi. Roma: Istituto della Enciclopedia Italiana, 1970–78.

Engels, Joseph. "Origine, sens et survie du terme boécien 'secundum placitum'." *Vivarium* 1 (1963): 187–14.

—. "La portée de l'étymologie isidorienne." *Studi Medievali* 3 ser., 3 (1962): 99–128.

Bibliography

Engle, Lars. "Chaucer, Bakhtin, and Griselda." *Exemplaria* 1 (1989): 429–59.

Evans, G. R. *Augustine on Evil.* Cambridge University Press, 1982.

—. *The Language and Logic of the Bible: The Earlier Middle Ages.* Cambridge University Press, 1984.

—. *The Language and Logic of the Bible: The Road to Reformation.* Cambridge University Press, 1985.

—. *Old Arts and New Theology.* Oxford: Clarendon Press, 1980.

—. "Wyclif on Literal and Metaphorical." *From Ockham to Wyclif.* Ed. Anne Hudson and Michael Wilks. Studies in Church History: Subsidia 5. Oxford: Basil Blackwell, for the Ecclesiastical History Society, 1987. 259–66.

Evans, J. Martin. *"Paradise Lost" and the Genesis Tradition.* Oxford: Clarendon Press, 1968.

Faral, Edmond. *Les arts poétiques du XIIᵉ et du XIIIᵉ siècles: Recherches et documents sur la technique littéraire du moyen âge.* Bibliothèque de l'École des Hautes Études: Sciences historiques et philologiques 238. Paris: É. Champion, 1924.

Ferguson, Margaret W. "St. Augustine's Region of Unlikeness: The Crossing of Exile and Language." *Georgia Review* 29 (1975): 842–64.

Ferrante, Joan M. *The Political Vision of the "Divine Comedy."* Princeton University Press, 1984.

—. "The Relation of Speech to Sin in the *Inferno*." *DS* 87 (1969): 33–46.

—. *Woman as Image in Medieval Literature.* New York and London: Columbia University Press, 1975.

—. "Words and Images in the *Paradiso*: Reflections of the Divine." *Dante, Petrarch, Boccaccio: Studies in the Italian Trecento in Honor of Charles S. Singleton.* Ed. Aldo S. Bernardo and Anthony L. Pellegrini. Binghamton, NY: Medieval & Renaissance Texts & Studies, 1983. 115–32.

Fish, Stanley Eugene. *Surprised by Sin.* New York: St. Martin's Press, 1967.

Fleming, John V. *An Introduction to the Franciscan Literature of the Middle Ages.* Chicago: Franciscan Herald Press, 1977.

—. *Reason and the Lover.* Princeton University Press, 1984.

—. *The Roman de la Rose: A Study in Allegory and Iconography.* Princeton University Press, 1969.

Floeri, Fernand. "Le sens de la 'division des sexes' chez Grégoire de Nysse." *Revue des Sciences Religieuses* 27 (1953): 105–11.

Flores, Nona C. "'Effigies Amicitiae . . . Veritas Inimicitiae': Antifeminism in the Iconography of the Woman-Headed Serpent in Medieval and Renaissance Art and Literature." *Animals in the Middle Ages: A Book of Essays.* Ed. Nona C. Flores. Garland Medieval Casebooks. New York and London: Garland, 1996. 167–95.

Forsyth, Neil. *The Old Enemy: Satan and the Combat Myth.* Princeton University Press, 1987.

Foucault, Michel. *The Order of Things: An Archaeology of the Human Sciences.* New York: Vintage Books, 1973.

Fowler, Alastair. *Spenser and the Numbers of Time.* London: Routledge & Kegan Paul, 1964.

Freccero, John. *Dante: The Poetics of Conversion.* Ed. Rachel Jacoff. Cambridge, MA: Harvard University Press, 1986.

—. "Dante's Ulysses: From Epic to Novel." *Concepts of the Hero in the Middle Ages and the Renaissance.* Ed. Norman T. Burns and Christopher J. Reagan. Albany: State University of New York Press, 1975. 101–19.

—. "The Fig Tree and the Laurel: Petrarch's Poetics." *Diacritics* 5:1 (1975): 34–40.

Freud, Sigmund. *Beyond the Pleasure Principle.* Trans. James Strachey. New York: Liveright, 1970.

—. *Civilization and Its Discontents.* Harmondsworth: Penguin, 1985. Vol. 12 of *Civilization, Society, and Religion.* Trans. James Strachey. Ed. Albert Dickson. The Pelican Freud Library. 251–340.

Friedländer, Paul. *Plato.* Trans. Hans Meyerhoff. 2nd edn. Bollingen Series 59. Princeton University Press, 1969.

Friedman, John Block. *The Monstrous Races in Medieval Art and Thought.* Cambridge, MA: Harvard University Press, 1981.

Friedman, Lionel J. "Jean de Meun and Ethelred of Rievaulx." *L'Esprit Créateur* 2 (1962): 135–41.

Froula, Christine F. "When Eve Reads Milton: Undoing the Canonical Economy." *Critical Inquiry* 10 (1983–84): 321–47.

Frye, Northrop. *The Secular Scripture.* Cambridge, MA: Harvard University Press, 1976.

Furrow, Melissa. "The Author and Damnation: Chaucer, Writing, and Penitence." *Forum for Modern Language Studies* 33 (1997): 245–57.

Fyler, John M. "*Auctoritee* and Allusion in *Troilus and Criseyde.*" *Res Publica Litterarum* 7 (1984): 73–92.

—. *Chaucer and Ovid.* New Haven and London: Yale University Press, 1979.

—. "Chaucer, Pope, and the *House of Fame.*" *The Idea of Medieval Literature: New Essays on Chaucer and Medieval Culture in Honor of Donald R. Howard.* Ed. James M. Dean and Christian K. Zacher. Newark: University of Delaware Press; London and Toronto: Associated University Presses, 1992. 149–59.

—. "The Fabrications of Pandarus." *MLQ* 41 (1980): 115–30.

—. "Froissart and Chaucer." *Froissart Across the Genres.* Ed. Donald Maddox and Sara Sturm-Maddox. Gainesville: University of Florida Press, 1998. 195–218.

—. "Love and the Declining World: Ovid, Genesis, and Chaucer." *Mediaevalia* 13 (1989 [for 1987]): 295–307.

— "Man, Men, and Women in Chaucer's Poetry." *The Olde Daunce.* 154–76.

—. "Nimrod, the Commentaries on Genesis, and Chaucer." *The Uses of Manuscripts in Literary Studies: Essays in Memory of Judson Boyce Allen.* Ed. Charlotte Cook Morse, Penelope Reed Doob and Marjorie Curry Woods. Studies in Medieval Culture 31. Kalamazoo: Western Michigan University, Medieval Institute Publications, 1992. 193–211.

—. "*Omnia Vincit Amor:* Incongruity and the Limitations of Structure in Ovid's Elegiac Poetry." *Classical Journal* 66 (1971): 196–203.

Bibliography

—. "St. Augustine, Genesis, and the Origin of Language." *Saint Augustine and His Influence in the Middle Ages*. Ed. Edward B. King and Jacqueline T. Schaefer. Sewanee Mediaeval Studies 3. Sewanee, TN.: University of the South, 1988. 69–78.

Gallacher, Patrick J. *Love, the Word, and Mercury: A Reading of John Gower's "Confessio Amantis."* Albuquerque: University of New Mexico Press, 1975.

Galloway, Andrew. "Authority." *A Companion to Chaucer*. Ed. Peter Brown. Oxford: Blackwell, 2000. 23–39.

—. "Chaucer's *Former Age* and the Fourteenth-Century Anthropology of Craft: The Social Logic of a Premodernist Lyric." *ELH* 63 (1996): 535–53.

Ganim, John M. *Chaucerian Theatricality*. Princeton University Press, 1990.

Gans, Eric. *The Origin of Language: A Formal Theory of Representation*. Berkeley, Los Angeles, London: University of California Press, 1981.

Gaunt, Simon. *Gender and Genre in Medieval French Literature*. Cambridge Studies in French 53. Cambridge University Press, 1995.

Gellrich, Jesse. *The Idea of the Book in the Middle Ages: Language Theory, Mythology, and Fiction*. Ithaca and London: Cornell University Press, 1985.

Genette, Gérard. *Mimologics*. Trans. Thaïs E. Morgan. Lincoln & London: University of Nebraska Press, 1995. *Mimologiques: Voyage en Cratylie*. Paris: Éditions du Seuil, 1976.

George, F. W. A. "Jean de Meung and the Myth of the Golden Age." *The Classical Tradition in French Literature: Essays Presented to R. C. Knight*. Ed. H. T. Barnwell et al. London: Grant and Cutler, 1977. 31–39.

Gillespie, Vincent. "Postcards from the Edge: Interpreting the Ineffable in the Middle English Mystics." *Interpretation: Medieval and Modern*. 137–65.

Gilson, Étienne. "*Regio Dissimilitudinis* de Platon à Saint Bernard de Clairvaux." *MS* 9 (1947): 108–30.

Ginsberg, Warren. *Chaucer's Italian Tradition*. Ann Arbor: University of Michigan Press, 2002.

—. "Ovid and the Problem of Gender." *Mediaevalia* 13 (1989 [for 1987]): 9–28.

Ginzberg, Louis. *The Legends of the Jews*. Philadelphia: The Jewish Publication Society of America, 1911–67.

Goldstein, Harvey D. "*Enea e Paolo*: A Reading of the 26th Canto of Dante's *Inferno*." *Symposium* 19 (1965): 316–27.

Goulburn, Edward Meyrick. *The Ancient Sculptures in the Roof of Norwich Cathedral*. London: The Autotype Fine Art Company, 1876.

Grayson, Cecil. "'*Nobilior est vulgaris*': Latin and Vernacular in Dante's Thought." *Centenary Essays on Dante*. Oxford: Clarendon Press, 1965. 54–76.

Green, Richard Firth. "Changing Chaucer." *SAC* 25 (2003): 27–52.

Greene, Thomas M. *The Descent from Heaven: A Study in Epic Continuity*. New Haven: Yale University Press, 1963.

—. "Dramas of Selfhood in the *Comedy*." *From Time to Eternity: Essays on Dante's Divine Comedy*. Ed. Thomas G. Bergin. New Haven: Yale University Press, 1967. 103–36.

Bibliography

—. *The Light in Troy: Imitation and Discovery in Renaissance Poetry.* New Haven and London: Yale University Press, 1982.

Grennen, Joseph E. "The Canon's Yeoman and the Cosmic Furnace: Language and Meaning in the 'Canon's Yeoman's Tale'." *Criticism* 4 (1962): 225–40.

—. "Chaucer and the Commonplaces of Alchemy." *Classica et Mediaevalia* 26 (1965): 306–33.

—. "Saint Cecilia's 'Chemical Wedding': The Unity of the *Canterbury Tales*, Fragment VIII." *Journal of English and Germanic Philology* 65 (1966): 466–81.

Grudin, Michaela Paasche. *Chaucer and the Politics of Discourse.* Columbia: University of South Carolina Press, 1996.

Guerri, Domenico. "Il nome adamitico di Dio." *Scritti danteschi e d'altra letteratura antica.* Ed. Antonio Lanza. Medioevo e Rinascimento, 1. 1908; rpt. Anzio: De Rubeis, 1990. 57–73.

Guerrieri Crocetti, Camillo. "Divagazioni sul *De Vulgari Eloquentia.*" *Nel mondo neolatino.* Bari: Adriatica Editrice, 1969. 361–77.

Guldan, Ernst. *Eva und Maria.* Graz-Cologne: Böhlau, 1966.

Gunn, Alan M. F. *The Mirror of Love: A Reinterpretation of "The Romance of the Rose."* Lubbock, TX: Texas Tech Press, 1952.

Haidu, Peter. "Repetition: Modern Reflections on Medieval Aesthetics." *MLN* 92 (1977): 875–87.

Hamilton, A. C. "Our New Poet: Spenser, 'well of English vndefyld'." *A Theatre for Spenserians.* Ed. Judith M. Kennedy and James A. Reither. University of Toronto Press, 1973. 101–23.

Hanna, Ralph, III. "*Compilatio* and the Wife of Bath: Latin Backgrounds, Ricardian Texts." *Latin and Vernacular: Studies in Late-Medieval Texts and Manuscripts.* Ed. A. J. Minnis. York Manuscripts Conferences: Proceedings Series 1. Cambridge: D. S. Brewer, 1989. 1–11.

— "The Difficulty of Ricardian Prose Translation: The Case of the Lollards." *MLQ* 51 (1990): 319–40.

Hanning, Robert W. "Chaucer's First Ovid: Metamorphosis and Poetic Tradition in *The Book of the Duchess* and *The House of Fame.*" *Chaucer and the Craft of Fiction.* 121–63.

—. "Roasting a Friar, Mis-Taking a Wife, and Other Acts of Textual Harassment in Chaucer's *Canterbury Tales.*" *SAC* 7 (1985): 3–21.

—. "The Theme of Art and Life in Chaucer's Poetry." *Geoffrey Chaucer.* Ed. George D. Economou. New York: McGraw-Hill, 1975. 15–36.

—. "Uses of Names in Medieval Literature." *Names* 16 (1968): 325–38.

Hart, Kevin. *The Trespass of the Sign: Deconstruction, Theology and Philosophy.* Cambridge University Press, 1989.

Haskins, Charles Homer. *Studies in the History of Mediaeval Science.* Cambridge, MA: Harvard University Press, 1924.

Hawkins, Peter S. "Adam." *Dante Encyclopedia.* 4–5.

—. *Dante's Testaments: Essays in Scriptural Imagination.* Stanford University Press, 1999.

Heilbronn-Gaines, Denise. "XVIII." *Lectura Dantis* 16–17 (1995): 266–76.

Bibliography

Herren, Michael W. "Latin and the Vernacular Language." *Medieval Latin: An Introduction and Bibliographical Guide.* Ed. F. A. C. Mantello and A. G. Rigg. Washington, DC: Catholic University of America Press, 1996. 122–29.

Hicks, Eric. "The 'Querelle de la Rose' in the *Roman de la Rose.*" *Les Bonnes Feuilles* 3 (1974): 152–69.

—. "Sous les pavés, le sens: Le dire et le décorum allégoriques dans *Le Roman de la Rose* de Jean de Meun." *Etudes-de-Lettres* 2–3 (1987): 113–32.

Hilberry, Jane. "'And in Oure Madnesse Everemoore We Rave': Technical Language in the *Canon's Yeoman's Tale.*" *ChRev* 21 (1987): 435–43.

Hill, Thomas D. "Narcissus, Pygmalion, and the Castration of Saturn: Two Mythographical Themes in the *Roman de la Rose.*" *SP* 71 (1974): 404–26.

Hindman, Sandra L. *Christine de Pizan's "Epistre Othéa": Painting and Politics at the Court of Charles VI.* Toronto: Pontifical Institute of Mediaeval Studies, 1986.

Hirn, Yrjö. *The Sacred Shrine.* Boston: Beacon Press, 1912, rpt. 1957.

Hirsh, John C. "The *Second Nun's Tale.*" *Chaucer's Religious Tales.* Ed. C. David Benson and Elizabeth Robertson. Cambridge: D. S. Brewer, 1990. 161–70.

A History of Twelfth-Century Western Philosophy. Ed. Peter Dronke. Cambridge University Press, 1988.

Hollander, Robert. *Allegory in Dante's "Commedia."* Princeton University Press, 1969.

—. "Babytalk in Dante's Commedia." *Mosaic* 8 (1975): 73–84.

—. *Il Virgilio dantesco: Tragedia nella "Commedia."* Biblioteca di "Lettere Italiane": Studi e Testi 28. Florence: Leo S. Olschki Editore, 1983.

Horowitz, Maryanne Cline. "The Image of God in Man – Is Woman Included?" *Harvard Theological Review* 72 (1979): 169–206.

Householder, Fred W. "The Primacy of Writing." *Linguistic Speculations.* Cambridge University Press, 1971. 244–64.

Howard, Donald R. *The Idea of the Canterbury Tales.* Berkeley, Los Angeles, London: University of California Press, 1976.

Hudson, Anne. *The Premature Reformation: Wycliffite Texts and Lollard History.* Oxford: Clarendon Press, 1988.

—. "Wyclif and the English Language." *Wyclif in His Times.* Ed. Anthony Kenny. Oxford: Clarendon Press, 1986. 85–103.

Hult, David. "Closed Quotations: The Speaking Voice in the *Roman de la Rose.*" *YFS* 67 (1984): 248–69.

—. "Language and Dismemberment: Abelard, Origen, and the *Romance of the Rose.*" *Rethinking the "Romance of the Rose."* 101–30.

—. "Words and Deeds: Jean de Meun's *Romance of the Rose* and the Hermeneutics of Censorship." *New Literary History* 28 (1997): 345–66.

Huot, Sylvia. *From Song to Book: The Poetics of Writing in Old French Lyric and Lyrical Narrative Poetry.* Ithaca and London: Cornell University Press, 1987.

—. "The Medusa Interpolation in the *Romance of the Rose*: Mythographic Program and Ovidian Intertext." *Speculum* 62 (1987): 865–77.

—. *"The Romance of the Rose" and Its Medieval Readers: Interpretation, Reception, Manuscript Transmission.* Cambridge Studies in Medieval Literature 16. Cambridge University Press, 1993.

Huppé, Bernard F. *A Reading of the "Canterbury Tales."* Rev. ed. Albany: State University of New York, 1967.

Ineichen, Gustav. "Le discours linguistique de Jean de Meun." *Romanistische Zeitschrift für Literaturgeschichte* 2 (1978): 245–53.

Interpretation: Medieval and Modern. Ed. Piero Boitani and Anna Torti. The J. A. W. Bennett Memorial Lectures, Eighth Series, Perugia, 1992. Cambridge: D. S. Brewer, 1993.

Irvine, Martin. *The Making of Textual Culture: 'Grammatica' and Literary Theory, 350–1100.* Cambridge Studies in Medieval Literature 19. Cambridge University Press, 1994.

—. "Medieval Grammatical Theory and Chaucer's *House of Fame.*" *Speculum* 60 (1985): 850–76.

Jackendoff, Ray. *Foundations of Language: Brain, Meaning, Grammar, Evolution.* Oxford University Press, 2002.

Jackson, B. Darrell. "The Theory of Signs in St. Augustine's *De Doctrina Christiana.*" *Revue des Études Augustiniennes* 15 (1969): 9–49.

Jacob, E. F. "The Giants (*Inferno*, XXXI)." *Medieval Miscellany Presented to Eugène Vinaver.* Ed. Frederick Whitehead, A. H. Diverres, and F. E. Sutcliffe. New York: Barnes & Noble, 1965. 167–85.

Jacoff, Rachel. "Intertextualities in Arcadia: *Purgatorio* 30.49–51." *The Poetry of Allusion: Virgil and Ovid in Dante's 'Commedia.'* Ed. Rachel Jacoff and Jeffrey T. Schnapp. Stanford University Press, 1991. 131–44.

Jacoff, Rachel and William Stephany. *"Inferno II."* Lectura Dantis Americana. Philadelphia: University of Pennsylvania Press, 1989.

Jager, Eric. "Did Eve Invent Writing? Script and the Fall in 'The Adam Books'." *SP* 93 (1996): 229–50.

—. *The Tempter's Voice: Language and the Fall in Medieval Literature.* Ithaca and London: Cornell University Press, 1993.

James, M. R. *Illustrations of the Book of Genesis.* Oxford: Roxburghe Club, 1921.

—. "Pictor in Carmine." *Archaeologia* 94 (1951): 141–66.

James, Montague Rhodes, and Eric George Millar. *The Bohun Manuscripts.* Oxford: Roxburghe Club, 1936.

Jameson, Fredric. *The Prison-House of Language: A Critical Account of Structuralism and Russian Formalism.* Princeton University Press, 1972.

Jarrell, Randall. *A Sad Heart at the Supermarket.* New York: Atheneum, 1962.

Javelet, Robert. *Image et ressemblance au douzième siècle, de saint Anselme à Alain de Lille.* 2 vols. Paris: Letouzey & Ané, 1967.

Jeauneau, Édouard. "Deux rédactions des gloses de Guillaume de Conches sur Priscien." *RTAM* 27 (1960): 212–47.

—. "L'usage de la notion *d'integumentum* à travers les gloses de Guillaume de Conches." *AHDLMA* 24 (1957): 35–100.

Jeffrey, David Lyle, ed. *A Dictionary of Biblical Tradition in English Literature.* Grand Rapids, MI: William B. Eerdmans, 1992.

Jenaro-MacLennan, Luis. *The Trecento Commentaries on the "Divina Commedia" and the Epistle to Cangrande.* Oxford: Clarendon Press, 1974.

John Paul II, Pope. "The Dignity of Women: Pope John Paul II's Letter." *The Tablet.* 1 October 1988: 1138–42.

Johnson, Douglas W. "*Verbum* in the Early Augustine (386–397)." *RA* 8 (1972): 25–53.

Jolivet, Jean. *Arts du langage et théologie chez Abélard.* Études de philosophie médiévale 57. Paris: J. Vrin, 1969.

—. "Quelques cas de 'platonisme grammatical' du VIIᵉ au XIIᵉ siècle." *Mélanges René Crozet.* 2 vols. Poitiers: Société d'études médiévales, 1966. 1:93–99.

Jones, Charles W. "Some Introductory Remarks on Bede's Commentary on Genesis." *Sacris Erudiri* 19 (1969–70): 115–98.

Jordan, Robert M. *Chaucer and the Shape of Creation: The Aesthetic Possibilities of Inorganic Structure.* Cambridge, MA: Harvard University Press, 1967.

—. *Chaucer's Poetics and the Modern Reader.* Berkeley, Los Angeles, London: University of California Press, 1987.

Joslin, Mary Coker, and Carolyn Coker Joslin Watson. *The Egerton Genesis.* London, Toronto and Buffalo: The British Library and the University of Toronto Press, 2001.

Jung, Marc-René. "Jean de Meun et l'Allégorie." *Cahiers de l'Association Internationale des Études Françaises* 28 (1976): 21–36.

Justman, Stewart. "Medieval Monism and Abuse of Authority in Chaucer." *ChRev* 11 (1975): 95–111.

Kamesar, Adam. *Jerome, Greek Scholarship, and the Hebrew Bible: A Study of the "Quaestiones Hebraicae in Genesim."* Oxford: Clarendon Press, 1993.

Kane, George. *Chaucer.* Oxford University Press, 1984.

Kaske, Robert E. "*Beowulf* and the Book of Enoch." *Speculum* 46 (1971): 421–31.

Katz, David S. "The Language of Adam in Seventeenth-Century England." *History and Imagination: Essays in Honour of H. R. Trevor-Roper.* Ed. Hugh Lloyd-Jones, Valerie Pearl and Blair Warden. London: Duckworth, 1981. 132–45.

Kay, Richard. *Dante's Swift and Strong: Essays on Inferno XV.* Lawrence: Regents Press of Kansas, 1978.

Kay, Sarah. "The Birth of Venus in the *Roman de la Rose.*" *Exemplaria* 9 (1997): 7–37.

—. *The Romance of the Rose.* Critical Guides to French Texts 110. London: Grant & Cutler, 1995.

—. "Women's Body of Knowledge: Epistemology and Misogyny in the *Romance of the Rose.*" *Framing Medieval Bodies.* Ed. Sarah Kay and Miri Rubin. Manchester University Press, 1994. 211–35.

Kelly, Douglas. *Internal Difference and Meanings in the "Roman de la Rose."* Madison: University of Wisconsin Press, 1995.

Kelly, Henry Ansgar. "The Metamorphoses of the Eden Serpent during the Middle Ages and Renaissance." *Viator* 2 (1971): 301–28.

—. *Tragedy and Comedy from Dante to Pseudo-Dante*. University of California Publications in Modern Philology 121. Berkeley, London: University of California Press, 1989.

Kieckhefer, Richard. *Magic in the Middle Ages*. Cambridge Medieval Textbooks. Cambridge University Press, 1990.

Kirkpatrick, Robin. *Dante: The Divine Comedy*. Cambridge University Press, 1987.

Kirwan, Christopher. *Augustine*. London and New York: Routledge, 1989.

Kiser, Lisa J. "Eschatological Poetics in Chaucer's *House of Fame*." *MLQ* 49 (1988): 99–119.

—. *Truth and Textuality in Chaucer's Poetry*. Hanover and London: University Press of New England, 1991.

Klemp, P. J. "'Now Hid, Now Seen': An Acrostic in *Paradise Lost*." *Milton Quarterly* 11 (1977): 91–92.

Klinck, Roswitha. *Die Lateinische Etymologie des Mittelalters*. Medium Aevum 17. Munich: Wilhelm Fink, 1970.

Klingender, Francis. *Animals in Art and Thought to the End of the Middle Ages*. Ed. Evelyn Anthal and John Harthan. Cambridge, MA: MIT Press, 1971.

Knowlson, James. *Universal Language Schemes in England and France 1600–1800*. University of Toronto Press, 1975.

Kolve, V. A. "Chaucer's *Second Nun's Tale* and the Iconography of Saint Cecilia." *New Perspectives in Chaucer Criticism*. 137–74.

Koonce, B. G. *Chaucer and the Tradition of Fame: Symbolism in "The House of Fame."* Princeton University Press, 1966.

Kooper, Erik. "Loving the Unequal Equal: Medieval Theologians and Marital Affection." *The Olde Daunce*. 44–56.

Kretzmann, Norman. "Aristotle on Spoken Sound Significant by Convention." *Ancient Logic and Its Modern Interpretations*. Ed. John Corcoran. Synthese Historical Library: Texts and Studies in the History of Logic and Philosophy 9. Dordrecht-Holland and Boston-USA: D. Reidel Publishing Company, 1974. 3–21.

—. "Semantics, History of." *Encyclopedia of Philosophy*. 8 vols. Ed. Paul Edwards. New York: Macmillan, 1967. 358–406.

Ladner, Gerhart B. *The Idea of Reform*. Cambridge, MA: Harvard University Press, 1959.

—. *Ad Imaginem Dei: The Image of Man in Mediaeval Art*. Wimmer Lecture, 1962. Latrobe, Pennsylvania: The Archabbey Press, 1965.

—. "The Physical Anthropology of Saint Gregory of Nyssa." *Dumbarton Oaks Papers* 12 (1958): 59–94.

Language Evolution. Ed. Morten H. Christiansen and Simon Kirby. Oxford University Press, 2003.

Lanham, Richard A. *The Motives of Eloquence: Literary Rhetoric in the Renaissance*. New Haven and London: Yale University Press, 1976.

Lawler, Traugott. *The One and the Many in the Canterbury Tales*. Hamden, CT: Archon Books, 1980.

Leach, Edmund. "Lévi-Strauss in the Garden of Eden: An Examination of Some Recent Developments in the Analysis of Myth." *Transactions of the New York Academy of Sciences* ser. 2, 23 (1961): 386–96.

Leff, Gordon. *The Dissolution of the Medieval Outlook: An Essay on Intellectual and Spiritual Change in the Fourteenth Century.* New York: Harper & Row, 1976.

Lehmann, Paul. *Die Parodie im Mittelalter.* Stuttgart: A. Hiersemann, 1922, rpt. 1963.

Leicester, H. Marshall, Jr. *The Disenchanted Self: Representing the Subject in the "Canterbury Tales."* Berkeley, Oxford: University of California Press, 1990.

—. "The Harmony of Chaucer's *Parlement*: A Dissonant Voice." *ChRev* 9 (1974): 15–34.

—. "Piety and Resistance: A Note on the Representation of Religious Feeling in the *Canterbury Tales.*" *The Endless Knot: Essays on Old and Middle English in Honor of Marie Borroff.* Ed. M. Teresa Tavormina and R. F. Yeager. Cambridge: D. S. Brewer, 1995. 151–60.

Leo, Ulrich. "The Unfinished *Convivio* and Dante's Rereading of the *Aeneid.*" *MS* 13 (1951): 41–64.

Leonard, John. *Naming in Paradise: Milton and the Language of Adam and Eve.* Oxford: Clarendon Press, 1990.

Leupin, Alexandre. *Barbarolexis: Medieval Writing and Sexuality.* Trans. Kate M. Cooper. Cambridge, MA and London: Harvard University Press, 1989.

Levitan, Alan. "The Parody of Pentecost in Chaucer's *Summoner's Tale.*" *UTQ* 40 (1971): 236–46.

Levy, Bernard S. "Biblical Parody in the *Summoner's Tale.*" *Texas Studies in Literature and Language* 11 (1966): 45–60.

Lewis, C. S. "Four-Letter Words." *The Critical Quarterly* 3 (1961): 118–22.

Lindberg, David C. *John Pecham and the Science of Optics: Perspectiva Communis.* The University of Wisconsin Publications in Medieval Science 14. Madison, Milwaukee, and London: University of Wisconsin Press, 1970.

Livesey, Steven J., and Richard H. Rouse. "Nimrod the Astronomer." *Traditio* 37 (1981): 203–66.

Lloyd, Genevieve. *The Man of Reason: 'Male' and 'Female' in Western Philosophy.* 2nd edn. London: Routledge, 1993.

Lonergan, Bernard J., SJ. *Verbum: Word and Idea in Aquinas.* Ed. David B. Burrell, CSC. University of Notre Dame Press, 1967.

Lo Piparo, Franco. "Sign and Grammar in Dante: A Non-Modistic Language Theory." *The History of Linguistics in Italy.* Ed. Paolo Ramat, Hans-J. Niederehe and Konrad Koerner. Amsterdam Studies in the Theory and History of Linguistic Science Series 3, vol. 33. Amsterdam/Philadelphia: John Benjamins, 1986. 1–22.

Lord, Carla. "The *Ovide Moralisé* and the Old Testament." *Tribute to Lotte Brand Philip.* Ed. William W. Clark et al. New York: Abaris Books, Inc., 1985. 95–102.

Lubac, Henri de. *Exégèse médiévale: Les quatre sens de l'Écriture.* Paris: Aubier, 1959–64.

Luscombe, D. E. "Peter Abelard." *A History of Twelfth-Century Western Philosophy.* 279–307.

Bibliography

Lusignan, Serge. "Le français et le latin aux XIIIᵉ–XIVᵉ siècles: pratiques des langues et pensée linguistique." *Annales E.S.C.* 42, no. 4 (1987): 955–67.

—. "Le Latin Était la Langue Maternelle des Romains: la fortune d'un argument à la fin du Moyen Age." *Préludes à la Renaissance.* Ed. Carla Bozzolo and Ezio Ornato. Paris: CNRS, 1992. 265–303.

—. *Parler Vulgairement: Les intellectuels et la langue française aux XIIIᵉ et XIVᵉ siècles.* Les Presses de l'Université de Montréal, 1986.

—. "La topique de la *translatio studii* et les traductions françaises de textes savants au XIVe siècle." *Traduction et traducteurs au Moyen Âge.* Ed. Geneviève Contamine. Paris: CNRS, 1989. 303–15.

Lutz, Cora E. "Remigius' Ideas on the Origins of the Seven Liberal Arts." *M&H* 10 (1956): 41–49.

Machan, Tim William. "Chaucer as Translator." *The Medieval Translator: The Theory and Practice of Translation in the Middle Ages.* Ed. Roger Ellis. Cambridge: D. S. Brewer, 1989. 55–67.

—. *Techniques of Translation: Chaucer's "Boece."* Norman, OK.: Pilgrim Books, 1985.

Maguire, Henry. "Adam and the Animals: Allegory and the Literal Sense in Early Christian Art." *Dumbarton Oaks Papers* 41 (1987): 363–73.

Mâle, Emile. "La légende de la Mort de Caïn – à propos d'un chapiteau de Tarbes." *Revue Archéologique* 3ᵉ série, 21 (1893): 186–94.

Mandelbaum, Allen, Anthony Oldcorn, and Charles Ross, eds. *Lectura Dantis: Inferno.* California Lectura Dantis: 1. Berkeley, Los Angeles, London: University of California Press, 1998.

Manetti, Giovanni. *Theories of the Sign in Classical Antiquity.* Trans. Christine Richardson. Bloomington: Indiana University Press, 1993.

Mann, Jill. "Jean de Meun and the Castration of Saturn." *Poetry and Philosophy in the Middle Ages: A Festschrift for Peter Dronke.* Ed. John Marenbon. Mittellateinische Studien und Texte 29. Leiden, Boston & Cologne: Brill, 2001. 309–26.

Manzalaoui, Mahmoud. "Chaucer and Science." *Geoffrey Chaucer.* Ed. Derek Brewer. *Writers and Their Background.* London: G. Bell & Sons, 1974. 224–61.

Marenbon, John. *Early Medieval Philosophy (480–1150): An Introduction.* London: Routledge & Kegan Paul, 1983.

Mariani, Valerio. "Commedia." *Enciclopedia Dantesca.* 2:79–118.

Marigo, Aristide, ed. *De Vulgari Eloquentia.* 3rd edn. Florence: Le Monnier, 1968.

Markley, Robert. *Fallen Languages: Crises of Representation in Newtonian England, 1660–1740.* Ithaca and London: Cornell University Press, 1993.

Marks, Herbert. "Hollowed Names: *Vox* and *Vanitas* in the *Purgatorio*." *DS* 110 (1992): 135–78.

Markus, R. A. *Saeculum: History and Society in the Theology of St Augustine.* Cambridge University Press, 1970.

—. "St. Augustine on Signs." *Augustine: A Collection of Critical Essays.* Ed. R. A. Markus. New York: Doubleday Anchor, 1972. 61–91.

Marrou, Henri-Irénée. *History of Education in Antiquity.* Trans. George Lamb. New York: Mentor, 1956.

—. *Saint Augustin et la fin de la culture antique.* Paris: E. de Boccard, 1938.

Martin, Priscilla. *Chaucer's Women: Nuns, Wives, and Amazons.* Iowa City: University of Iowa Press, 1990.

Maurer, Armand. "William of Ockham on Language and Reality." *Miscellanea Mediaevalia* 13, no. 2 (1981): 795–802.

Mazzeo, Joseph Anthony. "Dante's Three Communities: Mediation and Order." *The World of Dante.* Ed. S. Bernard Chandler and J. A. Molinaro. University of Toronto Press, 1966. 62–79.

—. *Medieval Cultural Tradition in Dante's "Comedy."* Ithaca: Cornell University Press, 1960.

—. "St. Augustine's Rhetoric of Silence: Truth vs. Eloquence and Things vs. Signs." *Renaissance and Seventeenth-Century Studies.* New York: Columbia University Press, 1962, rpt. 1964. 1–28.

Mazzocco, Angelo. "'La lingua ch'io parlai fu tutta spenta': Dante's Reappraisal of the Adamic Language (*Paradiso* XXVI, 124–138)." *Linguistic Theories in Dante and the Humanists: Studies of Language and Intellectual History in Late Medieval and Early Renaissance Italy.* Brill's Studies in Intellectual History 38. Leiden, New York & Cologne: E. J. Brill, 1993. 159–79.

Mazzotta, Giuseppe. "Dante and the Virtues of Exile." *Poetics Today* 5:3 (1984): 645–67.

—. *Dante, Poet of the Desert.* Princeton University Press, 1979.

—. *The World at Play in Boccaccio's Decameron.* Princeton University Press, 1986.

McClellan, William. "Bakhtin's Theory of Dialogic Discourse, Medieval Rhetorical Theory, and the Multi-Voiced Structure of the *Clerk's Tale.*" *Exemplaria* 1 (1989): 461–88.

McGerr, Rosemarie P. *Chaucer's Open Books: Resistance to Closure in Medieval Discourse.* Gainesville: University of Florida Press, 1998.

McKeon, Richard. "Aristotle's Conception of Language and the Arts of Language." *Classical Philology* 41 (1946): 193–206.

—. "Aristotle's Conception of Language and the Arts of Language (Concluded)." *Classical Philology* 42 (1947): 21–50.

—. "Rhetoric in the Middle Ages." *Speculum* 17 (1942): 1–32.

McKusick, James C. *Coleridge's Philosophy of Language.* Yale Studies in English 195. New Haven and London: Yale University Press, 1986.

McNally, R. E. "The 'Tres Linguae Sacrae' in Early Irish Bible Exegesis." *Theological Studies* 19 (1958): 395–403.

Medici, Mario. "I." *Enciclopedia Dantesca.* 3:345.

Mellinkoff, Ruth. "Cain's Monstrous Progeny in *Beowulf*: Part II, Post-Diluvian Survival." *Anglo-Saxon England* 9 (1981): 183–97.

Mengaldo, Pier Vincenzo. "Appunti sul canto XXVI del 'Paradiso'." *Linguistica e retorica di Dante.* Saggi di varia umanitá 21. Pisa: Nistri-Lischi, 1978. 223–46.

—. "L'elegia 'umile'." *Giornale storico della letteratura italiana* 143 (1966): 177–98.

—. "Gramatica." *Enciclopedia Dantesca.* 3:259–64.

Menner, Robert J., ed. *The Poetical Dialogues of Solomon and Saturn.* New York: MLA, 1941.

Bibliography

Menocal, María Rosa. *Shards of Love: Exile and the Origins of the Lyric.* Durham, NC, & London: Duke University Press, 1994.

Middleton, Anne. "Chaucer's 'New Men' and the Good of Literature in the *Canterbury Tales*." *Literature and Society: Selected Papers from the English Institute, 1978.* Ed. Edward W. Said. Baltimore and London: Johns Hopkins University Press, 1980. 15–56.

—. "Two Infinites: Grammatical Metaphor in *Piers Plowman*." *ELH* 39 (1972): 169–88.

Minnis, Alastair J. "*A leur fez cousines*: Words, Deeds and Proper Speech in Jean de Meun and Chaucer." *Medieval Heritage: Essays in Honour of Tadahiro Ikegami.* Ed. Masahiko Kanno et al. Tokyo: Yushodo Press Co., Ltd., 1997. 31–63.

—. "*De Impedimento Sexus*: Women's Bodies and Medieval Impediments to Female Ordination." *Medieval Theology and the Natural Body.* Ed. Peter Biller and A. J. Minnis. York Studies in Medieval Theology I. York Medieval Press, 1997. 109–40.

—. *Magister Amoris: The "Roman de la Rose" and Vernacular Hermeneutics.* Oxford: Clarendon Press, 2001.

—. *Medieval Theory of Authorship: Scholastic Literary Attitudes in the Later Middle Ages.* London: Scolar Press, 1984.

Minnis, A. J., and A. B. Scott, eds. (with the assistance of David Wallace). *Medieval Literary Theory and Criticism c.1100–c.1375: The Commentary Tradition* (1988). Rev. edn. Oxford: Clarendon Press, 1991.

Moi, Toril. "Desire in Language: Andreas Capellanus and the Controversy of Courtly Love." *Medieval Literature: Criticism, Ideology & History.* Ed. David Aers. Brighton, Sussex: Harvester, 1986. 11–33.

Moir, A. L. *The World Map in Hereford Cathedral.* Hereford: The Cathedral, 1970.

Monroe, William H. "A Roll-Manuscript of Peter of Poitiers' Compendium." *Bulletin of the Cleveland Museum of Art* 65 (1978): 92–107.

Moore, Philip S. *The Works of Peter of Poitiers.* Washington, DC: Catholic University, 1936.

Morey, James H. "Peter Comestor, Biblical Paraphrase, and the Medieval Popular Bible." *Speculum* 68 (1993): 6–35.

—. "Petrus Comestor." *Speculum* 68 (1998): 6–35.

Muratova, Xénia. "'Adam donne leurs noms aux animaux'." *Studi Medievali* ser. 3, 18:2 (1977): 367–94.

Murdoch, Brian. *The Medieval Popular Bible: Expansions of Genesis in the Middle Ages.* Cambridge: D. S. Brewer, 2003.

Murphy, James J. *Rhetoric in the Middle Ages.* Berkeley and Los Angeles: University of California Press, 1974.

Muscatine, Charles. *Chaucer and the French Tradition: A Study in Style and Meaning.* Berkeley and Los Angeles: University of California Press, 1957.

—. "Courtly Literature and Vulgar Language." *Court and Poet: Selected Proceedings of the Third Congress of the International Courtly Literature Society (Liverpool, 1980).* Ed. Glyn S. Burgess. Liverpool: Francis Cairns, 1981. 1–19.

—. "The Fabliaux, Courtly Culture, and the (Re)Invention of Vulgarity." *Obscenity.* 281–92.

—. *The Old French Fabliaux*. New Haven, London: Yale University Press, 1986.

Musurillo, Herbert, ed. *The Acts of the Christian Martyrs*. Oxford: Clarendon Press, 1972.

Myerowitz, Molly. *Ovid's Games of Love*. Detroit: Wayne State University Press, 1985.

Myles, Robert. *Chaucerian Realism*. Chaucer Studies 20. Cambridge: D. S. Brewer, 1994.

Nardi, Bruno. *Dante e la cultura medievale*. 2nd edn. Bari: Laterza, 1949.

—. "Due capitoli di filosofia dantesca." *Giornale storico della letteratura italiana* suppl. 19–21 (1922): 260–64.

Nencioni, Giovanni. "Dante e la Retorica." *Dante e Bologna nei Tempi di Dante*. Bologna: Commissione per i Testi di Lingua, 1967. 91–112.

New Perspectives in Chaucer Criticism. Ed. Donald M. Rose. Norman, Oklahoma: Pilgrim Books, 1981.

Newman, Barbara. *From Virile Woman to WomanChrist: Studies in Medieval Religion and Literature*. Philadelphia: University of Pennsylvania Press, 1995.

Nichols, Stephen G. "On the Sociology of Medieval Manuscript Annotation." *Annotation and Its Texts*. 43–73.

— "Prophetic Discourse: St. Augustine to Christine de Pizan." *The Bible in the Middle Ages: Its Influence on Literature and Art*. Ed. Bernard S. Levy. Medieval & Renaissance Texts & Studies 89. Binghamton, NY, 1992. 51–76.

Nims, Margaret F., IBVM. "*Translatio*: 'Difficult Statement' in Medieval Poetic Theory." *UTQ* 43 (1974): 215–30.

Nitzsche, J. C. "Creation in Genesis and Nature in Chaucer's *General Prologue* 1–18." *Papers on Language and Literature* 14 (1978): 459–64.

Nohrnberg, James. "Justifying Narrative: Commentary within Biblical Storytelling." *Annotation and Its Texts*. 3–42.

Nolan, Barbara. *Chaucer and the Tradition of the "Roman Antique."* Cambridge Studies in Medieval Literature 15. Cambridge University Press, 1992.

Nykrog, Per. "Obscene or Not Obscene: Lady Reason, Jean de Meun, and the Fisherman from Pont-sur-Seine." *Obscenity*. 319–31.

Nyquist, Mary. "Gynesis, Genesis, Exegesis, and Milton's Eve." *Cannibals, Witches and Divorce: Estranging the Renaissance*. Ed. Marjorie Garber. English Institute Essays n.s. 11. Baltimore: Johns Hopkins University Press, 1987. 147–208.

Obscenity: Social Control and Artistic Creation in the European Middle Ages. Ed. Jan M. Ziolkowski. Leiden, Boston & Cologne: Brill, 1998.

O'Connell, Robert J., SJ. *Art and the Christian Intelligence in St. Augustine*. Cambridge, MA: Harvard University Press, 1978.

The Olde Daunce: Love, Friendship, Sex, and Marriage in the Medieval World. Ed. Robert R. Edwards and Stephen Spector. Albany: State University of New York Press, 1991.

Olender, Maurice. *The Languages of Paradise: Aryans and Semites, A Match Made in Heaven*. Trans. Arthur Goldhammer. New York: Other Press, 2002.

Olson, Glending. "Chaucer, Dante, and the Structure of Fragment VIII (G) of the *Canterbury Tales*." *ChRev* 16 (1982): 222–36.

—. "*Inferno* 27 and the Perversions of Pentecost." *DS* 117 (1999): 21–33.

—. "Making and Poetry in the Age of Chaucer." *Comparative Literature* 31 (1979): 272–90.

On the Medieval Theory of Signs. Ed. Umberto Eco and Costantino Marmo. Foundations of Semiotics 21. Amsterdam/Philadelphia: John Benjamins, 1989.

Ong, Walter J., SJ. "Wit and Mystery: A Revaluation in Mediaeval Latin Hymnody." *Speculum* 22 (1947): 310–41.

Ovitt, George, Jr. *The Restoration of Perfection: Labor and Technology in Medieval Culture*. New Brunswick and London: Rutgers University Press, 1987.

Padley, G. R. *Grammatical Theory in Western Europe 1500–1700: The Latin Tradition*. Cambridge University Press, 1976.

Pagani, Ileana. *La teoria linguistica di Dante: "De Vulgari Eloquentia": discussioni, scelte, proposte*. Naples: Liguori Editore, 1982.

Pagden, Anthony. *European Encounters with the New World: From Renaissance to Romanticism*. New Haven & London: Yale University Press, 1993.

Pagliaro, Antonino. "Dialetti e lingue nell'oltretomba." *Ulisse II*. Messina & Florence: G. d'Anna, 1967. 433–65.

—. "La dottrina linguistica di Dante." *Quaderni di Roma* 1 (1947): 485–501.

—. "I 'primissima signa' nella dottrina linguistica di Dante." *Nuovi saggi di critica semantica*. Biblioteca di cultura contemporanea 51. Messina & Florence: G. d'Anna, 1956. 215–46.

—. "Teoria e prassi Linguistica." *Ulisse II*. 529–83.

Palmieri, Ugo. "Appunti di linguistica dantesca." *SD* 41 (1964): 45–53.

Pardes, Ilana. *Countertraditions in the Bible: A Feminist Approach*. Cambridge, MA: Harvard University Press, 1992.

Parker, Patricia. *Inescapable Romance*. Princeton University Press, 1979.

Patterson, Lee. *Chaucer and the Subject of History*. Madison: University of Wisconsin Press, 1991.

—. "The 'Parson's Tale' and the Quitting of the 'Canterbury Tales.'" *Traditio* 34 (1978): 331–80.

—. "Perpetual Motion: Alchemy and the Technology of the Self." *SAC* 15 (1993): 25–57.

Pearcy, Roy J. "Modes of Signification and the Humor of Obscene Diction in the Fabliaux." *The Humor of the Fabliaux*. Ed. Thomas D. Cooke and Benjamin L. Honeycutt. Columbia: University of Missouri Press, 1974. 163–96.

Pearsall, Derek. *The Canterbury Tales*. London: George Allen & Unwin, 1985.

—. *The Life of Geoffrey Chaucer: A Critical Biography*. Oxford: Blackwell, 1992.

Peck, Russell A. "Chaucer and the Nominalist Questions." *Speculum* 53 (1978): 745–60.

— "The Ideas of 'Entente' and Translation in Chaucer's *Second Nun's Tale*." *Annuale Mediaevale* 8 (1967): 17–37.

— "Public Dreams and Private Myths: Perspective in Middle English Literature." *PMLA* 90 (1975): 461–67.

Pelen, Marc M. *Latin Poetic Irony in the "Roman de la Rose."* Liverpool; Wolfeboro, NH: Francis Cairns, 1987.

Pépin, Jean. "Saint Augustin et la fonction protreptique de l'allégorie." *RA* 1 (1958): 243–86.

Pézard, André. *Dante sous la pluie de feu.* Études de Philosophie Médiévale 40. Paris: J. Vrin, 1950.

—. "Les trois langues de Cacciaguida." *Revue des études italiennes* n.s. 13 (1967): 217–38.

Phillips, John A. *Eve: The History of an Idea.* San Francisco: Harper & Row, 1984.

Pinborg, Jan. "The English Contribution to Logic before Ockham." *Synthèse* 40 (1979): 19–42.

Poggioli, Renato. "Tragedy or Romance? A Reading of the Paolo and Francesca Episode in Dante's *Inferno*." *PMLA* 72 (1957): 313–58.

Poirion, Daniel. "De la signification selon Jean de Meun." *Archéologie du signe.* 165–85.

—. "Les mots et les choses selon Jean de Meun." *L'Information littéraire* 26 (1974): 7–11.

—. "Narcisse et Pygmalion dans *Le Roman de la Rose*." *Essays in Honor of Louis Francis Solano.* Ed. Raymond J. Cormier and Urban T. Holmes. University of North Carolina Studies in the Romance Languages and Literatures 92. Chapel Hill: University of North Carolina Press, 1970. 153–65.

The Portable Medieval Reader. Ed. J. B. Ross and M. M. McLaughlin. New York: Viking Press, 1949.

Pratt, Robert A. "Chaucer Borrowing from Himself." *MLQ* 7 (1946): 259–64.

Pulsiano, Phillip. "Redeemed Language and the Ending of *Troilus and Criseyde*." *Sign, Sentence, Discourse.* 153–74.

Purdon, Liam O. "Chaucer's *Lak of Stedfastnesse*: A Revalorization of the Word." *Sign, Sentence, Discourse.* 144–52.

Quilligan, Maureen. "Allegory, Allegoresis, and the Deallegorization of Language: The *Roman de la Rose*, the *De Planctu Naturae*, and the *Parlement of Foules*." *Allegory, Myth, and Symbol.* Ed. Morton W. Bloomfield. Harvard Studies in English 9. Cambridge, MA: Harvard University Press, 1981. 163–86.

—. *The Allegory of Female Authority: Christine de Pizan's Cité Des Dames.* Ithaca and London: Cornell University Press, 1991.

—. "Words and Sex: The Language of Allegory in the *De Planctu Naturae*, the *Roman de la Rose*, and Book III of *The Faerie Queene*." *Allegorica* 2 (1977): 195–216.

Quinones, Ricardo J. *The Changes of Cain: Violence and the Lost Brother in Cain and Abel Literature.* Princeton University Press, 1991.

Rambeau, A. "Chaucer's 'House of Fame' in seinem verhältniss zu Dante's 'Divina Commedia'." *Englische Studien* 3 (1880): 209–68.

Rappoport, Angelo S. *Myths and Legends of Ancient Israel.* London: Gresham Publishing Company, 1928.

Ray, Roger. "Rhetorical Scepticism and Verisimilar Narrative in John of Salisbury's *Historia Pontificalis*." *Classical Rhetoric and Medieval Historiography.* Ed. Ernst Breisach. Studies in Medieval Culture 19. Kalamazoo: Mediaeval Institute Publications, Western Michigan University, 1985. 61–102.

Raybin, David. "Chaucer's Creation and Recreation of the *Lyf of Seynt Cecile*." *ChRev* 32 (1997): 196–212.

Bibliography

Réau, Louis. *Iconographie de l'art chrétien*. 3 vols. Paris: Presses Universitaires de France, 1955–59.

Reiss, Edmund. "Ambiguous Realities and Authorial Deceptions in Fourteenth-Century Fictions." *Sign, Sentence, Discourse*. 113–37.

—. "Chaucer's Fiction and Linguistic Self-Consciousness in the Late Middle Ages." *Chaucer and the Craft of Fiction*. 97–119.

—. "The Story of Lamech and Its Place in Medieval Drama." *JMRS* 2 (1972): 35–48.

Rethinking the "Romance of the Rose": Text, Image, Reception. Ed. Kevin Brownlee and Sylvia Huot. Philadelphia: University of Pennsylvania Press, 1992.

Reynolds, Suzanne. *Medieval Reading: Grammar, Rhetoric and the Classical Text*. Cambridge Studies in Medieval Literature 27. Cambridge University Press, 1996.

Richter, Michael. *Sprache und Gesellschaft im Mittelalter: Untersuchungen zur Mündlichen Kommunikation in England von der Mitte des Elften bis zum Beginn des Vierzehnten Jahrhunderts*. Monographien zur Geschichte des Mittelalters, 18. Stuttgart: Anton Hiersemann, 1979.

Ricks, Christopher. *Milton's Grand Style*. Oxford: Clarendon Press, 1963.

Riddy, Felicity. "Engendering Pity in the *Franklin's Tale*." *Feminist Readings in Middle English Literature: The Wife of Bath and All Her Sect*. Ed. Ruth Evans and Lesley Johnson. London and New York: Routledge, 1994. 54–71.

Rigby, S. H. *Chaucer in Context: Society, Allegory and Gender*. Manchester University Press, 1996.

Rist, John M. *Augustine: Ancient Thought Baptized*. Cambridge University Press, 1994.

Rizzo, Stefano. "Il *De Vulgari Eloquentia* e l'unita del pensiero linguistico di Dante." *DS* 87 (1969): 69–88.

Robertson, D. W., Jr. *A Preface to Chaucer: Studies in Medieval Perspectives*. Princeton University Press, 1962.

Robins, R. H. *Ancient & Mediaeval Grammatical Theory in Europe*. 1951; rpt. Port Washington, NY & London: Kennikat Press, 1971.

Robinson, Fred C. "The Significance of Names in Old English Literature." *Anglia* 86 (1968): 14–58.

Robinson, F. N. "Chaucer and Dante." *Journal of Comparative Literature* 1 (1903): 292–97.

Robinson, Richard. *Essays in Greek Philosophy*. Oxford: Clarendon Press, 1969.

Rosenberg, Bruce A. "The Contrary Tales of the Second Nun and the Canon's Yeoman." *ChRev* 2 (1968): 278–91.

Rosenberg, Joel W. "The Garden Story Forward and Backward: The Non-Narrative Dimension of Genesis 2–3." *Prooftexts* 1 (1981): 1–27.

Rothwell, W. "The Trilingual England of Geoffrey Chaucer." *SAC* 16 (1994): 45–67.

Rotta, Paolo. *La filosofia del linguaggio nella patristica e nella scolastica*. Turin: Fratelli Bocca, 1909.

Rowe, Donald W. "Reson in Jean's *Roman de la Rose*: Modes of Characterization and Dimensions of Meaning." *Mediaevalia* 10 (1984): 97–126.

Roy, Bruno. "L'humour érotique au XVe siècle." *L'Érotisme au Moyen Âge*. Ed. Bruno Roy. Montréal: Aurore, 1977. 155–64.

Rubinstein, Nicolai. "The Beginnings of Political Thought in Florence." *Journal of the Warburg and Courtauld Institutes* 5 (1942): 198–227.

Rudd, Gillian. *Managing Language in "Piers Plowman."* Piers Plowman Studies 9. Cambridge: D. S. Brewer, 1994.

Ruthven, K. K. "The Poet as Etymologist." *Critical Quarterly* 11 (1969): 9–37.

Salisbury, Joyce E. "The Latin Doctors of the Church on Sexuality." *Journal of Medieval History* 12 (1986): 279–89.

Salmon, Vivian. "Language-Planning in Seventeenth-Century England: Its Context and Aims." *In Memory of J. R. Firth.* Ed. C. E. Bazell, J. C. Catford, M. A. K. Halliday, and R. H. Robins. London: Longmans, 1966. 370–97.

Salter, Elizabeth, ed. *Nicholas Love's Myrrour of the Blessed Lyf of Jesu Christ.* Analecta Cartusiana 10. Salzburg: University of Salzburg, 1974.

Sarolli, Gian Roberto. "Dante 'scriba Dei'." *Convivium* n.s. 31 (1963): 385–422, 513–44, 641–71.

Scattergood, John. "Chaucer in the Suburbs." *Reading the Past: Essays on Medieval and Renaissance Literature.* Dublin: Four Courts Press, 1996. 128–45.

Schibanoff, Susan. "The New Reader and Female Textuality in Two Early Commentaries on Chaucer." *SAC* 10 (1988): 71–108.

Schildgen, Brenda Deen. "Dante's Neologisms in the *Paradiso* and the Latin Rhetorical Tradition." *DS* 107 (1989): 101–19.

Schless, Howard H. *Chaucer and Dante: A Revaluation.* Norman, Oklahoma: Pilgrim Books, 1984.

Schmidt, A. V. C. "Chaucer's *Nembrot*: A Note on *The Former Age.*" *Medium Aevum* 47 (1978): 304–07.

—, ed. *The General Prologue to The Canterbury Tales and The Canon's Yeoman's Prologue and Tale.* The London Medieval and Renaissance Series. University of London Press, 1974.

Schnapp, Jeffrey T. "Lectura Dantis: *Inferno* 30." *Sparks and Seeds: Medieval Literature and Its Afterlife: Essays in Honor of John Freccero.* Ed. Dana E. Stewart and Alison Cornish. Turnhout: Brepols, 2000. 75–85.

— "Paradiso." *Dante Encyclopedia.* 674–78.

— "Virgin Words: Hildegard of Bingen's Lingua Ignota and the Development of Imaginary Languages Ancient to Modern." *Exemplaria* 3 (1991): 267–98.

Schwartz, Regina M. *Remembering and Repeating: Biblical Creation in "Paradise Lost."* Cambridge University Press, 1988.

Schwarz, Werner. *Principles and Problems of Biblical Translation.* Cambridge University Press, 1955.

Scott, J. A. Review of Jenaro-MacLennan. *MLR* 71 (1976): 932–34.

Shankland, Hugh. "Dante 'Aliger'." *MLR* 70 (1975): 764–85.

Shereshevsky, Ezra. "Hebrew Traditions in Peter Comestor's *Historia Scholastica.*" *Jewish Quarterly Review* 59 (1968–69): 268–89.

Sherman, Gail Berkeley. "Saints, Nuns, and Speech in the *Canterbury Tales.*" *Images of Sainthood in Medieval Europe.* Ed. Renate Blumenfeld-Kosinski and Timea Szell. Ithaca and London: Cornell University Press, 1991. 136–60.

Bibliography

Shoaf, R. A. *Chaucer, Dante, and the Currency of the Word: Money, Images, and Reference in Late Medieval Poetry*. Norman, OK: Pilgrim Books, 1983.

— "'Unwemmed Custance': Circulation, Property, and Incest in the *Man of Law's Tale*." *Exemplaria* 2 (1990): 287–302.

Short, Ian. "On Bilingualism in Anglo-Norman England." *Romance Philology* 33 (1980): 467–79.

Sidebottom, E. M. *The Christ of the Fourth Gospel, in the Light of First-Century Thought*. London: S.P.C.K., 1961.

Sign, Sentence, Discourse: Language in Medieval Thought and Literature. Ed. Julian N. Wasserman and Lois Y. Roney. Syracuse University Press, 1989.

Sikes, J. G. *Peter Abailard*. Cambridge University Press, 1932.

Singleton, Charles S. *Dante Studies 1: "Commedia": Elements of Structure*. Cambridge: Harvard University Press, 1954.

—. *Dante Studies 2: Journey to Beatrice*. Cambridge: Harvard University Press, 1958.

—. *An Essay on the "Vita Nuova."* Cambridge: Harvard University Press, 1949.

Sisam, Kenneth, ed. *The Nun's Priest's Tale*. Oxford: Clarendon Press, 1927.

Skinner, John. *A Critical and Exegetical Commentary on Genesis*. Rev. ed. New York: Scribner's, 1925.

Sklute, Larry. *Virtue of Necessity: Inconclusiveness and Narrative Form in Chaucer's Poetry*. Columbus: Ohio State University Press, 1984.

Smalley, Beryl. "Andrew of St. Victor, Abbot of Wigmore: A Twelfth Century Hebraist." *RTAM* 10 (1938): 358–73.

—. "L'Exégèse Biblique du 12e Siècle." *Entretiens sur la Renaissance du 12e Siècle*. Ed. Maurice de Gandillac and Edouard Jeauneau. Paris: Mouton, 1968. 273–83.

—. *The Study of the Bible in the Middle Ages*. University of Notre Dame Press, 1952; rpt. 1964.

—. "Wyclif's *Postilla* on the Old Testament and His *Principium*." *Oxford Studies Presented to Daniel Callus*. Oxford Historical Society n. s. 16. Oxford: Clarendon Press, 1964. 253–96.

Smith, Lesley. "The Theology of the Twelfth- and Thirteenth-Century Bible." *The Early Medieval Bible: Its Production, Decoration and Use*. Ed. Richard Gameson. Cambridge University Press, 1994. 223–32.

Smithers, G. V., ed. *Kyng Alisaunder*. EETS o.s. 237. Oxford University Press, 1957.

Sommerfelt, Alf. "The Origin of Language: Theories and Hypotheses." *Cahiers d'Histoire Mondiale* 1 (1953–54): 885–902.

Southern, R. W. "Aspects of the European Tradition of Historical Writing: 2. Hugh of St. Victor and the Idea of Historical Development." *Transactions of the Royal Historical Society* 5th series, 21 (1971): 159–79.

—. *Platonism, Scholastic Method, and the School of Chartres*. The Stenton Lecture 1978. University of Reading, 1979.

—. *Robert Grosseteste*. Oxford: Clarendon Press, 1986.

—. *Saint Anselm: A Portrait in a Landscape*. Cambridge University Press, 1990.

—. *Scholastic Humanism and the Unification of Europe. Volume 1: Foundations*. Oxford: Blackwell, 1995.

Spade, P. V. "Ockham on Terms of First and Second Imposition and Intention, with Remarks on the Liar Paradox." *Vivarium* 19 (1981): 47–55.

Spicq, Ceslaus, OP. *Esquisse d'une histoire de l'exégèse latine au moyen age*. Bibliothèque Thomiste 26. Paris: Vrin, 1944.

Spitzer, Leo. "Speech and Language in *Inferno* XIII." *Italica* 19 (1942): 81–104.

—. "The Works of Rabelais." *Literary Masterpieces of the Western World*. Ed. Francis H. Horn. Baltimore: Johns Hopkins Press, 1953. 126–47.

Stakel, Susan. *False Roses: Structures of Duality and Deceit in Jean de Meun's "Roman de la Rose."* Stanford French and Italian Studies 69. Stanford: Anima Libri and Dept. of French and Italian, Stanford University, 1991.

Stam, James. *Inquiries into the Origin of Language: The Fate of a Question*. New York: Harper & Row, 1976.

Stegmüller, Friedrich. *Repertorium Biblicum Medii Aevi*. 11 vols. Madrid, 1940–80.

Stein, Arnold. *Milton's Answerable Style*. Minneapolis: University of Minnesota Press, 1953.

Steiner, George. *After Babel: Aspects of Language and Translation*. New York and London: Oxford University Press, 1975.

Stephens, Walter. *Giants in Those Days: Folklore, Ancient History, and Nationalism*. Lincoln and London: University of Nebraska Press, 1989.

Stillinger, Thomas C. *The Song of Troilus: Lyric Authority in the Medieval Book*. Philadelphia: University of Pennsylvania Press, 1992.

Stock, Brian. *The Implications of Literacy: Written Language and Models of Interpretation in the Eleventh and Twelfth Centuries*. Princeton University Press, 1983.

Strohm, Paul. *Social Chaucer*. Cambridge, MA: Harvard University Press, 1989.

Strubel, Armand. "'Allegoria in factis' et 'Allegoria in verbis'." *Poétique* 23 (1975): 342–57.

Tabarroni, Andrea. "Mental Signs and Representation in Ockham." *On the Medieval Theory of Signs*. 195–224.

Tambling, Jeremy. *Dante and Difference: Writing in the "Commedia."* Cambridge Studies in Medieval Literature 2. Cambridge University Press, 1988.

Tatlock, John S. P. "The Epilog of Chaucer's *Troilus*," *Modern Philology* 18 (1921), 625–59.

Taylor, John. *The "Universal Chronicle" of Ranulf Higden*. Oxford: Clarendon Press, 1966.

Taylor, Karla. *Chaucer Reads 'The Divine Comedy.'* Stanford University Press, 1989.

Taylor, Paul B. "The Alchemy of Spring in Chaucer's *General Prologue*." *ChRev* 17 (1982): 1–4.

—. "Chaucer's *Cosyn to the Dede*." *Speculum* 57 (1982): 315–27.

—. "The Parson's Amyable Tongue." *English Studies* 64 (1983): 401–9.

Terracini, Benvenuto. "Natura ed origine del linguaggio umano nel 'De vulgari eloquentia'." *Pagine e appunti di linguistica storica*. Florence: Felice le Monnier, 1957. 237–46.

Thurot, Charles. *Notices et extraits de divers manuscrits latins pour servir à l'histoire des doctrines grammaticales au moyen âge*. 1869; rpt. Frankfurt: Minerva-Verlag, 1964.

Todorov, Tzvetan. *Theories of the Symbol.* Trans. Catherine Porter. Oxford: Basil Blackwell, 1982.

Toynbee, Paget. *Dante Studies and Researches.* London: Methuen, 1902.

Trapp, J. B. "The Iconography of the Fall of Man." *Approaches to "Paradise Lost."* Ed. C. A. Patrides. London: Edward Arnold, 1968. 223–65.

Travers, Jean, OP. "Le Mystère des langues dans l'Église." *La Maison-Dieu* 11 (1947): 15–38.

Travis, Peter W. "Deconstructing Chaucer's Retraction." *Exemplaria* 3 (1991): 135–58.

—. "Symbolic Transformations in the *Canon's Yeoman's Tale.*" Unpublished paper. Medieval Forum, 1982.

Tuve, Rosemond. *Allegorical Imagery: Some Medieval Books and Their Posterity.* Princeton University Press, 1966.

Vallone, Aldo. "Il *silenzio* in Dante." *DS* 110 (1997): 45–56.

Vance, Eugene. "Chaucer's *House of Fame* and the Poetics of Inflation." *Boundary 2* 7:2 (1979): 17–37.

—. *Mervelous Signals: Poetics and Sign Theory in the Middle Ages.* Regents Studies in Medieval Culture. Lincoln: University of Nebraska Press, 1986.

—. "Saint Augustine: Language as Temporality." *Mimesis: From Mirror to Method.* Ed. John D. Lyons and Stephen G. Nichols, Jr. Hanover, NH: University Press of New England, 1982. 20–35.

Vincent, E. R. "Dante's Choice of Words." *Italian Studies* 10 (1955): 1–18.

Vogt, Kari. "'Becoming Male': A Gnostic and Early Christian Metaphor." *Image of God and Gender Models in Judaeo-Christian Tradition.* Ed. Kari Elisabeth Børresen. Oslo: Solum Forlag, 1991. 172–87.

Walcutt, Charles C. "The Pronoun of Address in *Troilus and Criseyde.*" *PQ* 14 (1935): 282–87.

Walters, Lori. "Appendix: Author Portraits and Textual Demarcation in Manuscripts of the *Romance of the Rose.*" *Rethinking the "Romance of the Rose."* 359–73.

Walther, Helmut G. "Utopische Gesellschaftskritik oder Satirische Ironie? Jean de Meun und die Lehre des Aquinaten über die Entstehung Menschlicher Herrschaft." *Soziale Ordnungen im Selbstverständnis des Mittelalters.* Berlin: Walter de Gruyter, 1979. 84–105.

Watts, William H., and Richard J. Utz. "Nominalist Perspectives on Chaucer's Poetry: A Bibliographical Essay." *M&H* n.s. 20 (1994): 147–73.

Weigand, Hermann J. "The Two and Seventy Languages of the World." *Germanic Review* 17 (1942): 241–60.

Weiss, Robert. "England and the Decree of the Council of Vienne on the Teaching of Greek, Arabic, Hebrew, and Syriac." *Bibliothèque d'Humanisme et Renaissance* 14 (1952): 1–9.

Wellek, René. *The Rise of English Literary History.* Chapel Hill: University of North Carolina Press, 1941.

Wetherbee, Winthrop. *Chaucer and the Poets: An Essay on "Troilus and Criseyde."* Ithaca and London: Cornell University Press, 1984.

—. "Convention and Authority: A Comment on Some Recent Critical Approaches to Chaucer." *New Perspectives in Chaucer Criticism*. 71–81.

—. "Latin Structure and Vernacular Space: Gower, Chaucer and the Boethian Tradition." *Chaucer and Gower: Difference, Mutuality, Exchange*. Ed. R. F. Yeager. English Literary Studies Monograph Series. Victoria, BC: University of Victoria, 1991. 7–35.

—. "The Literal and the Allegorical: Jean de Meun and the 'de Planctu Naturae'." *MS* 33 (1971): 264–91.

—. *Platonism and Poetry in the Twelfth Century: The Literary Influence of the School of Chartres*. Princeton University Press, 1972.

—. "The *Romance of the Rose* and Medieval Allegory." *European Writers: The Middle Ages and the Renaissance*. Ed. W. T. H. Jackson. New York: Scribners, 1983. 1:309–35.

—. "Some Implications of Nature's Femininity in Medieval Poetry." *Approaches to Nature in the Middle Ages*. Ed. Lawrence D. Roberts. Medieval & Renaissance Texts & Studies 16. Binghamton, NY: Center for Medieval and Early Renaissance Studies, 1982. 47–62.

Whitfield, J. H. "Virgil Into Dante." *Virgil*. Ed. D. R. Dudley. London: Routledge & Kegan Paul, 1969. 94–118.

Wilkins, Ernest Hatch, and Thomas Goddard Bergin. *A Concordance to the "Divine Comedy" of Dante Alighieri*. Cambridge, MA: Belknap Press of Harvard University Press, 1965.

Williams, Arnold. *The Common Expositor*. Chapel Hill: University of North Carolina Press, 1948.

Williams, Aubrey L. *Pope's Dunciad: A Study of Its Meaning*. London: Methuen, 1955.

Williams, David. *Cain and Beowulf: A Study in Secular Allegory*. University of Toronto Press, 1982.

Wolff, Philippe. *Western Languages AD 100–1500*. Trans. Frances Partridge. London: Weidenfeld and Nicolson, 1971.

Woolf, Rosemary. *The English Religious Lyric in the Middle Ages*. Oxford: Clarendon Press, 1968.

Young, Karl. "Chaucer and Peter Riga." *Speculum* 12 (1937): 299–303.

Yowell, Donna L. "Ugolino's 'Bestial Segno': The *De Vulgari Eloquentia* in *Inferno* XXXII–XXXIII." *DS* 104 (1986): 121–43.

Zeeman, Nicolette. "The Schools Give a License to Poets." *Criticism and Dissent in the Middle Ages*. Ed. Rita Copeland. Cambridge University Press, 1996. 151–80.

Zink, Michel. "The Allegorical Poem as Interior Memoir." Trans. Margaret Miner and Kevin Brownlee. *YFS* 70 (1986): 100–26.

Ziolkowski, Jan. *Alan of Lille's Grammar of Sex: The Meaning of Grammar to a Twelfth-Century Intellectual*. Speculum Anniversary Monographs 10. Cambridge, MA: Medieval Academy of America, 1985.

—. "The Obscenities of Old Women: Vetularity and Vernacularity." *Obscenity*. 72–89.

—. "Obscenity in the Latin Grammatical and Rhetorical Tradition." *Obscenity*. 41–59.

Index

Index

Index

Index

CAMBRIDGE STUDIES IN MEDIEVAL LITERATURE